WARLORDS

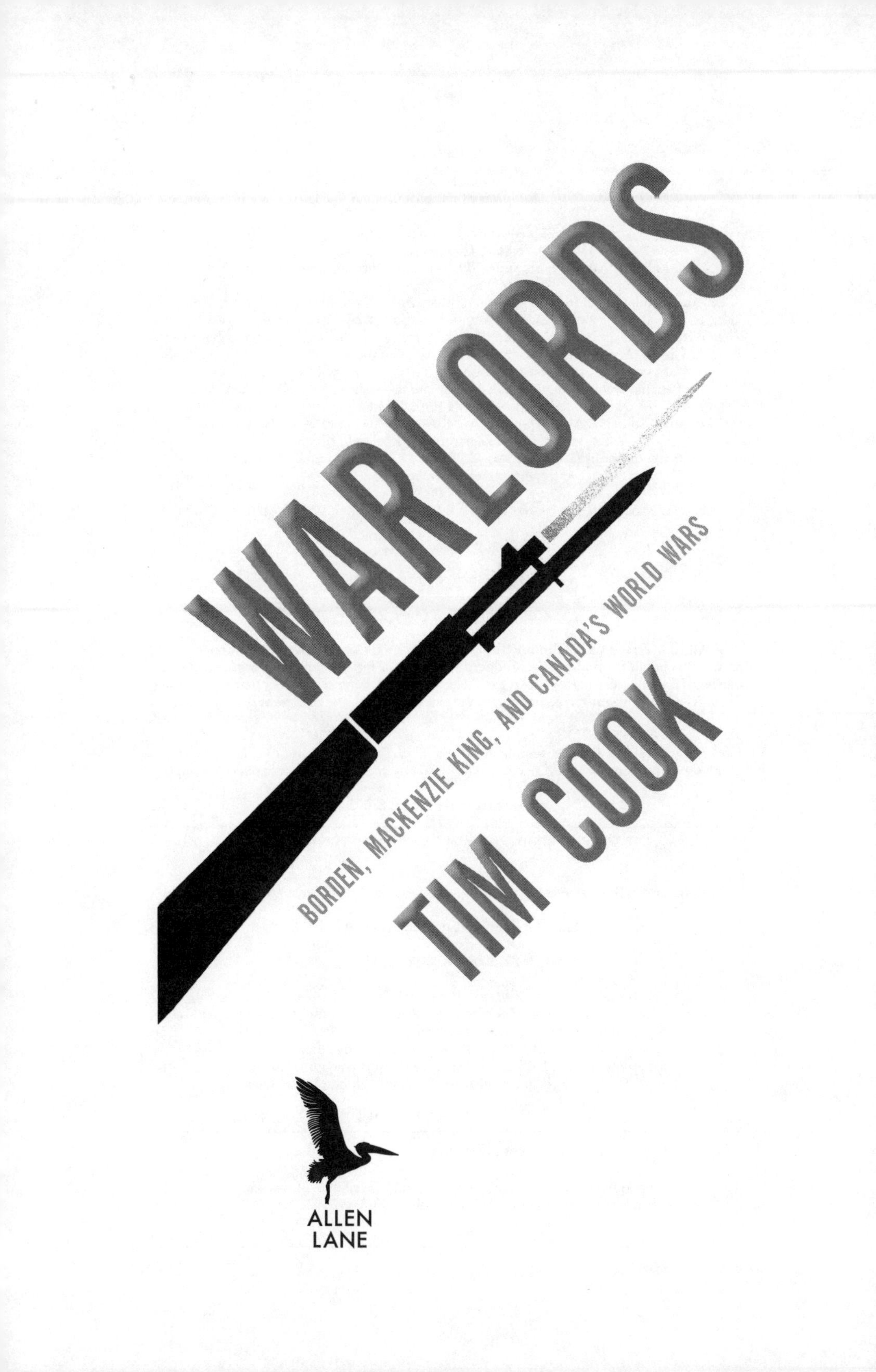
WARLORDS
BORDEN, MACKENZIE KING, AND CANADA'S WORLD WARS
TIM COOK
ALLEN
LANE

ALLEN LANE
an imprint of Penguin Canada

Published by the Penguin Group
Penguin Group (Canada)
90 Eglinton Avenue East, Suite 700, Toronto, Ontario, Canada M4P 2Y3

Penguin Group (USA) Inc., 375 Hudson Street, New York, New York 10014, U.S.A.
Penguin Books Ltd, 80 Strand, London WC2R 0RL, England
Penguin Ireland, 25 St Stephen's Green, Dublin 2, Ireland (a division of Penguin Books Ltd)
Penguin Group (Australia), 250 Camberwell Road, Camberwell, Victoria 3124, Australia
(a division of Pearson Australia Group Pty Ltd)
Penguin Books India Pvt Ltd, 11 Community Centre, Panchsheel Park,
New Delhi – 110 017, India
Penguin Group (NZ), 67 Apollo Drive, Rosedale, Auckland 0632, New Zealand
(a division of Pearson New Zealand Ltd)
Penguin Books (South Africa) (Pty) Ltd, 24 Sturdee Avenue, Rosebank,
Johannesburg 2196, South Africa

Penguin Books Ltd, Registered Offices: 80 Strand, London WC2R 0RL, England

First published 2012

1 2 3 4 5 6 7 8 9 10 (RRD)

Manufactured in the U.S.A.

LIBRARY AND ARCHIVES CANADA CATALOGUING IN PUBLICATION

Cook, Tim, 1971–
Warlords : Borden, Mackenzie King, and Canada's world wars / Tim Cook.

Includes bibliographical references and index.

ISBN 978-0-670-06521-9

1. Borden, Robert Laird, Sir, 1854–1937—Military leadership.
2. King, William Lyon Mackenzie, 1874–1950—Military leadership.
3. Canada—Military policy. 4. World War, 1914–1918—Canada.
5. World War, 1939–1945—Canada. 6. Canada—Politics and
government—1911–1921. 7. Canada—Politics and government—
1935–1948. 8. Prime ministers—Canada—Biography. I. Title.

FC555.C65 2012 971.061'2 C2012-903282-4

Visit the Penguin Canada website at **www.penguin.ca**

Special and corporate bulk purchase rates available; please see
www.penguin.ca/corporatesales or call 1-800-810-3104, ext. 2477.

ALWAYS LEARNING PEARSON

TO MY GIRLS:
PAIGE, EMMA, CHLOE, AND SARAH

CONTENTS

PROLOGUE

Two portraits flank the doors leading into Canada's House of Commons. Their subjects have been depicted by sympathetic artists as statesman-like, although with a hint of the common touch, charismatic yet stern, wise but judicious. On the left is Sir Robert Borden, prime minister of Canada from 1911 to 1920; on the right is William Lyon Mackenzie King, prime minister for most of the period from 1921 to 1948. The paintings are conventional, but the plaques attached to them are curious. Borden's caption reads: "World War I War Leader, 1914–1918," and King's is similar: "World War II War Leader, 1939–1945." No other dates are given. While the portrait captions of every other prime minister in the lobby contain their inclusive dates of service, only two, Borden and King, are defined solely by their wartime leadership.

Perhaps the description makes sense for Borden, who did little of note before the war, but it does not ring true for King, as Canada's longest-serving prime minister, with almost fifteen years of prewar leadership. Yet in both cases it is indeed the world wars that shaped their legacy. The portraits stand alone, as do their careers as war leaders. But there is value in examining the parallel stories of these two men, for when presented side by side, like their portraits, they reveal new meaning and continuing connections that animate some of the core themes of Canada's story.

Given the two men's prewar backgrounds and political record, few could have imagined Borden or King as wartime leaders. They were unmilitary in education, training, and, in the case of King, physical bearing. King admitted as much. "It seems odd to me to think of myself as a war leader," he wrote in his diary, during the sixth year of the Second World War. "Nothing could sound to me more remote."[1] Borden had a more commanding presence than King, but he relied on instinct rather than training, and he was appalled by the terrible slaughter in the Great War, describing it as "the suicide of civilization."[2] The burden of wartime leadership weighed heavily on them.

In the world wars against Germany and its allies, from 1914 to 1918 and from 1939 to 1945, the majority of Canadians were willing to pay almost any price to secure victory. A nation of "unmilitary people," as Canadians have sometimes been described, contributed more than 1.7 million men and women to campaigns and theatres of battle around the world; over 113,000 paid with their lives, and many more with wounds to the body and mind. Because of its part in the Great War, Canada was recognized as a country that had shed its colonial status and earned the right to control its own destiny. During the Second World War, Canada's enormous role in supporting its allies reinforced the nation's independence, and set the Dominion on a new trajectory towards prosperity and an international presence. Both wars were meant to defend the old order, but both ushered in massive disruptions:

government intervention in the form of income tax, health care, and conscription; changes to society through industrialization, enfranchisement, and patriotic unpaid labour; and the raising of large armed forces from a civilian base rather than professional service personnel. Contentious issues arose over the government's invocation of emergency powers under the War Measures Act, its management of dissenting minorities, and its attempts to balance the voracious demands of allies with what Canadians could be expected to bear. Some wartime actions, such as the conscription of young men for military service and the mistreatment of Japanese Canadians, are offensive to present-day sensibilities but need to be understood within their historical context, as do all the other difficult decisions the government either took or avoided.

Despite bookending a nearly thirty-year period of war, reconstruction, depression, and rearmament, the world wars exerted similar pressures and strains on Canadians, their society, and their leaders. This book does not attempt to judge Borden and King in comparison to one another, but instead to understand how they guided their country through two of the most disruptive periods in our collective history. In fact, a direct comparison is impossible because the two men led Canada at different stages of its economic and constitutional development. Nonetheless, they faced similar challenges, which shed light on the prime ministers' wartime actions and revealed their respective characters.

At the core of this book is the question of how prime ministers lead their country in times of war. Few would think of Borden or King as warlords, yet this is the role into which they were thrust. Neither was attracted to war. Neither had many friends or acquaintances in the armed forces. Their lack of interest in military affairs is typical of Canadian leaders. Only two ministers of national defence—the widely disliked and incompetent Sir Mackenzie Bowell and the unlucky and inconsequential Kim Campbell—have ever risen to the country's top job, providing evidence of how this difficult portfolio has been, for over 135 years, a graveyard of political aspirations.[3] But war weaves through Canadian history, driving change, creating nation-building events, and forcing a rapid, and at times cruel, maturation. Sir Wilfrid Laurier faced the South African War (1899–1902) while Louis St. Laurent led the country during the Korean War (1950–1953). During the Cold War, all of Canada's leaders had to deal with issues of defence and security. More recently, Brian Mulroney faced a war against Iraq in 1990–1991; Jean Chrétien sent Canadian troops as part of a NATO coalition attacking Serbian forces in 1999; and both Paul Martin and Stephen Harper have overseen Canada's ongoing decade-long contribution as a member of the multinational force in Afghanistan. Not one of Canada's prime ministers has had any senior military training, with its concomitant study of grand strategy, tactics, or logistics, and only a handful served in the country's armed forces, and none above the most junior of commissioned ranks. Since Confederation, only John Diefenbaker and Lester Pearson took up arms—in their case, during the Great War—and neither saw combat. If Canadians see themselves as an "unmilitary people" inhabiting a "peaceable kingdom," they have reinforced that image by electing unmilitary leaders.[4] For much of the second half of the twentieth century, Canadians were proud to embrace the role of international peacekeeper. Notwithstanding all these indications of Canada's peaceable legacy, any study of the nation's past reveals that Canadians have also turned readily to war in support of allies, alliances, international obligations, ideals, or humanitarian relief.

Like their portraits outside the House of Commons, Borden and King can be viewed individually, but also in close historical proximity. The challenges faced first by Borden and then by King offer insights into qualities of leadership, strategic vision, and necessary compromise, and into what animates and defines Canada as a nation, all set against the backdrop of the horrendous world wars, with their domestic and international pressures. Both leaders have been overshadowed in public memory by the earlier nation-builders and dynamic personalities, Sir John A. Macdonald and Sir Wilfrid Laurier, and, later, by the panache and imposing intellect of Pierre Trudeau. Borden and King deserve better treatment from historians, as well as clearer understanding by Canadians. Their political predicament, within the traumatic unfolding of total war, remains unique among the nation's highest leaders.

Borden and King governed Canada for a combined period of more than thirty years, ten of which spanned the agonizing world wars. Their actions in that critical time continue to resonate to this day, for these two unlikely warlords set our nation on a different course, one that has not yet reached its conclusion.

CHAPTER I

AN UNLIKELY LEADER, 1854–1908

The man who led Canada during the Great War came from the village of Grand Pré, Kings County, Nova Scotia. Born on June 26, 1854, into a loving if not wealthy family, Robert Laird Borden was anchored to his community. After he left to find success, he often looked back on Grand Pré with affection: "In all my journeyings throughout Canada and elsewhere in the world, I have yet to see any spot more beautiful than that which is still enshrined in my earliest memories."[1]

Such thoughts may not have preoccupied the younger Borden. Robert was an intense and serious youth, rarely known to joke or play games. While he helped his father, Andrew, work the farm, neither were men of the soil, and Robert admitted that he never mastered "the mysteries of building a load of hay," and found hoeing vegetables "extremely disagreeable" and the sawing of cordwood for winter fires "unpleasurable."[2] He resented the work, partly because it took him away from his studies.

Robert's mother, Eunice, was an avid reader, and there were rousing discussions of literature and politics in the house. Such talk stimulated the boy, and his parents often found him next to the fireplace reading late into the night, embers smudging his books and clothes. The emerging scholar was so dedicated to his studies that he drew up charts to schedule his day more effectively, which elicited some jibes from his normally compassionate mother. His younger brother, not nearly as gentle, teased him about the schedules that allotted time to reading, study, and even bathroom breaks. It is not surprising that Robert did well in school. He taught himself Latin and Greek, but was drawn to the law, which was a good fit considering his nature. The Bordens, however, could not afford to send him off to university, and he seemed destined to be a small-town teacher, a profession he had already entered at the tender age of fourteen.[3]

Although he liked the title "The Professor," bestowed on him by students in one of the single-room schools where he taught, Robert understood that teaching in rural Nova Scotia would leave him with few opportunities for advancement, either professionally or socially.[4] So in 1874 he began four years of articling in a prominent Halifax law firm. Much of the office drudgery fell to him, but he learned by watching, stumbling, and then succeeding.

He excelled, of course, standing first in the Nova Scotia bar examinations in 1877, ahead of some candidates who had attended schools such as Harvard. He continued to read voraciously, hoping, as he later reflected, "to give [him]self the equivalent of a university education."[5] He was given to quoting Horace and Virgil, a habit that was more common in the late nineteenth century than it is today, but he would still have stood out in a crowd of Haligonians.

While in his twenties, the handsome Robert, with a full moustache and mutton chops separated by a fashionable gap from his brown, curly hair, dabbled in the militia, for which he had turned out several times a week since 1874. He liked the camaraderie and needed the extra money, but he also joined, as did many others, because it was a good way to meet the rich and wealthy men who held higher rank. He was later commissioned and attended a short course at the School of Military Instruction.[6] He enjoyed the part-time soldiering, although this too, he knew, would not lead to worldly success. More promising was the time he made for the verbal sparring in the debating society of the Young Men's Christian Association.

In early 1879, Borden left Halifax to start a small rural legal practice in Kentville, Kings County, taking any and all cases that came his way. While he found arguing cases a "tremendous ordeal," he was a workhorse, and could be found in his offices from dawn to midnight, to the point where, in his words, "I would be in a condition of such extreme nervous tension that I could hardly eat or sleep."[7] The effort paid off when he was recruited in 1882 by the most prestigious Halifax firm of the day. The practice was headed by Sir Charles Tupper, a Conservative cabinet minister, long-time Canadian high commissioner in London, and future prime minister. Under Tupper's tutelage, and with the high-profile clients he brought in, Borden was soon a well-known lawyer in Halifax, taking cases to Ottawa to argue before the Supreme Court.

Borden believed that "to waste time is like wasting one's future."[8] He lived by this principle and barely had time for a social life. But it was his good fortune to meet Laura Bond at St. Paul's Anglican Church, where she was an organist and he was a member of the congregation. For Laura, Robert broke some of his punishing work habits and found time to go to the theatre, play tennis, and golf. The two were married in September 1889 and Laura was his lifelong love. The Bordens had no children, but Robert's brother Henry had a son, also named Henry, with whom the Bordens were close. Robert relied heavily on Laura, and she gave balance to his life. Yet while they enjoyed each other's company, and chatted about issues that animated their peers, they did not discuss politics or economics.[9] Those topics were reserved for his male associates at the club. There, in the company of his friends, Borden was known to swear, gossip, and generally let down his guard.

By the time he was in his early forties, Robert Borden was a man of some distinction. His dapper suits, erect bearing, and rugged face set him apart, but his hair apparently moved some women to fits of rapture. "That wonderful hair of his," wrote one female admirer, "must have brought the unctuous fingers of many masters, spiritual and otherwise, down upon it in commendatory pats ... I daresay that it was his mother's pleasure in it and the way she enjoyed running her fingers through it that made him realize—subconsciously at least—that his hair was a very magnificent asset."[10] No wonder Robert was a bit of a dandy, although the effect was offset by his deep, lugubrious voice, whose steadiness revealed the temperament of the inner man.

By the 1890s, Borden and the Tuppers, father and son, had the largest law practice in the Maritimes, and Borden, as a partner, was earning sums as high as $30,000 a year at a time when labourers made roughly a dollar a day.[11] The Bordens purchased a mansion on Quinpool Road in the western suburbs of Halifax in 1894, and they spent several weeks during most summers touring England and continental Europe. Gradually, with their financial and social position secured, Borden was drawn into public service: he became president of the Nova Scotia Barristers' Society in 1896, and later that same year, played an important role in organizing the Canadian Bar Association.

Politics beckoned. The Tuppers were involved heavily in the Conservative Party. There was a strong link between politics and the legal profession in the late nineteenth century. Almost all politicians were lawyers and almost all lawyers were associated with one of the major parties. Borden sympathized with his Liberal-minded parents, and it would have been natural for him to join the Liberal Party, especially with his famous cousin, Frederick Borden, later serving as minister of militia and defence in Sir Wilfrid Laurier's Liberal cabinet from 1896 to 1911. But Borden was drawn to the Conservatives after Liberal premier W.S. Fielding won the provincial election in 1886 on a platform of secession from Canada.[12] Borden hoped to see Canada grow stronger and he thought that Fielding was playing a dangerous game, even if he intended only to shake loose more concessions from Ottawa for Nova Scotia.

When Prime Minister Sir Charles Tupper—who was the fourth of four Conservative prime ministers during the five years since Sir John A. Macdonald's death in 1891—asked Borden to stand for election in 1896, Robert saw it as his duty to oblige. While he was well respected in Halifax, he had no passion for politics. His skills were not those of a politician: he had become an accomplished court orator, unfolding his arguments, one after another, moving logically and irrevocably to his conclusion, but he found stump speeches difficult and, at times, pointless. Hammering a few themes over and over again to embarrass, demonize, or denigrate one's political enemy did not agree with Borden, and at points during the 1896 campaign he admitted to "great nervousness and diffidence."[13] Perhaps none of it would matter, as the Conservative Party had been reeling since Sir John A. Macdonald's death a half decade earlier. The Liberal leader, Laurier, had solidified support across the country, and especially at the provincial level, where he piggybacked on the strong Liberal political organizations that were already in place. The eloquent French Canadian led his party to a sweeping victory over Tupper's Conservatives in 1896. In Halifax, Borden stood against the storm, while many of the Tory political faithful were swept away.

BORDEN DID NOT LIKE OTTAWA AT ALL, and he resented having to leave behind the ocean, his friends, and his club. His beloved wife stayed in Halifax, too, and he was lonely without her. For a while he lived with Henri Bourassa, the firebrand Liberal who would later become his ally and eventually a fervent opponent. Bourassa in particular and Ottawa in general exposed Borden to French Canadians. He enjoyed this mingling with people from across the country, but found many of the blowhards in Parliament hard to take and worried that ritual verbal exchanges were an enormous waste of time.[14] He resolved to stay in Ottawa for a single term, and then, having done his duty, hand his seat over to another Conservative who might better enjoy the privilege.

Despite his ambivalence about politics, Robert Borden worked hard on his party's behalf. He had deep reserves of energy to draw upon, even though he was frequently ill. Ottawa's miserable climate disagreed with him, but he also fretted over his impact in opposition, where the Conservatives would have little say in guiding the country for several years. In opposition, and as a new member, he did not have many duties and he continued to spend much of his time practising law. He was successful in both careers, and was soon recognized as a man who could shoulder a heavy burden. By the end of the first Parliament, Tupper had moved his young protegé to the front bench to better assault the Liberals. Despite his unhappiness, Borden's piercing eyes seem to burn with an inner light in photographs from this period in his life.

The restless Borden soldiered on for four years. His planned withdrawal from politics was the beacon that kept him going. But the thin ranks of Conservatives implored him to run again and the respite faded from view. There would be no relief unless, of course, he was defeated, and few Conservatives felt safe in going up against the Laurier-led Liberals. The Grits were a juggernaut, whose policies had encouraged a tidal wave of immigrants, developed the economy through railways and building projects, enjoyed for Canada a share in international prosperity and good times, and negotiated a course across the English–French fault lines that had been exposed in the Manitoba Schools Question over language rights and by Canada's participation in the South African War. The dutiful Borden ran again for his seat in Halifax in 1900 and won, even as the Liberals buried the Conservatives, including their leader, eighty-year-old Sir Charles Tupper, claiming a victory of 133 seats to 80.[15] The dispirited Tories needed a change.

Tupper and the party's inner circle well remembered the disastrous internecine fighting after Macdonald's death almost a decade earlier. There were no party conventions to elect leaders in those days, and it fell to Tupper to nominate his successor. There was a solid old guard to choose from, of whom the best and most respected was George Foster, a former minister of finance under Macdonald and several other Conservative prime ministers, but he and others had fought many battles since 1891, and Foster had been branded as disloyal when he led a revolt against the incompetent and unpopular Mackenzie Bowell in 1896. The Conservatives needed someone new.

Tupper turned to Borden. Even in an age when cronyism was the rule, to choose his law partner to take his place seemed beyond the pale. Borden, too, was taken aback, replying, "It would be an absurdity for the party and madness for me."[16] Supporters observed he had few enemies; skeptics sniffed that he had not been around long enough to create any. After much pleading, Borden accepted the position, but he told the Tory elite he would act as an interim leader for only a year, until a successor could be found in the ranks of the shattered party.

Borden's emergence as leader came as a shock to many in the party and to most political watchers across the country. He was hardly an inspiring choice. How would this slightly stuffy, deadly earnest political novice fare against the experienced and charismatic Liberal leader? Laurier had greeted Borden in the House of Commons with a cheerful quip: "I hope with all my heart he may continue to exercise for a long, long period, the function of leader of the Opposition."[17] For Borden's part, he did not really want the job, did not see what skills he could bring to bear on defeating the Liberals, and generally entered into the arrangement as a man marching to his own funeral.

Borden was virtually unknown outside Ottawa and Halifax. Those who did know him noted his lack of a killer instinct in the House. With speeches that lacked fire, Borden often failed to score points either against the Liberals or with his own party. His backbenchers needed the morale boost brought on by a verbal blast or a blazing denouncement of the government. Borden refused to embarrass the Liberals simply because he had to take an opposing point of view, and his leadership style was to delegate the role of critic to several of the Tory MPs who enjoyed preening in the House. His approach was sensible but hardly inspiring.

This is not to suggest that Borden was an anemic wallflower: his blood could boil under provocation, especially over issues of corruption or in demanding that Canada do its duty to the Empire. These were useful subjects upon which to take a stand, and occasionally skewer the government, but the Liberals held the centre ground, with Sir Wilfrid—knighted for service and to tie him more firmly to the British Empire—generally able to deflect and disarm the opposition. His party had backed Britain in its war in South Africa, and the country's emerging prosperity dulled accusations of financial corruption. The Conservatives could find few chinks in the Liberal armour.

"The nineteenth century was the century of the United States. I think we can claim that it is Canada that shall fill the twentieth century," charged Laurier passionately a few years into the Dominion's supposed century. The claim captured the popular imagination and was so often repeated that it was eventually handed down as truth that the twentieth century belonged to Canada.[18] It was hyperbole to the core, but it won the hearts of Canadians. Against this imaginative vision, Borden's carping was ineffectual. As Liberal supporter and gifted newspaperman J.W. Dafoe remarked, "Perhaps there never was a time when satisfaction with existing conditions and confidence in the future were so general as in the year 1904. There was hardly a cloud in the sky."[19]

The Tories suffered another electoral defeat in 1904. The Liberals won a majority of seats in the House of Commons, and

Borden's humiliation was made greater because he lost his own riding. Distraught, he offered to resign the leadership, but his colleagues, after glumly surveying their own ranks and finding no one more competent to take his place, declined to accept it.

"I have put all the hesitation and doubt behind me," wrote Robert Borden in December 1904. "I shall endeavour to do my full duty."[20] Having survived political and personal defeat, a rejuvenated Borden, with the backing of his party, found, contested, and won a safe seat in Ontario, and then began to recast the party. He needed a new platform and new candidates. In an important psychological shift that reflected his newfound passion, he also cut his ties to Halifax, giving up his practice and home. The Bordens moved into a mansion on Wurtemburg Street, overlooking the Rideau River in Ottawa. Borden was now a full-time politician and one who set out to govern the country.

It would be no easy task, but by 1906 the Liberals had been in power for a decade and the disease that afflicts long-governing parties, the inevitable smugness and corruption that come with being a winner and having little effective counterbalance, began to seep through the reigning body like a poison. Corruption was unearthed in relation to the rampant spending on railways, but the Conservatives would need more than a few scandals to dislodge the party that appeared to be leading Canada towards claiming the century as its own, and doing so amid widespread prosperity.

After almost no consultation with his party or other MPs, Borden crafted a new manifesto in the summer of 1907, which became known as the Halifax Platform. It demanded examinations for civil service jobs, in effect removing patronage from politics. Not everyone in his party was cheered by this prospect, which threatened to rob winners of the ability to reward their supporters, but the manifesto also called for honest elections, senate reform, free rural mail delivery, and public ownership of telephones. It was a dog's breakfast of issues meant to chisel support away from the Liberals. Borden's platform garnered some support in the influential newspapers and offered fighting points for Conservatives, but he continued to come across as the stern, somewhat moralistic aunt to Laurier's debonair, slightly rakish uncle.

In August 1907, Borden embarked on a two-and-a-half-month cross-Canada tour in which he spoke at almost a hundred meetings. Handshakes and kisses were exchanged in between cold chicken lunches and bountiful toasts. It was arduous and exhausting, but the Conservative campaign received strong press coverage. Laurier's acute political antenna quivered. The prime minister had learned from his great opponent Sir John A. never to move too quickly unless forced, but he now knew that after more than a decade of power, the Liberals had at times been sloppy in wantonly rewarding friends. Stealing the Conservative thunder—and some of their platform—Laurier adopted many of Borden's best ideas and placed them on the statute books. Tory electoral victory seemed a long way off; as Laurier rightly crowed to a crowd in Cornwall in 1908, "We have been twelve years in office, and these years will be remembered in the history of Canada."[21] On October 26 only 50.4 percent of the voting males agreed with Laurier, but that was enough in Canada's first-past-the-post system to garner 135 seats to the Conservatives' 85.

Borden had been Tory leader for more than seven years. He had brought the party back from despair, but it was still mired in the political wilderness, and he appeared to many party members to have reached the end of the road. The leader remained too reserved, too analytical, too rational. Borden believed he had "become a more effective speaker" since 1904, and many of his supporters agreed, but he still spoke with more grace than zeal.[22] He had never embraced the battles of the House of Commons. Perhaps one of Borden's colleagues summed it up best: ruthless Conservative brawler Sam Hughes said Borden was "a lovely fellow, very capable, but not a very good judge of men or tactics and ... gentle-hearted as a girl."[23]

Having come up short again—although the party added more seats to its previous total—Borden's leadership came under fire in his own party. "Failure is the unforgiveable sin of a political leader," he wrote later, and he was forced to confront usurpers.[24] Luckily for him, the coup was carried out incompetently and suffered from the glaring weakness that while regime change might be embraced by some of the disaffected, the traitorous rump had no one ready to take control of the party. Borden and his loyal comrades defeated the insurgency and the Conservative leader emerged stronger, more politically astute, and with a harder glint in his eye.

CHAPTER 2

DEFEAT AND VICTORY, 1908–1914

Robert Borden set himself the task of building a new and winning political agenda. In broad strokes, since Laurier's rule, the Conservatives had been associated more closely with the British Empire, while the Liberals appeared more friendly to recent immigrants and French Canada, although both parties blurred these messages and relationships when it suited them to do so. To make inroads into Liberal strength across the country, Borden fortified ties with the established political machines and grass-roots organizations in Ontario, New Brunswick, Manitoba, and British Columbia, which all had solidly entrenched Conservative premiers.

The Conservative Party got a boost from an international crisis. For over a century, the Royal Navy had ruled the waves. Its informal policy was to maintain a navy that was as strong as its next two competitors combined. But in 1906, it changed the rules. The Admiralty launched the battleship HMS *Dreadnought*, which outclassed every other warship in the world with its devastating guns, thick armour, and churning speed. The new battleship brought immediate glory to the Royal Navy, but it also made all other ships obsolete. Britain's policy of besting its next two competitors was much diminished, for the international tally of seapower suggested that Great Britain now led only by a score of 1 to 0. Rival Germany turned towards building its own battleships in order to claim, as its unstable Kaiser barked, its place in the sun. The arms race for global naval supremacy was underpinned by wild rhetoric and rampant nationalism.

Canada relied on the Royal Navy to protect it from all potential enemies (with the exception of the Americans, who could not have been stopped if they truly wished to occupy the Dominion), and so Britain's crisis became Canada's. Laurier had negotiated the potentially divisive South African War almost a decade earlier by dragging his heels until popular opinion obliged him to send an officially sanctioned, voluntary expeditionary force. In this new crisis, Laurier waited and refused to commit himself or the Canadian people. But the naval issue flared up again in 1909, with another round of fear-mongering in the press—both in Britain and then in Canada—driving frantic calls to meet the German threat.

Would Canada take a role, albeit gingerly, in supporting the Empire by creating an independent Canadian navy? Would it contribute money, ships, or resources to the Royal Navy, as a kind of paid protection? Or would it simply ignore these potential international conflagrations and its moral obligation to contribute to its own defence? Public discussion of these options forced Canadians to think about what was owed to Britain and, equally important, how Canada wished to project itself on the world stage.

Laurier's vision was of a nation inching slowly towards its

destiny. After the South African War, Canada's tiny army had been professionalized. New permanent branches, such as the medical and service corps, were created and then, in 1904, a militia council was established that reported directly to the minister of militia and defence, thereby strengthening civilian control and reducing the influence of the British general who traditionally commanded the militia.[1] In 1909, Laurier took another step on the march to autonomy by establishing the Department of External Affairs. The department was underfunded, understaffed, and small enough to be situated above a barbershop, but it marked a beginning. So too did the proposed creation of a Canadian navy, which was Laurier's answer to the international naval arms race. To the prime minister, it seemed the only solution that met the demands of imperially minded Anglo-Canadians while also fending off criticism from French-Canadian nationalistes. Laurier framed the creation of a navy as Canada assuming "a nation's responsibilities, among which was self-defence."[2]

Borden and his English-speaking Conservatives predicted that war with Germany was coming fast, and argued that the building of a Canadian navy—which he did not oppose in principle—would take too long.[3] Why was Laurier willing to sacrifice the safety of the Empire and Canada, Borden demanded, especially since any "tin-pot navy" would never stand a chance against Germany's dreadnought-class warships? Laurier, however, could not agree to give London a cash gift to build battleships, as Borden proposed. His enemies in Quebec would accuse him of paying a colonial tribute to London. And so his government introduced the Naval Service Act of 1910, which planned for a surprisingly robust navy of five cruisers and six destroyers, a fleet similar to Australia's, which was being constructed around this same time.

The Conservatives denounced Laurier for betraying the Empire. Quebec nationalistes, led by the one-time Liberal and now editor of the newly established newspaper *Le Devoir*, Henri Bourassa, took a different tack. They charged that any navy would inevitably serve with the imperials, and ultimately drag Canada into a global war. Bourassa offered few alternatives to Laurier's navy. His solution was for Canada to do nothing: no navy, no gift to Britain, no change in status. That policy might have suited Quebec, but it would never satisfy the rest of Canada. Laurier lamented his vulnerable, centralist position: "I am branded in Quebec as a traitor to the French and in Ontario as a traitor to the English … In Quebec I am attacked as an Imperialist, and in Ontario as an anti-Imperialist."[4] Yet the suave Laurier, who was pushed and prodded by the extremists on both sides, rode out the storm. The only significant damage the Liberals sustained was the loss in a November 1910 by-election in rural Quebec to one of Bourassa's nationaliste candidates, who lied openly that Laurier's navy would mean the conscription of Quebec's sons for imperial wars.

HOPING TO LEAVE THE NAVAL DEBATES behind, in January of the next year the Liberals presented to the House a tentative reciprocity trade agreement with the United States, which would open up new markets for Canadian goods by reducing the customs on manufactured products. It was a triumph. The Conservative Party already had been split by the naval debates, which had seen the Quebec rump break with the larger faction of imperially minded Tories. Now, as they faced another defeat, panic set in. Borden had to resort to the threat of resignation in order to force an artificial unity. Even then, Borden reported the "deepest dejection" among his colleagues in the caucus. Tory stalwart George Foster noted vividly that upon hearing the free trade news, "his heart had gone down into his boots."[5]

And yet, Borden refused to be cowed. He remembered how the old chief, Sir John A., had wrapped himself in the Union Jack in 1891, when the Liberals had talked of a possible trade deal with the United States. Now, in 1911, Borden adopted the same tactic, launching an assault on the Liberals for turning their back on King, country, and Empire, appealing to the unhappy manufacturers who prospered behind the high tariff wall, while at the same time keeping a rearguard action against at least four disparate groups in his own party that were manoeuvring to force his resignation.[6] In this five-front war, Borden's strong attacks propped up the flagging Tories and resonated in Ontario. Borden set out to rally the rest of the nation.

Over a twenty-one-day period in the summer, Borden spoke an astonishing 124 times in a western pre-election tour to rally the troops, offering an infusion of heady Canadian and imperial rhetoric to stoke the anger that was directed against the Liberal free trade deal.[7] Donations poured into party coffers, important businessmen joined the cause, and star candidates were attracted to the ranks for the forthcoming election. Laurier was forced to leave the country for two critical months to attend an Imperial Conference in London, but upon his return in mid July he resolved to drop the writ over the trade issue, setting the election for September 21. He hoped to catch the Tories by surprise. It was too late. Borden's men were on the march. The "Revolt of the Eighteen"—a group of powerful Liberals and business leaders, mainly from Toronto, who turned against Laurier's reciprocity deal in defence of their own interests—was deeply influential. The

Eighteen offered an important injection of financial and newspaper support for the Conservatives.

During the campaign, Conservative warnings about Laurier's reciprocity bill being the first step to American annexation were given an enormous boost by Champ Clark, the Democratic Speaker of the House of Representatives in the United States, who mused publicly—in defiance of President William Taft's opinion—"I hope to see the day when the American flag will float over every square foot of the British North American possession, clear to the North Pole ... We are preparing to annex Canada."[8] It was a very large nail in reciprocity's coffin. Conservative candidates used the damning comment with great flourish in every stump speech, inciting crowds to denounce Yanks, Liberals, and all manner of nefarious agents who sought to "annex" Canada.[9] Liberals denied the inflammatory lies, but the cries of disloyalty resonated widely across English Canada.

"We must decide whether the spirit of Canadianism or of Continentalism shall prevail on the northern half of this continent," hammered Borden, implying that free trade was akin to annexation.[10] Borden sensed an exposed enemy. The Conservatives stood for Empire, except in Quebec, where Borden muted his message in order to embrace the nationalistes. French Canadians were told to fear Laurier's navy, which would lead to the eventual conscription of their sons for overseas imperial wars, where they would be "disemboweled for the Empire."[11] The fight in Quebec was a different battle entirely. Borden visited Quebec only once during the campaign, all but handing over command to Henri Bourassa and his Quebec lieutenant, Frederick Monk, an intelligent if quarrelsome Roman Catholic constitutional lawyer from Montreal, who was first elected in 1896 and survived the

Liberal tide.[12] The anti-Empire French-Canadian nationalistes were improbable allies, but they drifted into the somewhat bewildered Conservative camp under the general principle "my enemy's enemy is my friend."[13] Yet, having only won eleven seats in Quebec in 1904 and again in 1908, Borden accepted his unlikely partners, as he could scarcely do worse than he had without them.

The election was fought on two issues: reciprocity in English Canada and the naval question in Quebec. But there was a third factor. The Liberals had been in power since 1896, and while they had guided the country through a prosperous period, scandals had accumulated over the years. There was a sense of entitlement in Ottawa and among Liberal grassroots organizations. Even the venerable Laurier had remarked, "Reforms are for Opposition. It is the business of Governments to stay in office."[14] Newspaperman J.W. Dafoe wrote astutely that the "Laurier government died in 1911, not so much from the assaults of its enemies as from hardening of its arteries and from old age."[15]

The Conservatives surprised most political watchers, and possibly themselves, by winning the election. Laurier could rightly be mystified by how the positive trade deal and the creation of a navy could provoke such sharp and irrational sentiments in Ontario and Quebec, but it would not be the first time a party was defeated for doing the right thing. After fifteen years in politics, the fifty-seven-year-old Robert Borden became Canada's eighth prime minister on October 15, 1911.

ACCORDING TO THE 1911 CENSUS, more than 7.2 million Canadians were scattered across the country, a majority of them in rural areas. In excess of two million immigrants had come during Laurier's fifteen years of leadership, with many drawn to the "Last Best West." The Dominion privileged British immigrants, but others, many from Eastern Europe, brought a new diversification to the social contours of the country.[16] Eight of the nine provinces that formed Canada (Newfoundland not yet having joined) were closely linked to the British Empire, through politics, arts, heritage, and parliamentary custom. While Quebec had its own traditions and culture and French Canadians formed close to a third of Canada's population, the Union Jack flew over the Parliament buildings and Canadians remained entwined with the Empire. Without the imperial connection, many feared that Canada would stand alone against the Americans.[17]

The Conservatives had been out of power for fifteen years, and while Borden had been able to entice some strong candidates back into the political fold since 1908, his new caucus was inexperienced. Voters do not usually think about the cabinet they are going to elect, but they are surely stuck with it once the government is formed. In the days after the victory, Borden was under siege from his own party members, old enemies and new friends, who came to the prime minister with palms outstretched.

Laura Borden protected her husband from the patronage seekers, refusing to let Tories press their case by phone and blocking them when they called unsolicited at the house, allowing the new prime minister to mull over his choices from late September to October 10.[18] Borden agonized over the strengths and weaknesses of his potential cabinet ministers, but he also needed to include representatives of diverse geographic, ethnic, and religious sectors. He wrote to one friend: "Until one actually enters upon the undertaking it is almost impossible to realize the difficulties and perplexities which confront any man entrusted with the task of forming a new cabinet."[19]

Borden had his favourites—successful businessmen such as A.E. Kemp and George Perley—but there was also the old guard, some of whom had fought hard for the party for years, or represented those who did, such as the Conservative provincial leaders who had been essential in delivering votes. Scarred provincial veterans such as Robert Rogers (known as Honourable Bob, because he was anything but), Sam Hughes (a military madman—or so said the Liberals—from the fringe of the party, but representing vote-rich rural Ontario), and Sir George Foster (who had served already in five prime ministers' cabinets) all came with liabilities, but also strengths. The hard-boiled Rogers made the jump from provincial politics in Manitoba and set to needling the Liberals, whom he hated. Hughes was ecstatic to be the defence minister, fulfilling a lifelong ambition, and attacked his duties with relish. Foster was furious about receiving trade and commerce, believing he was owed finance, the ministry he had held under Macdonald in the 1880s and 1890s. Foster was lucky to get a ministry at all, since Borden later described him as having the "political sense of a turnip."[20] Borden also brought in as railways minister the hardworking "Silent" Frank Cochrane, who had orchestrated the near sweep of votes in northern Ontario, and the popular if scheming John "Doc" Reid, even though he earlier had led a revolt against Borden's leadership. "Recalling Sir John A. Macdonald's maxim," wrote Borden, "one should never select a colleague by the standard of one's personal likes or dislikes."[21]

The all-important finance ministry went to Thomas White, who was not a career politician like many of the other Conservatives, but he had the support of the all-important Toronto Eighteen. The thought of the liberal-minded White holding a key ministry infuriated some of the old Conservative political warriors, but he would prove a good minister and best represented how non-traditional Tories were brought into the big tent party.

Borden had the added problem of having to reward the Quebec nationalistes. Bourassa turned aside Borden's probing offers of a seat in the cabinet, and was already wary of being linked to the Conservatives now that their common enemy had been defeated. Borden was left relying heavily on the uncharismatic, moody, and stubborn Frederick Monk. The cadaverous-looking Monk was a fierce nationalist, but he was not well liked by his English or French Conservative colleagues, who found him haughty, prickly, and insulting. He in turn was quick to take offence and long in carrying a grudge.[22] Nonetheless, he was the best of a weak pool from which to find the all-important French-Canadian leader, and he received the patronage-rich public works ministry. Borden found only two other cabinet spots for nationalistes: Louis-Philippe Pelletier was made postmaster-general and Wilfrid Nantel was appointed minister of inland revenue and mines. Neither was in the prime minister's influential inner circle.

There was no denying the cabinet's lack of experience. The Halifax *Chronicle* called it a "collection of mediocrities," and even with the passage of time it still did not come together, remaining a sum of its parts rather than something greater.[23] The Tories had little time to learn on-the-job before the country was in crisis. Within two years of Borden's victory, Canada followed a worldwide economic downturn and slipped into a recession. While immigrants continued to pour into the country (375,000 in 1912, 400,000 the next year), there were fewer jobs to occupy them. The railways that kept the isolated communities artificially linked east-to-west rather than along the more profitable north–south trade routes were feeling the pinch, and when trade slowed, the Canadian Northern, the Grand Trunk Pacific, and the Grand Trunk began sucking in federal funds to keep them financially afloat.

Borden's government found itself hemorrhaging on other fronts too. Laurier's navy was stillborn, with only two obsolete cruisers donated by the British, and in March 1912 Borden announced that he was killing the naval shipbuilding program. What he proposed to his colleagues, but not yet publicly, was to make a cash gift to Britain of $35 million to be put towards naval defence. He moved cautiously, however, knowing it would reveal the fault lines between nationalistes and imperialists in his own party. Even after a July 1912 visit to London—where Borden met with Prime Minister Herbert Asquith and many of his cabinet ministers, who expressed fear over falling behind in the naval arms race—Liberals and nationalistes at home were not convinced of the danger.

Frederick Monk argued against the plan in the caucus and cabinet. When he found no support with his colleagues, Monk, who operated almost independently from the English-speaking side of the party, unwisely demanded a nationwide plebiscite over the issue. This was, in fact, an option offered to the nationalistes by Borden during the election campaign, but a plebiscite was deeply unpopular with most of the new cabinet ministers, who believed it showed indecision and disloyalty to the Empire.[24] Aware that the party was already drifting into ineffectiveness, Borden denied Monk his plebiscite, much to the pleasure of some of his more rabid English ministers, who openly taunted the Quebec leader. Monk resigned on October 18, 1912.

Without a French-Canadian champion in cabinet, Borden lost what little influence he had in French Canada. Quebec politicians, at both the federal and provincial level, converged on the still-warm corpse of the party apparatus in Quebec, which led to an unseemly feeding frenzy, as Conservatives battled each other for control over funds, organizers, and the grassroots of the party. Borden looked on with disdain and disbelief, but could not rouse himself to do much other than wring his hands.[25] For the rest of his prime ministership, Borden engaged lightly with Quebec, and while he could force out some words in French, it was largely from memorization rather than understanding. He never overcame his view that Canada was a part of the British Empire and that Quebec had to accommodate itself to the larger nation. French Canada remained a mystery to Borden throughout his life.

With Monk gone and his English colleagues urging him to action, Borden introduced his Naval Aid Bill on December 5, 1912. Finally he made public the proposed $35 million donation to Britain for the construction of three dreadnoughts. The plan to build Canadian warships would be postponed indefinitely. Borden's naval bill set off a spectacular bloodletting in the House of Commons. The debates were endless, the overblown rhetoric moving from routine denunciations to salacious accusations. The Liberals, sensing an issue they could exploit, prolonged discussion until the talk degenerated into filibustering, with one Liberal member reading the Bible into Hansard to waste time. The Conservatives, in turn, rallied around the flag. As the Tory tone grew more strident, militaristic, and supportive of the Empire no matter the cost, the Quebec nationalistes who had joined them in

1911 began to waver, realizing that their shotgun marriage had them shackled to an imperial party. Many were looking for an annulment.

Fed up, exhausted, and angry, opposing MPs several times came close to exchanging blows in a partisan and alcohol-fuelled battle of "primeval passions," as Borden characterized it.[26] Borden himself was ill throughout the period. Boils that erupted over his body required daily lancing to release the pus and he was often seen in the House of Commons with his neck swathed in bandages. To end the opposition filibuster, the Tories invoked closure on April 9, 1913, in order to pass the Naval Aid Bill. It was the first time in Canadian history closure was used to end debate. Borden and his cabinet claimed the need for expediency in meeting the German threat, and for good measure sang "Rule Britannia" and "God Save the King," which only partially drowned out the cacophony from indignant Liberals screaming about the end of democracy.

Closure allowed the government to send the bill to the Senate (after another month of debate and delay), but the upper chamber was controlled by the Liberals, who had stacked it with party men over the preceding decade and a half. Borden hoped that loyalty to Empire would overcome the ill will engendered by closure. It was a naive wish. The Senate flung the bill back at the House and dared Borden to call an election over the issue.

Angry Conservatives accused the Liberals of deadlocking the government, but neither Laurier nor his senators were there to make Borden's life easy. A furious Borden read into the House on June 5 a quote from a German newspaper: "Whatever may be decided upon later, the actual decision of the Canadian Senate means at any rate a heavy moral and material loss for the defence of the Empire."[27] The Liberals shrugged it off, Laurier scoffing at the supposed danger to Empire. Their lighthearted taunts would come back to haunt them, but now, in the heat of battle, the Liberals were cheered by the thought of another election, especially with the naval question driving a wedge through Conservative ranks. The journalist Augustus Bridle characterized the Borden government as a "one-act farce."[28] The naval bill sank from sight.

The Tories continued to prepare for war, which both Borden and his minister of militia and defence, Sam Hughes, believed was fast approaching.[29] With Borden's support, Hughes poured money into building armouries and increased funds for the local militia units spread across the country that the minister believed were Canada's first line of defence.[30] As a member of the militia for almost fifty years, Hughes swore that the citizen-soldiers—men who would put down the plow to pick up the rifle—would rise to Britain's defence in time of need, and allow Canada to stride onto the world stage. Hughes was bombastic and bigoted, but he had enormous energy, was a compelling speaker, and was much loved by those he represented. These included the Orange Order, rural Ontario, and the militia.

Borden thought Hughes a bit of a crank, but one who got the job done, so the prime minister could focus on other pressing issues. Chief among them was the recession. With capital investment slowing, new construction declining, and the price of wheat, metals, and lumber all falling, the boom of the previous decade disappeared with the gurgle of an emptying tub. Soon the government was being blamed for fiscal mismanagement. The minister of finance, Thomas White, knew the country was spinning into a depression, but he had few tools with which to solve the problem.

He had neither a central bank, nor income tax revenue, nor Keynesian economic theory to work with. Instead of the government spending its way out of the predicament, White believed the only option was to reduce federal expenditures. This only hurt Canadians more, but White was essentially helpless.

In the summer of 1914, three years after taking power, Borden's Conservatives were a shambles. Laurier gloated at the prospect of an election, as certain as he was of victory as of anything in his life. How could he not be? The economy was depressed and voters blamed the Conservatives. The major Conservative legislation—the naval bill—had been blocked, along with several others for good measure, by the vindictive Senate. A frustrated Borden hoped to run on a proposal to make the Senate an elected body, but few across the country cared about its makeup. Borden's platform also featured the recycled plan to clean up the civil service by doing away with patronage appointments. This was viewed as sheer lunacy by many of his fellow Conservatives, who were aghast at the thought of losing some of the perks of power. When all these factors were taken into account, it seemed certain that the Conservatives would be cast back into the wilderness. Borden talked privately of retiring. Several ministers, such as Cochrane and White, were near physical collapse. The award of a knighthood for Borden in June 1914 did little to alleviate the strain. Sir Robert and his colleagues were sleepwalking to defeat.

CHAPTER 3

THE GREAT WAR, 1914

Sir Robert Borden was at a cottage in Muskoka during the warm days of late July, attempting to regain his strength and treat the carbuncles that plagued him. Like many Canadians who kept an eye on European politics, Borden had been aware of the assassination of the archduke of Austria, Franz Ferdinand, at the end of June, as well as the ongoing tension between the Austrian Empire and upstart Serbia, which was implicated in the murder. This boiling conflict between aggressive neighbours in a region of the world that had already seen a handful of wars since Borden had been elected prime minister now threatened to explode into a wider war.

When Germany gave unconditional support to its ally Austria, and Russia backed Serbia, it set off a chain reaction that saw a willing France, anxious to redeem its humiliating loss to the Germans in the Franco-Prussian War of 1870–1871, push belligerently into the escalating conflict. There was little time for diplomacy after the army commands of Europe implemented their lightning mobilizations, which called up the reserve armies of hundreds of thousands and then millions of civilians to back their core professional forces. On August 1, 1914, German armies crashed through Belgium's borders in the hope of encircling France's northern defences and armies. The invasion through Belgium brought Britain into the war through a sixty-year-old treaty with Belgium, as well as other alliance commitments.

Rushing back to Ottawa, Borden found himself on the night of August 4 the prime minister of a country at war. He had had no say over the matter. Neither had his cabinet nor Parliament, which was not sitting at the time. Nor had there been any information sent by Whitehall to update the Dominion.[1] Canada never declared war on Germany: as part of the British Empire it was drawn into the vortex that pitted the principal allies of Britain, France, Belgium, and Russia, along with their colonies, dominions, and protectorates, against the Central Powers of Germany and Austria, and later Turkey, with other opportunistic or unlucky small nations rushing to join the two alliance systems as the war progressed.

"Although the events of the past few days had quite prepared us for the result," remarked Borden about finding the country at war, "it came at the last as a shock."[2] Yet all were expected to do their duty as Borden had declared four years before: "So long as the English flag floats above Canada, Canada is at war when that flag is attacked."[3] Few in power questioned Canada's obligations to Empire or the need to defeat Germany. That nation was seen as dangerously militaristic and its aggression as a threat to the balance of power. A Germany that ruled Europe would soon threaten Britain. Canadians from all parts of the country stood by the Empire of which they were a part. Anyone who had reservations stayed silent, for fear of being accused of disloyalty or of suffering reprisals. Canada was going to fight, intoned the City Council of Winnipeg, in one of many responses from communities across the country, because "she was an integral part of the British Empire ... bound by the closest ties of blood and tradition to the Mother Country."[4] This was Canada's war.

The sudden declaration came as a shock to the bankers and financiers. The interconnected web of bond markets and stock exchanges were closed or disrupted. Before a single shot was fired, some doomsayers had predicted grave consequences, perhaps even worldwide financial collapse. It did not happen. The markets would be buoyed by war production. Still, few believed the warring nations would escape punishing debts.

In a time of emergency, the government's initial priority was not to raise an army but to secure its financial institutions. Would the panicked pull their money from the banks and crash the system? In fact, the Canadian people remained steady during the crisis, but Borden's cabinet had acted appropriately on August 3, a day before it was at war, by passing orders-in-council that guaranteed Dominion notes to fund the war effort, as well as wider powers that gave the government the right to "prevent any avoidable interruption of stable business conditions."[5]

And what did a country do when it was at war? Borden had presciently asked this of the small civil service earlier in the year. Under the guidance of the efficient Sir Joseph Pope, undersecretary of state for external affairs, a committee drew up a War Book, which offered guidelines for action.[6] The government now turned to it. Most departments followed their pre-arranged plans, although not the most important one, militia and defence.

Almost overnight, Minister of Militia and Defence Sam Hughes moved from the cabinet's periphery to centre stage.

Many viewed him as an unstable megalomaniac; most others saw him as simply a maniac. But he caught the frenzied tenor of the time. Hughes shouted and swore, in and out of the House of Commons. He made outrageous statements and was deeply bigoted against the French Canadians, Catholics, and anyone who questioned the role of the militia in Canadian society. He revelled in the British Empire, but bristled at British professional soldiers, believing they could not hold a candle to civilian soldiers, who were gifted, in his mind, with sharpshooting skills and a toughness born from working the hard land. That most Canadian militia men were drawn from urban centres never caused him to reappraise his views. While slightly buffoonish, Hughes was an imposing figure, who was a feared brawler in the House of Commons. Now, the hyper-patriotic minister offered citizens the chance to become soldiers. His ad hoc mobilization plan, which took authority away from district commands and gathered more than 30,000 recruits at Valcartier, Quebec, caused confusion, but it worked and captured the urgency and call for action felt by many. Despite Hughes's histrionics, Borden was deeply impressed by his bombastic minister, and glad to see him assume his duties with boundless energy.[7]

BORDEN WAS BRITISH TO THE CORE. He had been brought up on stories of Britain's great history, culture, and politics. His visit to England in 1912, when he met the elite of Edwardian society, had been a momentous occasion for him. He saw Canada as a proud contributing member of the Empire, and took it for granted that it would respond with assistance when Britain was threatened. And now, in August 1914, it was clear that Britain was in danger.

This was no minor colonial war, but one that involved Germany, aligned with other hostile states, whose actions threatened the British Empire. So when war was declared there was no surprise that Borden and his party caught the mood of the people by committing Canada to Britain's cause.

More surprising was how little opposition there was to war. The Liberals, too, backed Britain to the hilt. Even the influential Quebec nationaliste, Henri Bourassa, believed that France and Britain were engaged in a just war, and he pledged support, although he remained wary of a full wartime commitment to the Empire. Other prominent Quebec politicians were more enthusiastic: Montreal Mayor Médéric Martin proclaimed to French Canadians: "If you are needed it is your duty to fight."[8] There was nearly universal backing among the opinion-makers, although sometimes the arguments were presented differently. Conservative newspapers tended to proclaim their loyalty to the Empire and the need to support Britain in its time of need; Liberal papers echoed these sentiments, but placed more emphasis on upholding liberal ideas in the war against militarism.[9]

On the day war was declared, the cabinet immediately passed an order-in-council putting the two obsolete Royal Canadian Navy (RCN) warships, HMCSs *Rainbow* and *Niobe*, on active operations and under control of the Royal Navy.[10] *Rainbow*, on the west coast, was soon sent on a suicide mission to engage a modern German cruiser that was supposedly steaming for Vancouver. The threat proved to be illusory, but it inspired fear and consternation as Canadians imagined themselves as targets. The premier of British Columbia, Sir Richard McBride, took it upon himself to purchase two submarines from the still-neutral United States, which nearly doubled naval strength in a matter of days. Banks in Victoria and Vancouver moved millions of dollars inland, terrified homeowners took out insurance, and blasting was halted in connection with work on sewers in Victoria for fear of causing alarm. In this context, perhaps the submarines, boringly named *CC-1* and *CC-2*, had been worth their jaw-dropping price of $1.1 million—double the previous year's entire naval budget—as a prophylactic against fear.[11] Whatever the case, they are but a footnote to history, since the subs had no operational value. Canada's main war effort would be not at sea but on land.

Borden and his cabinet received word from the British a few days into the war that an initial contingent of 25,000 soldiers would be welcome. While Canada's expeditionary force would be organized, equipped, and paid for by the Dominion government, the Canadians would fight as part of the British army and would likely be commanded by a British general.[12] Borden would eventually leverage this contribution, and those that followed, in the Allied war effort to assert his country's demand for greater equality within the Empire.

An emergency session of Parliament was called to order on August 18. Laurier used the opportunity to express his loyalty to the Empire when he assured the House that "Canada, a daughter of old England, intends to stand by her in this great conflict ... When the call comes our answer goes at once, and it goes in the classical language of the British answer to the call of duty: Ready, aye, ready!"[13] It was stirring fare. The Loyal Opposition was living up to the first part of its name, although its fervour ensured that few were left to question the government's legislation.

The next day, the minister of justice, C.J. Doherty, introduced Bill C-2, the emergency war measures legislation. It allowed for censorship, trade restrictions, the arbitrary arrest of individuals without trial, and almost any other power that the government felt was necessary for the "security, defence, peace, order and welfare of Canada." With parliamentarians tripping over each other to appear more patriotic than the rest, there was very little debate about the authoritarian powers that would be afforded to the government.[14]

Liberal member of Parliament William Pugsley did have the gumption to question the government's right to suspend habeas corpus, the "dearest liberties of a British subject," but the government sidestepped the issue, suggesting that a committee would examine the bill in depth during second reading.[15] This was never done, and the bill was passed by both houses of Parliament by August 22 and proclaimed law on September 3.[16] The potentially most repressive law in Canadian history had been passed with minimal examination, and with unanimous support from parliamentarians. How was one to argue with MPs such as Liberal Michael Clark, who had a son in uniform: "Every man in the British Empire feels that he is fighting for the Empire and for the flag. But he is fighting for more than that. He is fighting for the principles that are at the root of the highest civilization; he is fighting for human freedom."[17] No MP ventured to challenge such fiery rhetoric.

There were few actions that the prime minister and his cabinet could not carry out legally under the War Measures Act. Buried in this extraordinary legislation was an enormous transfer of power from Parliament to cabinet, which could govern by decree. Through the use of orders-in-council—a formal recommendation by cabinet of an administrative decision to be signed by the governor general into law—the cabinet could pass legislation or create new agencies. Parliamentary debate and scrutiny were no longer required. In short, Parliament surrendered its role under this revolutionary bill.[18] For all intents and purposes, Borden's cabinet of fewer than two dozen men was now a law unto itself. Over the course of the war, these critical decision-making powers would be confined to the even smaller group of men who formed the prime minister's inner circle, and, during the war, at key points, decisions were often made by Borden alone.

"WE STAND SHOULDER TO SHOULDER with Britain and the other British Dominions in this quarrel," Borden told the nation.[19] During these early days of speculation and rumour, the prime minister was lauded by a prominent opinion-maker for his "special qualities of coolness, caution and concentration ... [Borden] rose to the occasion and did his dull duty in an adequate way, without fuss, or flurry, or excitement, [and this action] will be the high tribute of the future when the great issue, the tremendous strain, the silent labours, of this period come up for historic judgement."[20] While he had enormous energy and drive, he often worked himself to illness, and suffered from poor sleep or insomnia. But he remained a robust figure, with fierce, deep-set eyes, along with his thick, white moustache and hair. He was never seen in public without his high straight collar, tie, and suit. However, the more churlish gossip in political circles, as recounted by Ontario Liberal Newton Rowell, was that "Sir Robert Borden is an amiable man with good ideals but without decision of character, the courage or the outlook to fill the position of premier at this time."[21] Timid, uncharismatic, and vacillating, or so Liberals classified Borden. Neither his admirers nor his detractors would have pegged the prime minister as a warlord. Borden himself confessed that he was "not a military man."[22] However, Sam Hughes was, and he would initially lead the nation's war effort.

Sam Hughes strutted about in his colonel's uniform, barking out commands, raising soldiers in rank on a whim, while consigning others to the periphery. He appeared to be more of a general than a civilian minister. It rankled Hughes that he was in fact only a colonel, but he set in motion the wheels to have his rank raised, first to major-general, which set tongues wagging, and then to lieutenant-general, which led to gasps of incredulity. He faced down grumblers, punished the most vocal, and browbeat the rest.

Borden assured Canadians in a widely publicized speech in Halifax in December 1914 that Canada's new army would be composed of volunteers: "Under the laws of Canada, our citizens may be called out to defend our own territory, but cannot be required to go beyond the seas except for the defence of Canada itself. There has not been, there will not be, compulsion or conscription."[23] At the start of the war, no one dreamed of the need for compulsory service, as thousands of young and middle-aged men, the great majority of them British-born and with previous military experience, flocked to the new training camp at Valcartier near Quebec. But as the grim war progressed, Borden's promise would have to be revisited.

Hughes's "boys," as he liked to call them, were trained to march and shoot their Canadian-manufactured Ross rifles. Much of the senior officers' time, however, was spent sorting out the administrative mess the minister's improvised mobilization had created. They formed new units, looked for suitable junior leaders, and handled the complicated logistical challenges involved in setting up a brand-new camp, all in the few weeks before the First Contingent sailed for England. It was the largest single transfer of Canadians across the Atlantic up to that point in the Dominion's history. The initial 25,000 figure had ballooned to over 30,000; they would be followed over the next four years by another 420,000 men to make up the Canadian Expeditionary Force.

Canada's First Contingent arrived in England in mid October 1914 to cheering crowds. Their new British commander, Lieutenant-General E.A.H. Alderson, met the Canadians and was impressed by their ardour and desire for battle, while noting they were a little rough around the edges. But that is what everyone expected of colonial troops who were believed to be hard and reckless because of their years in the cold North American wasteland. While the Canadians wanted to go to the front immediately, the British decided wisely that the First Contingent needed more training. Alderson was especially critical of its officers, whom he characterized as "very ignorant and possessing no power or habit of command."[24] Borden worried about the general's observation, but he left the issue with Sam Hughes, who fumed at the attacks on his officers, many of whom were hand-picked by him, and he believed the harsh appreciation was nothing more than a British conspiracy. He took no action, but he soured quickly on Alderson. The Canadians spent the next four months training on Salisbury Plain, where they learned to soldier in muddy conditions brought on by nearly incessant rain.

THE GOVERNMENT ESTIMATED IN August 1914 that to put a soldier in the field would cost about $1,000 per man.[25] Much of this cost went towards equipment. Sam Hughes was the driving force in ensuring that his soldiers were provided with Canadian-made kit, but there were almost no available stocks. So he encouraged manufacturers to rev up production. Boot and coat manufacturers switched easily from civilian to military production, while the factory making the Ross rifle, Canada's national rifle, went into high gear. But much of the kit was soon found to be substandard: the boots dissolved in the mud and the Ross rifle malfunctioned in battlefield conditions. While these failures were lamentable, later scandal-mongers and investigators tended to forget the urgency to rapidly equip the Canadian forces and send them across the Atlantic. The nation was struggling with being thrust into a war for which it was almost completely unprepared.

Many of the scandals centred on Hughes's propensity to dish out contracts generously, but only to Conservatives. There is no doubt that Hughes disregarded Borden's prewar promise to rid the political system of patronage. The prime minister found this distasteful, but did not interfere, as his beliefs were not shared by most of his cabinet: "Astonishing how every minister reaches out for every available bit of patronage."[26] At this point in the war, however, there was little pressure to change the "old ways" of doing business.

Sam Hughes was also responsible for establishing Canada's munitions industry, and for this he deserved accolades. The fighting on the Western Front required an enormous expenditure of small arms and artillery shells. New Zealand, Australia, and South Africa were too far away to provide the necessary shells. In North America, Canada had no munitions industry, and the neutral Americans, with their established factories, were better situated than the Dominion to meet the demand. When the British placed contracts south of the border, however, Borden complained bitterly to London that they had overlooked Canada.[27] Hughes took it as a point of pride that Canada would meet this patriotic and profitable obligation. Unfortunately, the Dominion's manufacturers were reluctant to invest the funds to retool their industries for what was expected to be a short war.

Hughes, undeterred, used his considerable influence to cajole the manufacturers into assuming their responsibility to support the war effort. Technical challenges and shortages in skilled labour made progress slow, but gradually the industry came into its own. By 1917, it was supplying about a quarter of the artillery shells used by the British; in the last two years of the war it was turning out tens of millions of them. Hughes has often been condemned for the slow pace of development, but he was starting the industry almost from scratch. He laid the foundation, which would be built on by the more competent Joseph Flavelle after December 1915, for a sector that would create a quarter of a million jobs and make a significant contribution to the war effort.[28] This was one of the great success stories of Canada's war.

The war breathed new life into the Borden administration. The raising of the First Contingent had been haphazard and harried, but it had been accomplished. Canada had done its bit, and done it proudly. To an electorate now filled with patriotic fervour, Borden and Hughes, with White in the background scrambling to fill the nation's empty war chest, looked determined, competent, and in control.

Some opportunistic Conservatives, led by Minister of Public Works Robert Rogers, felt it was time to call an election and catch the Liberals while they were vulnerable. After all, Laurier's party had repudiated prewar military spending, torpedoed the naval bill, and scoffed at warnings that war with Germany was imminent. Borden toyed with the idea, but in the end felt that the inflamed passions of English Canadians on one side, and of anti-imperial French Canadians on the other, would lead, in his words, to "intense disunion and fierce controversy."[29] Borden also feared that such a blatant politically motivated election could backfire, especially as the Liberals were proving to be so cooperative in supporting the war. And so, to the annoyance of his more partisan colleagues, Borden embraced the role of statesman rather than politician, summoning Canadians to band together in a great national effort.

WHILE CANADA WAS STILL British at heart, the previous two decades had seen an influx of new settlers from almost every country in Europe. At the outbreak of war, there were roughly 400,000 German-born immigrants in the country and another 125,000 from the Austro-Hungarian Empire.[30] These were not insubstantial numbers in a population of less than eight million. While opponents of the war, and especially foreign ones, "made themselves scarce," according to the *Winnipeg Free Press*, a trickle of these new Canadians publicly sided with Germany, while others left the country via the United States to fight for the Kaiser.[31] On August 7, *The Globe* of Toronto, a Liberal newspaper, called for the registration of enemy immigrants and for rigid curfews, concluding hysterically, "Anyone disobeying these orders to be court martialled and shot as a spy."[32]

To the south, there were an estimated eight million German Americans, many of whom were stridently against the Allied war effort or demanded that the United States remain neutral. In early August, rumours circulated throughout the Dominion that

German Americans were massing for an invasion. Member of Parliament J.D. Hazen forwarded to the prime minister a report claiming that these terrorists "intend to muster 150,000 men along the border and invade in three or four places, destroy canals, the railroads, and grain elevators."[33] Although Borden was already feeling the strain of overwork, and was under the care of a physician, his common sense had not deserted him. He disregarded these paranoid alarms, believing rightly that the United States would never allow anything of the kind to occur.[34] He was ably supported by Sam Hughes, who ignored the invasion claims in his own blunt way: "This whole talk of German invasion through the United States is sheer insanity."[35]

Borden advocated publicly for calm, but potential threats were monitored. By mid October, about 8,000 militia men were posted to guard federal buildings, bridges, and power stations.[36] Trigger-happy guards shot a few trespassers, and a few high-profile, though ineffectual, acts of sabotage further heightened panic and stirred the ingrained nativism of many Canadians.[37] Fearful of potential enemies in their ranks, many Canadians called on the government to imprison immigrants from Germany and Austria-Hungary. Borden urged a sympathetic policy towards these Canadians, but pressure built and he caved to the demands. Under the War Measures Act, more than 8,000 "enemy aliens" were eventually interned in more than twenty isolated camps across the country, although by mid-1916 these numbers had been reduced to about 2,000.[38] Most of the internees were Ukrainians from the Austrian Empire rather than Germany, the British Empire's primary enemy. The Ukrainian internees, which included some families, were paid a pittance and put behind barbed wire. A few were even shot trying to escape. Few newspapers picked up on the sad irony that many of the Ukrainians had fled the repressive Austro-Hungarian Empire to start a new, peaceful life in Canada.[39] The strange imprisonment left hurtful scars in the Ukrainian community and was one of the war's dark legacies.

MANY CANADIANS VIEWED THE WAR as a crusade against the militaristic German people—the "barbaric Hun"—who sought to enslave Europe and destabilize the British Empire. Borden, too, believed in the justice of the Allied war effort.[40] He saw it as a war of good against evil, British liberty standing in the face of German aggression. "Canada, in common with all the Empire," he said, "is prepared to fight, and intends to fight, to the death."[41]

But Borden's battles were fought largely from Ottawa. His workload was enormous. There were few nights that the prime minister returned home before midnight, and his diary is replete with references to his exhaustion. With only a few assistants, and no formal Prime Minister's Office, Borden often responded in his own hand to correspondents. There was no shortage of citizens who wished to share their ideas on how to win the war, defend against nefarious agents, and address all manner of other issues great and small. Borden had a "genius for work," wrote Conservative member of Parliament Arthur Meighen, as the prime minister tackled file after file, chewing his tobacco, spitting away the brown juice into a spittoon at the foot of his desk.[42]

Gradually, the country was emerging from the prewar economic depression largely because of the ramped-up production of war supplies, which included everything from uniforms and razors to rifles and shells. Farmers would enjoy windfall profits the next year as their crops fed the Allied nations. The news from Europe, however, was grim. The war that many predicted would be over by Christmas was far from winding down. Million-man armies were being raised, and Canada would soon follow suit by turning to hundreds of thousands of young men to fill the ranks of the expeditionary force. Furthermore, in the heady days of August, the government had passed the most draconian legislation in Canadian history. The War Measures Act gave the government almost unlimited power over the citizenry, including censorship, the negation of civil liberties, and imprisonment without trial. In a war fought to preserve the old order, the conflict overseas was forcing the Dominion to change. How much further were Borden and the Canadian people willing to go? The only answer, as it was to turn out, was to the bitter end.

CHAPTER 4

A WAR FOOTING, 1915

The terrible nature of the war was brought home for Canadians in late April 1915. The First Contingent had trained in England for nearly four months before a pared-down force of about 18,000 soldiers, known as the Canadian Division, was sent to the Western Front in February 1915. There, the Canadians encountered for the first time the trench system that ran from Switzerland to the North Sea, some 700 kilometres. Burrowing into the ground like troglodytes, front-line soldiers learned that this was a war of the shovel as much as the rifle. Death came from unseen shells and snipers, and the strain of surviving in the mud, with the rats and lice, wore away at the strongest and most committed of men.

While serving in the Ypres salient in April, the Canadian Division faced the first major German offensive of the year on the Western Front, which was launched behind lethal chlorine gas that burned out the lungs of defenceless soldiers, none of whom were equipped with respirators. The Canadians fought tenaciously starting on April 22, in many cases purchasing time with their lives while British and French soldiers were rushed to the front. After four days of nearly constant battle, most Canadian units were relieved, but the carnage had been terrible. More than 6,000 Canadians were killed, maimed, or captured.[1] The shock of these losses swept over the Dominion, as Canadians found their newspapers filled with the names of their neighbours, brothers, and sons listed among the dead.

It was not until April 25, 1915, a full four days after the battle commenced, that Borden mentioned the Canadian stand at Second Ypres in his diary, and not until the 27th that he seemed to acknowledge the severity of the fighting, observing laconically, "casualties still coming."[2] Borden's apparent failure to appreciate that this had been the most costly battle ever fought by Canadians reveals how out of touch the prime minister was with what was occurring overseas.

The war was becoming a crusade. The Hun had overrun Belgium and put its civilians to the sword; they had occupied northern France and threatened the British Empire; and now they had savaged Canadians on the battlefield. Those on the home front uncommitted to the war were increasingly pressured to take a stand. Dissenters of prosecuting the war to the fullest were soon condemned by an angry and increasingly critical public that demanded that all Canadians support the war, no matter the cost.

The voluntary war effort brought tens of thousands of men into the forces, but the government had not been ready to deal with their dependents—the wives, parents, and children left behind. A civilian-run organization, the Canadian Patriotic Fund (CPF), had been established during the South African War a generation earlier to deal with similar problems, but now it faced challenges on an entirely new scale. The government encouraged it in its work, largely because it had neither the expertise nor the structure to deal with the war's impact on families.[3] Responding to calls to "Do Your Bit," Canadians donated tens of thousands of dollars to keep soldiers' families clothed and food on the table. As one contributor remarked, "Everybody felt they had to do something."[4] The publicists and propagandists emphasized the success of the voluntary distribution system, and ignored some early failures that had left some women and children begging and, in a few ghastly cases, elderly parents starving to death. Nor did the CPF highlight its role as a self-appointed regulator of social values. The middle-class women who allocated the funds watched their wards for signs of lavish spending, such as the purchase of hats or telephones, which might, it was believed, lead to lascivious behaviour. Rumours of infidelity and wanton drinking often caused the monthly stipend of roughly $30 to $50 to be cut off.[5]

While the Imperial Order Daughters of the Empire (IODE), churches, and charitable groups responded to the war with a fury of activity in raising money for soldiers' families or Belgian relief, they also used the great conflict as an opportunity to right social ills. Alcohol abuse had been the bane of social reformers for decades, but this new war provided an opportunity for groups such as the Woman's Christian Temperance Union (WCTU) to argue for a ban on drinking. Smoking, too, was regarded as a problem. "All who send cigarettes to the soldiers at the Front are partisans in a national crime," proclaimed one zealous member of the WCTU in October 1915.[6] Fervent abstainers worked to get hundreds of thousands of signatures on petitions demanding prohibition and presented them to local and provincial governments, or directly to Sir Robert Borden. One by one, all provinces with the exception of Quebec brought in temperance acts, and the federal government followed suit by making Canada dry by 1918. No government dared to touch the smoking issue. This terrible war was offering an opportunity to moral reformers to fight not only the Hun overseas, but also sloth, drink, and evil at home. They were remaking the social order.

PATRIOTISM GALVANIZED CANADIAN SOCIETY, but it did not pay the bills. The steady drain on finances remained one of the most pressing issues for Borden's government. Thomas White, who had taken over as minister of finance in 1911 at the relatively youthful age of forty-five, had been a Tory star candidate. He had a solid reputation as the managing director for the National Trust Company, and he represented an important shift of the centre of finance from Montreal to Toronto under the Conservatives.[7] Handsome, with piercing eyes, full moustache, and greying hair, the mild and friendly White was ill at ease in the House of Commons, where he never grew to enjoy the rhetorical attacks, feints, and parries of debate.

After White strengthened public confidence in early August by ensuring adequate credit and gold reserves for the banks, he sought new funds to pay for the war. The federal government had few methods of raising money other than through tariffs: White increased duties on commercial and luxury goods, but this alone was not going to be sufficient.[8] He turned to Canada's traditional lenders, the British, but they too were suffering from a credit crunch.

By the end of 1915, the idea that the war would soon be over had been smashed by the guns of the Western Front, and the Dominion was in desperate financial straits. White looked southward to the Americans, who officially remained neutral until April 1917, but sided, at times openly, with the Allies. However, nothing was for free. White blanched at the interest rates he was offered, but he had no choice but to accept them.[9] He borrowed $45 million in the summer of 1915. This was followed by the loan of $75 million in March 1916 and another $100 million in July of the next year. In late 1914, the finance department estimated that the war would cost $100 million a year. By 1917, the outlay was almost a million dollars a day.[10] Former minister of finance Sir George Foster could only shake his head at the extravagant spending: "We are approaching the billion dollar debt—yet no one turns a hair."[11] White knew that he was loading a heavy financial burden onto future generations, but the Dominion might not have a future at all unless battles were won in the present. What he did not realize at the time was that the war loans tied Canada to Wall Street as the Dominion's primary lender. This change would be critical for the country in cutting its financial tethers to Britain.

White also turned to Canadians for assistance. Wary of saddling the population with taxes or debt, for fear of the possible backlash, White issued government bonds that accrued value over time, usually 5 percent over several years. War bonds were floated by the government in 1915 and 1916, and oversubscribed by Canadians, who responded with "patriotism of the pocket."[12] In the summer of 1917, the first of the Victory Loans was intended to raise $150 million; Canadians purchased $400 million. Loans in 1918 and 1919 provided hundreds of millions of dollars more. Eventually $1.7 billion was raised in what White called the "greatest financial achievement of Canada during the war."[13]

Much of this money was funnelled back to England so that it could be used to pay for munitions and wheat purchased from Canada. "Canada the borrower has become Canada the lender," remarked the British Chancellor of the Exchequer.[14] It was fashioned as an elaborate kickback scheme, but it allowed Britain to receive necessary weapons and food, and Canada to keep employment and profits high. There were no easy solutions to the problem of paying for the war, and as more money was borrowed or printed, inflation began to rise. White pleaded with Canadians to embrace frugality: "Let the people of the Dominions, by thrift and economy, make their dollars fight the Huns."[15] That was a step in the right direction, but more would be needed than punchy slogans to keep the country financially afloat.

BY THE LATE SUMMER OF 1915, there was a growing awareness that the Dominion was in a fight for its very survival. Canada had raised and sent off a second contingent of troops and tens of thousands continued to flock to recruiting stations even though delays in finding equipment and experienced instructors had led to harsh criticism of Hughes, and to a lesser degree, Borden. These problems were exploited by the Liberals, who had caught scent of the administrative chaos.

Sir Sam Hughes, who was knighted in August 1915 for his wartime duties, was an easy target because of his extreme effusions and ill-advised actions. He had fed off the early praise and publicity, and was now unable to remove himself from the limelight. His outrageous statements about Canada defeating Germany on its own, or groan-inducing claims that the Canadians would teach the imperials how to fight, were fodder for his many enemies. Hughes was incapable of seeing the damage he wrought. The Toronto *Telegram* wrote that "Sir Robert Borden is a statesman of far different type than Major-General Hughes. He would rather keep his nose to the grindstone than pose in the spotlight."[16] Hughes was the jingoistic terrier. Borden held the leash, although sometimes too lightly.

Less than a year into the war, it became apparent that Borden would have to remove war supplies from Hughes's empire. It had never made sense that Hughes's relatively small department was responsible for military procurement. The products he obtained were often poorly made and led to Liberal-uncovered scandals. After a number of public attacks, Borden muttered to his diary, "Grits don't seem conscious that the country is at war."[17] While the Liberals supported the war effort, they also knew there could be an election at any time. The Conservatives tried to deflect the criticism by pointing out that it was the Liberals who long ago had saddled the Canadian militia with the Ross rifle, but the public was in no mood for finger pointing. Most Canadians were simply aghast that its citizen-soldiers were suffering because of government incompetence.

Hughes fought the loss of responsibility, and the normally reserved Borden was forced to put the minister in his place in a series of contentious meetings that brought Hughes near to tears. The War Purchasing Commission was established in May 1915 under the guidance of A.E. Kemp, a corpulent Toronto millionaire businessman and champion of the Orange Order, who lacked the flair (and instability) of Hughes but got the job done. Tenders were opened and bids were assessed, often with the assistance of experts from government departments. Inspections were carried out and contracts amended or cut if necessary. The commission saved millions of dollars over the next three years, or so thought Kemp and Borden.[18] With purchasing under control, Borden sought to deal with the corruption. He made an example of two Conservative parliamentarians who were read out of the party for profiting from their office.[19] More importantly, he began to realize that the expanding war effort required an enlarged bureaucracy, and the old ways of doing things—through rewarding the party faithful—were no longer acceptable in the context of an unlimited war effort in which tens of thousands of Canadian lives were at risk.

"Bad Luck Borden," as Grit propaganda had begun to label him, knew that Hughes had done important work in early August 1914 in establishing the Shell Committee, a body that funnelled and allocated Britain's million-dollar orders with Canadian companies. The initial output of shells had been slow, with Canadian companies plagued by shortages of experienced personnel and the necessary equipment.[20] The imperials had experienced similar problems that had led to major scandals. The Welsh Wizard, Minister of Munitions David Lloyd George, cleaned up the British war industry, addressing and rectifying the shell shortages that had embarrassed the government and cost lives on the battlefield. With similar problems in Canada, the Liberals smelled blood over the issue, with the aggressive, humourless, and sharp-tongued Frank Carvell, who had already earned the moniker "Lord High Executioner," dogging Hughes and the Shell Committee. In his grandstanding attacks in the House of Commons, he accused the government of trying to "cover up their tracks and whitewash and cleanse the character of the Minister of Militia and Defence" while they "refused investigations of things which any reasonable intelligent man knows are so dishonest that they would stink in the nostrils of every man in Canada."[21] Amid a cacophony of accusations that moved from profiteering to partisanship and incompetence, Borden was forced to establish a series of inquiries into the work of the committee.

Before the investigations were finished, however, the cabinet established a new Imperial Munitions Board (IMB) on November 29, 1915. It was headed by Joseph Flavelle, a long-time Conservative who had made millions in the pork and canned beef industry. Flavelle, who combined a ruthless business mind with his Methodist belief of self-denial and personal faith, made few friends with the munitions magnates. But he increased productivity by rewarding the successful and cutting contracts to dead-weight companies. Hughes wailed about losing influence, but Flavelle was a far better executive, even though he too acknowledged the enormous strain induced by the war, as all decisions were made "on an emergency basis," without time to ponder, let alone study, most judgments.[22] The IMB, which would eventually construct ships and planes as well, was, as the name suggested, an imperial body. While Flavelle's Conservative connections and earnest work ethic ensured the relationship was generally harmonious, the IMB was solely responsible to the British ministry of munitions. That the Canadian government would allow the British to oversee the largest single employer of Canadian workers with little federal oversight is a reflection of the colonial mentality that still prevailed in Ottawa. But the IMB was also a shield for Borden, who had been wounded in the attacks against Hughes and saw advantage in having an arms-length imperial body run the munitions effort.[23] Flavelle was one of the unsung heroes of the war, though his numerous enemies, who now numbered Sam Hughes, took every opportunity to damage his reputation.

Hughes made rash charges in public and fired off, in Borden's words, "extraordinar[il]y offensive and absurd letter[s]," which attacked Flavelle and almost anyone else.[24] Borden's continued support of Hughes was not always appreciated by other Conservative ministers, who wondered why the prime minister retained in cabinet a minister whose behaviour was so often an embarrassment. Sir George Foster wrote uncharitably in his diary after one August 1915 meeting: "The Prime Minister is undecided as usual." Foster wanted action, and could not stand Borden's proclivity to put off decisions, which he characterized as "Drift-Corroding drift."[25] Flavelle, who oscillated between admiring Borden and being frustrated by his inability to excite the nation as a war leader, thought the prime minister lacked "vision," "grip," and "vigour."[26] Foster and Flavelle were united, however, in their hatred of Hughes, and their comments about Borden were influenced by his handling of the unruly minister, who had moved from being a distraction to a full-fledged disaster. Yet like Laurier and Macdonald, Borden knew that political survival often depended on delaying decisions until the time to act was favourable, and despite the scandals, Hughes still remained the face of the war effort.

Even with all the struggles and strife, the prime minister had grown into the role of war leader. According to one political watcher, Borden "maintained an attitude of coolness and patience which was admirably suited to the times; refused to be rushed to action, or pushed back into inaction; pursued his settled policies quietly, persistently and with ultimate effectiveness."[27] Borden was not a jingoistic war leader, but Canadians did not appear to want that, if the backlash against Hughes was an indication of how war leaders should act. Staid and solid appeared to satisfy Canadians. Yet Borden remained deeply unconnected to the fighting overseas. While soldiers sometimes wrote to update him on events at the front or to gripe about senior officers or British slights, the prime minister had almost no contact with Lieutenant-General E.A.H. Alderson, who commanded the Canadian Division and, from September 1915, the Canadian Corps. Hughes had turned on Alderson, both because he wanted a Canadian in command and because the British general did not like the failure-prone Ross rifle, which Hughes favoured, and he whispered poisonous words to the prime minister. But Borden was in no position to gauge what made a good commander at the front. In fact, he had periodically inquired if he could dump Hughes as a minister and set him up as a battlefield commander, but the British recoiled each time at the proposal: Hughes had none of the qualifications to command a division and many characteristics that made him intolerable.[28] Borden took their answer in stride. He was not willing to press the British, but he also was curiously passive in assessing the generals who were commanding Canada's army, and expended little energy in filling the gap in his knowledge. Borden focused on the domestic front and relied on Hughes to oversee the fighting forces overseas.

EVEN AS CONTROVERSIES WORE AWAY at the Conservative government's reputation, recruitment continued to go well. Sam Hughes travelled the country in his private rail car, stopping in city after city to give patriotic—sometimes frothing-at-the-mouth-patriotic—speeches. Raging and shouting, joking and jostling, Hughes implored Canadians to do their duty. His message was echoed by thousands of people across the country. In the big cities, it was hard not to stumble upon a poster, a speech, a pro-war rally of some sort, all demanding that young men enlist. Yet, while tens of thousands signed up, hundreds of thousands more remained behind. One New Brunswick recruiting officer wrote around this time: "I find the same conditions [sic] in this district as prevails in other parts of Canada ... that recruiting is at a low ebb, and especially recruiting for the infantry. All who want to go have gone, and everyone who enlists now does so as a result of pressure."[29] For the moment there were enough soldiers, but the strain was beginning to show, as young men of soldiering age were drawn to high-paying jobs instead of to an army uniform.

Quebec—which held about a third of Canada's population—had initially greeted the war positively. Political leaders, both provincial and federal, spoke of French Canada's duty. Quebec's senior clergy were content to allow volunteers to enlist, but there was a marked lack of enthusiasm in the parishes. There was sympathy for France, which was occupied and suffering badly in the attritional battles of the Western Front, but there was no strong link to the mother country. France had played little role in Canada since the eighteenth century. Equally significant, Canadian soldiers fought in the British Expeditionary Force, and this did not encourage unilingual French Canadians to join. Moreover, there was not the same number of prewar militia units and militia officers in that province, and these had been the core of the new overseas battalions and batteries in the rest of Canada.[30] The war was never a draw for rural French Canadians, although several thousand enlisted in the first two years of the war, driven by the same motivations as English Canadians: a sense of duty, a belief in the righteousness of the cause, steady pay, or the desire for adventure.[31]

There was a noticeable drop in the number of recruits coming from Quebec in mid-1915, the result, it was thought, of worry over language issues. The Ontario government was enforcing Regulation 17, which would severely limit instruction in French within the education system. Most French Canadians saw the law as a brazen manoeuvre by the English-speaking majority to assimilate French-speaking Ontarians through the denial of their language. Education was a provincial matter, and so Borden could do little about the regulation. But nor was he inclined to act, especially with the provincial Tories and the opposition Liberals standing by Regulation 17. Nonetheless, French-Canadian MPs, both Conservative and Liberal, insisted on debating the issue in the House. The pressure ratcheted up when more than 5,000 protesters marched on Parliament on February 24, 1916. The prime minister delayed, but was eventually run to ground by his Quebec MPs, who implored for intervention; at the same time, the Orange Order, which was well represented in his cabinet and anti-French, urged him not to be drawn into the maelstrom.[32] Borden was not terribly sympathetic towards French Canada, and he was rather bewildered by all this whining when a war for civilization raged abroad.

Despite Borden's lack of interest, Regulation 17 continued to undermine the war effort in Quebec. Henri Bourassa, Armand Lavergne, and other French-Canadian nationalistes claimed the war that mattered to them was less about the Germans in France than the "Prussians of Ontario," who sought to destroy the French people by denying them education in their own language.[33] The outspoken Bourassa, editor of *Le Devoir* and well known because of his past battles with Laurier, argued that Canada had an interest in the "maintenance of the prestige, power, and world action of France and England," and so the nation should contribute to the Allied war effort, but within its ability to do so, and not to beggar itself or cause internal rifts between English and French.[34] These sentiments were thoroughly unacceptable to many English Canadians, who believed that their identity was shaped and underpinned by their association with the British Empire. Nothing less than a total war effort was acceptable. The Kingston *Standard* spoke for many when it lashed out that "Bourassa, The Dirty" was a "preacher of discord and strife, this snarling Ananias seeking to stir up rebellion in the hearts of his French-Canadian readers by making it appear that everything is wrong, everything vile, everything corrupt."[35] Bourassa was not easily cowed. He had the courage to speak in English Canada and to publish in English, which led to his message being widely disseminated. He may not have spoken for rural French Canada—and his paper was read primarily by the elite—but he was frequently singled out in English Canada as the "Arch Traitor of Canada" or saluted as "von Bourassa" for his supposed German sympathies. One newspaper claimed that the only solution to stopping his poisonous words was to ensure that the "skull of rebellion must be smashed."[36]

After the terrible casualties of Second Ypres, and a second costly engagement in the May 1915 Battle of Festubert, which left another 2,500 killed or wounded, Canadian attitudes hardened. The ongoing occupation of Belgium, with the reported atrocities committed against civilians—from the raping of nuns to the bayonetting of babies—enraged Canadians. The enemy's use of poison gas was seen as diabolical, and portrayed as such in newspapers, cartoons, and speeches, although little was made of it when the British and Canadians responded with their own chemical attacks from late 1915 until the end of the war. The sinking of the British liner *Lusitania* by a German submarine on May 7, the result of unrestricted warfare that sought to cut the logistical lifeline to Britain, was seen as another instance of the barbarous Hun shifting the war onto women and children. Borden reflected the sentiments of Canadians when he wrote angrily in his diary that "It seems nothing less than cold-blooded murder."[37] Almost 1,200 passengers were killed in the incident. Canadians were outraged at this blurring of lines between combatants and non-combatants, even as the nations of the world were moving progressively towards all-out war.

German-born Canadians continued to find themselves mistrusted and misused, and many were fired from their jobs in what was known as "patriotic dismissals."[38] Their stores and shops were less patronized and, on occasion, vigilantes sent harsh messages with fire and fist. Some Canadians pressed this anti-German patriotism to extremes: drinking beer was seen as disloyal; German music was banned; German Canadians changed their names and ethnic origin on census material; German teachers and professors were hounded from their schools and universities.[39] The residents of Berlin, Ontario, with its high proportion of German Canadians, engaged in a bitter debate before finally changing the city's name to that of the British war hero Kitchener. As more Canadians were killed or wounded, those on the home front were far less willing to tolerate dissent.

BORDEN ADMITTED IN HIS MEMOIRS that he had a "violent" temper, but he fought to keep it in check, to the extent that he was often characterized as being cautious and placid.[40] Still, as one journalist observed, "when the patient man was pushed too far by fools he exploded with cold violence."[41] Another close observer, Arthur Meighen, saw it differently: "When he came to a conclusion as to what was in the public interest, he wanted that thing done and was impatient of restraints imposed by the clamourings of what the Press calls 'public opinion.'"[42] As the war progressed, Borden consulted less frequently with his ministers, choosing to work with a smaller inner council and relying more heavily on his own judgment. Borden was becoming more imperious in nature within the Dominion's realm and, at the same time, increasingly frustrated by the lack of consultation from Whitehall.

In the first full year of the war, Borden was shut out entirely from the strategic direction of the war. He rarely complained, but he was furious that even basic information from the front was withheld by the British. The prime minister often found out about major military decisions, some involving Canadian troops, through newspaper accounts. In a much-publicized speech in Montreal in December 1914, he had told Canadians—and Whitehall too—that the day was soon coming "when the men of Canada, Australia, South Africa and other dominions will have the same just voice in these questions as those who live within the British Isles."[43] If Canadians were contributing treasure and blood to the Allied war effort, something had to change in Ottawa's relationship with the seat of power. To carry that claim forward, he needed to go to London.

Borden made his first wartime trip to Britain in July 1915. He was anxious to see the troops but also to consult with his counterpart, Herbert Asquith, who had recently formed a coalition government to better prosecute the war. There was much fearful talk in Canada and on Borden's ship, the *Adriatic*, that he might be making himself a target for the German U-boats, but he arrived in Liverpool unharmed, and recharged after having spent much of the voyage relaxing with some of his favourite friends: Latin classics, Greek poetry, English histories, and French novels.[44]

Borden met with the British prime minister and high-ranking officials. Asquith had led his country since 1908, but although he had been a successful peacetime politician, he was overwhelmed by the war, exhausted by the pace, and progressively unable either to lead the country or to project leadership to the public. Borden respected Asquith, but worried that the stress of the war had worn him down, dulled his thinking, and driven him to drink.[45] Moreover, he was not much impressed by the British administration of the war. "Procrastination, indecision, inertia, doubt, hesitation ... have made themselves entirely too conspicuous in this war," he wrote, adding that Canadian officials might inject more urgency into its conduct.[46] Asquith was uninterested in Borden's offer of assistance, however, and even less interested in including Borden in strategic decision making.

While Borden was disappointed with Asquith's response, an audience with the King reinforced his belief in the necessity of prosecuting the war to the bitter end, especially after the monarch referred, as Borden recounted, "in the most appreciative terms to the valour and heroism of the Canadian troops and declared that they saved the situation at the Second Battle of Ypres."[47] Borden also sat in on Asquith's cabinet meetings, an almost entirely symbolic gesture, yet noteworthy, as acknowledged by Asquith, who observed it "was a day for making new precedents." Borden was probably at home with the mundane discussions, but he might have sighed inwardly a few times over the heated if relatively trivial ministerial debates about whether or not Britain should add cotton to the contraband list.[48] Attending the cabinet meeting reaffirmed in Borden's mind that, at the most basic level, there was nothing happening in Asquith's councils of war that Borden and his ministers had not already talked about, and he felt himself an equal rather than a colonial.

Borden hobnobbed comfortably with politicians and royalty, but he was equally anxious to visit his soldiers. His attendance at parades and reviews, however, failed signally to electrify the troops. One Canadian general remarked, "Sir Robert Borden was here yesterday—he is too ponderous for soldiers."[49] He was more genuine when visiting the wounded, and tried to meet and talk to as many as he could in the limited time available, visiting an astounding fifty-two separate hospitals. Throughout these testing visits, he was shaken by the young lads putting on brave faces and smiling as they tried to rise from their beds to greet him. He met amputees and men who would never recover from their injuries. Borden said later, "it was the most deeply-moving experience of all my life."[50] This terrible war was laying waste to the best and brightest of the Dominion; Borden brooded on the thought and wondered if anything good could come of such horrendous bloodletting.

"I had gone from pillar to post, from one member of the British government to another, for the purpose of obtaining definite information as to when the British Empire would be in a position to throw its whole strength into the War," Borden wrote in his memoirs.[51] He encountered vagueness wherever he went. Borden was bewildered as to why the forces on the Western Front were stalemated and unable to advance except through the crippling loss of men from shot and shell. He wanted answers but he did not get them. The British were themselves unsure when new armies would be raised, trained, and ready for battle, and when enough artillery shells and heavy guns would be available to break the deadlock. Sometime in 1916, everyone hoped. Borden regarded this vague forecast to be uninspiring and unconvincing, and he pondered how he could continue to plead and cajole Canadians to do their bit for the war when he had so little sense as to how or when it would be won.

In early September 1915, Sir Robert embarked on the return journey to Canada. He spent hours staring out at the ocean from the upper deck of the ship as he contemplated the war, its strain on the country, and his own eroding health. The trip to Britain had been important: he had met with his imperial political counterparts and visited the brave and broken in hospital. He quickly developed an intimate bond with the "boys" in the hospitals, and their inspirational "triumph of the spirit over the dull pain and monotony of long, weary months."[52] He was too old to fight, but he would not abandon those who served in his place. Yet as part of his nation's sacrifice, Sir Robert Borden, the once-fervent imperialist, increasingly felt that Canada needed more in return for its gut-wrenching contribution to victory. Borden had told an audience in London that, with Canada's heavy involvement, a new commonwealth of "self-governing Dominions" was being forged.[53] The war would provide Canada with greater autonomy within the British Empire. Yet he was haunted by the question: how much was autonomy worth when measured in the blood of Canadians?

CHAPTER 5

DUTY AND STRAIN, 1916

A tired Sir Robert Borden returned from overseas in mid September to a mountain of work and an unending line of petitioners, but he made an effort to meet with Laurier and share some of his impressions. Both agreed that an election battle between Liberals and Conservatives was not only unhelpful but likely detrimental to the war effort. Despite much speculation in the press and by pundits about a 1915 election, Laurier and Borden agreed to extend Parliament one more year. The respected newspaperman J.W. Dafoe caught the pulse of the people: "Canadians could not bring themselves to the point of fighting one another while their sons and brothers were dying side by side in the mud of Flanders."[1]

While they talked of focusing on the war effort, both leaders had more persuasive reasons to postpone a summons to the polls. Borden worried about the fallout from the multiple scandals with which his administration had been scarred. He also needed to shore up the Quebec wing of the party. The prime minister had continued to search for French-Canadian ministers, since Pelletier and Nantel had resigned early in the war, and eventually settled on Thomas Chase-Casgrain, whom he appointed postmaster general and Pierre Blondin, who became minister of inland revenue. Both ministries were second-tier. Like their predecessors, these ministers would be far from Borden's inner circle, and the Conservatives remained extremely weak in Quebec. Laurier also wanted to avoid an election. He felt that English Canada would go with the Conservatives because they were perceived as the war party and intimately linked to Empire. Another year was needed, Laurier believed, to reveal the full extent of the Conservatives' ineptitude and to chip away at their reputation. Borden could live with the escalated state of tension between the parties, for it bought him breathing room, but he realized that the Liberals would not be accommodating for much longer.

More than 100,000 men volunteered to go to war in 1914 and the first half of 1915, but Sam Hughes and others believed that a change was necessary, one that empowered communities and the leaders within them to raise more local men to serve in newly formed battalions. Rooting new battalions in smaller locales allowed friends, co-workers, and church groups to enlist together. It also personalized the war effort and created more opportunities for politicians and the pulpit to exert pressure on young men not in uniform. Children were encouraged to harass older siblings. Patriotic leagues organized speakers' nights and rallies. Women held teas and dances to entice young men to don the khaki, while thousands more went into the workforce to fill the gap as men went overseas.[2] Special formations hoped to appeal to the uncommitted by focusing on the men's Highland heritage, their commitment to temperance, or their participation in sports. So-called "bantam battalions" recruited members five feet tall or shorter.[3] Prejudice against Natives or visible minorities was slowly put aside, after the supply of healthy white men, along with many of the feeble-minded, pigeon-chested, and flat-footed, had been exhausted. The message was relentless: "Do your duty." Those who did not enlist ran the risk of being labelled shirkers or slackers.

Senior staff at the Department of Militia and Defence warned Hughes and Borden that it would be a mistake simply to "go on adding to the number of regiments, batteries and battalions."[4] The fighting formations at the front needed fresh recruits to fill their gaping holes, but not whole battalions. While a 2nd and 3rd Division would be raised from these units and arrive on the Western Front by the end of 1915, and a 4th Division would be fighting the next year, most of the local battalions established in Canada from mid-1915 onwards were broken up overseas and used as reinforcements for those formations already at the front. It was a terrible shock to the local community leaders and the officers (usually one and the same), who were not wanted on the Western Front because of their high rank and lack of experience. The policy of recruiting units in Canada, and then breaking them up overseas, created much ill will towards the government.

It is unclear that Borden fully grasped the problem, although later in 1916 he told Hughes to stop recruiting battalions and focus on the recruits.[5] In 1915, however, Hughes weighed the options and kept on authorizing the new units, willing to leave the administrators in England to sort out the angry officers and bewildered privates after they arrived. An October 30, 1915, order-in-council increased the size of the Canadian Expeditionary Force from 150,000 to 250,000. A few months later, Borden announced to the nation, "It is for the future peace of the world that we fight to the end."[6]

As the year came to a close, Borden and his wife were laid low from a flu, with the prime minister also suffering agonizing pain through his back, hips, and legs from sciatica. Aching and feverish, Borden worried about the news from overseas, where the Germans seemed to be breaking through on the Russian front. He had also just returned from the United States, where he had been disgusted by the attitude of neutral Americans who were happy to help the Allies with munitions for a profit, but were unwilling to commit to the war. "No sacrifice, no endeavour," wrote an angry Borden in his diary.[7]

On December 30, Borden sent for Hughes, White, and John "Doc" Reid. He told them that Canada had to do more for the Allied war effort. With Britain on the verge of bringing in conscription, Borden told his ministers that he would issue a New Year's message announcing an increase in the size of Canadian forces to half a million. Hughes was no doubt ecstatic, but the prime minister took this extraordinary action without consulting the caucus, the cabinet, or any of the professional soldiers in Hughes's department, who had already claimed that such a force might be possible but would put a terrible strain on the nation's manpower.

With the male population between the ages of eighteen and forty-five at almost two million, it was possible to feed half a million into the war machine, but what about the estimated 700,000 farms growing war-winning food, the essential munitions work, or the thousands of other businesses, hospitals, and factories that needed labour?[8] Farmers claimed they could do more good on their farms than in uniform. What was the right balance? There was little attempt by Borden's government to study where the available manpower should go, and how it could best be allocated to win the war.[9] There is no indication in his papers or diary that Borden realized the enormity of the task. The decision to raise half a million men was his and his alone, and he placed faith in Canadians that they would rise to the occasion. "This announcement is made in token of Canada's unflinchable resolve to crown the justice of our cause with victory and with an abiding peace."[10] Finance Minister White later remarked that he had no idea how Canada would field such a large force. The cabinet "simply went on faith."[11]

Borden's announcement was greeted with excitement in parts of English Canada. Although an astonishing 220,000 young men had already enlisted, there had been much gnashing of teeth and wringing of hands by patriotic Canadians who saw the streets filled with men of military age.[12] Why were they not in uniform? Furthermore, while men were coming forward, were they the right kind of men? Of the first quarter million to enlist, contemporary manpower studies suggested that 62 percent were British-born, 30 percent were Canadian-born, and the remaining 8 percent consisted of a mixture of those from other Commonwealth countries, the United States, and everywhere else.[13] While many of those British-born individuals had resided in Canada for years, perhaps decades, it was still sobering to contemplate the relative dearth of Canadian-born recruits. From 1916, the number of Canadian recruits would rise, eventually bringing the total to slightly more than 50 percent, but in the first two and a half years of the war, Canadian-born—English or French—were slow to respond to the calls of King, country, or Empire.

Borden's 500,000-man pledge was a sign that Canada would support the Empire to the hilt. It was a steadying call by Borden, even though inwardly his anger escalated over the failure of the

British to vigorously prosecute the war, although this was no doubt exacerbated by his inability to access the inner councils of war in London. He wrote a letter revealing his frustration to George Perley, Canada's Acting High Commissioner in London, in which he accused the British civilian and military high command of "procrastination, indecision, inertia, doubt, [and] hesitation." Canada would not continue to be ignored. "It can hardly be expected that we shall put 400,000 or 500,000 men in the field and willingly accept the position of having no more voice and receiving no more consideration than if we were toy automata."[14] Borden was hardening his position on Canada's demand for a more significant voice in the Empire, although he had second thoughts about the letter to Perley, which he ordered him not to send on to the British. He did, however, include it in his memoirs nearly twenty years later, perhaps to appear more forceful than he was or, more likely, because it captured his feelings at the time.

The majority of parliamentarians responded positively to Borden's pledged manpower increase, and by the end of 1915, sixty-four MPs had enlisted or were going overseas. They joined a volunteer cohort of which roughly two-thirds were manual labourers, with professionals, businessmen, farmers, ranchers, and students forming the rest of the ranks.[15] But with skilled labourers back home, such as machinists, earning eight to ten times the salary of a private in uniform, the many profitable jobs created by the war worked against recruitment.[16] The remaining 1.7 million men of military age were unwilling to give up a job, or their family, or to put themselves in harm's way. This amorphous group from across the country—often identified as French Canadians, farmers, and recent immigrants—must have shifted uneasily at Borden's announcement. Some took solace from the prime minister's assurance that he would never impose conscription, a promise made credible by his conviction that forced service could frighten away potential American immigrants and do irreparable harm to French Canada.[17] But what would happen if the recruits stopped joining? Was the Ontario Liberal leader of the opposition, Newton Rowell, correct in stating, "Canada has profited the most and suffered the least from this war of any of the nations of the empire"?[18] Was the nation made up of gutless profiteers? Could Canada say it had done its share in the crusade and not be accused of shirking its duty to Empire, or worse, of having betrayed the soldiers already overseas?

IN EARLY JANUARY 1916, Borden instructed Hughes to create a system of recruitment that would "interfere as little as possible with the agricultural and manufacturing interests in Canada."[19] Borden was aware that simply taking every eligible man for overseas service would have a negative impact on the Dominion's ability to feed and arm itself and its allies. Selection of young men for service had to be carried out in a systematic way. But an oversight body that spanned the entire country was nearly impossible to establish. It is doubtful that Hughes had the mental capacity to carry out such overarching planning, and his own Department of Militia and Defence was far too small and centralized to manage it. When Hughes probed into establishing such a system, he barely consulted organized labour, and farmers refused, for the most part, to participate in any scheme that might see more of their sons or workers drafted, although they could not prevent their steady enlistment.[20] And so the recruitment officers across the country continued simply to pluck men from wherever they could find them, without recourse to any strategic plan that might have considered the proper allotment of men and resources in the unlimited war effort.

"Food is the most important of the sinews of war," claimed one farmers' newspaper. "The men on the farms of Canada do not need to go to the front to serve their country well in this crisis."[21] It was a sentiment with which Borden's government still agreed. With 60 percent of Britain's total caloric consumption coming from imported food, Canadian food contributions were soon to become a crucial component in the Empire's war effort.[22] Yet the hard life on the farm was often no match for the excitement and glory of overseas service, even when the dangers at the front were known. The appeal of the uniform exacerbated a trend that had worried farmers for years, as young men left rural areas for the bright lights of the city.[23] Such worries notwithstanding, productivity and the price of farm goods rose significantly in 1915. Wheat was an essential commodity and a crucial weapon in the war, although transportation to Allied countries remained a problem because of the lack of shipping and the threat of German U-boats.

Saturday Night magazine declared at the start of the war, "If it is possible for a country to benefit by the horror of war, Canada should be the one."[24] By the end of the first full year of the conflict, the depression of 1913–1914 had been beaten, as the war kick-started new industries and drove old ones such as steel and coal to expand output. Although Britain continued to turn to the United States for vast quantities of material, Borden and his ministers pressed the British at every turn to place orders with the Dominion and reward Canadians for their sacrifices.

By March 1915, some 200 factories were engaged in munitions work, with contracts totalling some $80 million. This was a significant economic stimulant, but it was centred around existing heavy industry, most of which was in Ontario and Quebec, with a smattering in the Maritimes, especially steel in New Glasgow and Sydney, but almost nothing in the West. This apparent hoarding of largesse enraged Westerners, especially when the new wealth slowly drove up inflation, which would eat voraciously into the spending power of all citizens and progressively worsen over the course of the war.

In response to a rising demand that the economic burden should be equally shared, Borden's government introduced income tax. White, who felt that the measure was too radical, resisted for as long as he could, but he was ultimately driven to adopt it. There were few protests and he appealed to the spirit of sacrifice: "at a time when mothers and wives are giving up their sons and husbands," all Canadians had a duty to do their part in winning the war.[25]

Businesses were hit first in 1916 with a tax on profits, which eventually raised about $200 million in revenue. The next year, individual Canadians were called on to pay taxes, although it was not an onerous burden.[26] The personal income tax was weighted towards very well-off Canadians: a married family man earning $3,000 a year paid only $20 in taxes in 1918.[27] While the cash generated was paltry, forming less than 3 percent of tax revenues in 1919, it was symbolic of the need to shoulder the war's load evenly.

The introduction of income tax was an important step forward in enlisting Canadians to pay the war costs—and then the postwar debt—but higher taxes would have brought down the inflation that was eroding disposable income.[28] From the start of the war to December 1917, there was a 65 percent increase in food costs, and they would jump again over the following two years.[29] White was focused on raising the money to pay for the war; inflation was a regrettable but, in his mind, unavoidable by-product that Canadians would have to endure.[30] The price of goods rose and Canadians felt the pinch as their purchasing power was diminished. The Department of Labour family budget index was set at 100 in 1913, fell to 98.7 in 1915, but then rose steadily to 147.2 in 1918 and 184.7 in 1920.[31] Inflation was hardest on soldiers' dependants and others on fixed incomes, and many found that the price of sending a father or son off to war was the forced sale of the family silverware or the loss of a business.[32]

Relative privation led Canadians to turn on one another. They looked for the profiteers in their midst. Government propaganda and a zealous desire to ferret out cheaters encouraged neighbours to spy on neighbours to ensure there was neither waste nor hoarding. An extra dollop of cream or spoonful of sugar added to a dish or a cup of tea was viewed as near treason. Militant labour was blamed for making trouble for hard-working folk. Farmers were accused of gouging city dwellers, even though they suffered crop failure in several sectors in 1917 and 1918. Grocers were suspected of conspiring to raise prices. And if it wasn't grocers, then some others, perhaps businessmen or factory owners, were thought to be making money hand over fist. Few understood how inflation worked, and it was easier, and perhaps more comforting, to accuse shadowy groups of profiteers, or other dark forces, of stealing money from the pockets of patriotic citizens.

In November 1916, Borden's Conservatives responded to the widespread discontent by appointing W.F. O'Connor, the man who had drafted the War Measures Act, as cost of living commissioner. O'Connor had the support of many Canadians, who wished to see him lead a crusade against the evils of inflation and expose the profiteers who benefited from their misery. O'Connor's report in August of the next year named many of the large food processing plants, including the pork-producing William Davies Company, which was headed by Joseph Flavelle. Flavelle's many enemies gloated at his embarrassment, and newspapers took to calling him "His Lardship" or the "Baron of Bacon." Canadians were willing to tighten their belts to achieve victory, but profiteering threatened to undermine the cause.

THERE WERE OTHER PROBLEMS confronting the government. The "Canadian Northern Nightmare," as Borden called it, took up a significant portion of the prime minister's time.[33] The Dominion's railways, especially the Grand Trunk Pacific and the Canadian Northern, were bleeding red ink. These lines had become a noose around Borden's neck, one that had been placed there by Laurier's Liberals, who had encouraged the extension of unsustainable railway lines in the previous affluent decade. This did not stop the Liberals from hammering the Tories on the issue every chance they could. One attack pamphlet claimed that "THE FACTS PROVE the Conservatives themselves are wholly to blame" for the railways' failures.[34]

Borden was handicapped by the record of previous Conservative railway scandals, most notably the kickback schemes that brought down Sir John A. Macdonald's government in 1873. No matter what he did now, whether he let the railways fail or bailed them out, Borden knew he would be giving the Liberals new ammunition with which to blast his government. In the heightened tension of the war, when ordinary Canadians were called upon to make do with less, Borden shuddered at the thought of sending tens of millions of dollars down the railway debt hole to keep millionaires in their mansions.

In May 1915, Borden returned to this vexing problem and considered the possibility of nationalizing the two ailing lines. Investigations into the nearly bankrupt companies revealed, according to one historian, a "shocking recital of fraud, duplicity, collusion, incompetence, and mismanagement."[35] But to let the railways fail would be a blow to Canada's national pride and would rock its financial markets. The Dominion had always relied on foreign investment and that would dry up if the railways were allowed to collapse and their stock became worthless. Moreover, there were likely to be secondary effects on the economy as thousands of men were thrown out of work and debtors went unpaid. The railway question continued to plague and divide his party: some members were thinking with their heads, others with their hearts, and still others, like R.B. Bennett, who had made a fortune as a corporate lawyer for the Canadian Pacific Railway, with their pocketbooks. A frustrated Borden went so far as to tell his colleagues in early April 1916 that he preferred to "resign and let the Grits clean up their mess."[36] He bought time by appointing a Royal Commission and, in May 1916, offered another $18-million bailout to the Grand Trunk Pacific and Canadian Northern, while acknowledging that the cash infusion would likely only forestall the inevitable. The Liberals raged a little, but since the mess was of their own making, Borden could mock them, saying that there was "No snap in their attack."[37] There was, however, "snap" in other assaults on the government, and especially in those aimed at Sam Hughes.

ROUGH, OUTSPOKEN, AND ABSURDLY EGOTISTICAL, the combative and combustible Sam Hughes inspired rage in Liberals. Many Conservatives disliked him too. Borden valued Hughes for his virtues, but was exasperated by his minister's "erratic temperament, countless indiscretions, absurd vanities" and complained that "his judgment was unbalanced and his temperament constantly led him into difficulty and controversy."[38] Echoing the prime minister, Flavelle remarked that Hughes was "possessed of remarkable physical energy and love of the spectacular. He has commanded wide attention, notwithstanding his vulgar brutality and coarse language." But his energy was offset by his instabilities. "I believe him to be mentally unbalanced," wrote Flavelle, "with the low cunning and cleverness often associated with the insane."[39]

Hughes had nonetheless risen to become the nation's war leader, inspiring Canadians to enlist and then supporting them in their service overseas. Inevitably, he became a target, and the Liberals baited and battered him over and over again in their newspapers and the House of Commons. Canadians were told that, while Hughes's soldiers marched on bad boots and carried a rifle that did not work, the minister dispensed largesse to crooks, extortionists, and scallywags.[40] Hughes had first been elected in 1892, and had been on the receiving end of much vitriol since that time, but few had seen such ferocious attacks as he sustained as minister. He fought back using any and all means at his disposal, sometimes peppering his arguments with loosely interpreted statistics, at other times impugning his attacker's patriotism. He dealt freely in mean insinuations and vicious rumours, even going so far as to attack the siblings of his political enemies. Increasingly, despite his desperate bravado, he came to be seen by many

Conservatives, and especially by his fellow cabinet ministers, as a liability. Yet, even as his old supporters slowly distanced themselves from him, Hughes continued to have a powerful patron in the prime minister.

Foster and Hughes had screaming matches in cabinet. Perley, Kemp, and White—Borden's most influential ministers—took every opportunity to speak ill of him when Hughes was not around. Utterly undaunted, Hughes carried on angering the British, the opposition, and many others with his outrageous and indelicate outbursts. When confronted with these indiscretions, he refused to back down. He justified his actions in long, rambling letters to Borden that outed nests of traitors in the cabinet, in caucus, in the press, and among the public. In one slashing attack, Hughes accused White of being "possessed of a sort of mental epilepsy; or rather that mental epilepsy controls him. He renders himself most obnoxious by his overweening vanity and egotism; and by his persistent meddling in other departments."[41] Borden ignored Hughes's assault on his friend, but by early 1916 Hughes's conduct could no longer be tolerated.

Most of Borden's cabinet believed, and many historians argue, that Hughes bullied Borden into keeping him on as minister. There is little evidence of this, other than the fact that Hughes was indeed intimidating, and Borden did not become leader of his party and then prime minister by being easily cowed. Borden put up with Hughes for so long because the minister had been loyal during the lean years when they were out of power and because Borden also relied on Hughes for military advice—far more than on the chief of general staff, Major-General Willoughby Gwatkin, who remained outside the prime minister's circle of advisors.[42] It was because the prime minister leaned so heavily on his minister (even though Hughes was desperately out of touch with developments on the Western Front) rather than on his senior general in Canada that Borden tried to save the beleaguered Hughes's career, telling him to tone down his rhetoric and offering to take over his department while Hughes fought off Liberal charges of corruption.[43] Hughes ignored the advice, or promised to change, and then continued in his maverick ways. Scandalous revelations continued to emerge unabated. In early 1916, the caucus turned on Hughes, and several members openly attacked the minister in his absence. Borden confided with some sadness to his diary on April 3, 1916: "It is quite evident that Hughes cannot remain in the Government."[44]

Yet there was no easy way to oust Hughes. To fire him would add legitimacy to the Liberal accusations of government mismanagement. It would also leave the fuming, scheming, and unstable Hughes, who already had a long history of attacking his own party, free and anxious to defend himself in the House, and among his network of newspaper contacts and supporters. Sir Robert rode out the caucus rebellion and kept Hughes on, while quietly seeking a discreet way to dump him. To others it looked like delay and weakness. Foster complained in late summer about "the same old trouble—a crazy Minister and a Prime Minister who will do nothing."[45] Borden had a different perspective; around this time, he wrote, "Very tired and weary of this life."[46]

Hughes went overseas again in August 1916, ostensibly to reorganize the chaotic Canadian training camps in England, where a number of generals had overlapping areas of control and were fighting over whatever crumbs of authority fell from Hughes's table.[47] But things had changed for the minister. He was met with a cold welcome from his boys, many of whom viewed him now as little more than a blowhard politician. The senior officers in the field were fed up with his meddling in military affairs, while the Canadian Corps commander, Sir Julian Byng, who had replaced Alderson in May 1916, tried to dodge the minister's demands for patronage appointments that hurt the combat efficiency of the fighting forces.[48]

Sir Sam's solution to the administrative mess in England—for which he was largely responsible—was to create another board consisting of his cronies. This move went against Borden's express orders: he had instructed his wayward minister to make no appointments or decisions until he had consulted the cabinet. When he found out from the morning papers what Hughes had done, Borden exploded. Hughes was immediately ordered home. On his return in late October, Borden told his shocked minister that he would rectify the mess by appointing a new minister of overseas military forces to administer the Canadian formations.

A somewhat vindictive Borden hoped that Hughes's long-time enemy, the anglophile millionaire Sir George Perley, who was comfortably ensconced as acting high commissioner in London, would manage the new organization. Poking Hughes in the eye appealed to Perley, but he was reluctant to take on the task of setting up a ministry from scratch, and wary of being subjected to attacks in the House of Commons to which he could not reply. But Borden was insistent and Perley finally agreed.[49] The Canadian Expeditionary Force would still serve as part of the British forces, but now it would be administered by Canadians—another sign of Ottawa's growing assertiveness.

Hughes, predictably, was furious. In his view, the establishment of the overseas ministry was an overt snub against him. And, in truth, it was. But the prime minister had carefully lined up his backers, including most of the party and caucus. An exhausted, overworked, and fragile Hughes had several stormy meetings with Borden through late October, in which he raged and ranted about the injustices done to him. A stony Borden would not be dissuaded. The final straw came in the form of an intemperate letter from Hughes to Borden on November 1, 1916, accusing the prime minister of lying and betrayal. The usually reserved Borden swiftly demanded Hughes's resignation.[50] Hughes was flung to the backbenches.

By this action, Borden at last showed his cabinet, the opposition, and Canadians that he had steel in him. Borden had led his country for two and a half gruelling years, but many of his ministers were succumbing to the pressure and collapsing from overwork and ill health. Some, however, stepped up. Perley thrived as the new minister of overseas military forces, while A.E. Kemp, the solid, smart, and hard-working leader of the Ontario wing of the party, took over from Hughes as minister of militia and defence.[51] Arthur Meighen's brilliant mind had been revealed since the beginning of the war, and he was moved from the junior minister position of solicitor general to secretary of state in 1917. Meighen remained a force in the House, where he was superb in the attack, skewering the Liberal critics in piercing speeches, much to the delight of Borden, who needed a political attack dog.[52] White was steady if brittle. Most of the other ministers were forgettable, unremarkable, or lamentable. Borden, however, remained an anchor. His stoicism and grit now grounded the nation. Having removed the knight leading his armies, Sir Robert Borden stepped into the breach. He would be Canada's warlord.

CHAPTER 6

BATTLE LINES DRAWN, 1917

What could be done to win the war? Sir Robert Borden felt he must again go to England to better understand the challenges facing the Allies and to find out why the losses on the battlefield were so high. But he had to take care of one loose end first. Sir Sam Hughes had been removed from the cabinet in November, but the ex-minister remained a powerful force, with many friends in the Conservative caucus and an explosive and vindictive personality. He had been in government for more than twenty-five years, knew party and war secrets, and could probably supply enough dirt to the Liberals to help them take down the government. After studying the situation coolly, Borden placed before Parliament the embarrassing and damning correspondence between Hughes and himself. It was awkward for Borden, because it publicized Hughes's growing insubordination and incompetence—which happened under his watch—but humiliating for Hughes, who was revealed to be a braggart and a bully.[1] The high-strung yet always dangerous Hughes, who thrived on battle and controversy, was declawed almost without a fight.

Hughes continued occasionally to make trouble for the Conservatives, but having lost the mantle of minister, he was much derided. After one of Hughes's attacks, Sir George Foster wrote that he was "in part unbalanced and absolutely untruthful."[2] Hughes had been called worse, but harder for him to take was that he was quickly seen as yesterday's man.

Borden had revealed himself to be an adept politician; now he would become a statesman. He increasingly saw Canada's sacrifice in the war as the impetus for greater national autonomy. The Canadian Expeditionary Force had become a source of pride. That the fighting force consisted almost entirely of volunteer civilian-soldiers was another sign of Canadians' service to King and country. Many at home who hoped to justify the cost of the war embraced the idea of Canada stepping out onto the world stage, even if that stage was the blasted, shattered landscape of the Western Front.

Borden had almost no interaction with the overseas forces. While Perley had earlier in the war tried to engage and include Borden in the enormous number of events and decisions affecting the overseas Canadian force, the prime minister had usually passed the duties back to Perley. Borden intervened only when it was a politically sensitive issue, such as when he championed Sir Sam Hughes's son, Garnet Hughes, to command the 5th Division in 1917, even though most of the overseas generals felt he was unqualified. Borden did not know what made a successful general, and usually avoided becoming embroiled in such issues, but he was not above exerting pressure for a political purpose, in this case to keep father Hughes from attacking the government. Garnet Hughes got the 5th Division, but he never made it to France because his formation was broken up for reinforcements.

Borden chose not to press the issue.[3] Nonetheless, Borden's actions in this instance represented the worst sort of political interference, and contravened his long-standing desire to put an end to patronage appointments, and this in an environment where lives were potentially on the line should an unqualified commander take over a formation.

STILL THERE SEEMED TO BE NO PROSPECT OF VICTORY in Europe. British prime minister David Lloyd George, who had replaced Asquith in late 1916, knew he needed more men from the dominions, but he realized that he had to offer something in return.[4] That quid pro quo would be a greater voice in the strategic direction of the war effort by the creation of the Imperial War Cabinet. The secretary to the cabinet, Sir Maurice Hankey, sniffed that inviting the dominion prime ministers to sit on a specially constituted cabinet would only waste time in useless pomp and ceremony. Canadian-born Andrew Bonar Law, who led the Conservative Party, was more dismissive, sneering to Lloyd George, "When they get here, you will wish to goodness you could get rid of them."[5] The dominion representatives saw their role as more than rubber-stampers, however, and viewed the Imperial War Cabinet as an important gesture, even if Lloyd George's smaller five-man war cabinet continued to make most of the strategic decisions. The Imperial War Cabinet was evidence that a fundamental shift had occurred in the relationship between the dominions and London. As one of Lloyd George's advisors said of the dominions: they were "fighting not *for* us but *with* us."[6]

The prime minister departed secretly from Halifax aboard the *Calgarian* in February 1917. It was a rough voyage. Borden was coming off one of his many colds and he slept poorly in his meat-locker-like stateroom; often he could find rest only in the ship's smoking room, where he curled up on a couch. He was anxious because he knew it was a bad time to be out of the country. The Parliament buildings had burned down on February 3, 1916. The cause of the fire remains a mystery to this day, but it was likely started by faulty wiring or a smouldering cigarette, and was not the work of German saboteurs, as was widely rumoured. He had other worries, too, brought about especially by the Liberals, who were unleashing a new round of attacks against the government's graft, profiteering, and supposedly reckless spending. But Borden left his ministers to fend for themselves in the improvised House of Commons now meeting in the Victoria Museum. He had had enough of partisan politics: Borden was going to renegotiate Canada's place in the Empire.

Lloyd George had called the dominion leaders to the seat of power out of desperation: the war was not going well and more troops were needed. Lloyd George also confessed to Borden that he hoped a council of influential prime ministers would strengthen his hand in dealing with his own generals, who openly showed their disdain for him and sought to curtail his influence over the war effort.[7] The inaugural meeting of the Imperial War Cabinet was convened in London on March 20, 1917. The U-boat campaign and future offensives on the Western Front occupied the leaders. There was no more airy talk of bringing the Hun to his knees in "one final push." Gone, too, in Sir Robert's mind, was the "timidity, vacillation and inertia" of the Asquith government.[8] Borden was told by one concerned British politician that "Lloyd George was virtually a dictator," although he had brought efficiency to the British war effort.[9] Sir Robert took note.

He did not want to go down in history as Canada's Asquith. He steeled himself for the long battle ahead: on the battlefields of Europe, in the meeting rooms of London, and in Ottawa's House of Commons.

While in London, Borden used his precious time to read the papers and reports at the war cabinet offices. For a man who was used to studying his way out of his problems, the overwhelming documentation that filled room after room was an indication of the complexity of the crisis. The war was constantly changing and not to the advantage of the Allies. The British and French armies were still recovering from the titanic battles of the Somme and Verdun in the previous year, where over a million Allied troops had been killed or maimed. They had recently been shocked by the abdication of the Russian czar and the Bolshevik revolution that followed in its wake. The loss of the Russian armies might make the war unwinnable.[10] The latecomer, Italy, which had joined the Allies in May 1915, in the hope of picking a few choice morsels, carrion-like, from Austria's corpse, found predictions of that crumbling empire's demise vastly overstated. It was now incurring shocking casualties in a series of battles with Austrian armies, but the Italians were at least tying down Germany's ally on that front. The Royal Navy blockade appeared to be strangling Germany, but it was difficult to see concrete results, and the combat efficiency of the German forces on the Western Front certainly had not eroded. Meanwhile, Germany's policy of unrestricted submarine warfare was putting Allied ships to the bottom of the ocean at an appalling rate: 694 merchant vessels carrying food and war supplies were lost in the first six months of 1917.[11] For a time it appeared possible that Britain would be starved out of the war.

The ongoing bloodletting and apparent bungling in the various theatres of war pressed the British civilian command to desperation and despair. The generals offered no way to end the war except to keep hammering the enemy. This was the same plan they had been following unsuccessfully for almost three years. Borden sought solutions, as he always had, through hard work and full days, which he described as "insistent and unrelenting often lasting until after midnight."[12] He was tired and dispirited, but not disillusioned. He would fight for a greater voice. His 130,000 dead and wounded countrymen were the markers he carried to remind him of his duty.

"Sir Robert was deeply stirred by the sights of the day," reported newspaperman Stewart Lyon. "He had seen many thousands of men inured to the life in the trenches, hardened veterans, while yet lads or young men."[13] As on his previous visit, Borden did not shy away from the hospitals, even though the broken men there haunted his nightmares. Guilt and anger tore at him: was it right to keep throwing the young manhood of the Dominion into the maw of war? Yet this guilt was also cut with pride. He felt a quickening of the pulse in Canada's achievement at Vimy Ridge. At that battle in northern France, four Canadian divisions, fighting as part of the 100,000-strong Canadian Corps, had captured the nearly impregnable German-held fortress over four costly days in April 1917. When news of the Canadian triumph was announced in the press, Borden crowed that in London it "aroused a universal tribute of admiration."[14] The 10,602 Canadian casualties suffered during the four-day battle were not played up in the press, or by Borden.

The Canadian prime minister held his own among the Empire's leaders and was soon a close ally of Lloyd George, who later described him as "always calm, well-balanced, a man of co-operating temper, invariably subordinating self to common cause, he was a sagacious and helpful counsellor, never forgetting that his first duty was to the people of the great Dominion he represented, but also realizing that they were engaged in an Imperial enterprise."[15] After nearly two months of constant meetings, Borden emerged as one of the more hawkish members of the "Cabinet of Governments," as he called the Imperial War Cabinet.[16] When there was talk of seeking a negotiated peace, Borden fiercely backed Lloyd George's position that only a strategy leading to Germany's total defeat was acceptable. Too much blood had been spilt for Borden to embrace any exploration of a negotiated peace.

Borden's conviction that Canada soon must seize control over its destiny was revealed in a speech in London when he expressed the "view that the constitutional development of the Empire will proceed along the path of equal nationhood and equal status."[17] With this end in mind, the most far-reaching measure adopted in this round of meetings was Resolution IX, of which South African Jan Smuts and Borden were considered the lead authors. Resolution IX boldly declared that when Germany was defeated, discussions would begin with "full recognition of the Dominions as autonomous nations."[18] Borden hoped these negotiations would eventually lead to the dominions controlling their own foreign policy, albeit within the British Empire as a unified voice of equals. As Sir Robert wrote after attending these conferences, Canada was now walking the road "from colony to nation."[19]

MILLIONS OF CANADIANS TOOK PRIDE in the Canadian forces, and especially in the battles won by the Canadian Corps. It was the nation's primary land army and by June 1917 it was commanded by a Canadian, Sir Arthur Currie. The corps had fought tenaciously at Mount Sorrel and at the Somme in 1916, and delivered victory at Vimy in April 1917. Canadian air aces Billy Bishop, William Barker, and Raymond Collishaw led the thousands of Canadians who flew in the British flying services. While Canadians were proud of their fighting forces, there were different opinions on the home front about how to back the war effort. The capture of Vimy Ridge had been recognized as one of the first large-scale successes of the war on the Western Front, but the battle also resulted in withering casualties. The Canadian Corps had been decimated at Vimy, and those losses could not be sustained without the Corps disintegrating over the course of the year. But in Canada the rush to enlist had slowed to a trickle, the number of enlistees sharply dropping in April to 5,328.[20]

While some 400,000 Canadians had enlisted by April 1917, more than 30,000 had been killed and almost 100,000 wounded, and more men were needed.[21] However, the farms had to be worked, munitions produced, and wartime goods manufactured. Those who wanted to enlist had done so, with tens of thousands more turned down as medically unfit, but more than a million men aged eighteen to forty-five had decided not to serve in uniform.[22] Many Canadians simply did not believe that the war was the necessary crusade that Borden and others called it.

At the same time, the war's supporters lamented the bleakness of the Dominion's future if the most loyal and dedicated young men went overseas and gave their lives, leaving behind only degenerates and deadbeats. From the hundreds of recruiting leagues and the tens of thousands engaged in the work of finding men to fill the ranks, there was an increasingly shrill call to invoke conscription. However, this call went against the accepted rhetoric about a just war to free the oppressed and restore liberal ideals. It was the enemy, Canadians had been told time and time again, who conscripted men within their militarized society. Would Canada's fight for liberty and justice become a war that enslaved its own people in a militaristic Canadian *Kultur*?

When an exhausted if determined Borden returned to Canada in mid May 1917, he was troubled by these issues. A few months earlier, he had written to Minister of Militia and Defence A.E. Kemp that "very strong pressure is being exerted in different quarters in the direction of conscription."[23] Should he force young men to fight against their will and break his promise to the nation, which might rip asunder the country? Or must he abandon the Empire in its time of need, undermine Canada's new status as a fighting nation, and break faith with the Canadians serving overseas? Perhaps there was a third unexplored option. By focusing on munitions and food, Canada could have a greater impact than by sending another division to the front or keeping the four already there up to strength. With the other dominions too far from Britain to supply this essential material, why did Canada not focus on becoming an immense storehouse of war materiel? In Borden's mind, the nation already was an arsenal of food and munitions, but that did not reduce its duty to send men to the front. Every exertion had to be made in this war that was critical to the survival of the British Empire. "It is for the future peace of the world that we fight to the end," remarked Borden.[24] In a fight to the finish, with the British Empire facing possible defeat, Canada could not shirk its responsibility. Two years earlier, in May 1915, a despairing Borden had written in his diary of the total war effort that threatened "the suicide of civilization."[25]

This was death by self-inflicted wound, and now Borden felt as if he had his hand on a dagger.

BORDEN HAD BEEN KEPT ABREAST of the failure in recruiting while overseas, and now, in May 1917, he steeled himself for taking the nation to a full and unlimited war footing.[26] In his mind, all Canadians had to share the terrible burden of the war. Equal citizenship demanded "equal service and sacrifice," urged one pro-conscriptionist pamphlet.[27] The nation was at war, and while Borden had tried to restrain those Canadians who cried out that anything less than total service was traitorous, he had now allied himself with them.

The prime minister raised two major issues with his cabinet on May 17: conscription and coalition. There were few objections to conscription, although his Quebec ministers were taken by surprise.[28] They pleaded that the party would be politically crucified in Quebec, and that it might be a quarter century before the Conservatives could ever win again in that province.[29] Borden acknowledged their warning, but was willing to sacrifice his party for the sake of the overseas soldiers. And the party, for the most part, was willing to follow him. One journalist after the war dismissed Borden by suggesting that "he was an influence; never a power."[30] The characterization was wrong. By 1917, Borden was a power unto himself. "Why will he not consult with any of us?," wrote a bewildered George Foster. "We could help him I think."[31] It was not the cabinet, not the party, not the constituents, but the warlord who decided to follow the path to conscription.

The prospect of forming a coalition with the Liberals was far more contentious. There had been talk of this in the newspapers and among some of the members in both parties for at least a year, but it remained deeply unpopular with many in the Liberal and Conservative rank and file. Borden championed the idea, but, somewhat ironically, he was not well connected throughout the Conservative Party machine. He had never gotten his hands dirty in the communities that fed upwards through their members of Parliament, and he left control of the grassroots organizations with regional representatives and bagmen. Sir Robert not only ignored the party structure but also had little time for the rank and file. This was no warm Sir John A.–like leader, who knew the entire caucus and asked after their family and friends. There were times when Borden did not even recognize fellow Conservative MPs outside the House of Commons. But the leader who pays little attention to his supporters soon finds, as Borden did, loyalty shifting and infighting erupting among them. He had firm backers, as most leaders do, among MPs who understood that Canadians generally chose leaders first and parties second. But a growing number who were ungenerous, unhappy, or ambitious refused to acknowledge their debt to Borden, and so the prime minister was often fending off party members who sought to undermine him or his policies.

These conflicts were exacerbated by the proposal for coalition, which was deeply unpopular with most Tories. Parties were formed and sustained through historic alliances and bloodlettings. Loyalty ran deep; the scars deeper. Borden knew this would be no easy manoeuvre, but he could see no other way to ensure stable political backing for conscription. Moreover, the strategy had proven successful in Britain, and had reduced party strife and bickering, at least publicly. The Conservative Party would battle over the coalition issue for months.

Borden returned to the House of Commons on the afternoon of May 18. The galleries were crowded. The House went silent when the prime minister rose to speak. He recounted his trip to England, his work with the Imperial War Cabinet, and his thoughts relating to Resolution IX. Then he pivoted to the question of manpower. He—like many Canadians—felt the "call from the wounded, the men in the trenches and those who have fallen." The country owed them a debt. With voluntary recruitment almost dead, the only solution was "compulsory military enlistment."[32] He would not break faith with the 400,000 Canadians defending country and Empire overseas, and the more than 30,000 who had already given their lives.

The Tory backbenchers rose together in a cheer. Many Liberals followed suit, while others pounded their desks in approbation, and in the gallery, Borden saw women and men crying. Silent were those parliamentarians who feared the political consequences of conscription, the violent passions that would be unleashed. Silent, too, were the masses of mothers, fathers, wives, and children who wondered if their loved ones would be taken from them in pursuit of victory.

"THERE IS BUT ONE COURSE to pursue if the honor of Canada is to be preserved," wrote the Toronto *Globe* in response to Borden's speech. "Until the war is ended Canada must be a nation in arms."[33] Many in English Canada would have cheered such sentiments, but few in Quebec would have done so. In the days following his announcement, Borden was shaken by the unrest and rioting in French Canada. In one demonstration of their discontent, for example, some 15,000 Quebeckers congregated at Lafontaine Park in Montreal on May 23. A series of speakers offered biting commentary on the war. A young journalist, Ubald Paquin, declared to the fired-up crowd that "Conscription is organized murder, systematically calculated and prepared in advance; it is the suicide of a nation; it is total oblivion, the mire of militarism and Imperialism; it is the sinister obliteration of a people and its personality."[34]

A worried Borden met with Laurier on May 25 with the offer of forming a political union. He made an extremely generous offer: he would remain prime minister, but Laurier would be his deputy and the cabinet would have an equal number of Liberals and Conservatives. Such parity would be deeply unpopular with the Tory backbenchers and many members of his cabinet, but Borden had made up his mind. If they did not like it, they could find a new prime minister. Borden was willing to sacrifice much of the Conservatives' power to avoid a damaging political battle, one in which Quebec would surely be a casualty.

Borden's offer was not motivated by altruism, however, as he and his ministers were unsure if they could win a conscription election. One after another, Conservative provincial governments had fallen to the Liberals during the war years—seven out of seven; at the federal level, the Conservatives had lost by-elections in most regions. Electoral success was by no means guaranteed, even with a wedge issue like conscription that might shatter the Liberal Party, which consisted of both those who believed that any burden must be met to win the war and those who spoke openly that Canada had done more than its fair share. In Australia, for instance, a plebiscite on conscription had been defeated, as would a second one. Borden wrote in his diary on May 25 that the consensus of the cabinet was that "we might be beaten by French, foreigners and slackers."[35]

While Laurier knew that union would allow him to rise above the relative ineffectiveness of the opposition and have a substantial role in directing the war, he felt deeply that conscription meant abandoning French Canada. Sir Wilfrid had always fought against the extremists, even when it had led to his downfall in 1911. Now, he was trapped between the English imperialists and some nationalists, who demanded victory at any cost, and their French opponents, who denounced any measure other than voluntary recruitment. Laurier asked for time to consider his options and consult the party.

Many of Laurier's English-speaking Liberals favoured union with the Conservatives. The seventy-seven-year-old leader, however, was personally opposed. He chastised the conscriptionists in his party for supporting a bill that would alienate Quebec and that might not be needed in a few months. But Laurier's hold on his followers had slipped considerably over the last few years. Newton Rowell, the Liberal leader of the opposition in Ontario, who combined carping with prissiness, believed that Laurier had "reached such an age and the condition of his health is such that I fear he cannot give the country the leadership it needs and demands."[36]

Laurier was right to worry about Quebec, but his reservations left him out of touch with the majority of English Canada. As J.A. Calder, the influential minister of railways in the Liberal Saskatchewan government, told him, "Unless something is done and done quickly we may find on our hands an election in which all the English-speaking provinces of Canada will be arrayed against Quebec."[37] Laurier knew that his refusal to form a coalition would force an election, and one that would split the country along linguistic lines. Would conceding ground now for possible gain in the future be the better choice, allowing him to work from within the Unionist government? Laurier's own words offer some insight: "If, at the present time, anybody can restrain and face the extremists, I think I am the man. Were I to flinch at all in the position which I always maintained, my usefulness would not only be gone, but my self-respect would be gone with it."[38] Perhaps Laurier also remembered that the French-Canadian ministers who sat in the Conservative cabinet had been ineffective in influencing Conservative policy. More importantly, he must have asked himself if French Canada would turn on him if he came out for conscription. This was a terrifying prospect, both for the party and Laurier's reputation, but where would Quebec go? Certainly not to Borden's party. And, as Laurier had admitted only a few months earlier, "to talk of civil war in Quebec is simply sheer nonsense."[39]

While Laurier considered his options, the Conservatives met in the last week of May to draft the conscription bill. Some desired to simply use the Militia Act, which had been on the statute books since 1868, and amended in 1904. It allowed the government to place the militia on active service in Canada, and beyond its borders in an emergency. However, the raising by levy or ballot of all men between the ages of eighteen and sixty—in Arthur Meighen's words, calling up recruits "chosen by lot, by chance, by hit and miss"—would sledgehammer the economy and disrupt communities and families.[40] The new bill, drafted by Meighen, would conscript a significant body of men, but would allow most of those in wartime industries or in agriculture to remain at their post, and provide some dispensation on grounds of religion or hardship. While the Military Service Act has been condemned widely over the years, it was certainly a more nuanced piece of legislation than the Militia Act.

Official figures based on the 1911 Census revealed that there were 760,453 single men and 823,096 married men between the ages of 20 and 45, including 401,882 identified Class I single males between the ages of 20 and 32, who would be the first to be selected for service.[41] With immigration between 1911 and 1917, there were likely several hundred thousand additional men. Of these 1.5 million men, 200,000 worked in the munitions industry and 917,000 men were engaged on farms.[42] The pool of manpower was therefore narrow, but the military was asking for only 100,000 men, at least through 1917. For Borden and for those who saw themselves as patriotic Canadians, it was clear that there were more than enough men to fill the ranks overseas without damaging the war effort at home, but only if the selection was made as scientifically and fairly as possible.

Laurier put off his answer until the first week of June, refusing to commit in the faint hope that the government might find a less muscular policy or that the war situation would alter the need for conscription. Anxious patriots condemned Borden for his patience, which was interpreted by many as a lack of leadership and a failure to know his own mind. Other party members took a different tack, flattering Borden by arguing that he could carry the country alone.[43] Borden would have none of this nonsense. He needed Laurier to placate Quebec.

They met on June 6. The prime minister had hoped the delay indicated that Laurier had been able to convince his caucus to embrace the offer, but now Sir Wilfrid told him a coalition was impossible. He would not join him in a union of the parties, even after Borden threw in the right to veto the makeup of the entire cabinet.[44] Never had a prime minister offered such power to an opponent. But now was the time, in Laurier's mind, to stand fast.

Laurier's essential objection had not changed since he wrote to one of his English-Canadian followers in early 1917: "In the present circumstances, Canada has certainly no reason to apprehend insurrection or riot, or invasion or war. It is physically and materially impossible for Germany to carry war into Canada."[45] Laurier could not support conscription that might destroy the unity of the Dominion when it was not physically threatened by enemy forces. Nor would he wreck his own legacy as a moderate and leader in French Canada. Borden disagreed with Laurier about the nature of the threat. If Britain lost the war, he believed, Canada would be forever imperilled by Germany and its allies. Damage to national unity had to be chanced if the nation, and the greater British Empire, faced defeat. Without Laurier's backing, however, Borden had no choice but to call an election.

CHAPTER 7

A COUNTRY TORN ASUNDER, 1917

The Prussian military theorist Carl von Clausewitz described war as a continuation of politics by other means. Now, in 1917, politics was a continuation of war by any means. All elections are contested fiercely, but this one proved to be savage. Few were interested in trying to understand the opinions or concerns of opponents. The contest was characterized by bitter arguments, wild accusations, shocking statements, and deliberate provocation. The strain of the war revealed the fault lines that ran deep through the Dominion.

On June 11, the Conservatives introduced the Military Service Bill. Borden framed the legislation as a debt owed to the overseas soldiers on behalf of all Canadians: "I will not shrink from the determination to support and sustain the Canadian troops now at the front." Moreover, as he warned, "If we do not pass this measure, if we do not provide reinforcements, if we do not keep our plighted faith, with what countenance shall we meet them on their return?"[1] Although no election had yet been called, the party machines went into attack mode. But not everyone would fight. One of Borden's last remaining Quebec ministers, E.L. Patenaude, gave up the political ghost and resigned, as did the Conservative deputy speaker, J.H. Rainville. Patenaude was the more important of the two: he refused to face his constituents, since he had long promised them there would be no conscription. He wrote in his resignation letter to Borden that conscription would "give rise throughout the country, to deep internal divisions, of long duration, and even detrimental to the needs of the present moment. Indeed it is better to keep the country united in the present effort, than to attempt a mightier one at the cost of national disruption."[2] Borden tried to convince him—and perhaps himself—that the Military Service Bill was no different from the Militia Act of 1904, which gave the government the right to call out able-bodied men, only now the government could do it with more precision. "I cannot imagine a more serious condition confronting our country and I cannot imagine a greater need for fighting beyond the seas in defence of our rights and our liberties," wrote Borden to his minister. "To prevent attack at home it is necessary to strike abroad."[3] Patenaude, and hundreds of thousands of other Canadians, had heard these pleas for three years but had seen no evidence that the Hun was set to invade. In this instance, and in many others, Borden's desperate words fell on deaf ears.

Borden sought replacements for those who had taken flight, but few prominent Quebeckers were willing to nail their flag to the Conservative mast. There would be no nationaliste support as there had been in 1911. Popular politician Armand Lavergne reflected the sentiments of many when he told the Quebec legislature, "not a soldier, a cannon, nor a cent should be sent from this country for the war."[4] The Conservatives' unlikely ally of 1911,

Henri Bourassa, knew that he could not influence Borden, and so he flip-flopped again, backing Laurier, whom he had as recently as September 1916 accused of being "the most nefarious man in the province of Quebec," for betraying Canadians and entwining them in the imperial web.[5] Bourassa's support of the Liberals further eroded Conservative influence in Quebec, but it allowed English Canada to link Bourassa and Laurier as a common enemy, to be condemned together. In fighting the election, the Conservatives would be largely devoid of French-Canadian voices.[6]

Many English-speaking Liberals wavered over the conscription issue. They faced an agonizing choice: either abandon the boys overseas or turn their back on their beloved leader. The young William Lyon Mackenzie King, poised to run in North York, thought conscription was the fairest method of dealing with the manpower question, but he stayed in the party and stood by his leader. Self-interest played a part in his decision: Borden declined to offer him the prize of a ministry when King secretly approached him.[7] His leader's advice was also a factor: Laurier told King he would control Quebec in the coming decades if he stood fast. He did, and he did. But King was a small fish at the time, and Borden ensnared other prominent Liberals. Laurier fought back any way he could, holding his party together and offering compromises, while rallying his MPs at meetings and conventions. In his charismatic presence, the quivering ranks promised fidelity; away from their leader, most Liberals suffered through long days and longer nights making anxious calculations. Many came to the conclusion that winning the war took precedence over all other considerations.

Borden's patience and tactical skill, not to mention the offer of ministries, pried many of the Liberals out of their party.

The defections included prominent Grits and future Unionist ministers Frank Carvell, Major-General Sydney Mewburn, and Newton Rowell, leader of the opposition in the Ontario legislature. All were long-time supporters of Laurier, and their crossing of the floor damaged the party—Carvell had been touted by some as Laurier's successor. While a number of Laurier's senior colleagues stayed loyal, they nonetheless backed conscription, revealing a hopelessly riven party. Borden's mastery of partisan politics was evident not only in his management of the dissenting Liberals, but also in his handling of disloyal Tories, especially the prominent cabinet ministers displaced to make room for the rebel Grits.

Dissatisfaction in Tory ranks flared when Minister of Public Works Bob Rogers, who hated the Grits with every fibre of his body, led a rebellion against the union. His animosity was returned viciously by Liberals, who thought him a symbol of corruption. He would have to go, Borden realized, if there was any hope of a union. Yet several ministers backed Rogers, and much of the rank and file saw him as a resolute party warrior, one who had brought much treasure into the Tory coffers. Rogers was a master backroom negotiator, and he gathered strength as he traded on years of built-up credit. Rumours were circulating that Rogers might have enough support in caucus to force Borden to back away from the idea of coalition, when the prime minister played his trump card, threatening to resign and appoint a replacement who was acceptable to the Liberals. This was brinksmanship and the stakes were high. In Borden's mind, without the Liberals, he would be gambling with the country's unity. To avoid an irrevocable rupture with Quebec, Borden was willing to bring down the Conservative house. Conservatives congregated to their clubs and talked it out over expensive whiskey. In the end, it was unthinkable that Borden would go. The caucus rallied behind him.

The dull and dour Borden, whom many regarded as unable or unwilling to engage in close-quarters political combat, had again outmanoeuvred an opponent. Much as he had done with Sam Hughes nine months earlier, Borden provoked Rogers into sending a letter that left him vulnerable. The prime minister slyly called Rogers's missive a resignation letter—and accepted it. The blindsided Rogers would sit with Hughes as a backbencher, and both could compare notes on how their leader had thrown them under a train and kept going as if nothing had happened.[8]

But what did the Conservatives—and the emerging Unionist Party—stand for? It was perhaps best summed up by a Liberal: Frank Carvell, a fierce and effective critic of the Tories for over a decade, told the House in late June, "I look at it as our duty to send all the men we possibly can, in order to make the war the success that the whole civilized world is praying that it will be. To the man who says: you are fighting for England in this war I say: we are fighting for ourselves in this war, no man reveres the autonomy of Canada more than I do; no man believes more strongly than I do that Canada should manage her own affairs."[9]

Most newspapers—including nearly the entire spread of English-speaking Liberal papers—were no less adamant in supporting Borden's Unionist Party and its war aims. The Halifax *Herald* argued forcefully, "The issue before the country is perfectly plain and clear-cut. A government has been formed for the one sole purpose of uniting all Canadians in one grand supreme effort to support and reinforce our gallant sons now yonder in France and Flanders, to assist in every possible way our Empire and our allies in the mighty conflict for the perseveration of civilization, and destroy once and forever the foul curse and a mad autocracy that would enslave humanity."[10] To side with the Liberals was to turn one's back on the soldiers, one's country, and one's civilization. The Liberal journalist, J.W. Dafoe, warned in the *Manitoba Free Press* that Laurier was supported only by pacifists, socialists, and the unpatriotic: "they will come together in the polling booth to stab their country."[11] Such defections were devastating.

The Liberals counterpunched during the conscription debate. They taunted Borden for going back on his word. They acknowledged that the fighting in Europe had become more costly with time, but queried, was Canada's existence at stake? Had the nation been attacked? There was more to Canada's war effort than supplying men for the imperial armies: what of the war-winning work of the farmers and munitions workers? Australia and New Zealand were sending men, but their distance from the battle front precluded the shipment of munitions and food at the same level of Canada's monumental effort.[12] Canada had taken up that slack and, in return, did that not mean that the senior Dominion could avoid drawing every young man from the farms? Where was the balance?

In a crusade, was it fair for the sons of one family to go and not another's? Yet what if it was not really a crusade, as many argued? At what point did the minority need to comply with the majority? Or was it the other way around? In a country of distinct regions, did the majority have to allow minority dissenters their right not to be included, especially in something as grievous as a war? Was the majority entitled to take men from their homes to put them in a situation where they might have to kill or be killed? This was the core of the issue: if the war was a crusade, then any burden must be borne. If it was not, conscription was not worth jeopardizing the fragile unity of the country. The debate continued throughout the summer, but Borden and his men finally demanded an end to the talk: Canadians were being killed on the Western Front, they argued, because of political inaction.

The Borden government finally used its majority in the House to invoke closure and shut down the discussion. The Military Service Act received royal assent on August 29. It called for 100,000 men to be drafted for overseas service, the first of whom would be unmarried men or childless widowers between the ages of twenty and twenty-four. It also created a mechanism for establishing local tribunals to which the conscripts could apply for exemption. While Borden was wearing down the sharp edges of the act in the hope of making it more palatable to voters, he also believed that the tribunals were necessary to keep workers in essential war jobs, to offer conscientious objectors a method to stay out of the army, and to accommodate those men whose absence from the home would leave dependents in distress.[13]

With this key legislation passed, Borden was inching towards an election, likely for December. The summer of debate and discord had revealed that there was only one credible issue, even though the Liberals tried to draw attention to the Conservatives' record of corruption and mismanagement. A vote for the Conservatives (later the Unionists) meant a vote for conscription; a vote for the Liberals was against it. It would be a contest in which patriotism trumped all other considerations. In Borden's inspiring words, "it shall be recorded of Canada that as at the first she never hesitated, so to the end she never faltered."[14] This was the crusading Borden's vision, but in reality an unknown, but high, proportion of the Dominion's citizenry was hesitating and faltering in the face of the terrible sacrifice demanded of them and their country.

BORDEN AND HIS PARTY were by no means assured a victory. There were more than 400,000 Canadians in uniform. Almost all of them were supporters of the win-the-war Conservatives, and all were ineligible to vote under existing laws. That had to be changed. Party strategists told Borden the military vote was critical, not just because the Conservatives were deeply unpopular in Quebec, but also because they were opposed by disenchanted farmers, trade unionists, and newly arrived immigrants who traditionally voted Liberal. The Military Voters Bill was introduced to ensure that all soldiers, including those that were underage or British-born, could vote in the coming election.

Laurier objected, but it was hard to make a case against extending the vote to the soldiers who were risking their lives in defence of liberty and justice. The Liberals were on firmer ground when they objected to the dubious decision to allow soldiers either to cast their vote for a specific MP in their home riding or to vote simply by party.[15] This dodgy measure meant that either party could use votes from this larger pool to tip the balance in close electoral contests, and this would surely assist the Conservatives since they were all but guaranteed a lion's share of the votes. The Liberal protest made little headway. Borden and his ministers were free to use the vote from the trench to offset that of the French.

While the Liberals were furious about the Military Voters Act, which became law on August 29, they erupted in nearly incoherent rage when they caught wind of a second bill introduced to the House on September 6. This bill, later the Wartime Elections Act, would shake the political landscape of the Dominion by enfranchising women and disenfranchising recent immigrants.

One of the many uncomfortable paradoxes facing Canadians in the Great War was the growing empowerment of women at a time when their political rights were limited. The traditional arguments against enfranchisement—that women could not handle the strain or make informed choices because of defects of mind or education—rang increasingly hollow. Canadian women had risen to fill the gap in the paid workforce, raised millions for soldiers' dependents, and had generally thrown their weight behind the war effort.[16] There were women's peace groups, but they remained as marginalized during the war as much as they had been ignored before the war.[17] However, patriotic women's organizations could not be so easily shunted aside.

Under the new Act, women with a link to a soldier overseas—widows, wives, and female relatives—would have the right to vote federally. Enfranchisement had come to women as a reward for their loyalty and, the more cynical remarked, as a deliberate attempt at scuttling the Liberal chances in the election. "If your husband or father is on the firing line," scolded an advertisement in the *Montreal Daily Star*, "he will have less chance of being killed or injured if we send more men to help them ... Vote to save your kin."[18]

Far more egregious than granting the right to vote to a narrow class of women was the withdrawal of that right from others. The Wartime Elections Act, in a brazen manoeuvre, took the vote away from immigrants from enemy countries (Germany and Austria) who had arrived since 1902 and who did not have a son serving with the Allies overseas. The author of the bill, Arthur Meighen, noted triumphantly in the House that the affected immigrants with "alien enemy blood" often had not had time to acclimatize to the nation and its sentiments, and therefore did not "have the same sense of Canadian and British nationalism as we have." Nor was it fair, Meighen argued wickedly, to force these enemy aliens to vote in support of a war that involved many of their "sons and brothers fighting in armies in Europe against us."[19] While most German Canadians in Ontario were not affected, as they had long-established communities, tens of thousands were disenfranchised in the West, where the 1916 Prairie Census revealed that 7.8 percent of the population was born in enemy territory. Moreover, any group of Canadians that had been exempted from service under the Military Service Act, such as conscientious objectors and Mennonites, also lost the right to vote.[20] An estimated 50,000 males were disenfranchised by the act.[21] The legislation combined some of the most democratic and antidemocratic decisions in Canadian history.

Liberals howled at these measures, arguing that the Conservatives were perilously close to emulating German *Kultur* and Kaiserism, contemporary terms to describe the enemy's proclivity to submit to military autocracy. The few Liberal papers that still backed the party—largely located in Quebec and New Brunswick—charged the Borden government with manipulating the electorate to create a "trial by a jury of its own choosing."[22] Borden's pit bull, Arthur Meighen, bit back, accusing Sir Wilfrid and the Liberals of caring more about enemy aliens than about Canadians sacrificing their lives for the Dominion's defence.[23] James Harvey, a prominent Manitoba Tory, captured the mood of many with his chilling pronouncement: "Today patriotism is greater than abstract justice or legal rights."[24]

Borden again cut off debate. Time was of the essence to the fighting men at the front. To wait, procrastinate, and blather on endlessly would lead to the death of more loyal Canadians. The

Conservatives invoked closure for all three readings, and the bill was signed into law on September 20. Parliament was dissolved on October 6, and an election was called for December 17. The Liberals and Conservatives took the battle to the hustings, in what would become the bitterest federal election in Canadian history.

BORDEN'S POLITICAL SKILLS and patience had enticed a number of key Liberals into the Unionist Party, which was formed officially on October 12. The entire process had been hideously complicated. The long-time Conservative and frequent critic of Borden, Sir George Foster, was impressed by the prime minister's ability to bring together Liberals and Conservatives, who had been "bred to party warfare for generations."[25] Borden revealed himself to be both a master strategist and ruthless tactician, and while Liberals complained that the new Unionist Party was just more of the same—corrupt Conservatives with a rump of traitorous Liberals—Borden had driven a wedge into Laurier's party the like of which had never been seen before.

The election mirrored the war overseas: vicious, unrestrained, and with blood everywhere. The *London Free Press* warned its readers: "Every vote cast for a Laurier candidate is a vote cast for the Kaiser."[26] The *Calgary Daily Herald* asked its readers: "Are you going to desert the boys at the front in their hour of need? ... You encouraged them to go; would it be fair or decent or honest to desert them now?"[27] The Toronto *News* moved a step closer to the lunatic fringe that had become mainstream: it printed a map of Canada with all provinces coloured imperial red except Quebec, which was cancerous black.[28]

The Liberal Party had been split by the formation of the Unionist Party, and with a weak party structure in several provinces, its power base remained in Quebec. The Liberals would pick up most of the seats lost in Quebec in the previous election because of the return of the nationalistes, but would that be enough? Laurier knew he could not stray far from his anti-conscription message, but he tried to convince the electorate in the rest of Canada that voluntarism could be revived. Most newspapers and Unionists sneered at the suggestion, arguing rightly that Laurier was employing sophistry or a smokescreen. Laurier even relaxed the conventional restrictions on his own MPs and candidates, who were allowed to vote with their conscience and speak in support of conscription. While this kept many of the patriotic as Liberals, it revealed a fragmented party, a condition exploited by the Unionist Party and press.[29]

The Unionists, in turn, could barely find candidates to run in Quebec. Chubby Power, a returned wounded veteran and Liberal, remarked that the Unionist candidates were frequently "threatened with bodily harm."[30] At one all-candidates debate, the minister of inland revenue, Albert Sévigny, was forced to flee an angry crowd that fired revolvers into the air and pelted the stand with rocks. When he ducked into a nearby hotel, most of the windows in the building were smashed, and he was forced to skulk out a servant's door in the rear. He was luckier than some. The home of fierce imperialist Lord Atholstan (the former Hugh Graham, editor of the *Montreal Star*) was dynamited.

All but shut out of Quebec, save for a few anglophone seats, Borden redoubled his efforts across Canada, and spread his time generously among the Unionist candidates. It was not uncommon for him to speak in three or four places in a single day, reiterating the same points over and over again, preaching to the choir of supporters and fending off the hecklers, before moving off by train or car to the next band of loyalists. While always fact-filled and well-constructed, Borden's lawyer-like briefs were generally dull and unimaginative. A contemporary writer described him as "unstageable, unspectacular Borden; the man from Halifax, the lawyer who was born to be a judge, the citizen who was never cut out for politics, the gentleman who ordinarily never could have got through life without becoming a churchwarden."[31] Controlled and even cold at the best of times, Borden became more tired during the election—fatigue added to the deep exhaustion of the previous three years—and his speeches lacked punch. Yet he was everywhere, despite death threats and added police escorts. In fact, he was so busy that for months he was almost completely cut off from information about the fighting overseas. In his personal diary, there is not a single reference to the battle of Passchendaele, where the Canadians fought in October and November in the slurry of porridge-like mud and rotting corpses. Sixteen thousand of his countrymen were killed and maimed in the fighting. Borden may have wanted greater access to the strategic direction of the war, but for a few months he barely acknowledged his nation's sacrifices.

THE UNIONISTS BELIEVED they owned urban British Columbia and Ontario, but the West and rural parts of Ontario were steadfastly controlled by farmers. And the farmers were not happy with either of the two parties, which they viewed as selling out their interests to city dwellers. The ongoing fear of rural depopulation had wormed its way deep into farmers' communities as sons, daughters, and farmhands left the land to enlist or work in higher-paying jobs in the urban areas.

Since the start of the war, farmers had been engaged in fierce battles on the agricultural front. As the price of food rose, bumped up by inflation and the selling of surplus harvests overseas, farmers were soon accused of profiteering. The renowned author and McGill professor Stephen Leacock described the farmers as "parasites," arguing that the government should intervene to reduce prices to the point where the farmers received enough of a return to cover just "food and clothes."[32] A chorus of shrill denouncements rose from urban newspapers claiming that farmers were gouging the public. Queen's University professor O.D. Skelton observed ruefully that he was "astounded ... by the violence of the anti-farmer sentiment among even educated people, resenting the alleged profiteering and selfish slackening of farmers on military issues."[33] Stung by the criticism, farmers fired back, observing that calls for higher agricultural production were useless if the army kept stealing their sons.[34] Crops were rotting in the fields for lack of hands.

Feeling exploited and underpaid for their back-breaking work, the farmers saw themselves as victims without a voice in Ottawa, even though more than half of the country's population lived in rural areas. If there had been a federal agricultural party towards which farmers could channel their support they would have, and so the Unionists and Liberals set to winning them over. Borden broadened the appeal of the Unionists to farmers by bringing in T.A. Crerar as minister of agriculture, an important gesture because Crerar was president of the influential Grain Growers' organization. It was a step in the right direction, but by November it appeared that unease over conscription was driving farmers into the arms of the Liberals. With electoral victory hanging in the balance, the Unionists cravenly changed their conscription policy, providing new exemptions to farmers' sons who were "engaged in the production of food."[35] The Liberals accused Borden of bribing farmers for their votes, and the Unionist justifications must have sounded weak after all the talk of the need to share the burden.

Many farmers also echoed organized labour groups in calling for a conscription of wealth.[36] If able-bodied men were to be taken against their will, why not co-opt the capitalists' wealth as well? The mainstream Toronto *Globe* endorsed the farmers' position.[37] Ottawa agreed, although the difference in degree of application was significant. Finance Minister White's business and personal income taxes levied in 1916 and 1917 were generally directed against wealthier Canadians or profitable manufacturers, but farmers and labour felt that the government had not gone far enough.

Like farmers, organized labour had become more militant during the war as the government and big business relied on workers for success at the front and at home. Many labour leaders hoped that the war would become working men's chance to take back their nation from the capitalists.[38] But the Canadian state was in no mood to lessen its control, or reduce support for business, and it used the war to hammer labour organizations. When the government broke strikes in Hamilton and Toronto in June 1916, using the powers afforded under the War Measures Act, and then prohibited newspapers from reporting on these repressive measures, labour realized that the state would challenge any demands for change.[39] The Canadian West was generally more radical than the East, and the government was more than a little concerned to hear the call to arms by Joe Naylor, leader of the British Columbia Federation of Labour, who demanded that "if our masters force us to fight let us fight for our own liberty."[40] He was, in effect, inciting an uprising against the state or capitalists, or likely both.

While labour opposed the Unionists, who were generally identified with prosecuting the war aggressively and with big business, one could not discount those labourers with fathers, sons, brothers, neighbours, and even co-workers in the overseas forces. With little fanfare, one-quarter of all of Western Canada's union members had enlisted for overseas service.[41] There were no clear-cut trenches in the open warfare at home.

WHEN WORD ARRIVED that the overseas forces would have the right to vote, many officers lectured their men that conscription meant punishment of slackers and some additional relief to the fighting forces. Captain S.G. Bennett of the 4th Canadian Mounted Rifles observed that the troops were inundated with propaganda, much of which was scoffed at as patriotic drivel, but enough of it "inferred that without conscription the Canadian Corps would dwindle away for lack of reinforcements and the men then engaged would probably have their leave seriously curtailed. This last effect was considered to be much too serious by those men who had not been on leave for over a year."[42] Combat veteran John Becker believed that Borden's track record was spotty at best and that he had done very little for the Canadian soldiers—especially with the Conservatives' defence of the Ross rifle—and "if conscription had not been the issue, very few votes would have been cast in France for a Government controlled by a Borden crowd."[43] As it was, he voted Union, as did 90 percent of his comrades.[44] The overseas service vote, which included nurses, was a powerful bloc and their influence was multiplied as they encouraged loved ones at home to support them with their ballots.

Overseas and at home, the Unionists took the fight to the Liberals. Borden's early plea for calm was forgotten in the heat of electoral battle and he incited his men to skewer Laurier for his alliance with Bourassa. The rhetoric during the final month of the campaign degenerated viciously. The message in English Canada, reiterated again and again, was that the Unionist Party would put Quebec in its place. While Borden had worried about the passions inflamed through divisive politicking, he gave no quarter in the final ruthless weeks of the campaign. "Our first duty is to win, at any cost, the coming election," he wrote in his diary, "in order that we may continue to do our part in winning the War and that Canada not be disgraced."[45]

Sir Robert and Lady Borden gathered in the Senate Chamber to wait for the election results that were coming in by telegraph on December 17. By the end of the day, the Unionists had swept the country, except for Quebec. Even without the soldiers' vote, which would not be counted until February (and would reverse the results in fourteen constituencies in favour of Borden's men), the Unionists captured smashing majorities in Ontario and the West, and split the Maritimes, although contests in individual ridings were sometimes very close. Old voting patterns based on ethnicity and religion defined many races, but the rural vote had been essential to swaying the tide, and English-speaking women were a factor too, voting in favour of the Unionists.[46] One hundred and fifty three Unionists were elected, but just three from Quebec. Laurier led eighty-two Liberals back to Parliament, sixty-two from Quebec.[47]

Sir Robert interpreted his victory in the "Khaki Election" as overwhelming support for conscription from the English majority. The vitriol unleashed during the campaign had rocked the country, however, and chest-thumping Unionist papers gloated at Borden's coup. "Patriotism, union, conscription and Britishism have triumphed; racialism, partisanship, bigotry, and slander have been trampled in their mire."[48] For the Liberals, the celebratory rhetoric must have been hard to bear. Witness the hyper-patriotic *London Free Press* editorial the day after the election: "The Flag will not come down. Canada's Allies will not be betrayed. The Canadian soldiers at the front will not be deserted. Quebec shall not rule Canada."[49] The Unionist win left French Canadians isolated and feeling bludgeoned into submission. Borden worried about his victory's legacy. He had counselled restraint going into the election, but in the end he had done little to control the frenzy. Perhaps no man could have. Yet it was Borden who had been willing to do nearly anything to win. He had intoned in the House of Commons that, with the exertions at home and overseas, "The nation is clothed with new dignity."[50] The overseas forces were carving out a name for Canada, but the disgraceful election made it much harder to hide the naked truth that the war was tearing Canada apart.

CHAPTER 8

THE DARK YEAR, 1918

Nineteen-eighteen opened with the guns still shelling the Western Front, and Canadians still dying in muddy fields. Russia was all but out of the war and seething in revolution and civil strife. The Germans were turning back towards the Allies in the West and would soon unleash a massive offensive. Following a year of slaughter in 1917, when British armies crashed fruitlessly into the enemy guns at Arras, Passchendaele, and Cambrai, war weariness rotted away at the morale of soldiers at the front and civilians at home.

Sir Robert Borden took a short vacation after the bitter election campaign, but soon returned to Ottawa. Even after his electoral victory, he must have been aware that nearly half of the voting population had gone against his party and policies. Conscription remained a source of anxiety and had to be handled with care. There were other problems. The previous year had seen a worldwide shortage of wheat, caused in part by the scarcity of farm labour, the result in turn of forty million men having donned uniform. Canadian farmers complained that production was down because they did not have enough help to bring in the crops.[1] They would just have to work harder, said the government. The less generous pundits sneered that lower supplies drove up prices, which benefitted farmers. In the name of efficiency, however, the Board of Grain Supervisors of Canada had been appointed in June 1917 to govern the all-important grain trade, fix prices, and make bulk sales to foreign markets.

Food shortages also demanded some oversight, and W.J. Hanna, a Conservative and former Ontario cabinet minister, was appointed food controller. He was to ensure the proper supply of food and to hector Canadians about unpatriotic hoarding. While such claims carried urgency, Canadians were anxious for Hanna to expose profiteers and reduce the price of food, which had been driven up by inflation. Hanna had no such influence, and soon his appeals to patriotism were largely ignored. Canadians were unwilling to accept his intrusion into their kitchens.[2] Hanna was replaced by the Canada Food Board in early 1918, which had little more success, although it was harder to vilify a board than a single man. Coal, gas, and wood were soon to be regulated, as most Canadians grudgingly went without, grumbling through "Heatless Mondays," and enduring the closing of schools and offices during the coldest days of February and March.

But no one was wasting away as they were in Germany, where the British naval blockade was curtailing the food supply to the point where gnawing hunger had given way to death from starvation beginning in 1917. In Canada, food shortages were a mere annoyance. In fact, the meatless and heatless days seemed to have resulted less from a requirement of forfeiting for the war's sake than from the working class's reduced spending power due to inflation. Sir George Foster observed of the circles in which he travelled in February 1918: "Yet how little we sacrifice!"[3] A sense of patriotism may have made the sacrifice more palatable, but for those who did not feel the pinch, there is little evidence that luxuries were given up.

The war was suddenly brought closer to home for Haligonians in early December 1917, when two ships collided in the harbour. One of the two was carrying tons of explosives and the result was the largest human-made explosion to that point in history. The shock waves crashed through much of the city. Structures shattered as if made of matchsticks, glass windows exploded into a million deadly shards, and secondary fires from burst gas mains burned much of the city. A shocking 1,600 people were killed and another 9,000 wounded. Many were blinded for life.[4] The survivors picked up the pieces and went on with their lives. Death and destruction were sadly familiar to Canadians, who already grieved for 40,000 dead soldiers. And there would be more.

Borden lamented the loss endured by his many friends in Halifax, but his attention was soon pulled in other directions. In early 1918, he was bombarded with one crisis after another—from the need to punish suspected profiteers to the agitation over prohibition, and from the debt-ridden railways to the ever-worsening food and fuel situation. And always behind them were "labour delegations, returned soldiers associations, women's associations, etc."[5] One of the most pressing issues was the need to sort out trade relations with the United States. The Canadian munitions industry relied on the United States as a source of supplies, but this had led to a trade imbalance of several hundred million dollars. Thomas White worried that the Canadian dollar would be devalued and, with little movement from the Americans to take remedial action, Borden was obliged to lead a delegation to Washington in February 1918. The party that had wrapped itself in the Union Jack in 1911 now trekked south, pockets turned out, palms open. The Yanks negotiated from strength, but a summit meeting between Borden and President Woodrow Wilson led to some important concessions on restrictive trade practices.[6] Borden did not get on easily with Wilson, whom he described in his diary as "stupid and indifferent."[7] Still, he persevered, while noting the irony that much of his work as a war leader was directed towards traditional fiscal and trade challenges. Though it was not immediately clear to Borden, Canada was being forced to embrace New York rather than London as its financial centre, which became one of the long-term effects of the war.

The relentless strain wore heavily on Borden. In the first two years of the war, he had found some time to fish and golf, but there was little room for vacation in the grinding months that followed. For exercise and recreation, he would walk with Laura to the farmers' market in Ottawa, and he often rode his bicycle to his parliamentary office. Once there, he worked unremittingly, chipping away at the daily mountain of correspondence from concerned citizens, suffering through cabinet and caucus meetings that tried his patience, and sparring with critics in and out of the House of Commons. Borden took solace in Sunday church attendance, and, as he committed to his diary, relieved tension there by singing loudly and "lustily."[8] But there was little respite for Borden, and he had few confidants other than Laura, who was often ill, and his equally hard-pressed friend, Thomas White. Both men worked long hours, and White always knew that his prime minister needed to chat when the weary Borden knocked on his office door and suggested they go for a walk. They would wander through the Parliamentary Library or, after the fire, around the streets of Ottawa. White steered Borden towards subjects other than the war, and the two men swapped their favourite Greek quotations or lines of poetry before returning to their offices, where they stoked the embers in the fireplace and went back to pondering how to manage the war and the economy.

After the brutal election campaign was over, White pleaded with Borden to let him retire. He was not sleeping and he was always ill. Borden, aghast at the thought of losing him, persuaded White to go to California on an extended vacation.[9] His absence was felt all the more keenly when White's replacement, A.K. Maclean, the former Liberal finance critic, floundered in negotiations with Washington and had to have his budget corrected by Joseph Flavelle. White was persuaded to return, even though he had not fully recovered from his exhaustion. Sir Robert worried about his friend. He had seen too many of his colleagues collapse under the strain of the war, but there was little opportunity for rest, and the prime minister too was succumbing to the unrelenting tension. But Borden drove forward, determined to see the war through to its end.

THOUGH THE UNIONIST GOVERNMENT eased the most pressing of the trade issues with the United States and addressed the budget shortfall by turning to Canadians again through the floating of bonds, it was hounded over the "hateful blood-tax law," as conscription was characterized in most parts of Quebec.[10] Under the terms of the Military Service Act, males aged twenty to twenty-four were the first to be selected for overseas service. But the act also set up tribunals before which conscripted men could appeal for exemption. There were more than 1,200 tribunals across the country, each consisting of two respected leaders from the community. And they were busy: more than 90 percent of young men appealed their call-up notice.

Almost all tribunal records were destroyed after the war because the government was afraid they reflected such vitriolic sentiment that they would be damaging to unity. Still, some evidence has survived. Torontonian Roy McCauley told Tribunal 353 on November 10, 1917, that his brother had been wounded at the front, leaving Roy as the only support for their mother. "What would become of your mother if you were to go out on the street and be killed by a motor car?" demanded the tribunal co-chairman, Judge John Winchester. "Don't look on the black side of things. Your brother is not dead, and instead of being killed you might come back with the Military Cross."[11] McCauley was drafted. But many others were given exemptions. Some were able to prove that their absence from their families would cause undue hardship, others that they held down important jobs that could not be filled by others. The tribunal hearings allowed for a humane application of the legislation, although much of this depended on the judges. In some cities and areas they were lenient, providing exemptions for almost all the men; in others, they took it upon themselves to see that the soldiers overseas were supported, and had little sympathy for those who stood before them. However, there were also thousands of conscripts who enlisted without facing the tribunals, and several thousand more—men outside of the conscripted age group—who continued to enlist voluntarily. All were soon sent overseas as much-needed reinforcements.[12]

Despite all their good work, the tribunals were criticized, especially for their sluggishness. Was there any other way to run them? Borden had desperately sought to avoid sweeping up all available men: "We are convinced that the selection should be based upon an intelligent consideration of the country's needs and conditions. We must take into account the necessities of agriculture, of commerce, and of industry."[13] More than 400,000 men already had been pulled from industry and agriculture, and more were needed. The government was trying to balance the competing demands for manpower. The bureaucratic apparatus to do this wasn't in place, and so the responsibility fell to the tribunals, which decided the fate of applicants one case at a time. It was no surprise that there were problems in how conscription, and especially the tribunals, were put into practice, nor that the draftees took the opportunity to appeal almost unanimously. But in addressing these problems, there were few other options open to the government, and no credible ones suggested at the time or since. In the end, conscription was the fairest method of allocating manpower, even if its implementation was flawed. If the process had been started in May 1917, when Borden announced the policy, new recruits would have been overseas by the end of the year; instead, they did not arrive until the summer of 1918.

THE MOOD IN QUEBEC was especially ugly. After the Military Service Act had passed, the worried Archbishop of Montreal had prophesied, "we are nearing racial and religious war."[14] The War Measures Act made it an offence either to impede or to oppose conscription, but there were constant rallies against the law, and few civil authorities were willing to risk their necks by jailing the leaders of the anti-conscription movements. Moreover, when the authorities tried to enforce the act, thousands of conscripted young men fled to the hills or were hidden from the authorities by their families, parishes, and communities.[15]

This tension came to a head in Quebec City on March 28, 1918. The unrest turned violent when an innocent man was arrested by the police for not carrying his exemption papers. Before he was released a few hours later, a crowd of several thousand protesters had gathered outside the police station. They burned the Military Service Registry office, where the records needed by the authorities to track down citizens for overseas service were kept. The mob spread throughout parts of the city, targeting and vandalizing English businesses. The local police officers were helpless to stop the crowd, and most of them wisely disappeared into the night.

Borden and his government had been receiving reports of unrest in Quebec for months, including some suggesting that secret societies were plotting to overthrow the government.[16] These worrisome accounts, when added to the periodic panics about German-American cross-border invasions, and about "enemy alien" uprisings in parts of the Canadian West that were heavily settled by Germans and Austrians, left the cabinet edgy and anxious. Quebec had sent just three Conservative MPs to Ottawa, and the province was represented in the cabinet by a single unelected senator. Never had a government—before or since—had less feel for the collective pulse of Quebec. Some in the party, made fearful by the Bolshevik revolution in Russia, formed an apocalyptic view of an imminent French-Canadian rebellion. When this fear of anti-government plotting was combined with a desire by many anglophones to put French Canada in its place because of its "disloyal" attitude, the demonstrations in Quebec seemed a harbinger of a full-blown insurrection.

On March 29, a second day of rioting featuring roving armed mobs left the shaken Quebec City mayor asking for military intervention. Borden's cabinet responded by ordering militia troops from English Canada to Quebec to restore peace and order, with instructions to use whatever force was deemed necessary. This was not an easy assignment. The winter's deep snow was piled more than six feet high in the streets, creating a labyrinth of white trenches. Wild rumours of uprising were mixed with accurate reports indicating that the rioters had broken into hunting and sporting stores and seized additional rifles and other weapons. The English troops, forced to patrol the city in small groups, and ignorant of the terrain and often the language, felt as vulnerable as they were.

On the night of April 1, huge mobs converged in the streets, while armed men could be seen on some of the rooftops. The militiamen formed up and were pelted with ice and frozen potatoes. At least one soldier was shot in the face, and, attesting to the level of violence, five were eventually sent to hospital.[17] After several minutes of open confrontation, the militia responded with fire from rifles and machine guns. Four of the rioters were killed; dozens of others were wounded. Canadians were killing Canadians on Easter weekend.

The shock rippled through Quebec and then the rest of Canada. Borden remained resolute, even though he found the strain severe and worried that it portended future unrest, and perhaps even civil war.[18] But he would not be cowed. The unyielding prime minister declared martial law on April 4, suspended habeas corpus, and declared that any male of military service age caught taking part in the riot would be conscripted into the overseas forces.[19] The mobs dispersed, but the protestors and rioters carried deep grievances back to their homes.

In the aftermath of the riots, the prime minister continued to strengthen the hand of the state. A month later, the censorship laws were tightened: it now was illegal to criticize the government's conduct of the war or to spread discontent by weakening the resolve of citizens.[20] In short, the new rules were not about protecting Canadians from enemy propaganda; instead, they targeted mainstream journalists who criticized the government. Dissent was now disloyalty in the eyes of the law.

The cabinet, with no discussion or vote in the House of Commons, had brought in an authoritarian state. Perhaps if Borden's party had enjoyed the benefit of a strong Quebec caucus, his actions would have been more restrained. Now he was playing to the worst passions in English Canada. However, in quelling the mobs, Borden's instincts were right: by dropping the hammer on Quebec, he forced the Church and the Quebec premier, Lomer Gouin, to intervene and call for calm. The unrest was smothered, but the coals of discontent continued to glow red.[21] The four dead protesters weighed heavily on the consciousness of Quebeckers. They became martyrs whose deaths overshadowed the hardship endured by thousands overseas and the service of hundreds of thousands at home. The Easter weekend killings left a powerful legacy of disunity and anger in Quebec.

ALTHOUGH THE WAR MEASURES ACT gave enormous power to the government, Borden and his ministers had been relatively restrained in applying it up to the last year of the war.[22] In 1918, however, the Unionist government turned to it more freely. In early April, for example, an order-in-council required able-bodied men between the ages of sixteen and sixty to be "engaged in some useful occupation." The anti-loafing law, as it was known commonly, was nearly impossible to enforce, but it revealed again that the Unionists were toughening up and accepting fewer compromises in prosecuting the war. Ministers did not need to justify their own actions to Parliament or the people; they simply passed orders-in-council that had the force of law. Few Canadians objected publicly, but fewer still had an effective voice with which to show their disapproval.

There was unrest in parts of Canada besides Quebec. The most obvious indication of this was the growing number of strikes. The government saw organized labour as an enemy. The high cost of living had added to the workers' burden, and even though the bureaucracy in Ottawa was unable to address the issue, leading members of the government, such as George Foster, were both angry and bewildered. "What spirit of evil animates these men ... to help the enemy?" he asked.[23] Labour leaders railed against the government, and against the hypocrisy that led to the conscription of bodies but not wealth, which allowed big business to profit at the expense of the workers.[24] These complaints were familiar, even though most profits were clawed back through taxes, but the reiterated calls for reform and accusations of seeming government duplicity added to the ill will that poisoned the Dominion.

The manpower crisis remained unresolved. The overseas commander of the Canadian Corps, Sir Arthur Currie, had already cannibalized the 5th Division in England for reinforcements, and all the senior Allied commanders expected the war to continue into 1919 and possibly even 1920. This grim assessment was given credence by a series of German offensives unleashed in late March 1918, in which hundreds of thousands of soldiers advanced behind earth-shattering artillery bombardments and clouds of chemical gas. Though the Canadians held their ground on the Vimy front, two British armies to the north were driven back. Within a few days of the opening battle on March 21, reports indicated that British forces were on the verge of collapse. Panic infected councils in Paris, London, and Ottawa.

Borden and his cabinet were still wildly disconnected from the fighting at the front. Never was this revealed more starkly than during the previous December, when Borden and his aide, Loring Christie, could not even put their finger on the total number of Canadians, to the nearest ten thousand, who were serving overseas.[25] In early 1918, Borden had been frustrated at the "complete lack of 'detailed intelligence'" relating to the war effort available to him, but nothing changed. When the German onslaught seemed to be breaking through the Allied lines, Borden's cabinet reeled in the dark.[26] Now, in the midst of this new crisis, which Borden classified as the most depressing of the entire war, how could he make a measured decision in response to desperate letters from a fear-mongering Lloyd George, who wrote that "the whole military future will depend upon our being able to refit and maintain our armies in time"?[27]

More men were needed. But why, Borden asked, was he having to fight this battle again, when he had already passed conscription? He was not willing to lose the war because of exemptions, tribunals, delay tactics, and soft-hearted judges. And so he turned to the House on April 17 and told the stunned MPs that the exemptions under the Military Service Act were cancelled. Farmers were furious, especially as planting season was fast approaching. Many MPs also saw it as an outrageous change of policy. They voted for it anyway: the need to forestall the doom that would be wrought by defeat weighed more heavily on their conscience than the act of betraying citizens at home.

"Many farmers accept the principle of conscripting single men with a fairly good grace," wrote a farmer from Burlington, Ontario, "but most of them are indignant with the Govt for breaking faith with them after having promised them exemption."[28] While some of the farmers' newspapers were muted by censorship, the farmers themselves protested the government's actions in meetings across the country. In January 1918, there had been a shortage of at least 35,000 farm workers in Ontario, Manitoba, Saskatchewan, and Alberta, and now it would get far worse.[29] A delegation of farmers was sent to Ottawa to meet with Borden on May 14, backed by tens of thousands of supporters. Borden refused to allow them to enter the House of Commons, which almost provoked a riot, and when the stony-faced prime minister listened to the leaders outside, he would not compromise. In his mind, "the supreme duty of the government [is] to see to it that these men [the overseas soldiers] are sustained by such reinforcements as will enable them to hold the line."[30] The farmers' plight was not helped by Unionist newspapers that sneered at their complaints, downplayed their claims of harvest shortfalls resulting from a lack of labour, and charged that their protest had more to do with profits than patriotism. The farmers seethed at the injustice. They had given their vote to the Unionists, only to find that the prime minister would barely acknowledge their complaints. Were they to face another four years of being ignored, even spurned? More farmers turned to the rapidly growing provincial farmers' parties, and, in 1920, to a new federal party, the Progressives.

The German offensive on the Western Front had been blunted

by late May, and Currie's Corps was up to full strength, having suffered only a few thousand casualties, which was light punishment considering how the British had been ravaged.[31] However, the influx of 47,509 conscripts in 1918, more than half of whom were absorbed into units in France and Flanders, provided an important stimulus to keep up the strength of the hard-fighting Canadian Corps, while other British and dominion forces were worn down to the bone.[32] Yet in Canada a timely, efficient, and controlled call-up of recruits was still lacking, and the government never effectively allocated men to the forces, business, or farms. This administrative failure detracted from the overall war effort.

In considering the Unionists' disastrous decision in April 1918 to revoke the conscription exemptions, it should be noted that Borden and his Union cabinet had no way of knowing that the German offensive would be stopped. Even with A.E. Kemp having replaced Perley at the overseas ministry to act as the government's eyes and ears, the information originating from the Western Front and London had suggested an Allied collapse was imminent, followed by catastrophic defeat. While the government soon backpedalled and promised to leave sons on the farm for the seeding season, Borden's stand must be understood within the context of the aftermath of the Quebec riots, the fear of insurrection they engendered, the labour unrest, and the panicky telegrams coming from his trusted informants overseas.[33] Nonetheless, the Unionists' drive to win the war at any cost was tearing the country apart.

IN LATE MAY 1918, Sir Robert was relieved to escape the cauldron that was Ottawa to take part in another round of Imperial War

Cabinet meetings. His government had struggled through bitter battles in the House of Commons, but had also achieved some important victories. It had established the Dominion Bureau of Statistics to provide more systematic data on the nation's economy and population; introduced regulations prohibiting the importation and sale of liquor; instigated a shipbuilding program for the government-owned merchant marine; passed into law a new civil service act that would reduce the number of ineffective patronage appointments; brought in appropriation bills to pay for the war by borrowing tens of millions of dollars; abolished the awarding of titles to Canadians; and adopted Daylight Saving Time to reduce electricity bills. Most of the important bills were applauded as essential to the war effort, but the idea of winding back the clocks by an hour in the summer resulted in sniping against the prime minister, who, it was said, had the hubris to replace God's Time with Borden's Time.

The prime minister and his entourage of advisors—Loring Christie, Arthur Meighen, and Newton Rowell—arrived in London on June 8. The Canadian prime minister was anxious to be updated on the status of the war, which had gone from bad in 1917 to worse in 1918. Russia was defeated and in the grip of revolutionaries. The British line on the Western Front had nearly cracked in the face of the sustained German operations of early 1918. The French remained in a fragile state after an army-wide revolt by the rank and file against their bungling senior officers had been barely suppressed the year before. And the Italian army continued to distinguish itself in finding new ways to lose battles on the Austrian front. This grim situation was leavened only by the arrival of hundreds of thousands of American soldiers.

And so Borden arrived in London at a critical time. Would he be told that the war could be lost? Had the Empire's sacrifice been in vain? If there was no prospect of victory, how could the Allied leaders ever justify the terrible death toll? Borden was angry and wanted answers. He had sacrificed much, and he had prevailed on his fellow citizens to sacrifice more. Defeat was, quite simply, not an option.

A few days after his arrival, the prime minister called on his corps commander, Sir Arthur Currie, for a more detailed assessment of the problems at the front. Sir Robert and Sir Arthur had met only a few times during the war and did not know each other as well as they should have.[34] But now Borden called on Currie to speak frankly. The big Canadian general, who had earned a reputation as an astute commander, obliged, telling the prime minister about the horror show at Passchendaele and, as Borden interpreted it, the "awful picture of the war situation among the British," which included "incompetent officers not [being] removed, officers too casual, too cocksure, no foresight."[35]

Borden used Currie's information and his own anger to blast the British high command in a fiery speech to the Imperial War Cabinet on June 13. The normally reserved Canadian prime minister was shaking with anger. He spat out his indictments and warned the politicians and senior Allied officers present that the Empire was in danger of losing the struggle if this ineptitude continued. "The future of this war in more senses than one depends upon our earnestness. We came over to fight in earnest; and Canada will fight it out to the end ... Let the past bury its dead, but for God's sake let us get down to earnest endeavour and hold this line until the Americans can come and help us to sustain it till the end."[36] When the Canadian prime minister was done, his colleagues congratulated him for his hawkish stand. David Lloyd

George could barely contain his smile: Borden had joined the battle the British prime minister had been waging unsuccessfully against the generals, especially the despised Sir Douglas Haig, the commander-in-chief of the British Expeditionary Force.

Borden argued forcefully for a re-evaluation of the strategic direction of the war, but he had no solutions. Neither did anyone else. The politician's desire for a second front had been tried with the Gallipoli campaign in 1915, and had failed miserably. And Lloyd George's punishment of Haig for the futile Passchendaele campaign, by withholding reinforcements in England in late 1917 and early 1918, had only weakened the fighting forces and contributed to the near-collapse. In the end, notwithstanding his fiery rhetoric, Borden and the other national leaders had little influence on the campaign. As it turned out, the German offensives of early 1918, in which they sustained more than 800,000 casualties, had crippled the Kaiser's forces. The Germans were susceptible to counterattack. This the Allies undertook, first with a French-led multi-army offensive on the Marne in July and then the British-led, but Canadian and Australian spearheaded, Battle of Amiens the next month. That battlefield triumph was the start of the Hundred Days campaign. Both sides fought tenaciously, paying a terrible price in lives. In Canada's case, the Canadian Corps of 100,000 soldiers suffered more than 45,000 casualties during the campaign. At the same time, the fortitude and fighting spirit of the Canadian forces allowed the Dominion's land army to cement its reputation as shock troops.

While Borden was in London, he was frequently annoyed by missives coming from his cabinet pleading with him to find solutions to the welter of issues and problems confronting the nation. These included the final negotiations on the nationalization of the railways, the management of labour unrest, the rising cost of living, and general war fatigue among Canadians. Equally important, without Borden to hold together the warring Liberals and Conservatives in the Unionist cabinet and caucus, few decisions were arrived at without agonizing discussions and angry denunciations. When Borden refused to leave London, rumours were spread to the effect that the prime minister was enjoying a holiday in England. These rumours were made harder to refute because much of his important work could not be advertised to the public. "Borden fiddles while Canada burns," sniped one bitter commentator.[37]

Borden's own cabinet of grafted and often incompatible parts was snapping the rotting sutures that held it in place. Borden might have held it together, but he believed he could play a more important role in London, especially in advancing Canada's claims to securing an "independent voice in her foreign affairs outside the Empire."[38] The drive for victory overseas finally was meeting success, but Canada was on the brink of self-immolation.

CHAPTER 9

PEACE, UNREST, AND A NEW VOICE, 1919–1937

Sir Robert Borden had gone back to Canada for a few months in the late fall of 1918, but was soon encouraged to return to England by Lloyd George, who sought his guidance and support. The Canadian prime minister and his small staff of ministers and advisors left New York on November 10. The next day, the ship received a wireless message that the Armistice had been struck. Borden took pride in having done his duty to Empire, Allies, and the Canadian forces overseas, but he worried about the hatred unleashed over four years of war, both against the enemy and within his own country. A reflective, but not optimistic, Borden wrote in his diary, "The world has drifted far from its old anchorage and no man can with certainty prophesy what the outcome will be ... another such war would destroy our civilization."[1]

Now that the enemy was finally crushed, Borden believed that Canada had to be involved in the negotiations that would decide Germany's fate, and it must do this as a member of the Allied powers, as it had been on the battlefield, rather than as a subordinate colony. The war was a transformative event for

Borden. While he had been positioning Canada to assume a stronger role in the Empire since the naval debates, it was not until he was confronted by the war's terrible brutality that he set his mind on achieving it. He believed that Canada's battlefield accomplishments were proof that the Dominion had advanced to full nationhood.[2] Loring Christie, Borden's advisor in legal matters and foreign affairs, penned an important memorandum for the prime minister on what the war had won for the Dominion: "Canada is not a colony, she is mistress of her own destiny. Canada is not a possession; the Canadian people and no one else are the owners of Canada with all the powers of disposition which that concept involves. Canada has a separate individuality, a will and power of her own, a self-respecting national consciousness—all manifested in a determination to recognize and shoulder her responsibility in the affairs of the world as a member of the family of nations which constitute the British Commonwealth."[3] This would be Borden's message to the British, and the world.[4]

BORDEN SET FOOT ON English soil in mid November. He was not sure what kind of reception he would receive. Was now the time to pursue Resolution IX? Even some members of his own party were unsure that Canada should claim an independent voice, worried that such an assertive stance would shatter the fragile British Empire after its recent exertions. Borden had no intention of burying the Empire, but felt that Canada could no longer remain a twilight nation, with one foot in the colonial camp while the other reached tentatively over the precipice, hoping to find solid ground as a self-governing nation.

The Great Powers—Britain, France, the United States, and Italy—had decided among themselves that each would have five delegates at the peace conference, with the minor powers, such as Portugal and Serbia, given fewer. But this meant Britain was forced to share its delegates with the dominions. There was outrage when Lloyd George announced to the Imperial War Cabinet that there would be only one representative from the dominions in Britain's group.[5] Canada, Borden reminded Lloyd George acidly, "had lost more men killed in France than Portugal had put in the field."[6]

Borden, along with the other dominion prime ministers, pressured the British leader to change his stance.[7] Lloyd George wrote how Borden demanded an "adequate voice in foreign relations, based on the principle of equal nationhood."[8] He was not agitating for outright independence, although he mused in his diary, "I am beginning to feel that in the end and perhaps sooner than later, Canada must assume full sovereignty."[9] At the conference, Borden knew that a separate but impotent voice meant very little; nonetheless, he needed the symbolic significance of equality with the small European nations. It was a narrow road to walk.

The British prime minister took the dominion representatives' demands to the Great Powers at the end of December 1918. After some hard bargaining, especially with President Wilson, who thought the British were simply stacking the deck with delegates who would echo imperial policy, a compromise was reached that allowed the dominions to be represented as independent entities. The tide turned when French premier Georges Clemenceau, upon learning "that these Dominions had put a million men in the field or in training, said that this record was enough for him."[10] Borden was less than thrilled by another statement made by Clemenceau to Lloyd George: "Come—And bring your savages with you."[11]

Most of the dominions received two representatives, although New Zealand had one and Newfoundland none. The dominion delegates, however, were denied a vote. Influence was still wielded by the Great Powers. This outcome was offensive to Borden, and he shared his frustration with his wife, describing Canada as "a nation that is not a nation." He planned to change that and he observed that with the terrible death toll still weighing heavily on him, the Dominion's participation in the international negotiations was "largely a question of sentiment." Still, sentiment was important. In Borden's mind, "Canada got nothing out of the war except recognition."[12] And this Borden fiercely refused to relinquish.

SIR ROBERT BORDEN WAS DEEPLY COMMITTED to the Paris Peace Conference. Perhaps too much so. While the European delegates profited from his guidance, his own country needed him more. Angry farmers, militant labour, and war-weary Canadians all demanded attention in the difficult aftermath of the war. Some were tempted to see Borden's absence as avoidance of the country's problems, but he viewed his presence in Paris as the capstone to Canada's war sacrifice. He was eager to embrace his role as international statesman, but he too quickly cast aside his more mundane position as domestic leader.

The negotiations were mind-numbingly complicated. Woodrow Wilson's Fourteen Points manifesto, put forward in January 1918 and seen by many as the template for the new world order, appeared to suggest that the United States would support the emergence of new, self-governing states such as Czechoslovakia or Estonia, especially after the disintegration of the Austrian empire and the drawing and quartering of Germany. Yet no one was sure—Wilson included—how new countries would be born, how borders would be drawn through independent countries, territories, and ethnic groups, and who would guarantee their freedom. There was also the bitter question of how to punish Germany. For some, reparations were not enough: there was talk of hanging the Kaiser (a proposal popular in France and Britain but horrifying to Borden), occupying German territory for years, and taking other measures, such as forcing Germany's leaders to admit guilt for the war and its millions of dead.

The Canadian delegation of fifteen arrived at the Hotel Majestic in Paris on January 11. The British had taken over the hotel, even installing their own staff because they feared spies. This meant that the food was typical British fare, all starch and blandness, and Borden ate out when he could. Paris was alluring to the Canadians who had been cooped up in damp and dreary London. Borden was enthralled by the monuments, buildings, and spirit of the people. He relished practising his French, more so than he ever did in Canada.

Negotiations, meetings, and consultations began in earnest in mid January. The Great Powers often retreated to closed-door meetings, excluding the dominion delegates, to hammer out important details. However, with Lloyd George pulled in many directions, Borden was sometimes asked to chair the British-led meetings or delegations. As Canada's long-service war leader, and as a politician known to have some influence with Lloyd George, Borden's patience, expertise, common sense, and knowledge were prized. Lord Milner, the British colonial secretary, wrote of Borden: "he is the only one of the Dominion P.M.'s, who, without ceasing to be a good Canadian, is capable of taking the wider view and whose judgment and influence are really useful on Imperial and International questions. He is not a showy man, but he is a man of weight."[13]

Sir Robert chaired the committee to determine Greece's borders, while other Canadian delegates, such as Clifford Sifton, a former Liberal cabinet minister under Laurier and long-time advisor to Borden, established international rules for ports, railways, and waterways. More importantly, Borden often took it upon himself to act as an intermediary between the American and British delegates, who tended to antagonize each other through their conflicting visions for the postwar world. Friction between them was inevitable, given that the United States insisted on Britain's divesting itself of colonies and protectorates, while the British resented the transparent American agenda of increasing American worldwide influence at the expense of the British Empire.

The Canadians participated in countless informal and formal conversations with their foreign counterparts. Borden played bridge regularly with South Africa's prime minister, Louis Botha, and the two talked as much about international relations, the role of the dominions in the Empire, and the threat of Bolshevism as they did about the classics and the annoying American delegation. The Canadians grumbled and groused at the British delegates, were hypersensitive to slights regarding their status within the Empire, and even pushed back against the imperial position. In these contests, they were urged on by the abrasive and unlikeable Australian prime minister, W.M. Hughes, but Borden more often did his best to assist the Empire, working with its delegates rather than against them.[14]

Borden was involved in these negotiations for nearly five months. Did his newly acquired expertise on Greece and Albania mean anything to anybody in Canada? Perhaps it showed maturity, or that Canada could engage with a wider international perspective? Or perhaps it was dust in the wind. Borden was more than a little miffed, for instance, when the multi-volume history of the Paris Peace Conference was published and he discovered that his name did not warrant inclusion in the index.[15] At the time, however, Borden traded on Canada's immense wartime contribution to secure separate status within the soon-to-be-created League of Nations and International Labour Organization. The latter was an attempt to strengthen the rights of labour—by establishing a minimum working age and acceptable weekly work hours—that crossed national boundaries. The former was more important and more contentious.

No one wanted to fight another Great War. The League of Nations was an attempt to reduce the opportunities for conflict by creating an international diplomatic forum. But despite the heady rhetoric, the League embodied an ideal that would prove impossible to realize. Even the wording of the founding document was forcefully contested. While Borden backed the League, he and the Canadian delegation objected fiercely to Article X of the treaty, which stipulated that "Members of the League undertake to respect and preserve as against external aggression the territorial integrity and existing political independence of all Members of the League."[16] Many nations besides Canada balked at this phrasing, which suggested they agree to a form of unified defence, but war-ravaged France refused to budge on the issue, demanding guarantees against future Teutonic invasions. Canada wanted peace too, but it certainly did not want to sign an international treaty that obliged it to fight automatically in a war between Italy and Austria or Germany and France. Borden tried to use his influence to remove the offending article and was roundly ignored. Canada might have had some influence in determining Albania's border, but the grand questions of war and peace were settled by the Great Powers. The treaty was too important to scupper over the issue, but it was certain that neither Borden nor any other Canadian leader would ever allow Canada to be drawn automatically into a European war.[17] Too many other countries felt the same way. Although Canada became a charter member of the League, the organization's goals would prove to be impossible to achieve. It was eventually rendered painfully irrelevant with the rise of the fascist dictators in the 1930s.

More successful was Canada's petition to have an independent signature on the Treaty of Versailles, which formally ended the war with Germany. The Treaty was much discussed, both at the time and ever since, largely because of its seemingly harsh treatment of Germany. However, for the French, the treaty did not go far enough; there was little that could assuage France's demands for full retribution after its awesome bloodletting and the considerable damage wrought to its occupied territory. The financial restitution exacted at Versailles bankrupted Germany, and the vanquished nation was further humiliated by the disarmament of its military forces and the war guilt clause, which obliged it to accept blame for starting the war. Many Germans found this bitter pill difficult to swallow and the issue was periodically brought up over the years, especially by Adolf Hitler and his National Socialist Party. Memories were short. Few Germans recalled the brutal 1918 Treaty of Brest-Litovsk imposed by Germany on the hapless Russians, which appropriated nearly 1.5 million square kilometres populated by more than 60 million people.[18] Grievance is not always rational.

The dominions, in the end, were invited to sign the Treaty of Versailles, albeit under Britain's name. Borden saw this as an important step forward for Canadian autonomy. The artist, Sir William Orpen, captured the historic proceedings of the June 28, 1919, signing in an enormous oil painting. Borden was portrayed as part of the group of statesmen in attendance, but his name was not among those on the treaty, since he had been forced to go home in May.[19]

Borden believed that Canada's wartime service had set in motion actions for greater responsibility and, sooner rather than later, the Dominion "must assume full sovereignty," but it had taken the Paris conference to show him that Canada could move easily within international circles. Borden's Canada had embarked upon a new path and emerged from its twilight status of Dominion to become a nation—in imagination if not full constitutional rights. This was Sir Robert Borden's greatest legacy, although it came with a heavy price.

WARTIME DIVISION AND DISCORD deepened the rift between English and French. The invoking of laws that press-ganged dissenters into the army and sent them overseas to fight in the trenches was the act of a despotic state. Even after the Armistice, thousands of conscription dodgers and deserters were still in hiding, unable to work or show their faces in public. An additional 15,000 men were in jail serving prison sentences for avoiding conscripted service, and it was not until December 22, 1919, that the Unionists passed a general amnesty for Military Service Act dodgers and deserters, and let the remaining men out of prison.[20] Nothing was done for those few who had been shot or killed in running battles with the police, as they tried to avoid being caught and forced into a uniform.

Although there was an amnesty for those who dodged conscription, the government continued to fear communists and a potential Bolshevik uprising.[21] Russia had succumbed to ideological revolution, and Canada's growing labour organizations appeared to be espousing the same ideals. Membership in trade unions was on the rise, there had been a sharp spike in the number of strikes, and the militancy of labour generally worried the government. Labour was increasingly angry over not receiving a fair share of industry's profits as wages had been corroded by inflation. The government neither understood, nor cared.

In October 1918, with Germany beaten on the battlefield and starving from the naval blockade, the Canadian cabinet passed a harsh order-in-council forbidding meetings of groups at which enemy languages were used and outlawing the publication of any document in an enemy language.[22] That same month, strikes were banned and men of military age who violated the ban could be compelled to enlist. It was nearly impossible to enforce, but the threat of such action revealed a government that was far less willing than earlier in the war to find common ground with its critics, an attitude that was carried into the peace.

But labour would not submit without a fight. After months of growing tension, in Winnipeg on May 15, 1919, the Winnipeg Trades and Labour Council sanctioned a general strike. Deep incubating anger and frustration welled up like an artery tapped: and the strike expanded to include more than 30,000 union members and then bled across the country. The government was terrified and saw communist bogeymen in every shadow. The Union ministers were desperate for Borden to offer some guidance, but he was in the middle of the Atlantic on his way home from Paris.

After reuniting with Laura, Borden was quickly back at work. But he was still out of touch with labour's grievances and the sour mood across the country when he spoke in the House of Commons on May 27. In the strikes, he saw insurrection rather than real grievances, and he promised a firm response. Borden's enforcer, Meighen, had gone west to Winnipeg to rally the troops and report on the general unrest; he would later describe what he saw there in viral terms: "epidemics of unrest and disorder."[23] Ottawa supported groups such as the Citizens' Committee of One Thousand, which was made up of anti-strike businessmen and self-described "better elements" of society, who claimed that the strikers were anarchists, revolutionaries, and Bolsheviks. The strike was the first wave, they warned, in the toppling of Canadian society. In Ottawa, the Unionists declared that, having won the war, they would not be guilty of losing the peace.

The Winnipeg General Strike occasioned large-scale demonstrations, destruction of property, the imprisonment of protesters, brutal battles between baton-wielding paramilitary forces and strikers, and finally death in the streets. By mid June, many of the strikers' leaders had been arrested, but that did not stop trigger-happy policemen on horseback firing into a crowd of boisterous protesters on what became known as Bloody Saturday, June 21. Neither Borden nor his cabinet seemed overly worried by the shooting. The prime minister merely expressed concern that more riots might be unleashed in another wave of violence.[24] The country had suffered much loss of life over the last five years, and the government's response was shaped by its own vague fears of communism and by poor information about what was happening in the West's largest city, but it is not simply a condemnation with the benefit of hindsight to suggest that Borden should have been more shocked by the killing of Canadians by Canadians.

The Winnipeg strike had seen veterans fighting veterans, which portended the fragmented future. The brotherhood of the trenches did not long survive the mean streets of Canada. The returned veterans came back to the Dominion in crashing waves, several hundred thousand arriving between February and June 1919. They grieved, as did the rest of society, for the more than 60,000 dead, and watched helplessly as several thousand more died of their wounds in the coming years. All this followed on the heels of the worst influenza epidemic in human history, which killed another 50,000 Canadians, and perhaps fifty million worldwide.[25] Families that had escaped the scythe of war were laid low by a flu that killed old, young, and healthy indiscriminately. War and then pestilence wreaked havoc on the country.

Gradually, the soldiers of the Canadian Expeditionary Force reverted back to their civilian occupations. After all they had been through, many expected to come back to a country changed, rejuvenated, and refocused. They believed they had been promised, or at least that they were owed, "a land fit for heroes." Instead, they found inflation, prohibition, and jobs that were mundane in comparison to the work overseas, and often overseen by managers who had not served in uniform and who now controlled their fate. Many veterans were rewarded with good positions but found themselves plagued by depression, anger, and, as one veteran-turned-journalist wrote, "that terrible restlessness which possesses us like an evil spirit."[26] There was no easy way to exorcise personal demons, and many veterans felt like ghosts in their own land, unable to recognize the country they left behind. The same might have been said of them by their families and communities. The war changed everything and everyone.

What was owed to the soldiers? One of the factors that had driven Borden to enact conscription had been the fear that 400,000 veterans would return home someday feeling they had been betrayed by their nation.[27] Almost from the start of the war, new government offices were created to care for the wounded soldiers. The Department of Soldiers' Civil Re-establishment, which was established in 1918 out of the ashes of the Military Hospitals Commission, was overwhelmed by the sheer number of veterans' claims. It responded in ways that were overly bureaucratic and sometimes callous, but it tried to deal with the tens of thousands of wounded veterans.[28] The less successful Soldier Settlement Act (1917) allowed for veterans to borrow money to purchase farms, but much of the available land was barren, and a soldier does not necessarily make a farmer. Within a decade, more than half of the farms purchased under the program had gone bankrupt, and most of the rest were struggling. In 1921, an economic recession hit veterans particularly hard, and by year's end one in five was unemployed; disabled men were even more likely to be jobless.[29] No wonder many veterans felt abandoned. Although Canadian veterans were better off than their counterparts in war-ravaged Europe, thousands fell through the cracks of the various medical or support programs, especially those with damaged minds and shattered spirits.

With rebuffed farmers, retreating French Canadians, militant labour, disenchanted veterans, and grieving families in every community, the Dominion slid further towards chaos. A year earlier, Newton Rowell had written worriedly to Borden, "People are not in a normal condition."[30] The new normal was to be anger, unrest, and disillusionment.

THE GREAT WAR SHATTERED EUROPE. Old empires—the Austro-Hungarian, the Russian, and the German—were dismembered. New countries emerged from the ruins. The mass slaughter of millions of young men left deep wounds on every nation. This was the case even in Canada, which was far from the fighting and the direct effects of war on civilians. The loss of more than 60,000 Canadians was a staggering blow for the nation of about eight million. Canadians tried to make sense of the war and, in the process, built memorials to the fallen, but many questioned what had been achieved in the four years of fighting. Canada had sought neither martial glory nor independence at the start of the war; its aim was simply to defend the British Empire. But it used its newly forged reputation as a fighting nation to demand greater recognition outside and within the British Empire. War involves destruction, loss, and shocking change, but it is also infused with unpredictable benefits, such as the creation in Canadians of a sense of pride in having stood as equals with Britain during the war. A new nation was forged from the valour and sacrifice of its people, but it had also been irrevocably riven as region was set against region. These contradictions did not sit easily with war-battered Canadians.

The Unionist Party was ill-equipped to deal with these postwar troubles. The 1917 Unionists had been unified only by their desire to win the war. Once the war was won, the partisan rivalries flared uncontrollably. Borden had brought the Unionist Party into the world through force of character, patience, and

RIGHT: A young Robert Borden, shortly after taking leadership of the Conservative Party in 1901. BELOW: A 1914 cartoon that argues the need for Canadians—"Everybody, Conservatives, Liberals, Independents, and Labour"—to band together to achieve victory in the war.

LIBRARY AND ARCHIVES CANADA, A027948[1]

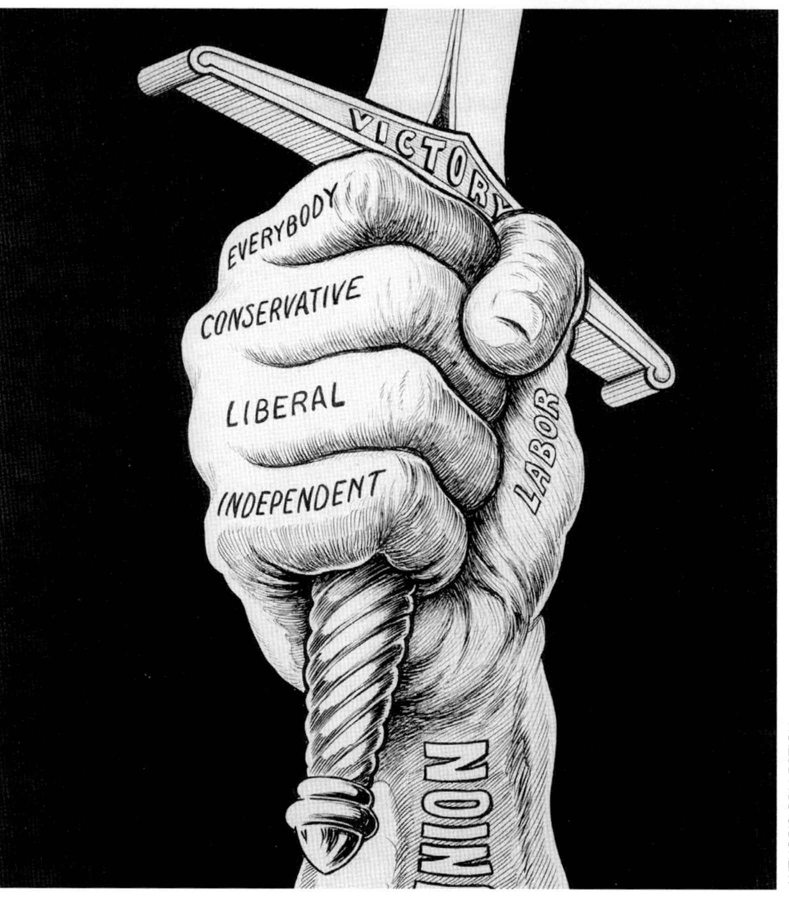

AUTHOR'S COLLECTION

AUTHOR S COLLECTION

LIBRARY AND ARCHIVES CANADA, C-020240

TOP: A determined Sir Robert Borden reviewing Canadian soldiers on a cold day in 1915.
ABOVE: The mercurial Minister of Militia and Defence Sir Sam Hughes dominated the early Canadian war effort, but, through his erratic and unconventional behaviour, was soon a liability to Borden's Conservative government.

AUTHOR'S COLLECTION

A 1915 Canadian cartoon that speaks to the importance of wheat as a weapon in the war against Germany.

AUTHOR'S COLLECTION

LIBRARY AND ARCHIVES CANADA, PA-002735

TOP: A Canadian cartoon caricaturing a German general condemning the success of the Canadian Shell Committee. In reality, the Shell Committee faced significant challenges in convincing Canadian industry to manufacture shells, but the committee, chaired by Sam Hughes, laid the foundation for Canada's enormous wartime production of munitions. RIGHT: Sir Robert Borden inspecting Canadian soldiers in France. Sir Arthur Currie, commander of the Canadian Corps from mid 1917, stands next to him taking the salute.

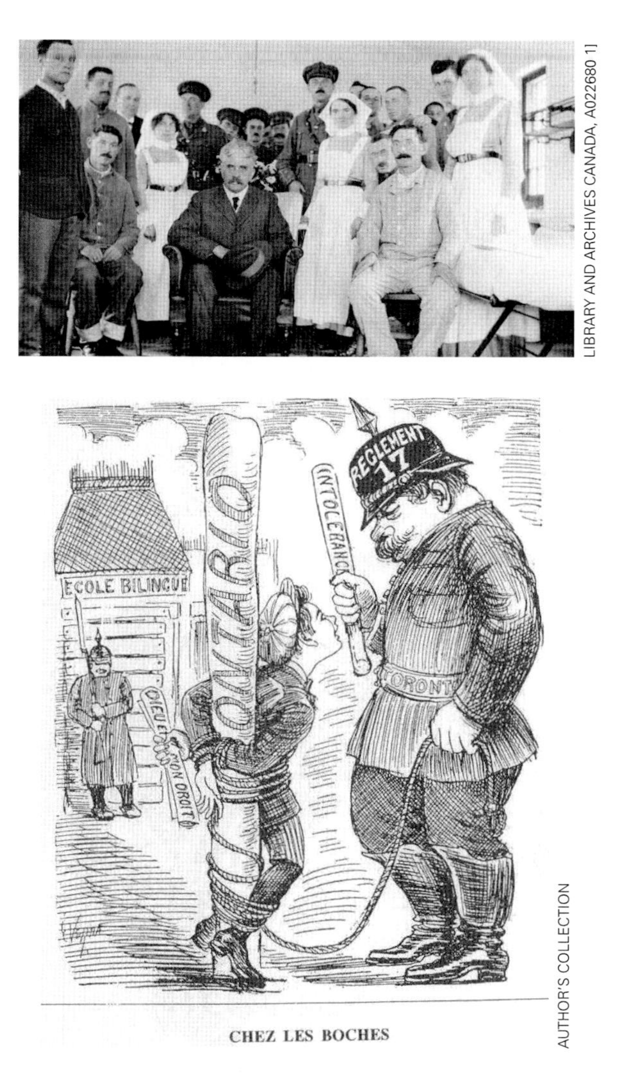

LIBRARY AND ARCHIVES CANADA, A022680 1

AUTHOR'S COLLECTION

TOP: A visibly moved Sir Robert Borden sits with wounded Canadian soldiers at an unidentified hospital. Borden's visit with the wounded convinced him of the need to invoke conscription to better support the overseas soldiers.

ABOVE: A 1915 cartoon depicting the Hun-like "Ontario" soldier prosecuting the innocent "Quebec" lad over language rights in schools in Ontario. Regulation 17, which removed French as a language of instruction in Ontario schools, dissuaded many French Canadians from serving overseas when they faced oppression in their own country.

TOP: Germany's Kaiser hands Sir Robert Borden an iron cross for his ruthless action in disenfranchising thousands of Canadians before the 1917 federal election.

ABOVE: A hardworking Prime Minister Borden fights the fire of the German menace to "Canada and Civilization," while a dithering Sir Wilfrid Laurier suggests a referendum over the Military Service Act that will bring in conscription.

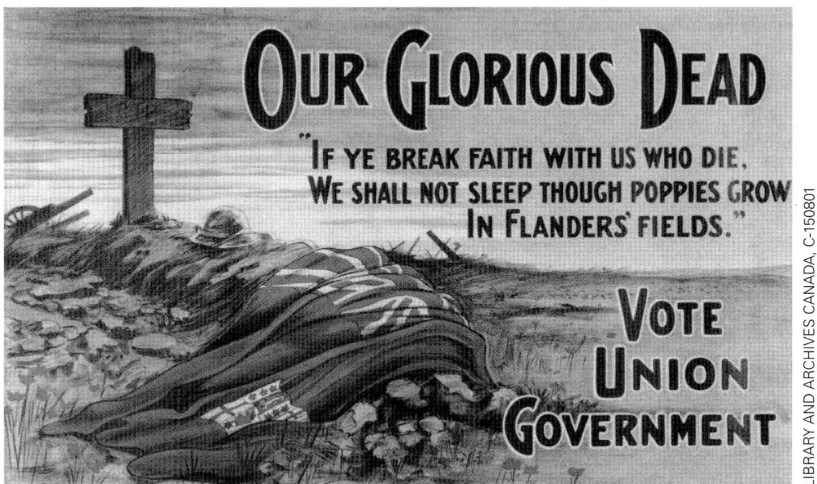

LIBRARY AND ARCHIVES CANADA, C-150801

TOP: A unionist poster that invokes John McCrae's famous poem, *In Flanders Fields*, and the grave of a Canadian soldier to demand that Canadians vote for the Unionist Party in the 1917 election to support the hard-pressed soldiers overseas.

RIGHT: A powerful cartoon that depicts a wounded and desperate Canadian soldier in France demanding that divisive politics be put aside to unify the Dominion in the pursuit of victory. This support can only be achieved, the soldier suggests in holding a ballot, by voting for the Unionist Party in the 1917 election.

AUTHOR'S COLLECTION

In this 1917 cartoon, a confident woman is using her newly received enfranchisement as a weapon to strike against the Hun and to vote for Sir Robert Borden's "loyal Government."

AUTHOR'S COLLECTION

AUTHOR'S COLLECTION

This scathing cartoon highlights a destitute soldier's family suffering under the strain of inflation while Borden does nothing to alleviate the problem other than to offer a "patriotic song" imploring them to sacrifice more in the name of victory.

political skill, but now, because of his exhaustion, indifference, and long absence during the war's immediate aftermath, he had effectively abandoned his toddler to a grim fate.

Liberal members began to leave the party. T.A. Crerar, who had been essential in winning the farmer's vote in the West, resigned in late May 1919 to form an agrarian protest party, the Progressives. Farmers also elected several provincial governments, including Ontario's. Borden had won over many of the farmers in 1917; a mere two years later, most had forsaken the party that they saw as abandoning them. The farmers were a political force to be reckoned with, although they would soon find that there were no easy answers to the vexing problems of trade, tariffs, inflation, and debt.

All of the money-losing rail lines, except the Canadian Pacific Railway, had been nationalized in June 1919 to form the Canadian National Railway. Hard-working Canadians were tired of bailing out the railway barons, and few objected, but the move saddled the state with a major financial burden. The railways were but one more steady drip into a sea of red, the nation's debt having increased from $750 million in 1914 to over $3 billion in 1921.[31] The country's sources of revenue were customs and excise duties, moderate taxes, and little else; Canada's total revenues in 1919 were $312.9 million.[32] The debt was another of the war's bitter legacies and a heavy burden.

The postwar years demanded new ideas and vigour. Some of the old guard apprehended the need and stepped aside. Thomas White ached to leave politics. He pressed Borden for permission to retire and this time the prime minister let him go, with White departing later that summer. New Brunswick Liberal Frank Carvell also resigned as minister of public works, his once promising political career destroyed when Liberals refused to forgive him for his betrayal. He was joined in retirement by other Liberal ministers who turned tail on the steadily dissolving Unionist Party. The centre might have held if Borden had been willing to fight harder to keep it together. But the prime minister had neither the energy nor the willpower; he was a spent force. And he knew it.

Sir Robert drew up his resignation letter in June 1919. Unionist MPs reacted with visceral panic. They begged the tired leader to continue. He did. The Unionists staggered onward. They had little direction, in part because Borden disassociated himself from the day-to-day operations, as well as significant policy and legislative decisions. Borden was prime minister in little more than title.

"ON BEHALF OF MY COUNTRY I stood firmly upon this solid ground; that in this, the greatest of all wars, in which the world's liberty, the world's justice, in short the world's future destiny were at stake, Canada led the democracies of both the American continents. Her resolve had given inspiration, her sacrifices had been conspicuous, her effort unabated to the end. The same indomitable spirit which made her capable of that effort and sacrifice made her equally incapable of accepting at the Peace Conference, in the League of Nations, or elsewhere a status inferior to that accorded to the nationals less advanced in their development, less amply endowed in wealth, resources and population, no more complete in their sovereignty and far less conspicuous in their sacrifice."[33] These lofty words were part of Sir Robert's speech to the House on September 2, 1919, when he presented the Treaty of Versailles for debate and ratification. This was Borden's manifesto; it was a summation of the nation's sacrifice and what it received in return for its shattered youth and lost generation.

The Liberals criticized the treaty, but it was an exercise in sound and fury rather than substance. Laurier had passed away in February 1919, and now his party, too, was in turmoil. Some Liberals, such as D.D. McKenzie, the interim party leader, tried to portray Borden's work as destructive of the British Empire. Another splinter group, led by Ernest Lapointe, a fiery member from Quebec, argued that membership in the League of Nations would drag Canada into more conflicts. Surely this was a Conservative conspiracy, the logical extension of conscription. Unionist guffaws did little to quell the fear in Quebec—and in many other parts of the country, for that matter—of further foreign entanglements. The House argued heatedly, but with the Liberals divided, and with Borden having won Canada the right to sign the treaty, there were few who seriously believed that Parliament would not approve it. The treaty was accepted in the Canadian House of Commons. However, the debates revealed that the war had done little to chart Canada's course ahead, and quite a bit to obscur it. What would Canada's role be on the world stage? War weariness infected most Canadians, who were too focused on their own lives to worry much about constitutional negotiations or the next steps in Canada's long march to full autonomy.

Borden needed to escape the drudgery. He had been prime minister for almost nine years, and leader of the Conservatives for a decade more before that—not bad for a man who initially intended to serve a single term as a backbencher. But now he was done. Laurier's death signalled the end of an age. Borden's poor health left him believing that his days too were numbered. He came to the conclusion that he must pass the torch to someone else to lead the nation over the fractures and fault lines towards a new age.

None of Borden's colleagues had risen above the fray to position themselves for power, although Meighen seemed the likely successor. And so when Sir Robert presented another resignation letter to the cabinet on December 16, 1919, along with the explanation that his doctor warned him that every day he stayed in office was another day he spent digging his own grave, his Unionist colleagues again reared up in panic. They begged that he stay on, even if he required an extended vacation.

They should have let him go. With the Liberal rats re-ratting—to use Winston Churchill's memorable phrase uttered in similar circumstances—by returning to their party, the Unionists needed a new man. Yet either because of their desperation and pleading, or out of vanity, Sir Robert acceded to the party's wishes. The offer of an extended hiatus left the nation essentially leaderless again. As the acting prime minister, Sir George Foster remarked gloomily in early January 1920, when Borden was on a holiday of indeterminate length in Florida, "So now we are launched on a troubled sea without chart, compass or captain."[34]

When Borden returned to Ottawa in May, over five months after he had left, the Unionists had lost key by-elections and more senior members, including the redoubtable one-time Liberal, Newton Rowell, who announced he would retire at the end of the session. The sixty-five-year-old Borden soon reverted to his workaholic ways, slept badly, and was urged again by concerned doctors to retire. It was time. He began to think seriously about his successor: either White or Meighen was the obvious choice. Borden favoured White, though the ex-minister of finance had already retired back to Toronto. The caucus supported Meighen as the more inspired leader, no doubt swayed by his opposition-eviscerating speeches in the House.

On Dominion Day, July 1, 1920, Borden again announced his retirement. No one tried to stop him. The Unionist Party's death march had to end. Borden continued to favour White as the best choice of leader. He did not think that Meighen could ever regain Quebec after having been such a vocal champion of conscription—although, in reality, it was unlikely that the leper-like Conservatives would find traction in that province for at least a generation. Borden did not much care, at any rate, what other Conservatives thought. He would decide, and Borden went to the governor general in early July to ask him to summon Sir Thomas White from Toronto to offer him the prime ministership. A somewhat bewildered White met with Borden and the governor general, but his health had been ruined by the war and he had no desire to lead the country.[35] Meighen took up the mantle on July 10, becoming, at age forty-six, Canada's youngest prime minister to that point in the nation's history, and hoping soon to lead his renamed National Liberal and Conservative Party to victory.

HAVING MORTGAGED HIS HEALTH and perhaps the unity of the country, what would Borden do in retirement? Few who saw him off in the summer must have believed he had long to live. However, Borden surprised everyone, again, as he had throughout his life, and he took easily to his life out of public office. He had been wise with his investments in land, stocks, and his law practice, and the Bordens had no need to worry about money. As the elder statesman of the party, he was called on by Conservatives for advice and guidance, especially on relations with Britain and the United States, where his name carried considerable clout.

The Bordens kept an active social calendar. Sir Robert was forced to respond to the occasional journalistic muckraker dredging up his wartime decisions, but he fought back against attackers by supplying rebuttals to Conservative MPs, especially the ever-loyal Sir George Perley, who spoke on his behalf in the House of Commons. Little of the mud stuck, at least outside of Quebec. In 1927, an informal poll in the national magazine *Maclean's* ranked him as one of the "Greatest Living Canadians."[36] He was also continually buttered up by businesses, boards, and universities, with one private medical firm hoping to entice him in the early 1930s to lend his name to their company, since he was the "most famous Canadian at present alive."[37] Borden picked and chose what appealed to him, accepting in 1928 the presidency of the Crown Life Insurance Company and the Canadian branch of Barclays Bank, and four years later he became chair of Canada's first mutual fund, the Canadian Investment Fund. There were many more opportunities and appointments that he turned down. Borden periodically lectured in Canada and abroad about constitutional issues and foreign affairs. He published two books, *Canadian Constitutional Studies* (1922) and *Canada in the Commonwealth* (1929), the latter highlighting Canada's road to nationhood, a status, Borden argued, that positioned the Dominion firmly within the British Commonwealth. His international prominence as a statesman was unmatched by any Canadian politician before him.

Like most Canadians, the Bordens were hard hit by the 1929 stock market crash and near-decade long depression, but the former prime minister had either sufficiently diversified his portfolio or simply had enough money to ride out the disaster. "There is nothing that oppresses me," Sir Robert wrote to Lloyd George in 1932. "Books, some business avocation, my wild garden, the birds and the flowers, a little golf, and a great deal of life in the open—these together make up the fullness of my days."[38] He had great interest in tracking the birds that lived on his two-and-a-half-acre property close to downtown Ottawa. In true clinical form, he made a list of the two dozen or so that he discovered, as well as the various wild flowers that he admired, and which, next to his books, he described as providing the "greatest pleasure of my old age."[39] His nephew, Henry Borden, recounted that his uncle "in his later years enjoyed the company of younger people with whom he would talk, discuss, and laugh as if they were his equal in learning and experience."[40] The former prime minister was known to make snow angels with the local children, to the merriment of all.[41] He had mellowed considerably, as he puttered around in casual clothes and, in the summer, slept in a hammock under the stars, waking to greet the dawn.

The former prime minister was interested in history as well as his place in it. Borden was made president of the Canadian Historical Association in 1930, and that small body of professional historians was doubtless elated to have such a prominent Canadian enrich their shallow ranks. More than a decade into his retirement, with his body strong and his mind sharp, Sir Robert turned to penning his memoirs, a task that neither Macdonald nor Laurier, both of whom died in political harness, had time for.[42]

Like his friend David Lloyd George—whose memoirs he read, as well as those by every other major figure who published during his time in office or in the war's aftermath—the former prime minister looked to settle some old scores.[43] He was gracious to most Liberals, but had harsh words for some of the old-school Conservatives, especially Rogers, Foster, and Hughes. Borden was generous in praise of Canadian soldiers but had little to say about their commanders, even Sir Arthur Currie, who had led his national army in the field. He may have felt the fighting men had little appreciation for the stress he faced on the home front. In 1934, he wrote to one of Currie's supporters, "In reading, from time to time, articles written by men who served at the Front, it has occurred to me that they were and are very far from realizing the almost insurmountable difficulties, the intense perplexities and the exhausting anxieties which constantly oppressed those who were holding the line in Canada ... In recent months I have gone over my diary [for the war years]. As I grasped the record of those years, each seemed to me the most trying and exhausting until I recalled and grasped the significance of the next."[44] Borden's memoirs—which were edited by Henry Borden and published the year after his death in 1938—provided a strong narrative of his life and times, and the tumult that he and his government suffered through during the war.

Sir Robert's health deteriorated during the mid-1930s. His sciatica left him with pain in his back and legs, but he was not bedridden, and he continued to garden, walk, and golf. In early 1937, however, he declined quickly and he passed away on June 10. One of Borden's last instructions was to his nephew: "none of this Sir stuff at the cemetery, just plain Robert Laird Borden, born Grand Pré, N.S.—1854; died Ottawa, Ontario,—1937."[45] A few days later, on June 12, the body of Robert Borden was carried from his Ottawa home in a procession that was viewed by thousands of Canadians, representatives from all levels of government, his former cabinet ministers, and an estimated thousand Great War veterans in uniform, honouring the nation's warlord as he moved to his final resting place in Beechwood Cemetery.

THE PRIME MINISTER OF THE DAY, William Lyon Mackenzie King, was not present at Borden's funeral. He was in Europe, trying to determine how Canada would respond to the deepening international crisis. Nazi leader Adolf Hitler, anxious to restore Germany as a European power after the humiliations of the Great War, was preparing to expand his agenda of Pan-Germanism and anti-Semitism beyond the country's borders. It was becoming all too apparent that another world war was on the horizon. In Canada, a new warlord would soon be required to lead the Dominion in defence of the British Empire, democratic ideals, and national sovereignty.

CHAPTER 10

MAN OF DESTINY, 1874–1930

Canada's longest-serving prime minister, William Lyon Mackenzie King, was born with rebel blood coursing through him. His mother, Isabel Grace, was the daughter of William Lyon Mackenzie, who had led the uprising in Upper Canada in 1837 against the political elite, a loose Tory conglomerate of wealthy landowners and public office holders. Mackenzie was a political firebrand, but not much of a military leader, and his rebellion was ended quickly and ignominiously. He fled to the United States to escape charges of treason, and languished there in poverty before returning to Canada under the protection of a general amnesty in 1849. Mackenzie cultivated a keen sense of injustice towards the Tory elite in Canada, which he passed on to his daughter Isabel, the last of his thirteen children.

In turn, and not surprisingly, Isabel instilled a fierce respect for her rebel father's actions in her son, William Lyon Mackenzie King, who was born on December 17, 1874. While close to his father, John, who was a lawyer, occasional lecturer at Osgoode Hall law school, and author, Willie, as he was known to his family and friends, always felt a deep link to his grandfather. It was not just the name they shared: all who knew young Willie could sense his pride when talking about his family's fight against Tory oppression. Although the young King was the rebel's grandson, he also remained a proud British subject, revelling in the Empire's history, literature, and political traditions. Throughout his life, he could always square the apparent contradiction.

Isabel was a dominant presence in her son's life. She photographed well, with her large eyes, delicate mouth, and wavy hair. Deeply religious, she imparted to her son her Presbyterian beliefs, which included penitence for past, present, and future sins. King would be burdened by guilt his whole life. Isabel also demanded success, although her Willie did not need to be pushed too hard. He always strove to be at the top of his class. There was no denying his intelligence or drive. As a young student, he was known as a persuasive and effective orator. Around the age of thirteen, he started to sign his name as William Lyon Mackenzie King.

William did well at school, and continued to excel at the University of Toronto, where he enrolled in 1891. In his spare time, he dabbled in journalism for the major Toronto papers, his beat being crime and investigative news stories. A conscientious student, he also was physically active as he skated and played cricket and football. He had many friends and was generally convivial, although he had an annoying tendency to blame others when he periodically failed.[1] William was a well-rounded student, if perhaps a little cocky and too sure of his own success.

After graduating with first-class honours in 1895, King also received his L.L.B., though he had decided he did not want to practise law. He had succeeded beyond all expectations, except perhaps those of his mother and himself. Later, he took degrees at the University of Chicago and then at Harvard, where he readily absorbed the ideas and theories of socialism, liberalism, Marxism, and theology.[2] He holds the most university degrees—a BA, law degree, two MAs, and a PhD—of Canada's prime ministers.

King's engagement with liberal idealism, underpinned by his Christian beliefs, drove him to help the less fortunate. When he returned to Toronto from Chicago in the summer of 1897, he worked as a reporter for the *Mail and Empire*, where he wrote a series of blistering articles on the exploitation of women workers in sweatshops. The articles found their way to Laurier's cabinet, and changes in government contracts were effected. King had begun to make his name as a champion of the oppressed.

And he came to know his subjects. He lamented over the fate of fallen women. He walked the streets of Toronto at night, just as later he would trawl through Chicago, anxious to persuade the prostitutes he met to engage in a more wholesome lifestyle. These interactions also led to secret anguish and, in his words, a "fierce war of flesh and spirit."[3] There is some evidence to suggest that he paid for sexual relations with women, or perhaps he only gave them money in the hope of curbing their wayward conduct. Either way, he frequently was overcome by shame because of his sexual thoughts.[4] He did not easily stray from Isabel's influence and the repressive guilt she had instilled in him. However, his life was not without female companionship, and he had a relationship with a nurse while he was a graduate student in Chicago in 1897; but it did not work out, largely because of his mother's overbearing influence. After taking another degree at Harvard in political economy in 1898, his life almost seemed too busy for romance.

IN THE SUMMER OF 1900, while taking a sabbatical from his Harvard PhD on labour relations and working conditions, King was offered the post of deputy minister of the Department of Labour. It was an astonishing opportunity for a twenty-six-year-old, and so was the offer made simultaneously of a professorship at Harvard. He chose Ottawa.

The new deputy minister was not a towering figure at five foot seven, but with his hair cut short and parted in the middle, and his smooth face not yet etched with stress or run to fat, he was an eligible, intelligent, and handsome bachelor. He wrote excited letters home, which encouraged his mother to swoon over his success. Isabel's other son, Max, prospered too: he served in the South African War, became a doctor, authored a medical textbook, but died at a relatively early age of tuberculosis. Max's character allowed him to move away from his mother's long shadow, and so she turned further towards Willie, whom she relied on to release her from the drudgery of her domestic unhappiness. And he did. He paid off family debts and purchased train tickets so she could visit the capital. When she was there, they shopped together, dined out, and met the political elite.[5] Willie was a model son.

King had an immediate impact in Ottawa. He founded and edited the *Labour Gazette*, a record of the labour relations in Canada. In a government sympathetic to business, he was concerned with the working man and pressed the minister to draft legislation to relieve the plight of workers. He was, for example, the architect of the 1907 Industrial Disputes Investigation Act, a significant step forward in the field of labour relations. King was sympathetic to those who faced exploitation. But this was turn-of-the-century Ottawa, and such reforms were still offset by an avalanche of legislation that favoured business and owners.

In carrying out his duties, King came to rely on his assistant, Henry Albert Harper, known to his chums as Bert. Bert and Rex, as King's close friends called him, had a deep relationship, although there was no evidence of homosexuality, as some have intimated over the years. They went to parties together, walked in the Gatineau hills, read poetry to each other, and ruminated about how to lead better, Christian lives.[6] The two became inseparable.

But fate intervened. In 1901, at a governor general's skating party, a young woman fell through the ice. Bert leapt in to save her and both were swept away to their deaths. Rex was devastated. He pined for his friend and eulogized him in a fawning book, *The Secret of Heroism*. King used his influence to create, in 1905, a statue of Bert portrayed as Sir Galahad. It was erected on Wellington Street in front of the Parliament buildings, where, somewhat bizarrely, it stands to this day, while statues of Canada's prime ministers are relegated to the periphery. King eventually dealt with his grief, but he never made another close male friend.

AFTER EIGHT YEARS AS A CIVIL SERVANT, King was recruited by the Liberals to run as a candidate for Parliament. Laurier, at the height of his political dominance, was looking for men to rejuvenate his cabinet. In the 1908 election, King campaigned diligently, and was supported by a strong Liberal grassroots organization, as well as the party's national record. He won the Waterloo North seat, which was a bit of a shock for the Tories, who had held it for more than a decade. A year later, King was sworn in to the cabinet as minister of labour. He was not yet thirty-five years old, a mere child among the grey beards who sat at Laurier's table. A success by any standard, some found King aloof and priggish. He was both, but he also was wise enough to lie low in the talented cabinet, and to ally himself with the prime minister, with whom he became increasingly close. Laurier and his wife took a shine to the young man, whom they mentored over tea and cakes at their mansion, Laurier House, located in Ottawa's fashionable Sandy Hill. King, not unnaturally, was thrilled by their attention.

King proved to be an adequate minister, but the Liberal defeat in 1911 took him down with it. He was too bright and diligent, however, to wallow for long. In 1909, Harvard had granted him a PhD for a series of labour reports and manuscripts and now, two years later, he put out feelers hoping for a renewal of the offer of a professorship. There was no opening, but he was soon earning money through speaking engagements and writing, and he continued to oversee the Liberal information office and newsletter. From his perspective, he was simply treading water until Laurier inevitably swept back into power.

THE GREAT WAR CHANGED EVERYTHING. King did not serve. At thirty-nine when the war began, he would have been old for the trenches, and few could imagine the squat, professorial, and earnest scholar as an officer at the front, even though other prominent, older Canadians were in uniform, usually in non-combat roles. Instead, King returned to the United States, where he had, since June 1914, worked as a labour mediator and consultant to the Rockefeller family. Throughout his early political career, political hecklers taunted King for not having served in the war. He would claim, somewhat lamely, that his work eased labour tensions in the United States and therefore facilitated greater output of war material.[7] In a country where a third of the male adult population between eighteen and forty-five was in uniform, King's lack of service and his residency in the United States left him politically vulnerable.

The Rockefellers were among the worst of the "Robber Barons," known for their exploitation of workers and their hostility to unions. After a series of brutal strikes in the Rockefeller companies and factories, where beatings and murders were common, King was brought in to ease tension. It was no easy task, and King sustained some bruises to his ego when he was publicly excoriated as a company man. Nevertheless, he succeeded in defusing the tension between management and labour. King also became a brilliant manipulator of the Rockefeller "brand," working like a modern-day public relations consultant to rehabilitate the Rockefellers in American society.[8] For his wild success he was paid a king's salary. But his heart remained in Canada, and he travelled frequently to the Dominion during the war years, and remained active in the Liberal Party by editing its journal and speaking frequently at grassroots meetings.

These were difficult times in King's private life. His sister, Isabel, died in 1915, and his father John passed away in August 1916. His mother's health declined sharply in this same period, and King increasingly felt alone. The grief-stricken forty-one-year-old was desperately trying to finish off his magnum opus on labour relations and class harmonization, which would become his book *Industry and Humanity.* The writing did not come easily in the summer of 1916, largely because much of what King sought to present was not grounded in fact or reality. The accumulated stress, lack of companionship, and general anxiety left him restless during the days and sleepless at night. In the guarded language of his diary, King intimated that he was plagued by unfulfilled sexual urges and oppressed by guilt over masturbation or nocturnal emissions. He turned for help to medical specialists in the United States.

King was admitted to hospital at Johns Hopkins on October 30, 1916, and he stayed under care for almost two weeks. He was nervous and overwrought. He also told his doctors that he periodically felt shocks passing through his body, which he believed allowed "other people [to influence] him by electric currents."[9] This rather distressing reported symptom was coupled with psychiatrists' observations about King's high intelligence, his "sensitive nature," and his deeply religious outlook on life. The psychiatrists also noted that King was worried about his political future, about finishing his book, and about his fragile emotional state. After putting him through a battery of tests, the doctors concluded that he suffered from a stunted sex life exacerbated by an "intensely religious and spiritual trend of affection, which only once became focused away from his mother on a nurse, unfortunately without response on her part."[10] But after almost a fortnight of treatment—for which expenses were paid by the Rockefellers—King put the nervous disorder behind him. He did not again report any worrying symptoms of being controlled by others, and continued to advance from one success to another. However, either because of ill luck, overwork, or a difficult personality, King lost interest in actively seeking a female partner, even though he continued to talk of having a wife and family with whom to share his life.[11]

King also fretted over his inability to fulfill his political destiny. When he learned that there would be an election in 1917, he left the Rockefellers and returned to Canada to run for a seat in North York. Although King had almost crossed the floor to join Borden's Unionist Party (and continued to believe that conscription was the fairest method of allocating manpower for the war effort), he stayed loyal to Laurier. King and the Liberals were crushed, the thrashing made more bitter in King's mind because his mother died the day after the ballots were cast. He would later conflate her passing and his defeat. As his grief faded, however, he came to believe that her spirit would watch over and guide him. Despite two electoral defeats, King was by no means done with Canadian politics.

LAURIER'S DEATH IN EARLY 1919 left the fractured Liberal Party in ruins. A new chief was required to heal wounds. In the sweltering heat of August 1919, Liberal candidates faced off against each other in Ottawa for control of the party in its first leadership convention. Almost ten years of opposition had reduced the pool of younger candidates, while most of the old guard had been tainted by the conscription issue, over which almost all had gone against Laurier. The leading candidate was Laurier's long-time finance minister, W.S. Fielding. But Fielding was old, at seventy, and had supported conscription during the war.

Because of his work in the United States and his electoral defeat in 1917, the forty-four-year-old King had avoided much of the strife that had shattered the party. King positioned himself as a leader of compromise and conciliation. The labour expert could also point to his book, *Industry and Humanity*, published the year before to some acclaim, though it was that rare combination of preachy and impenetrable.[12] In the book, King argued that the principle and practice of conciliation would lead to partnership and harmony in the ongoing disputes between labour and industrial capitalism, creating a fairer collective society, and, more optimistically, fashioning an intellectual framework to end conflict and war. The book contained a lot of woolly thinking and outright gibberish, as well as a series of mystical diagrams that tracked, in a spiritually influenced, pseudo-scientific manner, how the constellation of principles underlying peace, work, and health would bring balance to society through a series of immutable laws and dictums.[13] While King's book has been much ridiculed, it was forward-thinking, even radical, for the time. It went through several editions, and remained an anchor-like manifesto that he turned to throughout his political career whenever he engaged in discussions of social policy and the role of government in the lives of Canadians.[14]

Whoever won the leadership race would find themselves dealing with a nation mired in debt, with tensions between English and French at the breaking point, with labour at daggers drawn with industry, and with farmers turning their backs on the traditional parties. Conciliation was desperately needed. King had fewer weaknesses than the other candidates, and he could command the respect of the influential Quebec wing, which represented the party's chief hope. King prevailed in a surprise victory, although few Unionists cared, or worried.

KING WON THE LIBERAL LEADERSHIP with the support of the Quebec wing, yet he barely spoke French and had a long-honed Presbyterian bias against Catholics. If he was to survive for long as the leader of a federal party, he needed a Quebec lieutenant. King went beyond simply appointing a leader for the French wing. He made a conscious decision to make his Quebec lieutenant his second-in-command, thereby giving him significant control over all MPs in the Liberal caucus.[15] While it was shrewd to share power in order to solidify his own position, the move also demonstrated King's faith in his own abilities, and his eye on the long game.

King found his man in Ernest Lapointe, who, standing more than six feet tall and massive in girth, was a colossal presence both figuratively and physically. Lapointe had first been elected in Quebec in 1904, had learned English while in the House of Commons, and had acquired a reputation as a champion of French rights in Ottawa. He had opposed conscription in the Great War, while still believing that Canada had a role to play in the British Empire as a maturing nation advancing steadily towards autonomy. Lapointe had swayed the Quebec wing to support King at the convention, so it was no surprise that he became King's Quebec lieutenant. In English Canada, Lapointe garnered widespread respect. Over time, in French Canada, the press and people viewed the party leadership as consisting of King and Lapointe in tandem.

As party leader, King began to unify the Liberals, while also attempting to chip away at support for the National Liberal and Conservative Party (the former Unionist Party now almost entirely formed of Conservatives), which was led, after 1920, by Arthur Meighen. Sharp-minded and hard in the attack, Meighen had been a workhorse for Borden during the war. Meighen did not suffer fools at any time, but there was something about King that particularly irked him. It might have been King's sanctimonious, muddled, and meaningless pronouncements, often carried on for hours, but everything that the leader of the opposition did or said raised Meighen's hackles, and he took great delight in verbally eviscerating King in the House. The mumbly and monotone

King was slow on his feet and, facing Meighen, looked like a schoolboy in the presence of his master, even though the two men were the same age. When King tried to go after the government, as one journalist remarked, he offered "ponderous, shapeless, labyrinthine speeches that had no beginning, no middle, almost no end." Meighen, in turn, was "calm and metallic, his diction letter-perfect, his sentences sharpened to penetrate like talons, his arguments marshalled clause by clause in neat syllogism, his irony corrosive, his loathing of King naked."[16] Playing over the thrashings he endured in the House again and again in his own mind, the humiliated King grew to hate Meighen.

Meighen had other worries. He carried enormous liabilities as the architect of conscription; he had made himself the enemy of immigrants by arguing for their disenfranchisement; and he had won no friends among organized labour during the Winnipeg General Strike. Some Tories also viewed him with suspicion because he had been responsible for drafting and defending the legislation that saddled the state with an ever-tightening noose of debt from the newly nationalized railways, while also angering much of Montreal's financial community, which turned off the flow of funds to the party. The economy, meanwhile, was staggering as it shifted production from guns back to butter, and none of this was made easier by the collapse of grain prices and high inflation. Meighen sought to reduce the rampant unemployment, which was perhaps as high as 20 percent (the precise figure is unknown because of a lack of Dominion-wide statistics), but the war's huge debt gave him little room to manoeuvre. Meighen's devotion to a high protective tariff offered relief to Ontario and Quebec (the latter already lost to his party) but did nothing for much of the West.

After eighteen months as prime minister, Meighen called an election for December 1921. King did not appear to be a threat. The respected journalist J.W. Dafoe, who consistently bet against King in the 1920s, remarked of the Liberal leader, "His political amateurishness in view of the position he holds is almost unbelievable."[17] But the election campaign revealed wide discontent among Canadians. The West spurned the two major parties and elected representatives of the new protest party, the Progressives. Much of Ontario went Conservative (the National Liberal and Conservative Party), but there were Liberal and Progressive strongholds, and the Maritimes were split. For the first time in the Dominion's history, however, all 65 ridings in Quebec voted Liberal, revealing that the conscription wound ran deep. In the end, the Progressives won a stunning first-time 64 seats, the National Liberal and Conservative Party dropped to 50, and the Liberals carried a solid 116, a few short of a majority when the independent MPs were counted. There were many reasons for the victory, but the most convincing was that the nation, and especially Quebec, was not yet willing to forgive Meighen and the Conservatives for their role in the Great War and, perhaps more importantly, for the postwar debt and disillusionment.

PRIME MINISTER AT FORTY-SEVEN, William Lyon Mackenzie King set about governing the Dominion. While some of the party elite remained unhappy, King healed many of the rifts by accepting most of the Unionist Liberals back into the fold and by forming his cabinet around the old guard to offer stability and continuity with the last years of the Laurier regime. The prominent Liberal organizer Vincent Massey observed, "Although Mackenzie King commands but little respect, and has few friends, even in his own party, he seems on the whole, to have selected a reasonably good Cabinet."[18]

From 1921 to 1925, the King government proceeded at glacial speed on the domestic front. With Canada's wartime debt at $3 billion—about a third of the government's budget was directed towards paying it off each year—King did not feel that he could spend his way out of financial problems. (This was before the age of Keynesian economics, when the spending might have been rationalized.)[19] A reserved government was also in keeping with King's personality. He preferred a sober, cautious, slow unfolding of debt reduction as he carefully guided the damaged country with the first minority government in its history. He governed with Progressive support and tried to lure the party into the Liberal fold with small rewards, such as lowering the tariff rate on farming machinery, but it was modest tinkering. King was in no hurry.

As the domestic front was slowly brought under control and prosperity returned to most areas of the country, King remained wary of international entanglements. He revelled in the "richness of the inheritance of partnership in the British empire," but he reigned in his enthusiasm in matters affecting external affairs. He believed British imperialists had dragged Canada deeper and deeper into the Great War, to the point that the nation had been split apart by the conscription crisis, and they might do so again in another conflict.[20] For King, there was a difference in the liberal ideals underpinning, as he saw it, the imperial mission to civilize and stabilize the world and that of the more damaging, imperial adventurers—irresponsible politicians and warlike generals—who besmirched and bungled the march of progress. Serving as both prime minister and secretary of state for external affairs, King firmly controlled how Canada would act and react to matters on the world stage, when it would back the Empire and when it would shun the imperial mischief-makers.

The Chanak Crisis of 1922 tested the young prime minister. During the Great War, Turkey had fought on the side of Germany and Austria, and been on the losing end in 1918. But Turkey had re-emerged rapidly in the war's aftermath, its military and political leaders driven by a nationalist ambition to reclaim lost glories and reverse recent humiliations. A revitalized Turkish army defeated Greek forces in 1922, and pressed forward to threaten British and French garrisons in the Dardanelles sector, where the British had fought the costly Gallipoli campaign in 1915 and early 1916. Turkish pressure came to a head in September 1922, when the French gave ground but British forces refused to retreat from a few outposts, especially an exposed one at Chanak on the Asiatic shore of the Dardanelles. Under the direction of the bellicose Colonial Secretary Winston Churchill and Prime Minister David Lloyd George, the British rattled sabres, promised to reinforce the garrisons, and threatened war. Realizing that projecting power that far from England would be difficult and costly, the British sent telegrams to the dominions requesting diplomatic support and military forces. But in a clumsy attempt to pressure Wellington, Canberra, and Ottawa, London leaked its request to the press before the communiqués arrived in the dominion capitals.

King and his cabinet regarded these actions with disdain and then anger. Laurier had passed on many lessons to King, but few were as strong as the need to be wary of imperialists dragging "Canada into the vortex of militarism."[21] But King did not need Laurier's ghost to remind him that, for Canadians, another war was unthinkable. The prime minister would not send his countrymen to fight for Britain's reputation or, in his words, "to play the imperial game."[22] As leader of the opposition, however, Arthur Meighen issued the rousing cry, "Ready, aye, ready." This had been Laurier's rallying call in 1914, and it still resonated with many imperially minded Canadians, although now, in the face of more than 60,000 Canadian wartime dead, even more Canadians must have seen this perspective as too jingoistic, even tinged with colonial subservience, and quite likely to lead the same generation of Canadian boys to new battlefields.

King was wary of turning his back on Britain and incurring the wrath of parts of English Canada, and yet unwilling to risk alienating Quebec or war-weary Canadians generally.[23] He chose a bold course of action: he would delay. "Parliament will decide," he said, but Parliament was not sitting, and so any action that depended on parliamentary approval would have to wait for weeks. The stirring echoes of "ready, aye, ready" faded into history, replaced by prevarication and caution. It was the right choice. The crisis burned itself out quickly: Lloyd George found little support in Britain for his aggressive stance, and he was soon forced out of office. "It would be a good thing for England if she could get rid of Churchill," too, wrote King.[24] The inexperienced Canadian prime minister was left shaken by what he saw as London's attempt to ensnare Canada in another war.

STUNG BY THE LASH, and backlash, from Chanak, King refused to chart a definite course, simply hoping that the ship of state, while not exactly rudderless, would drift along in the right direction. While Borden had seized the opportunity during and after the war to give Canada the right to act, King embraced independence as the right *not* to act. As one American observed, Canada "wished to get all the benefits of the protection afforded her by geography, by membership in the British Empire, and by friendship with the United States without assuming any responsibilities."[25] However, it was difficult for the country's leader to avoid taking action when he was personally invited to the seat of power. The 1923 Imperial Conference was an occasion for pomp and celebration, but one that sought to reinforce the ties of Empire and find common ground in a single policy on issues of defence. The British had achieved good results in the past when dominion prime ministers were separated from much of their cabinet and staff, and then both feted and pressured to embrace London's decisions. King girded himself for battle.[26]

Borden had left a legacy of pursuing a relatively aggressive foreign policy, one that combined autonomous action in a national context and cooperation within the Empire. What was King's vision? He had to take a stand. And he did. "The decision of Canada on any important issue, domestic or foreign, we believe should be made by the people of Canada."[27] And there it was. After much dodging and debating, King had staked out Canada's claim to autonomy. Parliament would decide. Canada would conduct matters according to its own interests and not, automatically, as part of a pan-Empire strategy. That was clear, except that there was more to King's position. The Canadian prime minister issued another unequivocal pronouncement at the conference: "If a great and clear call of duty comes, Canada will respond, whether or not the United States responds, as she did in 1914."[28] And there it was, again; another unambiguous statement that seemed to contradict the first, but did not. The British, in their desperate attempt to achieve imperial unity, especially on questions of mutual defence, missed King's pledge, and instead remembered only his constant embracing of contradictions, his search for wiggle room, and his platitudinous utterances that carried neither weight nor substance. British foreign secretary Lord Curzon, one of the more belligerent imperialists, wrote that the obstacle to any progress, in his mind, had been "Mackenzie King, the Canadian, who is both obstinate, tiresome and stupid."[29] Maybe so, but King had achieved his goal of staking out Canada's right to act independently.

KING DID NOT DRAW ATTENTION to his actions upon returning to Canada, although he had been impressive at the conference, with long-time critic J.W. Dafoe remarking that "my regard for him has perceptibly increased ... He is an abler man than I thought; he has more courage than I gave him credit for."[30] Although King had not turned his back on the Empire in staking out Canada's right to decide its own destiny, neither did he advertise his lack of cooperation with London, as such actions did not win elections in English Canada. But he had made his point, stood by his principles, and could avoid imperialist adventures for the foreseeable future. Meanwhile, his political prospects got a boost when, in 1923 and 1924, the economy rebounded. The return of prosperity throughout much of the country was assisted by the revoking of prohibition and the influx into government of new liquor taxes. The Progressives withered, partly because they refused to act like a national party: their MPs adopted diverse, often contradictory policies, ultimately proving that the sum of the parts was far less than the potential of the whole. However,

King could see that Meighen was rebuilding the Conservatives. The 1923 Tory victory in Ontario was an indication, perhaps, that voters were turning against the Liberals. King was anxious for election day, October 29, 1925.

The once athletic King was older and plumper now. His hair was thinning, but a curled lock sometimes crept down his forehead. One journalist of the day wrote that King's "face looked featureless, puddinglike, and weak ... The black suit, in the antique style which never changed, fitted perfectly. The long, starched cuffs almost covered the plump little hands, as delicate and soft as a woman's."[31] He cut a weak figure, but as prime minister for nearly five years, he could boast of his experience, though seemingly he had governed by doing little. Economic recovery had been slow, but it had happened, with inflation under control but the nation mired in debt. While King offered little to the electorate, Meighen argued vehemently for high tariffs to keep Canada from being overwhelmed by American goods. Much of this was a rerun of the 1921 election.

It turned out that the electorate had, indeed, soured on the Liberals and their do-little ways. The Conservatives elected 116 MPs, the Liberals 99, and the Progressives a much-reduced 24, with a smattering of independents. King lost his seat in North York, and the defeat sparked a mutiny in the ranks, where support for the Liberal prime minister had dropped off steadily over the previous year.[32] Unpopular in his own party and now defeated as an MP, the prime minister's career appeared to be over. There was talk of enlisting as party leader either Lapointe or the dashing premier of Saskatchewan, Charles Dunning. But Lapointe refused to abandon King, and he cajoled the Quebec wing to prop up the vulnerable leader. Dunning did not yet have a federal seat; even as others urged him on, he took some time to think it over and refused to go for the kill. Somehow King rallied the demoralized party. But this was not his most audacious manoeuvre. King refused to resign: he believed he could govern with the support of the remaining Progressives. It was an astonishing claim. Canadians waited, mouths metaphorically agape, as the beaten prime minister continued to lead his much-reduced party and nation as if neither he nor the party had been defeated.

The governor general was Sir Julian Byng, the one-time commander and hero of the Canadian Corps. Baron Byng of Vimy was much admired by Canadians, and especially veterans. He was a simple man—King George V's nickname for him had been "Bungo"—who believed in fair play, honesty, and doing what was right. In Byng's eyes, it was not right for King to hold on to the prime ministership after having lost the election. The governor general encouraged his prime minister to resign, using as strong words as he dared. King refused, gently, but refused nonetheless. He could govern, he assured Byng. He would not hand over power to his hated rival.

King moved forward cautiously, with the backing of the Progressives and independents. Incredibly, he did this while waiting four months for a by-election, a time during which he could not sit in the House of Commons. Under King's command, the Liberals unrolled an old-age pension scheme in 1926, something that King had talked about in his manifesto at the 1919 convention, but about which he had done almost nothing. When issued to Canadians the next year, the pensions were ungenerous and often denied to the most needy due to the stringent proofs of hardship that were required, but they were a step in the direction of a social safety net.

Finally, in June 1926, King asked Byng for the dissolution of Parliament and an election. The government was on the verge of being defeated in the House after a sustained and withering Conservative attack over a scandal implicating bribe-taking customs officials that shamed King's government and eroded Progressive support. The governor general refused. It was his right, but governor generals normally did as their prime ministers asked. In Byng's mind, Meighen had won the 1925 election, only to watch helplessly as King had stolen it. Now it was Meighen's turn to lead. King protested, but Byng stood firm and so Meighen became prime minister again on June 29.[33] His minority government was in immediate difficulty because he commanded little support among the Progressives. Some brilliant political posturing by King further embarrassed the Conservatives in the House of Commons, and within a few days the Meighen government collapsed. Byng was forced to accept Meighen's resignation and call an election.

King could barely conceal his gloating as Meighen looked foolish in another defeat. Moreover, Byng's rejection of King's advice now appeared spurious and ill-conceived. But the Conservatives were not helpless. They attacked the Liberal record of corruption, and King knew the charges were hard to avoid and harder to explain. He chose offence over defence, and rewrote the script for the campaign. The message went out to Liberal MPs and party newspapers that Byng, by his refusal to follow the advice of his prime minister and dissolve Parliament, was engaged in an imperial conspiracy to claw back control of the Canadian government. It was grievously unfair, but in tarring Byng, King also managed to portray Meighen as a British boot-licker. Chanak was dredged up by both sides; so too was the war. Lord Byng kept a dignified silence, but his infuriated wife categorized King as a power-hungry "scurvy cad."[34] Many veterans, too, were outraged at how Byng was treated, but King kept on message. A plurality of Canadians was swayed by King's accusations, or perhaps they simply thought that Meighen had blown his chance; whatever the case, King and the Liberals were returned with a slight majority of 128 seats, including 60 of Quebec's 65 seats. It was the Liberal Party machine at the grassroots that had saved King, but to many he looked like a high-stakes gambler or a grand strategist. King had other thoughts on the matter. On election day, he had prayed and read his Bible. He was drawn to a passage that seemed to portend the day's victory: "There shall be a resurrection of the dead." The comforting words were a sign, he wrote in his diary, of the "presence of the spirits of the loved ones guiding and guarding me."[35] The victory, in King's mind, had been destined.

KING HAD STARTED WRITING a diary in 1893, and with few breaks, he kept at it until his death in 1950. This incredible document, spanning some 30,000 pages and numbering about 7.5 million words, reveals a thoughtful and conflicted man, who poured out his soul on the pages with sometimes disturbing frankness.[36] The diary, in part, was a record of events to which he referred for guidance, but it soon became a daily ritual that had to be met. King purged his tormented soul each night by putting down his thoughts and deeds, capturing grievances, offering petty observations and justifying his own crippling self-doubt. The diary was a way for him to work through problems, and the countless passages where he documented his own failings reflected his desire for self-examination and improvement. At the same time, he had an amazing capacity to deceive himself, or to make sense of the day by slighting others and putting himself in the best light. Pages were filled with windy rhetoric and moralizing platitudes used to justify his sometimes cruel or self-serving political decisions. At other times, he was excessively hard on himself, deriding his lack of skill at public speaking or his acts of moral compromise. "The Record," as he called his diaries, has become the single most important privately created document in Canadian history, providing deep insight into Canadian society and politics over a more than fifty-year period. It also reveals King, warts and all.

Though King was a bachelor, he continued to have a strong friendship with Joan Patteson, a bank manager's wife in Ottawa. Rumour-mongers speculated that she was his mistress, but there is no evidence of this in King's diary, except for a tantalizing section in September 1920 that was ripped from the book. Hints elsewhere suggest that there may have been a brief and guilty affair, or, more likely, something that came close to it. Whatever the case, the Pattesons—both Joan and her husband, Godfroy—and King moved past the incident, and he was later to say that his devoted friend Joan, who was several years older than him, "filled the place of his mother in his heart."[37]

Joan introduced King to spiritualism in the early 1920s, and he quickly became a believer. Many middle-class Canadians had turned to spiritualism after the traumatic Great War, their grief at their losses driving the search for an afterlife.[38] Some were intrigued by the modernist thinking associated with seeking out the souls of the departed, while others simply dabbled in it as a parlour game. King had always paid attention to signs and symbols that offered a glimpse into the future. He was obsessed by the magical significance of numbers, and especially the hands on a clock face. He felt a secret thrill when a glance revealed the hour and minute hands lined up, or when they conformed to other patterns that he found pleasing. As one of King's secretaries revealed, "to him there was no such thing as chance: in this ordered universe every person, every happening, a falling leaf, the position of the hands of the clock in his study, had secret meaning for the discerning eye and ear and mind."[39] This continual search for hidden codes was evident throughout his life. It became even more important to him as he took on greater responsibility.

While King looked for the portents in his everyday life, he also sought out assistance from those he thought watched over him. He remained deeply connected to his mother, believing that she continued to direct him from the "other side." King and Joan Patteson first experimented with table-rapping in the early 1930s, when he was leader of the opposition. It soon captured his imagination. The activity involved a complicated form of communication with the spirits through guided raps on the table. He engaged in seventy-five sessions in 1937 alone.[40] The spirits provided clues and guidance on many matters, from politics to economics, and sometimes a sheepish King was urged to shed his extra weight. These sessions filled empty holes in King's life, but they occasionally revealed his sickening self-regard, as when he and Joan summoned the spirits of Lady Byng and Sir Robert Borden, both of whom reached across the great divide to apologize for having wronged King in life: Lady Byng for her visible meanness to King after he destroyed her husband's reputation, and Borden for having supposedly spread the lie that King had sought a cabinet position in 1917 (which evidence suggests he probably did, at least before Borden turned him down and he returned to Laurier's side). In these wretched acts of self-deception are stark examples of King's unbounded narcissism mixed with haunting self-doubt.

King also made secret visits to mediums across North America and the United Kingdom. In these sessions, his mother and grandfather offered advice, as did his heroes Gladstone and Laurier, and an assortment of other Liberal leaders in Britain and Canada who had crossed over. King wrote that they and "others are guiding me," although it is important to note that he did not believe they were controlling him.[41] Even when the ghostly messages were maddeningly oblique, or simply wrong, the prime minister's faith was little shaken. And, attesting to the respectful nature of the media at the time, no reporter ever outed the prime minister during his time in power, and King's staff, while aware of his increasing obsession with the supernatural, kept silent on the topic.

If King found solace in the spirits, he also finally found a great love in the land of the living. His dog, Pat, arrived in 1924, as a gift from Joan Patteson, and soon the Irish terrier was a constant companion. Pat, and the two dogs with the same name that replaced him after his passing, were among King's most important relationships. They brought him much joy and, judging from his diary, helped to soften his character. Witness this passage, which is not unique: "Little Pat came up from the bedroom and licked my feet,—my dear little soul, he is almost human. I sometimes think he is a comforter dear mother has sent to me, he is filled with her spirit of patience, and tenderness & love."[42] King believed fervently that the original Pat contained elements of his mother's spirit. Whether enjoying solitary reading, engaging in the rituals of his religious faith, or playing with Pat, King spent much of his free time without contact with others.

That is, except for the spiritual communiqués, which involved his close friends, the Pattesons, and his departed loved ones and heroes. Perhaps it was because he was lonely that spiritualism held such an important role in his life.

AFTER HIS ELECTORAL DOMESTIC VICTORY, King turned his attention to the upcoming September 1926 Imperial Conference. Sir Robert Borden had urged an internationalist approach to foreign policy in the 1926 Rhodes Memorial Lecture, saying that "each nation stands at the threshold of every other, that all frontiers touch one another throughout the world, that there can be no hermit nation and no hermit continent."[43] King's view was much closer to that of his friend and advisor, Senator Raoul Dandurand, who claimed in 1924 that Canada "lived in a fireproof house, far from flammable materials."[44] Canada's hermit would take that message to London.

The London representatives made one last effort at the conference to establish the principle of the Empire speaking with a single voice. The dominions, especially South Africa and Northern Ireland, were having none of it. In this dissenting group, the noncommittal King was seen as a moderate, bringing balance and a spirit of compromise to the discussion. It was a position that he dearly loved—that of the helpful fixer who committed to nothing. One senior British civil servant described King as the "umpire of the Conference," although he was, of course, an umpire with an agenda.[45] He believed Canada's association with the British Empire was a positive one, and that the Empire was an "agency of peace for goodwill throughout the world," but at the same time he was terrified of being drawn into colonial wars.[46] He sought to loosen the shackles from London, without actually pushing for any wording that implied "independence."[47] In the end, the conference built upon the sentiment of Borden's Resolution IX from 1917 and came to an agreement that the dominions were "autonomous Communities within the British Empire, equal in status."[48] It would take another five years for the parties to hammer out the details, but the 1931 Statute of Westminster would eventually codify the terms of the resolution, giving the former colonies full control over their own foreign policy. Change was slow, but King was comfortable with that—it allowed him to study the landscape and ensure there was nothing lurking in the underbrush to politically blindside him.

King missed the signs that the decade-long period of prosperity was coming to an end. Almost everyone else did too. Speculators in land and stocks watched with dismay and then horror as the bottom fell out of the stock market at the end of October 1929. Panic sell-offs drove Wall Street into a death spiral, and all the other major money markets sank with it. Strong companies were decimated; weak ones disintegrated and hundreds of thousands of jobs disappeared. Everywhere workers were let go, wages were frozen, and then reduced.

The Liberals were unsure of the ramifications of the economic crash, but they knew their political mandate was running out at a desperate time. King weighed the party's steady success throughout the 1920s, plus the possibility that the economic fallout might get worse. When he was nudged along by one of his trusted fortune tellers, who predicted electoral triumph, he decided to call an election for July 28, 1930.[49]

King ran a good campaign, but unemployment was biting deep, and already Canadians sensed that they were living through something uniquely bad. The Conservative leader, the pompous if energetic R.B. Bennett, was also an unexpectedly forceful opponent. A dominating orator, he used his immense wealth to propel himself across the country, giving one barn-burner of a speech after another.[50] Bennett hammered away at the Liberals for having done almost nothing for the economy, while promising financial relief for Canadians. In a memorable and oft-repeated phrase, Bennett undertook to "blast" Canada's way into world markets.[51] His words captured the imagination of many Canadians, though Bennett offered little concrete evidence of how his incendiary plan would be realized, especially as country after country was erecting high tariff walls. In the end, King had to defend his inactivity while Bennett offered pie-in-the-sky plans.

The Conservatives won the election, taking 137 of the 245 seats. King was dismayed to find himself in opposition, having lost to the one-man party of Bennett, whom he despised, describing him later as "a dog of a man" and "a horrible creature."[52] But King was leaving Bennett to deal with a shattered economy and the growing anger, unrest, and hopelessness that would characterize the Great Depression. After almost nine years in power, King had served almost as long as Borden, although his accomplishments had paled in comparison. But he considered that his destiny in guiding Canada was far from over. He would be back.

CHAPTER 11

NO COMMITMENTS, 1930–1939

In the depth of the Depression, about a third of the Canadian workforce was unemployed, and almost everyone else suffered in one way or another. Farmers were evicted from their land or, with crashing wheat prices, simply abandoned their blighted fields. Young men rode the rails looking for jobs, driven out of one urban centre after another. There was almost no state relief, and even the charities became mean-spirited out of desperation, as they sought to drop the undeserving from their long lines or forced others to justify their wretchedness. The grinding poverty forever scarred those who lived through the period. It was not a good time to be prime minister of Canada.

R.B. Bennett was almost totally ineffectual in leading the nation during the first half of the Dirty Thirties. While his government spent unprecedented millions on relief, it was sopped up in the poverty sponge, with little effect. At an imperial economic conference in 1932, Bennett tried to batter the British into lowering tariffs in the hope of stimulating trade. A miffed British delegation dropped a few tariffs, but Bennett's promised blasting operation turned out to be little more than a pathetic scratching at closed doors.

Bennett's term lurched towards a miserable demise. But with the need for an election looming in 1935, he underwent a deathbed conversion. Bennett—sickly, drained, and deserted by his cabinet—gave a series of radio addresses in which he said that capitalism was broken and only a massive government injection of funds into the economy could create jobs and restore faith. It was a step in the right direction, but too little, too late. Much of what he proposed was unconstitutional, as well, since the responsibility for social welfare rested with the provinces, which were both jealous of their domains and almost bankrupt. Bennett offered to reform society, while the Liberals offered little more than a memorable slogan: "King or chaos." Canadians had lived through chaos; in October 1935, they chose King.

The national political landscape was crowded with new parties. During the Depression, intellectuals, leftists, farmers, workers, and radicals had come together under a loose conglomeration known as the Co-operative Commonwealth Federation (CCF), which called for a new social order based on economic equality and workers' rights. Their leader, J.S. Woodsworth, was a minister, a champion of social justice, and a pacifist. King watched the CCF warily, as he had the now-defunct Progressives, but he made few concessions to their program. He was content to govern with his majority of 178 MPs. In the West, desperate Albertans turned to the Social Credit Party, which offered hope by pledging cash injections to all. However, the Social Creditists had no plausible budget to deliver their funds and King was horrified by their promises, which he believed reeked of socialism. King blocked or obstructed the Alberta policy whenever he could.

Despite the lean times, or because of them, King saw himself again as a force for prudent money management. Order rather than chaos, a doctor rather than a dictator: it sounded right, but Canadians needed more than rhetoric to get back on their feet. The dream of a nation on the rise, stepping boldly towards its destiny, had suffered grievous blows in the last five years, and King offered few solutions other than to ride out the storm.

THE WORLD, TOO, had become a more dangerous place. Japan had armed itself, was bullying neighbours, and had subjugated Manchuria in 1931. It would fight a series of bitter campaigns in China—a conflict that became a full-fledged war in 1937, in which hundreds of thousands of Chinese civilians were massacred. Germany had pulled itself out of staggering financial destitution brought on by the Great War's debts and rampant inflation. Adolf Hitler, an angry and charismatic war veteran, clawed his way into power by preying on the German people's fears, fabricating hidden enemies, and solidifying his position through brute force, a process completed in 1933 when he became chancellor, and later dictator. Almost immediately he rearmed the country. He postured aggressively and murdered dissenters. Europe trembled.

Benito Mussolini led Italy down a similar path. Il Duce, "the Leader," restored pride in Italians who felt they had been cheated of land and spoils during the Treaty of Versailles negotiations. Like most dictators before and after him, he had visions of expanding his empire—or in Italy's case, reclaiming the nation's role as a world power. In need of a weak opponent, Mussolini was gathering his military forces for an invasion of Abyssinia (Ethiopia) in 1935.

The League of Nations—created in the aftermath of the Great War to usher in peace and punish aggressors—had failed to prevent the Japanese military incursions into China and had been impotent in curtailing Germany's rearmament. Could Mussolini now be stopped? Who would stand against him? Over the preceding decade and a half, Canada had made little impact at League meetings. King or his representatives could be counted on only to give moralizing speeches about how the Dominion and the United States had found ways to embrace peace, while Europe was still wedded to war. Now, in the middle of a new crisis, few anticipated anything different: the British Foreign Office noted that "Canada can be expected to be the least active of all the Dominions."[1]

But the representative of the Bennett government at the League of Nations, Howard Ferguson, a former Conservative Ontario premier, surprised naysayers by urging a strong stand against the Italians at several meetings in September 1935—a month before King's return to power. Ferguson and others knew that brinksmanship diplomacy might lead to war with Mussolini, but if Western Europe and the Commonwealth implemented economic sanctions, the dictator would surely be forced to temper his violent stance. Even after King won the election, Canada's advisory officer in Geneva, W.A. Riddell, a doctor of theology in the United Church of Canada and an experienced delegate to the League, argued for forceful sanctions.

The position taken by both Ferguson and Riddell represented a departure for Canada. Oscar Skelton, undersecretary of state for external affairs and close advisor to King, cautioned against sanctions because they might drag the nation into war. Skelton had advised King periodically since 1911, and then closely at the

1923 Imperial Conference, and was finally enticed away from Queen's University in 1925 to serve as senior mandarin at the Department of External Affairs. The owlish-looking Skelton, with his glasses and thinning hair, was somewhat distant and retiring in manner, but brilliant in his commentary, pursuing matters, in Lester Pearson's words, with "quiet determination."[2] And while Skelton took pride in British traditions, he was a firm believer that Canada should control its own destiny. He worried constantly about British designs to lump Canada and the other dominions together in pursuit of a single imperial foreign policy.[3] Skelton was mistrustful of the imperially minded politicians, and all they stood for, and throughout the 1920s and much of the next decade his caution was echoed by King's own sense of Canada's place in the world.[4]

In Geneva, Riddell ignored Skelton's missives that urged inaction and pushed forward with sanctions, including a ban on shipments of oil, which would hurt Italy's economy and war machine. Notwithstanding Canada's long-standing reluctance to lead on any issue, Riddell persuaded other delegates to act decisively. A package of sanctions became known as the "Canadian proposal," and was widely publicized in early November. It was a diplomatic coup for Canada—the nation's greatest up to that point in its rather stunted international history—but it was in direct conflict with Skelton's messages and government policy.

Ernest Lapointe was especially twitchy at the possible ramifications of Canadian-led sanctions, and he knew that Quebec was hostile on religious grounds towards any embargo that might draw Canada into a war against Catholic Italy.[5] Most Canadians objected to Mussolini's warlike behaviour, but would likely have sided with Lapointe when he asserted during the election campaign that "Abyssinia was not worth the life of a single Canadian."[6] Could Canada's pathetic military even raise an expeditionary force? Would anyone but the wretchedly unemployed fight? The embarrassing answers to these questions were left unspoken as Lapointe made his case to King that Canada should not be leading the sanctions charge. King agreed, although several of his ministers were furious at the thought of Canada retreating from its bold stance in supporting Britain, which had also demanded action against the Italian dictator.

Lapointe announced in early December 1935 that the "Canadian proposal" was Riddell's personal opinion and did not represent the government's view.[7] Delighted Italian newspapers thumbed their nose at the League of Nations. British and European opinion-makers skewered Canada for its cowardice, but the government's cringing about-face was soon forgotten when secret talks between France and England revealed that they too would not go to war against a Great Power to save an African nation.

The Abyssinian affair was far from Canada's finest moment. But King was confident that the humiliation would soon be forgotten. "It is what we prevent, rather than what we do that counts most in Government," he told his diary.[8] It was as close to a political creed as King ever uttered and, in this case, Canadians seemed to support it. King reiterated the theme when he stood in the House of Commons and asked if the "honourable members think it is Canada's role at Geneva to attempt to regulate a European War."[9] The answer was as obvious as it was callous. Secure in their fireproof house, few Canadians were willing to shed blood for Abyssinia, and that country fell to the Italian tanks, guns, and chemical weapons.

Encouraged by Mussolini's unpunished aggression, Hitler reoccupied the Rhineland in March 1936, eliminating a buffer zone between Germany and France that had been established by the Treaty of Versailles. The French and British howled, but once again, few were prepared to go to war. King remarked in the House, with uncharacteristic forthrightness, "In a word, the attitude of the government is to do nothing."[10] Emboldened by the Allies' weakness and timidity, Hitler continued to rearm and to spout his war rhetoric, while liquidating political opponents, Jews, and deemed undesirables. In Spain, communist Republican forces and fascist Nationalists, backed by German and Italian forces, fought in a civil war from 1936 onward, in which millions of innocent civilians were caught in the path of the pitiless armies and city-bombing air forces. Canada was both anti-communist and anti-fascist, and so it passed legislation forbidding Canadians to fight in the war.[11] Several thousand communist and left-leaning Canadians left the country to enlist in international forces and fight on behalf of the Republicans, but King would not be drawn into another nation's civil war, or any other conflict for that matter.

WHILE SHUNNING THE MAD Europeans who stumbled from one war to the next, King set about cementing positive relations with the United States. One of King's first acts of business after his re-election was to go south to visit President Franklin Roosevelt. Before he left, he talked to the American minister in Ottawa, Norman Armour, reportedly saying that with Canada at the crossroads between Britain and the United States, he "wanted to choose 'the American road if [they] made it possible for him.'"[12]

King was adept at telling others what they wanted to hear, and this was one of those cases. He sought a beneficial trade agreement, but he would not give up the connection with the British Empire. He did not have to. Roosevelt expended the political capital to do the deal. Trade barriers and tariffs were dropped on a number of agricultural and manufactured goods, and while it was not a treaty—which the American Senate would have had to ratify—King called it one, and basked in the satisfying result of his diplomacy. King had been urged on by the influential Skelton, who thought that freer trade had the potential to shape a "North American mind" among Canadians, and to reduce the Empire's impact on the Dominion.[13] The Americans, too, believed that trade deals like this might pry Canada out of Britain's clutches. In 1938, a more extensive trade agreement further solidified the relationship between the two nations.[14]

Roosevelt and King were wildly different characters. The American president was a dashing, relentlessly cheerful, and charming former governor and secretary of the navy. The Canadian prime minister was virtually his opposite. But the two men got along. Roosevelt treated King with respect, even if he uttered the occasional snide remark behind his back, and the perennially insecure King was positively humbled to be in the president's presence.[15] Theirs would be a friendship that spanned the war years, and it was extremely beneficial to Canada.

Roosevelt had always liked the northern Dominion. He had vacationed for many years at a summer home on Campobello Island in New Brunswick, and he felt an obligation to the country that had always greeted him as a hero. On August 18, 1938, when he was in Kingston receiving an honorary doctorate from Queen's University, Roosevelt took the opportunity to remind

Canadians, Americans, and the world that the two countries stood together in mutual respect, and that he would not accept a threat to that relationship, even in times of war. "The Dominion of Canada is part of the sisterhood of the British Empire. I give to you assurance that the people of the United States will not stand idly by if domination of Canadian soil is threatened by any other empire."[16] Here was a pledge of American protection. Most commentators, newspapers, and Canadians in general were thrilled by the gesture, as it acknowledged that Canada was both part of the British Commonwealth and an integral part of North America. However, a vulnerable Canada, helpless in its own defence, would have less influence with the giant to the south, and even the least hawkish senior mandarins and members of cabinet soon realized that Canada needed the capacity to defend itself lest the Americans in times of war simply move north, organize a forward defence on Canadian soil, and swallow the nation in the name of mutual security.[17]

BRITAIN'S LEADERS WERE WORRIED about the prospect of another war with Germany, and called the dominions to prepare for the onslaught. King set off for the May 1937 Imperial Conference aware of their anxiety. It was one hundred years since his grandfather had led an uprising against the Tory government forces, and he found it supremely ironic that now he—with "rebel blood coursing through" his veins—might be called upon to save the Empire he loved.[18]

He revelled in the pageantry of King George VI's coronation but remained cautious at the conference that followed. The British high commissioner in Ottawa warned his counterparts in

London that "the ministerial and official Canadian instinct ... is ... to play for time and to find reason for *not* co-operating."[19] With his old fears rising to the surface, King hastily retreated from any suggested proposal for an Empire-wide plan of defence. As the delegates tried to hammer out a mutual understanding, King quibbled over every phrase, sentence, and paragraph, insisting on rewrites to water down meaning and to provide escape clauses at every juncture. He all but refused to offer an expeditionary force and would not even commit to munitions production, one of Canada's critical contributions during the Great War. "No commitment" was King's implicit or explicit response on nearly every issue, and his was the decisive voice at the conference.[20] "I gave them no quarter," wrote King, a little too smugly, considering that the British and the dominions left the conference having made almost no preparations for the looming war.[21]

King's nimble sidestepping of military commitment drew him naturally to backing British prime minister Neville Chamberlain's policy of appeasement towards Nazi Germany. War had to be avoided at nearly any cost. Another generation should not be marched into the trenches and the horror that they represented. Another generation should not have to face a crippling conscription battle. In the midst of these discussions, with tension rising on every side, King, surprisingly, received an invitation to meet with Adolf Hitler. Skelton was skeptical about a visit that could anger Canadians in its acknowledgment of an aggressive dictator whose ambitions clearly extended to surrounding territories, which he was willing to take by force. Nonetheless, the prime minister, who was pleased to see himself as a conciliator and peacemaker, decided that he might be able to head off the coming disaster with a timely exchange of words.

And so occurred one of the strangest diplomatic missions in Canadian history.

Both King and Hitler came from poor backgrounds; were bachelors, successful authors, and self-made success stories; spoke openly of their love for their mothers; and shared a belief in mysterious forces. Many of the prime minister's acquaintances were aware that one of his flaws was blindness to flattery, and worried that King would be seduced by the German dictator's powerful charisma. After two days during which he toured youth and labour camps, and visited the Berlin Zoo and the Olympic Stadium, King met Hitler on June 29, 1937. What was scheduled to be a short interview was extended to nearly ninety minutes. King inwardly swooned when Hitler promised that Germany had "no desire for war."[22] Like many before him, he was drawn to Hitler's magnetic personality, and he would later write that the Nazi was "a man of deep sincerity and a genuine patriot." He had a "very nice, sweet smile," and his eyes had a "liquid quality ... which indicates keen perception and profound sympathy."[23] King's schoolgirlish description still has the power to make one squirm. Little came of the meeting, however, although King later said to Chamberlain—who, like Hitler, did not think much of King—that if Germany attacked Britain, "Canadians would swim the Atlantic" to defend her.[24]

In March 1938, Hitler annexed Austria, despite a series of concessions made by the West. The democracies rearmed aggressively throughout the summer, but politicians and generals were aware that their nations had neither the strength nor the will to stop the German dictator. With Britain unprepared for battle, and the dominions noncommittal in offering military support, Chamberlain felt compelled to negotiate with Hitler on behalf of the Western world. The Munich Agreement of September 1938 was a distasteful affair born of desperation and weakness. The Western allies handed Hitler a large portion of Czechoslovakia—the Sudetenland, a border region where many German-speakers lived—in the hope that the dictator would be satisfied. The appeasers rationalized that the sacrifice of the few was worth the safety of the many, and France and Russia skulked from their treaty obligations with Czechoslovakia. "Peace for our time," claimed Chamberlain.[25] The British people breathed a collective a sigh of relief. So did King, who published a message saying that "The heart of Canada is rejoicing tonight at the success which has crowned your unremitting efforts for peace."[26] The Czechs were abandoned to a cruel fate.

ONE OFFICIAL BRITISH REPORT described King as "the world's champion fence sitter," but the Canadian prime minister had endorsed Chamberlain's peace plan.[27] At the same time, King realized that Hitler might not stop with Czechoslovakia. He cringed at the thought of another total war, but he would not abandon Britain in a time of crisis. King embraced conciliation, negotiation, and appeasement, and he found shows of force distasteful and dangerous, but he was finally willing to commit himself. In his diary, King wrote revealingly in September 1938 that "it was a self-evident national duty, if Britain entered the war, that Canada should regard herself as part of the British empire."[28] After years of dodging and equivocating, King finally let the curtain drop: if Britain went to war, Canada would march in step.

After Munich, King wanted to commit Canada to supporting a robust British response if Hitler broke his promises again, but he found the cabinet much more cautious, with many of the isolationists and neutralists content with further inaction. Skelton urged King to avoid making any such commitment without debate or discussion.[29] King asked Lapointe for his opinion in a letter written on September 23, 1938. Lapointe, whose opinion mattered more than any other, reacted with visceral anger to the proposed announcement, sending a sharp retort to King insisting that the government stick to the message of "Parliament will decide." King backed down, even though he believed that providing a solid front against Hitler was "one of the great moral issues of the world, and that one cannot afford to be neutral on an issue of this kind."[30]

While Hitler did not likely care what Canada did—especially since King spoke softly and carried a twig—he might have taken note if Britain had been backed strongly by the dominions. That did not occur, largely because of King's refusal to commit to a unified defence, although South Africa and Ireland also refused London's requests. And so Hitler, who was disappointed at being cheated of his desire for war, went back into his lair, prize in hand, knowing that he had humiliated Western Europe and could probably do it again. But Chamberlain was not as naive as he has often been portrayed, for he now had written guarantees that Hitler was done with his aggressive march to enlarge the Fatherland. If the dictator broke the agreement, as many suspected he would, the Western world would be easier to rally in the defence of the small nations who were cast in the role of future victims.

THE EUROPEAN STATES were preparing for war. Not to do so was folly. Hitler's record as chancellor was pitted with broken promises and outright lies. Yet, for all King's talk and earnest diary musings, there was little evidence of urgency on the part of the Canadian government to rearm. Canada's army lacked trucks and tanks; the navy was unable to defend its two coasts; and the air force flew shockingly obsolete warplanes.[31] Canada was nearly defenceless and the chiefs of staff were all but muted in pleading their case to King, since Skelton acted as a buffer to silence them.[32] However, Skelton did not have to obstruct too vigorously, for King had an instinctive loathing of military men. Worse, in his mind, rearmament would lead inevitably to war, or critics would argue that this was the case and the move would be used against him. In spite of his resolve that Canada could not avoid another war that involved Britain, he was afraid to engage Canadians in a conversation about the coming crisis for fear of what it might stir up across the Dominion.

This frustrated the British to no end. King was seen as shirking his duty, but he was supported by his two most influential ministers, Ernest Lapointe and Minister of Finance Charles Dunning, who were steadfast in arguing against a further increase in defence spending.[33] Quite apart from the predictable objections from Quebec, how would the cabinet explain the transfer of essential funds to the manufacture of weapons of war when the nation was still suffering from the Depression? King refused to chance such criticism. Even though he had a solid majority in the House, King acted as if he had a minority. In the process, he showed little leadership and no passion in convincing anyone that the nation was vulnerable.

The defence budget crept up from a pittance in 1935, but King capped it at $35 million in the critical years between 1937 and 1939. This was less, for example, than the government paid out in pensions and medical care for Great War veterans, and was a far cry from what was required to rearm Canada for a worldwide war.[34] King was aware of the shortfall, and in November 1938 he confided to his diary that in spite of new funding, "our defence was wholly inadequate and ineffective."[35] His government put money into building modern destroyers and upgrading coastal fortifications, which he could present as protecting the nation's borders, at the same time placating the anxious Americans, who worried about Canadian defence capabilities. But King did not believe he could make other armament upgrades, especially to the army, and he frankly did not want to.[36] As a consequence, Canada was criminally unprepared for war, a war that King had agreed was nearly unavoidable by late 1938.[37] Appeasement had bought time, but King and his timid cabinet had wasted it, all the while huddling from the cold reality that was blowing out of Europe.

FOR YEARS, KING SHELTERED BEHIND a policy of no commitment, placating Canadians and confusing Whitehall. Malcolm MacDonald, secretary of state for dominion affairs and later an influential high commissioner to Canada, wrote that King was "over-sensitive, over-cautious, over-suspicious" in his relations with London, especially in matters of defence and diplomacy.[38] King refused to allow Canadian troops to engage in joint planning exercises with their British counterparts, even when his military advisors pleaded that it was essential. While Canada controlled its own destiny, the British were left wondering, especially after the 1937 Imperial Conference, if a King government would come to the aid of Britain in war. King's string of public refusals to commit to any unified defence left Maurice Hankey, the secretary to the

British cabinet, observing matter-of-factly, "It would be disastrous if we laid our plans on the assumption that we could count upon Canada, and then when the day came we found that we had been building on false premises."[39] The irony, of course, was that King personally believed that Britain had to be supported. Publicly, he found it impossible to say so.

King's obfuscating ways changed in early 1939, when he again wanted to offer public support for Britain, prepare his party for increased military expenditures, and alert Canadians to the growing European crisis. He was now ready to act. In a speech to Parliament on January 16, 1939, King echoed the words of Laurier a generation earlier: "If England is at war we are at war and liable to attack. I do not say that we will always be attacked; neither do I say that we would take part in all wars of England. That is a matter that must be guided by circumstances, upon which the Canadian parliament will have to pronounce and will have to decide in its own best judgment."[40] Here was King's policy, and for once it was not wrapped up in a cocoon of dithering and contradictory statements. Yet this was also a shock to many Canadians, and King had to fend off attacks from both the pro-war and antiwar segments of society, as well as Quebec nationalistes who accused the prime minister of reducing Canada to its pre-Westminster colonial status.[41] He had not done so, as he made clear when he said that Parliament would decide, but he was again reminded that defence issues provoked controversy in Canada, even when war was on the horizon.

On March 20, after Hitler had broken more promises and swallowed what was left of Czechoslovakia (save for that portioned off to Poland), seizing key territory, armaments, and heavy industry, an angry King told the House of Commons that

Canada would come to Britain's aid if "bombers [were] raining death on London" or if its citizens faced a cross-channel invasion.[42] King was firming up support, and he and Lapointe spoke to Parliament—and all Canadians—at the end of the month, on the 30th and 31st, telling the nation that war was coming and that Canada would not let Britain face Hitler's armies alone. The once-cautious Lapointe realized that Germany would not stop until it dragged Europe into war, and King believed he must now act, notwithstanding the reluctance of some in the cabinet, although both promised that conscription would never be invoked.

While another war was "sheer madness," said King, a world dominated by Germany was unthinkable.[43] At the back of King's mind was the knowledge that if Britain was overrun, and Canada somehow survived, it would almost certainly fall into the American sphere of influence and might even be annexed.[44] With King and Lapointe singing from the same hymn book, while still placating their English and French constituents, the country was moving towards war, fairly united, and likely to be protected by the United States should it be invaded. At the same time, King's refusal to make the case and spend the political capital for rearmament had left Canada vulnerable as it marched to war against Germany, then the most powerful military nation in the world.

CHAPTER 12

TO WAR, 1939

War came with much warning in September 1939. For at least three years prior, Hitler's feral violence and relentless treachery humbled and humiliated the other world leaders. They sought to reason with him, and then bribe him. He lied to them and when they called him out, he ignored them. As Hitler's sociopathic one-mindedness in moving towards war became apparent, the Western allies despaired but realized that he could not be stopped without force, especially after Germany signed a non-aggression pact with Russia on August 23, clearing the way for war.

Canadians faced a grim reality when Germany invaded Poland on September 1, 1939. Fearful, disorganized, and unready, Britain nonetheless declared war on September 3, after having guaranteed Poland's safety less than a year earlier in a desperate bid to stand up to Hitler. How would Canada respond?

The country had changed since the "war to end all wars." It had grown up. In 1939, about 3.5 out of the 11.5 million Canadians called themselves French, but Canada remained a British nation, one with a rich inheritance reflected in its history, political traditions, and culture.[1] A popular royal visit from King George VI and Queen Elizabeth in the months before the war had strengthened the royal bond. Millions of Canadians believed that as soon as Britain declared war, Canada should automatically join the colours. Others portrayed this as Canada's war: they saw the Dominion as a proud nation in the British Empire, one that needed to act for itself on the world stage. Of course, there were also those who wanted no part of the coming bloodbath.

King told the cabinet again on September 1 that "if Britain was at war then Canada would be at war." In his mind, "this was what the people of Canada expected."[2] However, Canada—and King's cabinet specifically—would decide the extent of the nation's commitment. None of this was a surprise, even with King's tendency, as poet Frank Scott later sniped, to do nothing by halves that could not be done by quarters. King had, in fact, remained surprisingly consistent in his statements about defending Britain in the face of a significant threat. This was the spirit of the speech he had given at the Imperial Conference in 1923 that had affirmed the Dominion's support of Britain in a major war, and of several pronouncements since then. Yet with the deep scars of conscription and the widespread unpreparedness of the military, and with key cabinet ministers and advisors shivering against commitment, King prepared the nation cautiously. He was comfortable with caution.

"Parliament will decide," had been King's position—and his shield, even though he believed that neutrality was not an option. At a press conference on September 1, a tired King, his voice "grave, low, firm," according to one journalist, read out a statement indicating that Parliament would be recalled for a special war session on September 7, a date King secretly liked because he believed it was lucky.[3] But in the meantime, King told the reporters that Canada would defend its borders against aggressors, with the armed forces—the militia, naval service, and air force—put on alert.

King could be proud of how he had acted in these dark days. He was following the advice of Skelton and Lapointe, but he also knew in his own mind what was required. He spoke forcefully in cabinet and kept skittish ministers from bolting, which was no easy task, as the strong Quebec wing—and Quebec newspapers—associated any war with the likelihood of conscription, notwithstanding King and Lapointe's pledges to the contrary.[4] He was pleased with himself and privately surprised at "how timid some members of Council [cabinet] were to declare that we were prepared to fight for freedom."[5] That evening, as King was driven to Kingsmere, his rustic retreat in the Gatineau hills, he stared into the sky and watched as the sun was setting. As he pondered the future, he saw in the clouds "very distinctly a knight like a king (not a crown but the kind of head gear worn by the King at the time of coronation ...)—it seemed to me a sign dear Mother or others were sending me, of something having been well done today and a promise for the future—some approval toward the good for which I have been striving."[6] King was an odd bird, needing odd encouragement, but he had united the Liberal Party and positioned the nation for war. And it was he who was responsible for these developments, even if he wished to acknowledge the assistance of others, real or imagined.

KING STILL HOPED THAT WAR would be avoided, and he continued to believe, bizarrely, that Hitler was a misunderstood man of peace, who had been provoked to war by the Poles. Seeking guidance from beyond, on the night of September 2 the prime minister engaged in one of his table-rapping exercises.[7] A nameless spirit told him that Hitler had been shot dead. He was amazed and relieved, but he looked for confirmation. His mother's spirit soon came to her son's aid, adamantly assuring him that war would now be averted. King rejoiced. Only the next day did he find out that he had been deceived by his guides.[8] A worried King, who had been swept away emotionally by the incident, was concerned that even the spirit world was destabilizing. Later, he blamed a malignant force for leading him astray. It is perhaps instructive that around this time, King's closest advisor, O.D. Skelton, told a senior military officer that King "did not think that we were about to find ourselves at war… 'He plays his hunches.'"[9] And perhaps, at times, they played him.

King knew that the majority of Canadians would not allow Britain to go it alone, and he had said as much in a radio address on September 3. However, the French-Canadian nationaliste press demonized the government and singled out Lapointe as a traitor to his people. Within a few days, antiwar crowds in Quebec milled angrily in the streets and, at one point, shouted for the death of King and Lapointe.[10] In English Canada, Tory newspapers, especially in Toronto, condemned King for his unwillingness to go on record and support Britain to the hilt, which, they claimed, left the country humiliated and rudderless.[11] Damned if he did, damned if he didn't, King waited.

King and Lapointe were given a more friendly reception from fellow MPs on the 7th. Robert Manion, a Great War veteran, family physician, and Bennett's replacement as leader of the Conservatives, urged the country to mount a strong war effort.

The Social Credit Party concurred. The CCF went through a series of painful internal debates, its leader, pacifist J.S. Woodsworth, pleading in his caucus for peace, but he found himself standing almost alone. He resigned as leader and was replaced by the much-respected M.J. Coldwell. In the end, King knew that dissension would not come from outside his party, but from within its ranks, and chiefly from his Quebec MPs. Lapointe, citing King's strong statements against conscription, deployed his considerable charisma to calm his comrades. In private talks and addresses to the French-Canadian caucus, he pleaded that if Quebec MPs voted against supporting Britain in a war, the party would be destroyed in English Canada, and would likely give way to a Conservative or Union government. Most of the dissident MPs were mollified, but all eyes in the House fell on King to reassure his party and inspire the nation.

King's speech to the House on the second day of the special war session was dreadful. He remained a nervous talker, even after having given thousands of political speeches. He agonized over his text and hated to stray from his carefully prepared notes. He droned on in a wearying monotone that occasionally was pitched high or was broken by an audible wheeze. When King did wander from what he had written, he was often very good, but he was never a comfortable performer. On this occasion, in what he described as "the most important speech of my life," he read the prepared text, his round face pale and almost expressionless, his hand fidgeting with the black ribbon of his glasses.[12] The talk was drab, uninspiring, even painful, and a bizarre misreading of what was needed. The opposition looked on with ill-concealed dismay and his own members cringed despairingly, before everyone lost interest. By the fourth hour, MPs on both sides of the House were either chatting openly among themselves or sitting stupefied as this seemingly weak man mumbled his way through his scripted text, trying to reassure the nation that he would lead the country through the coming crisis.

The government's honour was saved by Lapointe. On the third day of the session, the big bear of a man rose from behind the desk he shared with King and spoke with passion and force, using English so that his message was not lost on the majority of the members. Throughout his speech he turned his back to the opposition, facing his own party, focusing on the Quebec wing. His face was contorted by the effort, his hands clenched and unclenched, and spittle and sweat flew from his heaving body. "I hate war with all my heart and conscience, but devotion to peace does not mean ignorance or blindness." Neutrality was impossible, he said, because it would aid the enemy and weaken the Empire. But with this rallying cry also came a promise, directed at both English and French members across the House: "If Canadians go to the front line of battle, they will go voluntarily, as Canadians under the control of Canada, commanded by Canadians, and maintained by the Dominion of Canada."[13] He would never stand for conscription. He sat down to thunderous applause. King was weepy over Lapointe's moving words.

On September 10, parliamentarians voted on whether the country would commit itself to Britain's side in war. It was a week after Britain had declared war on Germany. Although it was not a recorded vote, the MPs were nearly unanimous, with only a handful of dissenting Quebec MPs and a few lone voices pleading for peace or isolation. "We are a nation in the fullest sense," intoned King, "a member of the British Commonwealth of Nations, sharing like freedom with Britain herself, a freedom which we believe we must all combine to save."[14] While Canadians would never have taken up arms if Britain had not stood its ground against the Nazis, now the self-governing nation of Canada was at war: in defence of Britain, in defence of liberal ideals, and in defence of its own sovereignty.

ON SEPTEMBER 3, the cabinet had put in force the War Measures Act and the supporting Defence of Canada Regulations (DOCR), which broadened the government's ability to fully prosecute the war. The DOCR allowed for censorship, surveillance, and detention of potential enemy aliens; prohibited statements that hindered recruitment; and, perhaps most disturbingly, gave the minister of justice the right to detain without charge anyone who might act "in any manner prejudicial to the public safety or the safety of the state." King was uncomfortable with the sweeping powers, but he did not like to go against Lapointe, who, as attorney general, enforced the legislation.[15] Communist and fascist organizations were to be targeted, which was fine with most of the ministers, and few objected to locking up Canadians who sided openly with the enemy. Those who were innocent had few supporters. Such tough action also helped the King government look serious about prosecuting the war, especially to its critics, who were already arguing for a coalition government that included more seemingly hard-minded Conservatives.[16]

King would never allow Conservatives in his government, but he also knew that he had to strengthen the critical portfolios of defence and finance. The finance minister, Charles Dunning, who had once been touted as King's replacement, by coup if necessary, was broken in health, and had retired before the war. The current minister of national defence, Ian Mackenzie, was a well-liked bon vivant who had an affinity for fast cars and strong drink. But he was no warlord, and he had been plagued by scandals. Even in early September, King's ministers were saying openly to journalists that Mackenzie had to go.[17] Like Borden, King needed key lieutenants to help shoulder the burden: a Thomas White at finance and a military-minded minister to lead the war effort, although preferably someone more stable than the maniacal Sam Hughes.

An obvious choice for either portfolio was Colonel J.L. Ralston, a decorated Great War battalion commander, a leader in the veterans' community, and defence minister from 1926 to 1930. With his box-like jaw and fierce eyes, Ralston looked like the pugilist that he was. He closed his lucrative legal practice in Montreal and rushed to Ottawa, where he became, almost immediately, with Lapointe, C.D. Howe, and later J.L. Ilsley, one of the leaders of the cabinet. Ralston chose finance over defence, and many believed, including King, that Ralston could be the next prime minister.[18] He was the type of man to prepare the nation for a war for which it was deeply unready, and especially for the "long grinding economic struggle" it would entail.[19]

Norman Rogers was King's choice as defence minister. Lanky and thin, the former Great War veteran and Rhodes Scholar had been King's private secretary in the late 1920s, and then a professor at Queen's University. He had a powerful intellect and was generally well liked, having won over the cold-fish King who had trouble extending genuine warmth to any of his colleagues, and especially to young ones.[20] Rogers proved hard-working and conscientious, but within a few months *Winnipeg Free Press* journalist Grant Dexter was reporting multiple rumours that he was working himself towards a breakdown.[21] The task of raising a military force from scratch, and this time one that included the navy, air force, and army, was nearly crippling in its complexity.

Charles "Chubby" Power, another Great War veteran, long-time Liberal MP, and cheerful party bagman, was a close second to become defence minister, but the abstainer King worried about his colleague's proclivity for binge drinking; Power periodically went off the rails and disappeared for days.[22] "Chubby had an extraordinary capacity to elicit loyal and even enthusiastic support from many who would not have tolerated some of his weaknesses in anyone else," wrote Jack Pickersgill, a senior civil servant who worked closely with King. "His irreverence and wit appealed to me, and I soon learned that they were merely the outward screen of a thoughtful and philosophical mind with the shrewd judgment of the character and capacity of others."[23] The gregarious, chain-smoking, Irish–French Canadian moved from pensions and national health to postmaster general, and he continued to exert heavy influence over the Quebec wing, especially with his promise that he would not be a part of a government that brought in conscription.

C.D. Howe, a tough-talking businessman with enormous drive and capability, was essential to the war effort—one in which the supply of munitions and war materiel was to be more crucial than the raising of vast armies, navies, and air armadas. Howe well earned his moniker as "minister of everything," and he would soon oversee all wartime production. J.L. Ilsley, who was minister of national revenue, but later the essential finance minister, was not close to King, but he was a critical member of the cabinet. T.A. Crerar and J.G. Gardiner were long-time ministers, and then there was the host of lesser lights who sat at the cabinet table, generally because of the need for regional representation. Many were past their best-before date, and King would find ways over the coming months and years to bring in new blood. But the key position in the cabinet was held by King's closest political ally, Ernest Lapointe. King relied heavily on Ernest—King always pronounced his name with the English emphasis, "Er-nast"—deferring to him on almost all matters related to Quebec, as well as on issues that affected the Liberal Party.

Within a few months, a concentration of authority rested in the Cabinet War Committee (CWC), which was headed by King and included Lapointe, Ralston, Rogers, Ilsley, Howe, and a few others. The CWC and the larger cabinet had the power to pass orders-in-council, which, for the most part, circumvented Parliament's authority. As in Borden's war, power was concentrated among the few. It should be noted that the service chiefs of staff were not standing members of the committee, and were rarely invited to attend.[24] Through this system, King and his ministers would manage the war effort, but they, in turn, were often isolated from what was occurring overseas or within the branches of the army, air force, and navy.

In the larger cabinet, the need for consensus was important to King, who did not expect cabinet to behave as an echo chamber. He knew that his ministers were not his obedient subordinates, but King was adept at managing them, with their shifting priorities, loyalties, and support of the war effort. In King's words, the most important quality in political life was the need to "endure with patience ... endure to the end."[25]

King typically arrived late to the cabinet meetings, ensuring that everyone was there and talking before him. As the prime minister passed through the red baize door to the Privy Council chamber, he took his place at his high-backed chair at the circular table. The ministers put out their cigarettes because King forbade smoking in his presence. King let Lapointe speak first, followed by the ministers in sequence around the table. King usually allowed a full discussion to develop, and he had that rare ability to suffer fools. But he had his tricks. One was to encourage ministers with whom he agreed to speak first, thereby making it harder for others to go against the grain. Cabinet Secretary Arnold Heeney wrote that King cleverly "altered the normal order to give place to matters he considered of special urgency or importance. Indeed, it was quite clearly understood by all that the Prime Minister could bring up whatever he wished, whenever he wished."[26] While King did not like confrontation, he was shrewd and canny, and he had certain "tells," often revealing his frustration by impatiently playing with the short, stubby pencils with which he liked to write. When he was ready, he simply shut down the conversation. King always had the last word in the cabinet, and he used his time to sum up events. In his fierce desire for agreement, he would often simply conclude arguments as he saw fit, telling the cabinet they were of one mind and ready to go forward unified. "He was a master of leading the cabinet towards decision," wrote Paul Martin, a minister late in the war. "Such was his prestige and authority that as soon as Mr. King began speaking one or two of my colleagues would vigorously nod their heads in agreement—no matter what they themselves had said before."[27]

BUT WARS ARE NOT RUN by ministers alone. The apparatus of government had evolved and changed since the Great War. As King wrote early in the conflict, "We were fortunate in having experienced the past war to guide us through this one, and to avoid mistakes being made."[28] In this new war, the deputy ministers of most departments were strong, able, and quick-minded, and all had taken away lessons from the Great War. O.D. Skelton at external affairs; W.C. Clark, the deputy minister of finance, as well as other dedicated "Ottawa Men" brought a new level of professionalism to running critical departments. King, too, was ably supported by advisors, who assisted with policy, legal interpretation, speech writing, and general advice. During the course of the war, Arnold Heeney, Walter Turnbull, and Jack Pickersgill all held important positions in the Prime Minister's Office.[29]

And King was a demanding master, although he could be generous and thoughtful, keeping and attending to a lengthy Christmas card list, and freely sending flowers, telegrams, and small gifts to mark births, deaths, and weddings. "He covered me with whipped cream and bullshit," remarked one aide who tired of King's constant flattery.[30] At the same time, King's odd personality left him brooding over seemingly insignificant slights. A minor quip or joke said in his presence could send him off in rants, although these usually went no further than his diary. He was easily mortified: mention of pregnancy left him squirming. Perhaps if he had had a wife with whom to talk these things over, he might not have sounded like such a martinet or emotional cripple. At the same time, King often sought praise, and gushed over trivial compliments. Journalist Tom Blacklock, a member of the press gallery in the 1920s, observed that King was "such a pompous ass that an orangutan that would flatter him could choose its own reward."[31]

King's daily routine usually involved a late start to the morning, but he often worked long into the night. To meet his needs, King's secretaries were summoned to Laurier House after dinner, to work for several hours. He rang the cabinet ministers or his staff at any time. Arnold Heeney remarked that "virtually no personal or family occasion was immune from King's interruption," and, while usually charming, he expected "immediate attention."[32] This is not an unusual trait in workaholics in positions of power, but King had the bad grace to constantly complain that he did not have enough support from his staff—and this of a group that regularly worked twelve-hour days. King's petty and choleric attitude was hard for his staff to stomach, and one remarked that working for King was "all industry and no humanity."[33] He was fussy and fastidious, selfish and self-absorbed, a natural blamer who shifted responsibility onto others and then complained of how he had been let down—all the while whining that he was unassisted, unappreciated, and standing alone against the storm. Unlike most prime ministers, who cultivate a group of admirers and champions, and ready-to-die-in-a-ditch loyalty within their inner circle, William Lyon Mackenzie King was loved by few.

KING HAD BEEN SCARRED by the terrible slaughter of the Great War. He never forgot how the withering losses had brought in conscription and nearly torn the country apart, as well as sent him and the Liberals into defeat. The young King had perceived the necessity and justness of that war, but, like his mentor Laurier, he had not been willing to sacrifice all in the name of victory. Now, as a war leader in a potentially more destructive conflict, he clung to similar ideals. Canada would supply food and munitions to the Allied war effort, but King was anxious to limit the deployment of large fighting forces, for fear that the inevitable casualties would lead to conscription. But the experienced King also knew that the expanding war effort would be difficult to control, and he offered a revealing aside in his diary: "I have no doubt Borden was sincere in believing conscription was necessary."[34] The long, drawn-out, and costly campaigns of the Great War had necessitated a change in policy. No one could be certain what would happen in this new conflict, although few were naive enough to predict a short war.

Despite all the signs pointing to another war involving Great Powers, ideologies, and cultures, King refused to be drawn into an unfettered war effort. He made it clear to his cabinet, if not the general public, that Canada's war would be one of limited commitment. The phrase "limited liability" was not coined by King, and perhaps not even uttered by him, but it has been ascribed to him and accurately describes his policy. Canada would stand by Britain in its time of need, but as an independent nation it would first safeguard its shores and become a fortress for war production.[35] This proposition was not as smarmy as some critics have suggested. King had, after all, led Canada united to Britain's side, but in the process he had declared war on the greatest military power in the world, with almost no military forces at his disposal. Unlike some of the hawks in Canada, King was perhaps wise to play down the nation's military commitment.

While King believed this had to be Canada's approach to war—supporting Canada's allies but not sending large forces overseas—he was wary of articulating these thoughts. Many Canadians would view such a limited war policy as an attempt by the King government to profit from war while letting others suffer the losses. King was soon confronted by such sentiments, and he slowly lost control over the size of the Canadian overseas military forces. But if there was to be a fighting component to the war effort, he was adamant that Canada was to exert influence over its forces through an overseas headquarters and national commanders, although he quailed at any thought of being involved in the strategic direction of the war.[36] The British resisted the idea of Canadians fighting independently, and would eventually have them under their overall command in most theatres; at the same time, London was only too happy to comply with King's desire to shed responsibility for any strategic influence, for the officials there had no interest in sharing power with the dominions. A more aggressive Canadian war leader would likely have wrung some concessions from the imperials, when there were opportunities to do so. King was too busy ducking for cover to make the effort.

As the King government determined the nature of its military commitment, the prime minister was shocked to find that the army brass had plans for an expeditionary force of 60,000. King had hoped to avoid sending even a single 20,000-strong division overseas, and to place the focus instead on the navy and the air force.[37] However, he was overtaken by events as tens of thousands of Canadians enlisted in the first month alone. A division of infantry of the Canadian Active Service Force, renamed the Canadian Army (Overseas) in November 1940, would have to be sent to Britain.

Yet there were other ways of limiting Canada's commitment. The military chiefs of staff asked for a $500-million budget; King's cabinet had rejected the demand as too expensive.[38] The forces would get half of what they had requested. Canada was still suffering through the lingering effects of the Depression, and there were almost no munitions contracts from Britain, which was attempting to jump-start its own stagnant war industry.[39] The opening months of the conflict saw Canada adopt an unheroic, penny-pinching approach to a war that was already looking grim. King tellingly observed in his diary that Britain and France might not "be saved from destruction" unless some armistice—and by this he meant surrender—was achieved with Germany.[40]

WHEN ROOSEVELT ANNOUNCED on September 1 that the United States would remain neutral, King professed to be "terribly shocked and surprised" at the shirking of duty. However, King's long-time friendship with the American president paid dividends.[41] In the days before Canada declared war, Roosevelt had taken the opportunity to offer support to his friend, "Mackenzie." (Much as he appreciated the president's using his given name, King never had the heart to tell him he preferred Rex. King, in turn, never felt comfortable calling the president "Franklin," although he managed to get this out a few times after screwing up his courage.) Whatever they called each other, King and Roosevelt used Canada's brief bout of neutrality, between September 3 and 10, as an opportunity for Canada to purchase essential war materiel, especially much-needed aircraft, before the Dominion became a belligerent and therefore unable to receive war goods from neutral America. While the Americans remained officially neutral, they continued to side with the Allies, and King would sometimes act as the hinge between the Americans and the British, especially during the first two years of the war.[42]

With the United States helping Canada rearm, the energetic, charismatic, and brilliant Andrew McNaughton was picked by

Norman Rogers and King to command the 1st Canadian Division. Tall, lean, and soldierly, McNaughton had served his country in the Great War as an innovative gunner, and had risen to chief of the general staff and then head of the National Research Council. McNaughton believed that firepower and scientific principles, when applied properly on the battlefield, would minimize Canadian casualties. King was impressed by the general, especially because he told King what he wanted to hear: that Canada's war effort could be achieved without resorting to conscription.[43] Although McNaughton was a forceful personality who wanted the nation to be represented in the coming ground war, King slept better with the assurance that his overseas commander understood the limits on Canada's engagement.

It was no easy task for the prime minister and his cabinet to put the country on a war footing. Part of the problem was King's failure to energize the nation. Cunning, sometimes conniving, in his political manoeuvres, King was hamstrung by his fear that stirring up the passions of Canadians would lead to greater exertions, ultimately forcing him to create a large fighting force. So he kept to his calculated policy of obfuscation, while privately acknowledging in late September 1939 that his prewar cautious military policy had done grave damage to Canada's ability to prosecute the war.[44]

Australian prime minister Robert Menzies, who visited Canada in 1941, was not impressed by King: he "is not a war leader, possesses no burning zeal for the cause, and is a politician who possibly prefers to lead from behind."[45] Another Canadian journalist-turned-soldier mocked him as "the furthest thing imaginable from a national wartime leader."[46] King was certainly not a traditional warlord, but he was never pressed hard by the opposition to lead from the front or rouse the nation to a patriotic fervour. The Conservatives could only nip from the sidelines, and their early calls for greater military involvement and sacrifice rang hollow as the war on the Western Front stagnated after Germany's initial success in Poland. Although the federal Tories were ineffectual, King worried about the situation in the two most populous provinces. Here, he faced skilled, forceful, and antagonistic leaders: Maurice Duplessis in Quebec and Mitchell Hepburn in Ontario.

Duplessis was a fierce opponent of King and the Liberals. The Quebec premier was a hard-drinking bachelor, who was known for living riotously, dispensing cash to buy votes or silence opponents, and running the province with an iron hand. "Le Chef" had united several political parties to create the Union Nationale, which won the 1936 election against the corrupt and disorganized Liberals, and now, in late September 1939, Duplessis called a snap election to be held in October. He hoped to stir up Quebec's fears that Ottawa, armed with the War Measures Act, would centralize power to the detriment of Quebec, and, for good measure, he accused the King government of planning, at some point, to impose conscription. Duplessis had another motive in going to the polls: he had nearly bankrupted the province and wanted a new mandate before the true financial disaster was revealed. King was horrified: he had brought the nation into the war unified; now the premier, through this "diabolical act," sought to take Quebec out of the war.[47]

When King's cabinet met on September 25, the senior Quebec ministers responded angrily to Duplessis's opportunism. A furious Lapointe and Power argued that a Duplessis victory could only be viewed as a want of confidence in their ability to represent Quebec in Ottawa. "If Duplessis wins," warned Power, "the war is over, so far as Quebec is concerned."[48] The two ministers threw down the gauntlet, and they were joined by their influential colleague, P.J.A. Cardin, the minister of public works. The Quebec ministers would work with the provincial Liberals to defeat Duplessis. This was an all-or-nothing gamble, mixed with blackmail. If Duplessis won, King's Quebec ministers announced publicly that they would resign, leaving Quebec powerless in Ottawa, and with no one, supposedly, to hold off conscription.

King was terrified. He preferred a compromise, and he knew that a mass resignation of the Quebec ministers would force his government to form a union with the Conservatives and the other opposition parties.[49] King tried repeatedly to talk his ministers out of their high-stakes gamble, but they could see no other way to impress upon Quebec that a vote for Duplessis was, in effect, a vote for conscription. When King realized that his ministers would not be swayed, he unleashed the federal party machine to help Adélard Godbout's provincial Liberals.[50]

The uncharismatic Godbout was overmatched by Duplessis. He needed the influential and pugnacious Lapointe, Power, and Cardin to bolster him, and they soon took over the fight. It was a brass-knuckle campaign. Lapointe was on point, swearing to the electorate that the Quebec ministers were "the rampart between [them] and conscription," while Power was the backroom man, dispensing cash and favours, and Cardin, an eloquent and invigorating speaker, applied steady pressure on potential supporters and those who wavered.[51] For a time, it looked as if Duplessis was unstoppable, positioning himself as Quebec's strongman instead of Godbout, whom he derogated as little more than an Ottawa stooge. But the federal pressure turned the tide. When ballots were counted on October 25, the provincial Liberals had a landslide win. King not uncharacteristically congratulated himself for the cabinet's hardline stand—even though he had argued against it—but he also praised his Quebec ministers as heroes who had saved the country from what he termed the fascist "Union Nazionale."[52]

King was also engaged in a long-simmering war with Premier Mitchell Hepburn. "Mitch" was a larger-than-life figure. Loud and boisterous, reckless and self-destructive, he drank heavily and partied deep into the night, and often with questionable characters and good-time girls. The Ontario premier looked a lot like King, with his round face and receding hair, and years of drink had left him with a corpulent body. He was a Liberal, but had fallen out with King after the 1935 federal election. Hepburn had campaigned vigorously on behalf of the federal party and had played a widely acknowledged role in delivering dozens of seats from Ontario, which he had won handily in the previous year's provincial election. In compensation for his work, the brassy Hepburn demanded that King place one of his cronies in the cabinet. King refused, instead appointing C.D. Howe and Norman Rogers from Ontario, both of whom proved to be exceptional ministers.[53] Hepburn took the rejection personally. He launched a series of lowdown snubs and high-profile attacks that led to internecine strife within the party structure at the federal and provincial levels.[54] Hepburn's aggression was brazen and embarrassing, and each time King took note, smouldered inwardly but did not respond. He knew that something would have to be done eventually, but he kept his powder dry.

WITH THE ALLIED AND AXIS ARMIES facing off against each other, Britain needed to strengthen its air force. It turned to its senior dominion as a vast training centre that was far from the threat of German aerial attacks, but close enough to transport trained flyers to the battlefront. In response to a late-September letter from British Prime Minister Neville Chamberlain, the cabinet agreed that negotiations on the proposal should begin, although both King and many of his ministers were disappointed that the request had not come earlier. They wondered if training aircrew could have been Canada's primary contribution to the war effort, a notion dovetailing nicely with the concept of limited liability.

Lord Riverdale headed the British mission to Ottawa. He was a poor choice. The disagreeable industrialist from Sheffield was either poorly briefed or simply assumed that he could dictate terms to the Canadians. From the start, it was clear that the British were desperate to preserve their limited supply of dollars for essential war purchases in the United States, and they sought to push the cost of the plan onto the Canadians, hoping the Dominion's patriotism would overshadow financial constraints. The Canadians did not take well to the bullying and were horrified at the massive financial burden, which was estimated at close to $1 billion, several times the total prewar federal budget. This was not a good start.

King and Riverdale met for the first time on October 17, and during their conversation, Riverdale made an unfortunate reference to "your scheme." King was taken aback, and then outraged, his prejudice against presumptuous British imperialists confirmed. The usually restrained King made his position clear: Canada had made no promise except to discuss the possibility of exploring a plan—which was pure King!—and it would decide on its level of commitment depending on several issues, including its cost. This, he emphasized, was far from being Canada's "scheme." King would write in his diary that night about Riverdale's "railroading style." "These people ... from the Old Country ... seem to think that all they have to do is to tell us what is to be done."[55] King sniped at the British emissary publicly, too, referring to Riverdale, as one journalist observed, "with a slight hesitation, as if he could not rightly remember" his name, while at other times calling him Lord Riverfield or Lord Riverbank.[56] These were the types of slights that King had honed over the years, in particular the disrespectful misnaming of opponents. King was backed strongly by Ralston, who told him Canada could not foot the bill without being "financially bled to death."[57] The nation was already beggaring itself over the initial war effort and had yet to see much reciprocation from the British. Negotiations limped on.

"Ambitious" was not a grand enough word to describe the program. The British envisioned dozens of training schools spread across the country, almost all of which required the construction of new airfields. At one point during the heated discussions, while fretting over the enormity of the project, King had uncharacteristically lost his temper in a meeting and blurted out that Britain must pay the majority of the training cost, because "this is not our war."[58] It was a poor choice of words: King had already committed his nation to Britain's side, but the comment deeply shocked the negotiators. "The best thing that could happen to parliament hill," one disgruntled British delegate was heard to say after one testy round of negotiations, "would be for the Germans to drop a large bomb on top of it."[59]

Lester Pearson, then a senior Canadian diplomat in London, commented, "The haggling that occasionally went on over financial matters in those early days was more fitting for a marketplace than for two countries fighting and working together in a war for survival." However, the difficulty, as Pearson noted, "was that we did not know yet that it was a question of survival."[60] Despite the ugly negotiations, by mid November the two sides had worked out an agreement by which the Canadians made much of their aid conditional on Britain's placing orders for war materiel in Canada and buying wheat.

The final sticking point, once the cost was divided up, was the demand by King, Rogers, and Ralston that newly trained Canadian airmen fly in Royal Canadian Air Force (RCAF) squadrons, and not go into the Royal Air Force (RAF), where they would be "lost." Ralston was adamant that, unless Canadians served as part of the RCAF and under their own commanders, "there would be a fear among our men that they would be sent into such places as Passchendaele as in the last war, and their lives unnecessarily sacrificed."[61] Perhaps more accurately, they did not want a repeat of the situation in the Great War, when 20,000 Canadians had fought in the British flying services and not in identifiable Canadian units. The British blinked. They agreed to the creation of RCAF squadrons, although in the course of the war, RAF senior command often ignored the deal and continued to siphon off the majority of Canadian flyers to serve in British squadrons.[62] It was the principle that mattered to King and the cabinet, and the RCAF would eventually have eighty-five squadrons—fighter, naval, transport, and bomber—flying in multiple theatres of war and in home defence. Even with this immense aerial exertion, the RCAF served under RAF command, meaning that Canada's air marshals or civilian politicians would have no influence over air strategy, much like the generals and admirals.

The terms of the British Commonwealth Air Training Plan (BCATP) were finally hammered out on December 16, 1939. The two delegations held off signing the accord until a minute after midnight on the 17th, to coincide with King's birthday, and the old boy was pleased. King had bullied his way to victory, often railing and occasionally screaming at the British delegates, leading one of the bruised British intermediaries to note King's "pitiful sort of pettiness."[63] The weeks of hard bargaining, recrimination, and wrangling left a bad taste in everyone's mouth, but they revealed that the British had to treat Canada as an ally, although perhaps not as their equal.

By war's end, Canada had agreed to pay the lion's share of the BCATP, which amounted to $1.6 billion out of $2.2 billion.[64] The first trainees arrived at flying schools in the spring of 1940, and an astonishing 131,500 airmen from across the British Commonwealth and the United States would eventually be trained, as well as 80,000 ground crew. It was not hyperbole when President Roosevelt later described Canada as the "aerodrome of democracy."

THE LIBERALS HAD SWEPT THE VOTE decisively in 1935, but another federal election was required sometime in 1940. Though King had gone through periods of unpopularity, he could claim credit for having guided the nation through the chaos of the Depression's late stages and for bringing a unified country into the war. The Conservatives rightly highlighted the military's unpreparedness—for which King was indeed responsible. But the Phony War—the phrase used to describe the months of inaction after Germany's successful war against Poland—had allowed the Dominion to avoid direct fighting, except on the oceans, where the Royal Canadian Navy was contributing to the Allied war effort. Having raised a division for overseas service and established the BCATP, King knew that his stock would never be higher.

But he needed an issue upon which to go to the electors, and he had a problem: King had promised Manion on the last day of the special war session, on September 12, that Parliament would meet again before an election was called. He was now kicking himself, because a new session would give the opposition parties an opportunity to question the Liberal government's war preparations—what had and had not been done. King was worried too that he remained an easy target for news editors, hecklers, and cartoonists, all of whom might pillory him for his uninspiring leadership. He needed to squirm out of his pledge. But as King pondered his predicament, he was given a gift by the unpredictable Mitch Hepburn, who continued to see King as a hesitant opportunist, leading a party of equivocators who were more interested in placating Quebec than in fighting a war against evil.

On January 18, 1940, Hepburn stood up in the Ontario legislature in a fit of pique and condemned the Liberal government in Ottawa. His statement included a personal accusation: "Mackenzie King has not done his duty to his country—never has and never will."[65] Even those who had followed Hepburn's long-standing vendetta against King were shocked by the attack, and many startled Liberals bolted from the legislature so as not to have to choose between the prime minister and the premier. The party whip hounded the skulkers back into the legislature and, in the end, with Hepburn staking his political career on the vote, an overwhelming majority passed the motion censuring the federal leader, with the delighted support of the provincial Conservatives.

News of the charge soon found its way to Ottawa. King called Heeney and Pickersgill to his office. Pickersgill described the scene: "Pacing up and down the library like a caged tiger, he told us that he had decided Parliament would be dissolved that day. It was the most dramatic display I ever saw of the forceful and almost violent will of that man generally considered weak and mild. Heeney and I were overawed and scarcely uttered a word."[66] While King had found his election issue, he still had the prickly problem of having promised another parliamentary session to Manion. King pondered the matter, and was still working on the Throne Speech the night before Parliament was to meet on January 25.

At the opening of Parliament, the governor general, Lord Tweedsmuir, better known as the celebrated British author John Buchan, stunned members, as he read King's words calling for an "immediate appeal to the country." It was a shock, but most of the MPs interpreted "immediate" to mean several weeks at least. Later in the day, however, King rose to address the House. After a mild preamble, his voice hardened as he informed the gathered MPs that the government had been challenged by a vote of non-confidence from Ontario, and that he could not continue to lead with this threat of disunity unanswered. Parliament would be dissolved that day.

King sat back down as the House exploded. He kept his glasses off to blur the angry faces of the opposition across from him and stared nonchalantly at the ceiling. But he could not fail to hear the howls that rose to a cacophony, lashing the government for its dishonest manoeuvre, for gagging Parliament, and for thumbing its nose at the democratic process. Liberal backbenchers were bewildered because they too had been kept in the dark. In

King's mind, however, he had kept his promise to Manion: there had been a parliamentary session, although it had lasted only as long as it took for King's procedural sucker punch to knock the opposition to the ground. Later, King lamented to his diary, in language that was over-the-top even for him, "Nothing hurts me more than when the situation becomes personal and one's own position becomes misrepresented. That, of course, is the hardest cross to be borne in public life. It was the cross of all others, that Christ himself had to bear."[67]

Canada's messiah survived the opposition's fury, and he went confidently into the election campaign. The Liberal Party's two main messages, "Win the war" and "Preserve Canadian unity," were what the broad spectrum of Canadians wanted to hear.[68] Another suggested, although unused, slogan was "What is your alternative?"[69] That was too brazen, but it summed up the thoughts of much of the electorate, most of whom could not chance a vote for Social Credit or the CCF. That left only the Conservatives, who blasted the government over its lacklustre record (which actually appeared quite strong when laid out in its entirety) and its underhanded dissolution of Parliament, and who stressed the need for a unified national government. To French-Canadian ears, this last point seemed to suggest an arrangement uncomfortably similar to the Unionist government of 1917, which had brought in conscription. Quebec scurried for Liberal cover. As one Ottawa insider reported: "King is just as unpopular in the country as anyone, but the country knows that King surrounds himself with good men."[70]

After a month on the hustings, the Liberals were swept back into power on March 26 with a commanding majority: 181 of the 245 seats (and 64 of 65 seats in Quebec). They also held

51.5 percent of the popular vote. Few Canadians—in either English or French Canada—were willing to accept the Conservatives' claims that a greater exertion was needed by the Dominion at this point in the war. Having achieved the greatest landslide victory up to that point in the nation's history, the prime minister could justifiably claim that he had no reason to form a coalition government: the best minds in the country were already gathered under the Liberal banner. King would face the coming storm with a unified party, an opposition in disarray, and his mandate supported by a majority of Canadians.

CHAPTER 13

THE REAL WAR, 1940–1941

Germany's attack of France on May 10 was not a complete surprise—Denmark and Norway had been invaded a month earlier—but the ferocity of the assault left the world reeling. The Nazi blitzkrieg operations, based on lightning-fast armoured thrusts and infantry carried forward in motorized vehicles and supported by dive-bombing Stukas, pierced deep into the French lines, moving past areas of resistance, disrupting command and control. In the face of this ferocious advance, the French retreated or surrendered, with their lines of defence collapsing.

The German invasion of France precipitated a momentous development in Britain, when Neville Chamberlain handed over power to Winston Churchill. The new prime minister was as much a warrior as a politician: as the former, he had served in several military campaigns; as the latter, he had been First Lord of the Admiralty, while falling in and out of favour with his party. This new war was a second chance for Churchill to exercise power—or a third or fourth one, depending on how one counted the opportunities won and lost in his political career. He took office on May 10, 1940, and set about rallying the British nation.

Churchill's appointment was ominous for William Lyon Mackenzie King. King was under no illusion that he compared favourably to the warlike Churchill, whom he had mistrusted for years because of his bellicose statements and affinity for military action. Less than a year earlier, King had labelled him "one of the most dangerous men I have ever known."[1] Churchill inspired; he made those around him, and those who listened to him, feel larger than they were. This was required in war, especially one that Britain was losing. Canada was without a similarly rousing leader. "It will not be long before an attack gets worked up against me along lines very similar to that which Chamberlain has had to endure," wrote a fretful King.[2]

King had already weathered calls for him to step down and allow a more warlike leader to take his place, and now he faced a new round of questions. He dug in. "When he is encountered with a really serious and urgent crisis," wrote one British diplomat of King, "the weak side of this character comes to the top, and he becomes badly scared and, as so often happens with such natures, he tends to vent his alarm in fury upon anyone who is near him or whom he chooses to regard as responsible for his difficulties."[3] King looked for enemies, real or fabricated, but several decades of politics had taught him also how to effectively mount a flinty resistance.

When speaking in the House of Commons, King was mediocre at best, and sometimes downright terrible, but he loved to preach to the choir. When he was in front of his Liberal caucus, he listened carefully to their comments and spoke forcefully of his political mission. It is revealing that King, unlike many prime ministers, including Borden, faced few revolts from his Liberal members of Parliament. He managed his caucus as effectively as he managed his ministers. Now, his message was clear and consistent: Britain and France desperately needed Canadian support, and King would spare no expense in giving it. But—and this was important for the French Canadians—he would never endanger the unity of the country by enacting conscription. His passionate defence of his ideals almost always met with a standing ovation. While never a bare-knuckled brawler, King fought the latest "conspiracy," as he labelled it, by rallying the party, which stood behind him firmly.

CANADA'S WAR EFFORT in this period was summed up by the governor general, Lord Tweedsmuir, as "half-detached and half-embroiled."[4] While that assessment did not accurately describe the Canadian government, which was scrambling to meet multiple obligations in issues with respect to finance, security, and defence, many Canadians were barely affected by the war, even though tens of thousands had already enlisted. But this detachment changed with news of the intensifying action overseas, as the Nazi forces overran France. Canadians prepared themselves for the lean years ahead of toil and sacrifice.

In King's vision of Canada's contribution to the war effort, munitions and supplies were always the key pillars, and he looked to C.D. Howe to become, in effect, the minister of domestic wartime production. Howe was born in the United States but came to Canada as a young man, where he eventually made a fortune designing and building grain elevators. A self-made millionaire, his intelligence was matched by his management skills: he was knowledgeable, aggressive, and, at times, ruthless.

However, he was no machine, and friends found "C.D." to be jovial and passionate. He even had a soft spot for detective novels, which he ran through at lightning speed. When first elected prime minister in 1935, King had quickly made him a minister: Howe's background in industry offset a weakness in the cabinet, few of whose members (including King) had any business sense. Tough, forceful, and relentless, Howe was comfortable in delegating work to trusted subordinates. In April 1940, King appointed him minister of the Department of Munitions and Supply, a mammoth department that took over the purchasing and production of war supplies and materiel.[5]

Howe, with King's blessing, set about transforming the Dominion into "the arsenal of the Empire."[6] Given tax breaks and credit for investment, Canada's dormant and decrepit industry responded with increased productivity. Howe brought into his department a number of experienced business leaders who became known as the "dollar-a-year-men," because that was their salary. He selected both Liberals and Conservatives, a practice that made the rabidly partisan King uncomfortable, but the prime minister rarely interfered in Howe's actions. Despite the billions of dollars spent on government contracts, there was almost no graft or profiteering, and much of the credit for this went to Howe and his non-partisan operation.[7]

Output was slow in 1940, largely because the neutral United States and cash-poor Britain were buying little, but contracts were accumulated steadily throughout the war, eventually putting every able Canadian to work, and pulling the Dominion from the muck of the prewar Depression into wartime prosperity. Canadian firms and businesses built everything from munitions to bombers, from tanks to destroyers. More than 800,000 CMP (Canadian Military

Pattern) trucks were manufactured in Canada for the Allies. It was a staggering accomplishment, with an equally eye-popping price tag. Yet as Howe told his officials in June 1940, "If we lose the war nothing will matter ... if we win the war the cost will still have been of no consequence and will have been forgotten."[8]

Howe oversaw his empire with sublime confidence: when there were challenges, he blasted through them. For instance, when Canadian industry suffered a shortage of synthetic rubber, Howe set up a Crown corporation to manufacture more. Other Crown corporations followed; Victory Aircraft, Eldorado, and Polymer were some of the most efficient of these government-run businesses, producing aircraft, uranium, and rubber. He created twenty-eight in total, and several of them continued to operate after the war.[9] From 1940 to 1942, the value of war production rose from $310 million to $2.6 billion.[10] The next year, 1.2 million Canadians were working in war-related industries. Howe moved mountains during the course of the war, and the nation's industrial mobilization was among Canada's most important contributions to its wartime allies.

As the situation in Europe worsened, the cabinet was showing signs of strain. The expanding war effort had put enormous burdens on Norman Rogers, who was much diminished in health and mental energy. There were renewed calls to lessen his load and to create assistant ministers for the air force and the navy. King supported the idea, and on May 23 the cabinet agreed to the appointment of Chubby Power as the minister of national defence for air. He would oversee the air training program and the expanding RCAF. King was also fully aware that Power, as a Great War veteran, had often talked about how his voluntary wartime service had led him to the conviction that he would never be responsible for sending young men to fight against their will.[11] Although a naval counterpart was still needed, Power was another stalwart for King in balancing off the demands from the Tory press and from many Canadians for conscription.

King's able protegé, Norman Rogers, died in an aircraft accident on June 10. For King, a man of signs and symbols, it portended a grim future—this was also the day that Italy declared war on the Allies. The distraught prime minister took time from his busy schedule to visit Rogers's widow and two young children, trying to comfort them with readings from the Bible. Later that night, he wrote, "No loss could possibly be greater for the Ministry."[12] King's diary entries tended to be emotional, but Rogers had been among his closest political friends and had carried a heavy load. His sentiments were heartfelt. He also knew, however, that his cabinet, which had already been accused of being an "old government with old policies," needed an injection of new blood.[13]

In the aftermath of Rogers's death, and urged on by a personal report from Churchill to the effect that the French army was on its last legs, King needed his best man to take over national defence. In finance, Ralston had been tough; in defence, he would be tougher. And while Rogers had accepted King's lead in adopting the policy of limited engagement, Ralston would be far more insistent and difficult to coerce than his predecessor. Because Ralston had imposed such stringent control over the nation's purse strings as finance minister, King believed he would not tolerate the expense of a large expeditionary force. King was wrong.

Ralston's replacement at finance was J.L. Ilsley, a competent and hard-working Nova Scotian, who became one of the unsung heroes of King's cabinet. Ilsley led an austere life, and was widely regarded as dour, though in private he was quite pleasant and would mimic other cabinet ministers, to the delight of his loyal staff.[14] Despite Ilsley's success—or because of it—King did not enjoy his company and often treated him callously.[15] Though Ilsley was initially overshadowed by Ralston, whose appointment was met with approval from across the country, he would play a critical role in the war effort. Most Canadians realized that in the face of France's catastrophic defeat the war would get far worse before it got better, and leaders like Ralston would be needed to guide the armed forces, especially now that Britain was on the new front line.

At about the same time, King's most important political ally, Ernest Lapointe, was on the verge of collapse. "The lines in his face are deeper and he has lost much weight," wrote journalist Grant Dexter. "His shoulders sag more than I have ever noticed them and there is a hurt look in his big brown eyes."[16] Few knew that Lapointe had suffered a nervous breakdown as France fell under Nazi occupation. He blamed himself for a lack of defence preparations and for supporting a policy of isolation that effectively abandoned the mother country. Exhausted and spent, he came to King several times in an emotional state, unable to go on; each time King comforted him, said the right words, and sent him back to work.[17]

Some of the strain on Lapointe came from the necessity of dealing, as justice minister, with the unpleasant issues of censorship and national security. In a war to preserve liberal democratic ideals, the state had embraced draconian measures. As a Roman Catholic, Lapointe had been bred to be mistrustful of communists, and he showed little compunction in cracking down on those in Canada, even more forcefully than on the identifiable fascists in Montreal and Toronto. Other labour and ethnic groups also were outlawed, with little ensuing uproar. As one mid-1940 *Winnipeg Free Press* editorial remarked, "the temper of Canada has changed. It has hardened and we have shed our tolerance."[18]

The most high-profile arrest was of Montreal's mayor, Camillien Houde, a giant of a man at over 300 pounds, extravagant in dress and character, who for years had ruled by gift and by graft. A populist by nature, he spoke against the war effort, advising on August 2 that French Canadians should refuse to register their names for a national list of available manpower, labelling it "unequivocally a measure of conscription."[19] This was a crime under Defence of Canada Regulations and, in spite of fear of public unrest, the King cabinet was unanimous in having him arrested and thrown in jail. Houde was interned without trial for the next four years. Somewhat surprisingly, there was little backlash from French Canadians for imprisoning Houde, though it provided some fodder for antiwar editorialists.[20] While the prime minister might ruminate regretfully about such internments—"how excruciatingly cruel a thing war is"—he had little hesitation in backing Lapointe, and such actions were a sign of the emerging determination in the King cabinet.[21]

CANADIANS READ ABOUT THE DEBACLE in France with growing dismay and then horror, and were fearful for Canadian lives when elements of A.G.L. McNaughton's 1st Division made a brief foray to the continent in mid June. The troops saw no action and could do little to reverse the tide, so retreated back to England. With Britain facing a potential invasion, King was pressured to order additional forces overseas. Even as he lamented to his diary that

"We could have used our money more effectively if it had all been confined to air and naval services," the 2nd Division crossed the Atlantic to defend Britain.[22]

Seeing that the collapse of France was likely imminent, the British government asked Ottawa to send all of its available destroyers to guard against a possible cross-channel invasion. The cabinet agreed to this on May 23, though it meant stripping Canada's coast of its four most modern warships (and later three more and most of its modern fighter planes) and left the Dominion vulnerable. "It is right we should strike with her the last blow for the preservation of freedom," wrote King in his diary, but he also realized that he now would have to turn to the Americans for protection.[23] King informed Roosevelt of the grave situation, basing his report partly on British military and diplomatic intelligence. Several diplomatic missions to the United States over the coming days helped to solidify Canada's position as a useful mediator between the neutral United States and desperate Britain, although this linchpin role would come with a price.[24]

King was confronted with a difficult decision. He had long sought to play a role in the North Atlantic Triangle, acting as an honest broker between Britain and the United States.[25] To some degree, King was well suited to the task, and at the start of the war, with the Americans remaining neutral and drawing British ire for not shouldering their part in the fight against Hitler, the Canadian prime minister helped to soothe bad relations. But for a natural born trimmer who skirted commitment his whole life, the role of middleman required that he speak truth to power, or commit himself, on occasion, to action.

The Americans responded to Canada's missions to Washington with a pessimistic assessment of France's chance of survival and a warning by the president that he and his advisors believed that Britain was unlikely to withstand the German juggernaut. Neutral and isolationist America would shed tears for a conquered Britain, but what concerned them most was the prospect of the victorious Nazis acquiring Britain's dominant navy. With the combined might of the German, British, and French fleets, Hitler could threaten North America.

In this delicate matter, Roosevelt asked his friend "Mackenzie" to convey to his British counterpart the American suggestion that, should Britain's land defences fall or its cities be obliterated, its fleet of warships must flee the doomed island kingdom and regroup in Canada or Bermuda. "I instinctively revolted," wrote King in his diary, "against the thought of losing faith in Britain, but also shoving the nation while it was down. My reaction was that I would rather die than do aught to save ourselves or any part of this continent at the expense of Britain."[26] While King had been accused by sneering Tories throughout his political career of being pro-American, he believed in the sanctity of the Empire. It was the reason he had taken the country to war. It was the reason he would now not abandon Britain when few outside the island gave it much chance at survival.

King knew that Roosevelt was using him as a stalking horse. But instead of agreeing with the American prediction of Britain's imminent collapse, King tried to convince Roosevelt to send fighter planes to replenish Britain's air arm, which had been shot down over the continent. Unlike the Canadians, who sent off the cream of their navy, the Americans would not denude their limited military resources, pleading a shortage of aircraft. The shortage was real enough, but America was also neutral, and therefore safe for some time, while Britain would soon be the lone European bulwark against Nazism.

With time running out, King agonized over his letter to Churchill, desperate to find the right words. In the end, he felt that Churchill, aware of King's discomfiture, would appreciate his position.[27] The British bulldog did not. With the Allied armies retreating in France, Churchill did not need a self-serving American administration—seemingly supported by a skittish Canadian prime minister—prodding him not so gently into abandoning his country to enslavement under the heel of a mad Austrian corporal, as he often dismissively referred to Hitler.

Churchill's reply to Roosevelt's administration was perhaps the greatest oration of his life. On June 4, he gave his spine-tingling, "We shall fight on the beaches" speech, which he hammered home with the resounding cry, "We shall never surrender." The next day, a chastising letter arrived in Ottawa, in which Churchill admonished King that "We must be careful not to let Americans view too complacently prospects of a British collapse, out of which they would get the British Fleet and the guardianship of the British Empire, minus Great Britain."[28] Indeed. And to reinforce his point, Churchill warned a little wickedly that should Britain be overrun, there was no telling what the replacement quisling government of the day might do in cooperation with Germany. Perhaps that was something that King might raise with the Americans. The United States should send military aid, like Canada, instead of hedging its bets or wagering on Britain's defeat. The Americans reacted badly to Churchill's veiled threat, oscillating between anger and discomfort. The British prime minister had made his point. King, in his windy, self-deluded way, thought he had somehow brought the two sides together. He had not. And he was to find that linchpins can also sometimes find themselves caught in a vice.

AFTER THE FALL OF FRANCE at the end of June and the miraculous escape of the British Army from Dunkirk, everything changed. Canada was on the front line. King worried that if Germany took control of the French navy, there was a "real possibility of invasion of our shores."[29] The senior dominion was now Britain's most powerful ally. King once again took it upon himself to see if he might bring Britain and the United States together. But after Churchill's rebuke, King was more cautious about his role, writing at one point that he was a "medium of communication," who might channel their energy to better see each other's point of view.[30]

King visited Roosevelt several times in 1940 and early 1941. The two most pressing issues were defence and finance. In both cases, Britain's desperate weakness drove Canada into the American arms, although King always kept his head, and his heart, with the British Empire. While King and the Canadians felt reasonably certain that Roosevelt would fulfill his 1938 promise to stand by the Dominion if it was invaded—the Canadian prime minister worried about turning the country into an American protectorate.

In August 1940, Roosevelt invited King down to Ogdensburg, New York, to discuss issues of hemispheric defence, and especially the pressing deal that would see the United States give Britain fifty old destroyers for access to Empire-wide naval bases. While the bases-for-destroyers deal was between the British and Americans, Roosevelt felt that King might help in the negotiations. The

Americans could spare the destroyers and coveted the critical bases, which would allow them to better protect trade routes with their warships and, later, sea-patrolling aircraft. Accordingly, on August 17, King slipped away from Laurier House, got a haircut, picked up the American ambassador Jay Pierrepont Moffat, and drove the roughly 80 kilometres from Ottawa to Prescott, before crossing the border and pushing on into New York State. He was received in the president's private railway car, where Roosevelt was preparing his campaign for an unprecedented third term as U.S. president. While the two men were different in character and temperament, the American president genuinely liked spending time with the Canadian prime minister, perhaps because King was a good listener, who rarely asked for much. After a dinner of enormous steaks, the two leaders swapped old political stories and shared reminiscences of their time at Harvard until after midnight. Amid the pleasant chat, King was able to put in a good word for the British, again highlighting the importance of the bases-for-destroyers deal, although he bided his time in pushing his own aims.[31]

The president and prime minister met again the next morning, August 18, and King broached the issue that Canada, too, could use some military assistance. Since Roosevelt had long worried about continental defence, he listened intently. King soft-pedalled the request, as he was wont to do, highlighting Roosevelt's own claims of being short of aircraft and warships, but King passed along a memo prepared by Ralston, listing equipment and supplies that Canada was desperate to obtain from American markets. The president read it over carefully and promised to help.

Roosevelt also believed that, to ensure the successful defence of North America, Canada and the United States needed to work more closely together. In one of the epoch-changing moments in Canadian–American relations, with the leaders' lemonade glasses half filled and the sun beating down outside, the president drafted an agreement on the back of a piece of paper that he plucked from the wastebasket. The brief statement proposed the creation of a commission—the Permanent Joint Board on Defence (PJBD)—that would give Canada, at least in appearance, an equal voice with the United States in protecting North America.[32] The Americans, for their part, hoped that the PJBD would be a vehicle they could use to pressure Britain if it collapsed before the Nazi onslaught, and to ensure that the Royal Navy would steam to North America (preferably the United States) rather than fall into Hitler's hands.[33] The six sentences in the unsigned press release would become the framework for the next seventy years of Canadian–American defence relations.

The prime minister returned to Ottawa as a hero. His ministers were thrilled by the plan to ensure more integrated defence and additional military supplies, even though King had not consulted either them or the British. Almost all of the newspapers supported it too, although Arthur Meighen, still a prominent Tory voice even though he held no seat in the House of Commons, claimed King was handing the nation over to the Yanks. Winston Churchill similarly bristled at the bilateral defence agreement, which seemed to suggest that Canada was abandoning the Empire. Canada was not, but Britain's vulnerability had driven the Dominion to look south for protection. King attributed his success to hidden forces and the "Hand of Destiny," but it was his own hand that guided the nation to this important victory.[34]

THE GERMANS HAD OCCUPIED PARIS, and France was about to surrender, when King was astonished to learn during the Cabinet War Committee meeting of June 17 that the former anti-conscriptionists, Power and Lapointe, and most of the English-speaking ministers believed it was time to call out every available man for obligatory military training in defence of the country, although not overseas service. There had been talk of home defence conscription for some time, but King had done his best to suppress this in the cabinet. France's cataclysmic defeat changed everything, and even the Quebec ministers were onside, convinced that French Canadians would now see the war as a struggle for survival. Nonetheless, it was ironic that it was King and his party, not the dreaded Tories, who inched towards the most effective "mobilization of all resources."[35]

After hurried drafting of the legislation, on June 18 and 19 King defended the National Resources Mobilization Bill in the House, where he spoke with more than usual passion. Behind the scenes, King and Lapointe steadied the Quebec wing by underlining that the bill was about defending Canada and that the Liberals were against overseas conscription. Under the terms of the bill, men between the ages of twenty-one and forty-five were required to register and subsequently undergo one month of military training. This was far from the full conscription feared by many, but for some it must have seemed like the first tentative step on a slippery and steep slope, especially after the army complained that a month was not long enough, and the length of training was extended to four months. Nonetheless, the cohorts of conscripted men still remained relatively small—about 74,000 in uniform at the peak of the process in 1944—and in 1940 there was no shortage of recruits for overseas service.[36] On the whole, King escaped criticism for reneging on his long-time non-conscription pledge, although a fierce and articulate Quebec pressure group, La Ligue pour la défense du Canada, argued relentlessly against overseas conscription. But for King, the cabinet, and most Canadians, everything changed when Britain was threatened and Canada found itself as the ranking ally in the war against the Nazis.

Throughout the fall of 1940, the army brass grumbled that the Canadian soldiers in England were getting stale, even as tens of thousands enlisted during the European crisis or were diverted into home defence by the new National Resource Mobilization Act (NRMA). While Rogers had been in close agreement with King in his desire to keep Canadian forces from battle, Ralston had his own strong opinions on the role of the army, and, urged on by his generals, he wished to see it serve in North Africa with British forces. One astute political watcher believed that the army high command in Ottawa, led by Major-General Harry Crerar, had cornered Ralston: "He is perpetually the amateur civilian dealing with the expert. If he overrules the expert on points of major policy, he must assume that he is better qualified to decide. This is a very difficult position for a minister to take. If he accepts the advice—suspending his own judgment because he lacks military training—he has ceased to be minister, the generals are in charge and Cabinet control has been forfeited."[37] The intelligent and forceful Ralston was not so easily railroaded, but he quickly became a fierce champion of the army. In early December 1940, the war committee, at Ralston's urging, mulled over the idea of ordering Canadians to battle. King recoiled from the thought and refused, declaring, "We owe it to our men to seek to protect their lives."[38] He agreed that Canadians should defend

Britain, but he did not want to fight in North Africa, which he thought was little more than an attempt to hold on to the outer reaches of the British Empire. It was another of King's odd justifications: Britain was surely fighting for more than its Empire in Africa, both to defeat Germany and to protect the oil reserves in the Middle East, but King was adamant. Commitment to that theatre of war would result in Canadian deaths, and could easily lead to the army demanding more and more men. King would wait; he ordered the army to do the same.

BECAUSE OF ITS POLITICAL IMPORTANCE to the Liberal Party, Quebec was never far from King's mind, but there were other tensions in federal relations with the provinces as well. Duplessis had been banished and Hepburn put in his place, but the centralization of power in Ottawa was leading to increased friction with the provincial capitals. One of the most important commissions in Canadian history, the Royal Commission on Dominion–Provincial Relations, had delivered its report in May 1940, after three years of study and consultation. The commissioners had argued for a drastic change in the fiscal relations between the federal and provincial governments. The wealthier and larger provinces reacted with visceral anger to the Rowell-Sirois report, as it was commonly known, even as it argued that Canadians deserved uniform national standards of services and care. To achieve equal services, however, the provinces were required to withdraw from collecting income tax from individuals and businesses so that the federal government could better coordinate their efforts and, in these desperate times, pay for the war and control inflation. In return, the federal government would supply a balance of payments to the provinces, which would ensure continuity and greater fairness.

King met with the provincial leaders in mid January 1941, though he never thought the provinces would accept changes in their taxing powers.[39] It seemed at first that his caution was justified: Ontario's flamboyant and provocative Hepburn, supported by the premiers of British Columbia and Alberta, set out to scuttle any federal intrusion into provincial spheres. King and his ministers suffered much abuse; yet even as King faced defeat, the provinces acknowledged, in between their posturing and griping, that the federal government had the right and the need to meet its growing wartime obligations. As King noted philosophically, "Like all these things, it is not a choice of perfection, but the lesser of two difficult situations."[40] Additional negotiations secured for the duration of the war an agreement on wartime tax arrangements, which authorized the federal government to take over provincial debts and allocate payments to poorer provinces. After further meetings, it was decided that these transfer payments would continue into the postwar years. The new taxation powers helped to fill the federal coffers, but King continued to wring his hands over the prospect of a costly war, questioning "whether Canada will be able to maintain the burden she is assuming."[41]

Meanwhile, Britain had burned through much of its cash reserve and was desperately short of funds to purchase munitions in North America. While Roosevelt backed the Allied cause, the American policy, hardened by an ungenerous Congress, apparently was to bleed Britain white, demanding that it liquidate securities and assets in the United States. Not surprisingly, this prompted ill feelings in Britain: as the nation fought for its survival, the neutral Americans—who winked and nodded at the Allies and passed them goods secretly—took the opportunity to fleece the British of their wealth. This draining of Britain's treasure, capital, and securities had a profound effect on Ottawa, because Britain would soon be unable to pay for Canadian goods. The Dominion's war industry was employing tens of thousands of Canadians, and was continuing to expand under C.D. Howe's guidance, but a bankrupt Britain would be disastrous. Finance Minister J.L. Ilsley and Governor of the Bank of Canada Graham Towers explained the growing crisis to King and then urged on the prime minister to appeal to the Americans.

After much negotiation between Britain and United States, in which King had played a small role by pleading for the support of Britain, in early January 1941 Roosevelt proposed that the United States supply the Allies with munitions, ships, and aircraft without charge for the duration of the war. In his folksy way, he sold the move publicly as the lending of his garden hose to a neighbour whose house was on fire. The situation was, of course, far more complex, and Roosevelt's announcement reaffirmed the unstated fact that the United States had sided with the Allies. The enormous program, known as Lend-Lease, involved the arming of Britain, China, the dominions, and later Russia in the war against the Axis powers and took three months to pass through the U.S. Congress. It eased the immediate prospect of Britain's financial collapse, although Britain would be paying off the debt for the next sixty-five years.

King was delighted that the Americans were helping the British, and he also believed that these actions would eventually bring the United States into the war, as the country was now tied economically and morally to Britain. He was also rightly proud of his own involvement. In communications with Roosevelt, King had consistently argued in favour of the Americans supporting the British. Churchill and several of his key ministers sent along telegrams of thanks to King, and despite the somewhat customary and anodyne nature of the letters, King practically burst with pride when he received them.[42] He kept them in his wallet, pulling them out to show to his ministers and staff, and even to guests and visitors at parties and official functions.

Canada faced its own pressing financial issues. Generous American support to Britain meant that the British were likely to divert their purchases from Canada to the United States, where the goods were free, at least in the short term.[43] This would hurt the Canadian munitions industry.

In April 1941, King made a personal visit to the White House. With Roosevelt's encouragement, he met senior staff, including Secretary of State Cordell Hull and Secretary of the Treasury Henry Morgenthau. King informed the Americans that the Canadians were "in a very bad way." His nation was importing American raw materials and then sending the Dominion's war products to Britain, which the latter could not pay for. A well-briefed King proposed a barter of sorts, which would allow Canada not to spend its precious dollars, and instead receive American raw materials, as Britain did under Lend-Lease, since it was producing the material for Britain.[44] King sought aid, but he was wary about going to Uncle Sam cap in hand. And he was not a little bit angry that it was his nation that sent treasure and manpower to Britain to defend against the Nazis while the Americans lined their pockets. Though King knew the war would be lost without American aid, he noted that he "was stronger than ever for the British connection as far as Canada was concerned."[45] But even with this firm connection of the heart, Britain's vulnerability was driving Canada reluctantly into American arms.[46]

An invitation from the president allowed King to extend his trip and visit Roosevelt at home in Hyde Park, New York. The two men met to work out a financial deal that would allow Canada to continue to back the British. They talked about the war, and Roosevelt continued to confide in the Canadian about his own political problems. While they sat on the veranda staring out at the Hudson River and sipping iced tea, King worked in his own concerns, especially the political fallout from Lend-Lease.

Although Roosevelt appeared to be listening sympathetically, King wondered if the president understood the gravity of the situation, but after dinner, he and Roosevelt sat down for another round of talks. Almost as an afterthought, Roosevelt asked for a piece of paper and requested that King draft a few lines summing up what they had been discussing. King scribbled notes as Roosevelt stared out into the darkness. With slightly trembling hands, King handed the sheet to the president, who took it in rapidly. Yes, it would do. The note read, in part, that "in mobilizing the resources of this continent each country should provide the other with the defence articles it is best able to produce." The United States also agreed to purchase $300 million a year in Canadian raw material and supplies, with these dollars covering off Canada's purchasing south of the border. When the agreement was typed up later that night, Roosevelt wrote in pencil: "Done by Mackenzie and F.D.R. at Hyde Park on a grand Sunday, April 20, 1941."[47]

After months of apparently fruitless negotiations with the United States by lower-level politicians and diplomats, King's colleagues were truly amazed at his breakthrough. The Hyde Park

Declaration ensured that there would be a continuing market for Canadian goods in the United States, and sufficient raw material for Canada to produce war materiel for Britain and the other wartime allies.[48] This was King's monumental victory, but also one that changed the terms of economic relations between the two countries. While still tethered to the great island kingdom by bonds of culture, history, and blood, Canada had taken a significant step towards becoming a North American nation, further entwined through goodwill, trade, and economics—all brought together through the desperate situation of the war. And no one, not even King, who always seemed four moves ahead of his allies and opponents, was quite sure how this new relationship would play out.

CHAPTER 14

THE WAR INTRUDES, 1941–1942

Prime Minister William Lyon Mackenzie King's firm commitment to Britain's defence, along with his productive negotiations with the Americans, placed him high in the regard of many Canadians in the summer of 1941. He had proven he could walk a fine line, supporting the Allied war effort while not alienating Quebec, which, in poll after poll throughout the war, believed that Canada was already being pushed too hard in supporting Britain.[1] But despite the worry in French Canada, the Dominion's contribution to the military campaign against the Axis powers had gradually escalated. The Canadian navy protected the convoys from U-boats across the Atlantic; the air force joined the Royal Air Force in fending off the Luftwaffe and was soon sending bombers to attack German cities; and the army protected the island nation against invasion. All told, King and his government could look proudly upon the nation's war effort. Even as King occasionally fretted over his own inadequacies, he reminded himself that he had a robust mandate from the people and, despite the NRMA and increased income taxes, their lives had not been disrupted significantly. A study of civilian attitudes around this time observed that Canadians, unlike in the last war, were far less willing to demand the imprisonment of German Canadians or to harass young men to enlist.[2] Most Canadians must have agreed with King's policy of limited liability. That would change over time, and King would be forced to change his views too.

THE WAR WAS WEARING ON CANADIANS, and especially on those carrying the burden of leadership. King's long-time senior advisor, Dr. Oscar Skelton, died of a heart attack on January 28, 1941. His loss was a blow to King, the government, and the country. Skelton had been a link between Laurier and King, and had helped to bolster and articulate King's nationalistic views. While King and Skelton had drifted apart a little in the late 1930s over Canada's commitment to the Empire, their professional relationship had not suffered. Norman Robertson, who would have a long and rich diplomatic career, succeeded Skelton as undersecretary of state for external affairs. He exhibited good judgment time and time again, and he, along with Pickersgill, Heeney, and, from 1944, General Maurice Pope, played key roles in advising the prime minister.

With Skelton and Rogers gone and Lapointe in failing health, King relied most heavily on Ralston, who had vast responsibilities as defence minister. While most were awed by Ralston's intellect and work ethic, he was not an efficient manager, and rarely delegated responsibility. "Stiff and unbending, meticulous and demanding," he worked incredibly long hours, which worried friends who feared that he might soon burn out.[3] King needed to lighten his load. Power was a success as minister of defence for air, but King wanted a strong minister to take over the expanding Royal Canadian Navy. The popular Liberal premier of Nova Scotia, Angus L. Macdonald, agreed to serve in June 1940. Known as "Angus L." to friend and foe, he was one of the leading lights of the Liberal Party. The new minister ran and won in Norman Rogers's riding of Kingston and was soon a critical member of the cabinet, serving as minister of national defence for naval services. Although Ralston was the minister and Power and Macdonald nominally were junior ministers, they got along well (all were veterans, lawyers, and long-service politicians) and ran their own departments with little interference. Power remained a confidant of King, while Ralston pulled away increasingly due to his frustration with the leader. Angus L., meanwhile, had never been a King man, and he found the prime minister's manner aggravating, his inaction perplexing, and his avoidance of decisions unleaderlike.[4] Macdonald, touted by the media as a star, never lived up to the hype, and found Ottawa stifling and his leader intolerable.

The navy expanded rapidly during the war, from about 3,000 permanent and reserve sailors to an astonishing 96,000 by war's end. There was also a frenzy of activity in Canadian shipyards, which the King government encouraged because it led to greater industrialization and job growth. The initial focus was on minesweepers and corvettes. Churchill dubbed the latter as "cheap and nasties," and they were.[5] Small but robust, they could be manufactured quickly to be deployed against the U-boat threat. One hundred and twenty-three Canadian corvettes fought against the Axis powers, serving in most theatres of battle. As the war progressed, Canada built or acquired larger and more powerful frigates and destroyers, many of which took part in hard-banging sea battles with German surface raiders in the last two years of the war. The key to victory, however, was the dangerous run across the Atlantic. If the U-boats severed the lifeline from North America, Britain would be starved into submission. Almost any price would have to be borne to avoid such a fate, but that did not make it any easier on the sailors who risked their lives day in and out.

In the summer of 1941, King's diary revealed his own exhaustion, which had been building for months. He had seen close advisors die, and the unending strain of the war effort was wearing him down. His beloved dog Pat was in decline, and would lie down for the last time in July. King was devastated by the loss. He poured his grief into his diary, in page after page of handwritten passages that reveal a man on the edge of losing his self-control. Pat had been a constant companion, and now he was one more who had gone to the "Great Beyond." There were several times in the summer of 1941 when King, wracked with worry and self-doubt, believed he should resign and let the more warlike Ralston or Macdonald take over.[6] Even though King often used the threat of resignation to gauge his ministers' reaction, and then savoured the protests that soothed his ego, he agonized over the coming political battles that he knew could not be avoided. He felt more alone than ever.

THE WAR TOOK A GRIM TURN on June 21, 1941, when German forces attacked their ally, Soviet Russia. Yugoslavia and Greece had fallen to the Nazis in April. Could Russia hold out? It appeared unlikely, largely because the Russian dictator, Joseph Stalin, had murdered much of his military high command in retaliation for supposed conspiracies. Moreover, even though Stalin had been given British intelligence showing that German armoured divisions were massing on the Russian border, the dictator had been bizarrely passive. The prospect of having to fight the nearly invincible Wehrmacht paralyzed him in thought and action.

The initial stunning success of German blitzkrieg forces crashing through the Russian lines, shattering dozens of infantry divisions, destroying squadrons of aircraft on the ground, and throwing the defenders into disarray, led most professional soldiers to predict that the ill-trained and poorly-led Russians would last for a few weeks at best. Mass surrenders involving hundreds of thousands of soldiers—more than in the entire British Army—early in the campaign confirmed the pessimistic appreciation. However, Hitler's mad action in the east bought time for the Allies to regroup in the west, and soon it was clear that while the Russians had been savaged, they were not finished. As the Soviet forces retreated into the vast Russian plains, the pursuing German armour slowed to a near stop. Generals Mud and Winter saved Stalin in 1941. And the Russian soldiers, even though they were poorly led, criminally armed, and almost always surviving on starvation rations, revealed a tenacity that shocked the Germans. There would be no lightning defeat of the Russians.

The potential disaster on the Eastern Front led to new calls for greater Canadian military involvement. King, feeling the pressure, made an effort to engage the newspapers to highlight the armed forces' already considerable deployment. While King had never had a press or public relations advisor, he was adept at ingratiating himself with influential commentators. He knew all the journalists in Ottawa, and most across the country, and he often arranged face-to-face meetings with them. The prime minister invited reporters for private talks at Kingsmere, his 200-hectare sanctuary in the Gatineau hills, or to Laurier House, a spacious mansion in downtown Ottawa that he had inherited from Lady Laurier in 1921. He filled the Ottawa house with hideous knick-knacks, ugly paintings, and gaudy furniture, giving it the appearance of a mausoleum, but it was his sanctuary.

King was noncommittal and evasive with groups of journalists (one of them said he was as "informative as a gagged clam"), but he was more forthcoming in intimate settings.[7] He cultivated strong one-on-one relationships, and sometimes slid scoops to individual reporters. They, in turn, often treated him kindly in their columns, at least the ones who were not strongly partisan. King also listened to their advice, especially to that of J.W. Dafoe, editor of the *Winnipeg Free Press* and one of the nation's most intelligent and influential writers on foreign affairs. King's relationship with journalists went both ways. Relying on the hammer of censorship, his strong personal relationships, and his ability to freeze out those who criticized him, King often used the newspapermen to get out important stories. It is perhaps revealing that next to his bed at Laurier House he kept a phone and a long list of names and numbers, including that of a veterinarian, key ministers, and many journalists.[8] King was the complete politician. Every waking hour of his adult life was spent cementing his own political position and that of his government and party.

WHILE KING MANAGED THE DOMESTIC SCENE adeptly, he was far less certain about his role on the international stage. Although

British Empire and Commonwealth strategy was formulated in London, the prime minister blanched at the idea of going overseas, feeling that such a trip would be misconstrued in Quebec. He also worried privately that an extended absence would cause him to lose control of the party or fall victim to a palace coup. Perhaps more disturbing to him, the notion of a meeting of prime ministers was strongly reminiscent of the Imperial War Cabinet of the previous war. King believed correctly that the subtle and overt imperial pleas and charms that accompanied those meetings had dragged Borden and the country deeper into that costly conflict. And so King avoided the half-hearted calls for such a gathering from Churchill, who really did not want to consult the dominion leaders anyway. The Canadian prime minister stood behind what he had written a year earlier: "My first duty is to Canada ... Keep our country united."[9]

Nevertheless, the war was by now so all-encompassing that international issues were always intruding on the domestic. King received a shock on August 6. The British high commissioner to Canada, the very able Malcolm MacDonald, called on King to tell him that Churchill and Roosevelt planned to meet in Placentia Bay, Newfoundland, to hammer out the Western allies' grand strategy. King was not asked to attend what came to be known as the Argentia Conference, even though the United States had not yet entered the war and Canada was providing both men and treasure for Britain. Churchill did not want King pestering him or getting in the way when he needed to focus his attention on the Americans, whom he was courting openly. Churchill took King for granted and, at this stage in the war, viewed the Canadian prime minister, as Malcolm MacDonald remarked, "with a touch of contempt, as a pigmy."[10]

King was furious that the two great powers had left him out of the summit, especially as it was being held on his doorstep. The more he reflected on the snub, the more his rage was "unbounded," as one journalist reported in a private communication. He knew the opposition would use his exclusion from the meeting to embarrass him.[11] The British pleaded that if Canada was invited, the other dominions would demand the right to participate too, but this did little to assuage King's bruised ego. The prime minister wrote that he found it "extraordinary" that Churchill would push "Canada completely to one side—simply saying that we would be told what had been done, though having no voice in the arrangements."[12]

At Argentia, the Americans and British drafted the outlines of what would become known as the Atlantic Charter. The document laid out international agreements on finance and cooperation, but also implicitly bound the United States more tightly to the Allied war effort, and, quite remarkably, put Canadian naval forces under American command in the Western Atlantic. Despite the important work at the conference, the still dismayed King complained to Malcolm MacDonald that the callous treatment of him and his government was the "way in which the British lost their friends, wanting them in foul weather and ignoring them in fair."[13] King had to do something to combat the impression in Canada that he was being ignored by the great powers. He planned a trip to England.

KING FRETTED ABOUT A TRANSATLANTIC TRIP. Sea travel was not an option—C.D. Howe had almost been killed when the ship he was travelling on had been attacked by a U-boat the previous year.

King would have to fly. This would be a novelty: King, in his more than sixty-five years, had never been in the air. And so a Liberator bomber was outfitted with a heated cabin, where King could rest along with a few advisors. He was nervous before takeoff on August 19, but calm during the flight. He took solace from the idea of the plane slipping the bonds of earth, in an almost angelic manner, and the words that came to his mind were "Terrestrial and celestial; seeing a new heaven and a new earth."[14]

Upon his arrival in Scotland, King was driven to London, where he stayed in a palatial suite at the Dorchester Hotel. His most important engagement was at 10 Downing Street to meet Churchill. The two had never been friends, and while they were career politicians and loved the British Empire, their approach to politics and war was at opposite ends of the spectrum. Warned by Malcolm MacDonald to treat King cautiously and with respect, Churchill unleashed his charm, greeting King like a long-lost brother. If their friendship was feigned, the gratitude on both sides was real.

Like Borden a generation before him, King was invited to the war cabinet and made to feel welcome. Accolades and praise for the Canadian war effort and for its critical contribution as the arsenal of the Empire were heaped upon him, and King fairly swooned with pleasure. His worries about being dragged into a deeper commitment were unfounded, he decided, even though the war could hardly have been going worse for the Allies, as they suffered defeat upon defeat on almost every front. Churchill, having been briefed on King's guarded nature, asked very little of the Canadian, even going so far as to suggest that this was a war of machines and industrial might rather than of cannon fodder. King nearly danced with delight. Later events would prove, however, that the infantry and large ground forces were necessary for victory, and that most of the theatres of war would, if they had not already, degenerate into attritional campaigns and battles, far different from the "lightning" battles of 1939 and 1940.

King found himself warming to Churchill. The two swapped political stories, shared the lines of poetry that moved them, and even revealed to one another their favourite hymns. At a dinner party at Churchill's estate, an imbibing Winston shuffled across the drawing-room to the sound of big band music emanating from the radio. Soon, arm in arm, the fat, old, and balding British and Canadian prime ministers danced an awkward jig. The crowd of politicians and military men laughed along hysterically, and wicked Winston kept King up far past his normal bedtime.[15]

The Canadian prime minister also used his overseas trip to meet his soldiers and airmen. King had a comforting talk with corps commander A.G.L. McNaughton. The Canadian general reiterated that he did not think conscription would ever be necessary, and that "unity was more important than all else."[16] This pleased King to no end. But McNaughton also asked the prime minister to address the troops at Aldershot on August 23. King shuddered at the thought. He began to sweat and felt physically sick. "I would have given anything not to have to speak," he wrote.[17] Despite King's visible discomfort, McNaughton knew that it would be disastrous if word leaked out that the Canadian prime minister had been at the training camp and had not reviewed the troops.

King's instinct was right. His party arrived forty minutes late to review the thousands of soldiers who had been called to await his arrival in the rain. When he waddled to the speaking stand, he was met by a smattering of applause and some loud, anonymous boos, which set off a round of glib whispers and taunts. It was humbling, although King recovered, later ascribing the boos to Toronto Conservative officers seeking to score political points.[18] Still, his game had been thrown off, and he made a dull speech. He rushed from the field as soon as possible, worried about how the opposition and their papers would use the embarrassing event to question, yet again, his wartime leadership.

Although King wrote about being impressed by the young men in uniform, he was deeply uneasy around military personnel. His lack of service in the Great War had dogged his political career, leaving him open to endless snipes about his loyalty, patriotism, and manhood. In some dark level of his already conflicted soul, these barbs led him to pull back from interactions with those who served in uniform. They were chalk and cheese, and when three days later King next addressed a mass of soldiers, he nearly fainted from the pent-up anxiety. In the tense minutes leading up to his address, he recounted that he "felt what was like a dart pass through my bowels."[19] He broke out in a cold sweat. There was no booing this time, but when he was led to the microphone to speak to the thousands of soldiers, he was, in his own assessment, "really in a condition of agony and fright."[20] Not surprisingly, he made a poor job of it, never quite finding the words either to inspire his audience or to communicate how the nation was backing them.

What to make of this paralysis? King had his own private insights: "I really felt too moved at the thought of all this young life being possibly destroyed to be able to give proper expression to my thoughts. I cannot talk their jargon of war."[21] Canada's wartime leader could not mouth the expected platitudes and patriotic phrases that normally rolled easily off politicians' tongues.

Moreover, his discomfort around the soldiers was a reflection of his ongoing worry about how far to commit the nation and how many more young men would be thrown into the cauldron of battle.

KING RETURNED HOME to a conflicted and suffering country. The massive mobilization of manpower and resources was leading to labour unrest. Rising inflation was eating into the spending power of citizens, just as it had done disastrously in the last war, and this led to widespread charges of profiteering. Something had to be done. One radical option was to put a cap on wages and prices, so that both were kept artificially low. King felt it was far too drastic a move and that it would leave him and the party exposed dangerously if Canadians refused to accept the controls.[22] Jack Pickersgill commented that King was "initially suspicious of new ideas, and indeed, of any kind of novelty."[23] Although he had five university degrees, King was no intellectual, and he governed himself not by study but through instinct. In this case, he was exceedingly wary of any untried intrusions into the lives of Canadians. But his resistance was overcome finally in a mid-October meeting with the able W.C. Clark of the finance ministry and Graham Towers of the Bank of Canada, who were backed by Ilsley; all warned of dire consequences if the economy was not checked.

Labour leaders were initially wary and combative, but the prime minister was at his best when meeting with them—conciliatory and calming, but also emphatic in stressing that runaway inflation would eventually cripple the nation. King gave a well-received public broadcast on October 18 that hit the right note in stressing the danger of an uncontrolled economy and the steps the government was taking to meet the threat. The cap "will affect the daily lives of each one of us."[24] The freezing of prices and wages had never been tried before, but it was carried out, with the support of most Canadians. They grumbled and groused but nevertheless realized that they were better off in Canada than their comrades-in-arms, friends, and loved ones in bombed-out, always-on-the-verge-of-starving Britain. With ever-escalating taxes soaking up much of Canadians' purchasing power, inflation was managed effectively. King deserves credit for standing behind the novel and controversial legislation: it could not have been implemented without his commitment. And it worked. Of all the Allied countries at war, Canada was the most successful at controlling inflation.[25]

However, the manpower issue continued to divide the cabinet. Canada now was fighting hard on the oceans and in the air, and had created a large overseas army. With its factories booming, there was a labour crunch. The cabinet was at loggerheads over how best to apportion the available manpower between the fighting elements and the home front.

The army especially demanded more and more men. While King had the utmost respect for Ralston, he worried that he was being led by the senior generals, who wanted larger formations. Ralston admitted as much in late 1941 to journalist Grant Dexter: "[I am] minister but must act upon the advice of [my] staff of professional soldiers. Being a civilian, [I cannot] set aside [my] advisors simply because [I] disagreed with what they said. They know; [I] did not know."[26] Despite his unease, Ralston argued relentlessly for a big army, to the point that other ministers like Macdonald, Power, and Ilsley were forced to push back.

The army, as they saw it, was expanding almost beyond control, gobbling up financial and manpower resources. King did not like to confront Ralston, and so he often used his other ministers to run interference, although his views were well known. Ralston was no empire-builder, but he believed in supporting the service personnel overseas in their fight against Hitler. He was coming around to the position that conscription would be necessary if the army needed the manpower to fully prosecute the war.

Conscription was the bridge too far for King. He had made countless promises to Canadians, and especially to Quebec, that he would never enact conscription. He was firm in his own mind that official compulsion would lead to "civil war." A victory overseas would be pyrrhic if it was achieved through the dismemberment of the Dominion. Few could argue with this. But was the country on the brink of civil war? There was no indication of that. King exaggerated the danger, but he simply did not believe that an all-out war effort was required. The fall of France had ushered in a period of fear and anxiety, but when Britain survived that first, desperate year, most Canadians expected the Allies would hold out until the Americans were eventually dragged into the worldwide conflict. For King, the international war had to take second place to the one at home. In adopting this position, King was bolstered by a late-1941 opinion poll that revealed 61 percent of Canadians were satisfied with Canada's war effort and slightly more approved of King's wartime leadership. Ominously, however, 60 percent of Canadians also believed that conscription was necessary.[27] King tried to navigate his way through the apparent puzzle of what Canadians thought about the war.

Around this time, King lost one of his most important

champions in the fight to hold off conscription. Ernest Lapointe was hospitalized in mid November with pancreatic cancer. King made several trips to see the dying Lapointe in Montreal. They reminisced about past political triumphs, talked of their brotherly love, and shed tears. King and Lapointe had been the closest of allies, but not outside of politics; they had rarely called upon each other socially.[28] Still, there was a special bond between the two men, and now, in his final parting, the sentimental, Presbyterian King told his old, Catholic friend, "Ernest, we will see each other again," beyond the great divide.[29] The man who had put him in power in 1919, kept him there in 1926, and delivered Quebec time and time again, passed away on November 26. King's grief was mixed with a shrewd understanding that unless a suitable Quebec lieutenant were found, the government would be in jeopardy, as King certainly could not command the province.

With his anchors, Lapointe and Skelton gone, King was adrift in the storm. He was tired, talked of depression, and was truly saddened by the loss of those closest to him. One unsettling passage in his diary reveals the dark dogs that snapped at him: "sick at heart ... The strain is terrible—mental fatigue and physical combined, but depression as well, and feeling of being left alone, old colleagues gone or going, no one to help, and alone at Laurier House ... no one to talk with."[30]

IN THE WANING DAYS OF 1941, Quebec had to be reassured that it still had a voice at the cabinet table, and that conscription was not the next step in the march to total war. King turned first to P.J.A. Cardin as the obvious replacement for Lapointe, but Cardin had recently suffered a heart attack that left him incapable of taking over Lapointe's heavy duties. He had also made enemies among prominent English cabinet ministers by suggesting that it would not be a bad thing for Canada if Britain was defeated in the war, because it would irrevocably cut the shackles of empire.[31] Chubby Power was already influential, but his fondness for the bottle left the moralizing King unwilling to put the party's future fully under his bibulous control.[32] King was disappointed when he could not pry the Liberal provincial leader, Adélard Godbout, out of Quebec City, but then the name Louis St. Laurent was advanced by senior Quebec politicians.

King knew of the handsome and dignified sixty-year-old St. Laurent through his work on the Rowell-Sirois report and his high-profile court cases, but the lawyer had no political experience. One might have thought that the professional politician in King would have held that against St. Laurent, but he didn't, with his uncanny instinct again leading him. King offered St. Laurent a cabinet position and an opportunity to have a profound impact over the direction of the war. Like Ralston before him, St. Laurent recognized that the war was a national emergency and he was willing to give up time with his family, community, and law practice. St. Laurent agreed to join the cabinet as minister of justice on December 9, two days after an event that would change the war effort for both the Allies and the Axis powers.

After years of tension and escalating acts of aggression, the Japanese attacked the American naval base at Pearl Harbor on December 7, 1941. The "day that will live in infamy," as President Roosevelt called it, was ironically the Allies' salvation. The Americans finally entered the war, a move for which the president had been slowly preparing the nation since September 1939. King's reaction to Pearl Harbor was one of shock, but he also understood, as did Churchill in London, that the enraged Americans would not stop until the Japanese were defeated.[33] Both worried that the Japanese attack would lead the Americans to direct all their military might towards the Pacific. The British were saved by Hitler's monumental stupidity. The Nazi dictator declared war on the United States on December 11, in one of the greatest strategic blunders in military history. While Hitler's motivation has never been clear—though it surely involved a mixture of hubris and hatred—the declaration allowed the surprised Roosevelt administration to turn its attention to Germany and Japan in a two-front war.

Pearl Harbor overshadowed the other Japanese offensives in the Pacific theatre, but these were also swift and successful. Fast-moving infantry following behind surprise aerial bombardments combined to drive the British, Dutch, and Americans back on several fronts. Poor morale and weak leadership saw one garrison after another fall to the Japanese enemy the British had derided for years.

Two Canadian battalions of almost 2,000 soldiers were caught in the fighting. The Winnipeg Grenadiers and Royal Rifles of Canada had been sent to garrison Hong Kong, a British Crown colony, arriving only five weeks before the Japanese assault. King had been convinced by Chief of the General Staff Harry Crerar, who was backed by Ralston, to involve the army in more active operations. Senior British generals and mandarins had believed for years that the isolated garrison was doomed in the face of any sustained attack, but in the months before the Japanese offensive, Churchill and his staff had engaged in "deterrence of desperation."[34] By sending the two Canadian battalions, along with two of the Royal Navy's capital ships, the battleship and battlecruiser

Prince of Wales and *Repulse*, the British high command hoped to cow the enemy. They did not, and it was a flimsy pretext upon which to gamble Canadian lives, though the act was widely supported by the press.

Upon hearing of the Pearl Harbor invasion on December 7, King called a cabinet meeting for later in the day. He contacted the leaders of the opposition, and considered recalling Parliament, which was out of session. The cabinet decided on a declaration of war against Japan that same evening, even before action was taken by the American Congress. Canadians had, after all, been attacked. But King's forthrightness caught some of his ministers flat-footed.

The Canadians, with British and Indian troops, fought bravely in Hong Kong, but they were damned from the start, with no chance of reinforcements.[35] Although King did not know the full extent of the Japanese savagery after the surrender of the garrison on December 25, which saw the cold-blooded execution of wounded prisoners and the rape of nurses, he did not seem to anguish over their fate. And yet this was the same man who wrote long passages in his diary about small talk at diplomatic functions and worked himself into a lather when he turned down a friendly drink from Roosevelt, wondering if he had hurt the president's feelings because of his own pledge of abstinence during the war. The pages of King's diary are nearly barren of references to the Hong Kong debacle, although he expressed his relief later in 1942, when his government was exonerated by a royal commission. To the extent that he acknowledged the defeat, King shifted the blame onto Crerar, interpreting it as an example of the need to rein in the army from committing Canadians to future offensive operations. He seems to have spared few thoughts for the 1,975

Canadians committed to that doomed theatre, or for the 1,418 who returned to Canada nearly five years later, most of whom suffered grievously from physical beatings, debilitating disease, and the psychological brutality of horrific imprisonment.[36] King's gaze was always directed firmly on domestic issues in Canada, and he continued to know little, and seemingly care less, about what was occurring to the Canadian forces overseas.

CHAPTER 15

UNLIMITED WAR, 1942

In the aftermath of the Japanese attack on Pearl Harbor, the war went global. Although the Allies were strengthened immeasurably by the Americans, Britain and the United States were soon reeling from a string of humiliating defeats at the hands of the Japanese. In the three months of war with Japan, the British lost 166,000 men, 130,000 of whom were taken prisoner.[1] With America on the back heel as it organized new armies, navies, and air squadrons to meet the Japanese threat, the only good news in late 1941 and early 1942 was that Stalin's forces had survived against the German onslaught.

The expanding war gave new urgency to the task of protecting Canadian soil. However, the U-boat battle had drawn most of the RCN's warships to the east coast, leaving British Columbia vulnerable to a Japanese naval or amphibious assault. Vehemently anti-Asian ministers like Ian Mackenzie were already warning about sabotage by Japanese-Canadian fifth-columnists, who would aid the enemy.[2] Aware that the growing unrest about Japanese Canadians had to be contained, but not willing to act drastically, King put off action as the cabinet wrestled with the war planning for 1942.

A week before the Japanese surprise offensives against Pearl Harbor and other sites in the far east, Ralston had brought forward a proposal for an army program that consisted of a six-division overseas force.[3] King was uneasy with the idea, rightly noting that a bigger army, when combined with the steady growth of the air force and a navy that wanted larger and more powerful warships, meant a greater chance that conscription would have to be imposed at some point. Ralston disagreed, saying the men would come voluntarily, but, he warned, they ultimately had to come if Canada was not to shirk its duty. This the prime minister could not accept. He reiterated his recurrent threat that he would resign before his government brought in conscription, and he was backed by most of the cabinet.[4]

Ralston, in turn, continued to demand the larger army, and always with the unspoken threat of his own resignation if he was denied. The defence minister was increasingly frustrated with King, and more so as he became exhausted from constant toil over his many files. Lester Pearson remarked that Ralston "worked every day, all day, and never seemed to relax."[5] How could he? Lives were on the line. His son was in uniform. Hundreds of thousands of other parents' sons and daughters were serving their country. The Great War soldier and postwar champion of veterans' rights would not break faith with those who risked their lives for their country, and he increasingly refused to play what he believed were King's delaying games.

It was the same old argument between the cabinet's two most powerful personalities, although the prime minister was weakened by the loss of Lapointe, who had always stood against Ralston's large army. Although King still thought that the nation's remaining resources should go into manufacturing and farming, and he was backed strongly by C.D. Howe and T.A. Crerar, he finally allowed himself to be convinced that the army should continue its expansion when Chief of the General Staff Lieutenant-General Kenneth Stuart assured him that voluntary recruitment would fill the ranks.[6] Ralston had won. The army got its "big" overseas force, which grew, at its peak, to an astonishing 495,073 men and women, eventually consisting of five divisions and two armoured brigades.[7] This would be the largest land formation in Canada's history. It was also the seed of future crises.

THE WAR OF WILLS WITH RALSTON came to a truce at the end of December, when Churchill arrived in North America. The British bulldog had gone to Washington, where he and Roosevelt, along with their chiefs of staff, worked on the joint strategy, now that Japan was in the war and loosely aligned with the Nazis. Canada had not been invited to the conference, even though, up to a few days before, the Dominion had been Britain's ranking ally. A disappointed King refused to rock the boat, but he nonetheless bristled at Churchill's "supercilious English attitude."[8]

King knew a political opportunity when he saw one, however, and he raced to Washington with several ministers on Christmas Day. King and his entourage arrived to encounter a tense standoff between the British and Americans over the Free French, who, with British approval, had recently occupied the tiny French islands of St. Pierre and Miquelon, off the Atlantic coast of Newfoundland. The Americans were outraged that such action had been taken in their backyard without their knowledge, their anger made hotter by their intense dislike of the pompous Charles de Gaulle, leader of the Free French. [9] When the Americans pressured the British to remove de Gaulle, Churchill was in no mood to entertain their whining, rightly seeing this as the inconsequential sideshow that it was, especially with British colonies and protectorates falling like hay before the Japanese scythe in the Pacific theatre. King, too, refused to be bullied by the Americans on the issue. Nonetheless, he remained worried about the entire affair and how it would play out in Quebec, which had influential politicians and newspaper editors sympathetic to Vichy France, the French government that worked with, and for, the German occupiers.[10] Tempers among the Allies were eventually cooled, and the Americans retreated from their hardline position. Relations with the French were made clearer in late 1942, when Vichy France openly sided with the Nazis during the North Africa campaign, thereby provoking the Allies to cut diplomatic ties and declare Vichy an enemy.

Even as the tempest swirled among them, Churchill, Roosevelt, and King remained friendly and courteous, although the unsaid assumption was that the Canadian prime minister was there as a junior ally, not a principal. King would later mutter to his diary that, with the media focused on Churchill and Roosevelt, there was a tendency to "crowd both Canada and myself off the map."[11] Indeed there was, but King had to come to grips with that—and he knew it—and so he kept his objections to his secret journals.

But King could also take advantage of Churchill's celebrity status. After the Washington meetings, Churchill was enticed to Ottawa, where he was greeted as a hero by adoring Canadians. The cigar-chomping Churchill, riding in an open car, enjoyed himself too, flashing his famous "V-for-victory" symbol with his two fingers to roaring crowds. King copied it for a while, but stopped when he realized he looked silly. John Diefenbaker, then a young Conservative MP, was little impressed by anything King did. When a sycophantic Liberal backbencher turned to him at an event attended by King and Churchill and gushed, "'Isn't that wonderful. There is Mr. King making that sign that Churchill has made his. They are together.'" Diefenbaker replied gruffly, "The V has different meanings. For Churchill it means Victory: For King it means Votes."[12]

Churchill addressed a joint-session of the Senate and the House of Commons on December 30, 1941. Anyone who was anyone in Ottawa was crammed into the House. Although the British prime minister was worn out and occasionally fumbled the words from his prepared text, what all who were there remembered was his soon-to-be-famous remark about British resolve. Churchill mused about the dark days in the aftermath of France's collapse, when, he claimed, defeatist French generals talked maliciously about how Britain would be next to fall. The Germans, they said, would wring Britain's neck. Churchill, pausing for effect, looked up from his text to stare down the elite of Canada, before spitting out his next words contemptuously: "Some chicken. Some neck." The audience gasped, roared, and lurched to their feet with shouts of joy.

King had been prime minister for more than fifteen years and Churchill for a mere two; nevertheless, Churchill overshadowed King at every turn. But simply being mentioned in the same article or breath—and King was wise enough to introduce Churchill wherever and whenever he could—helped raise the Canadian's profile. Churchill suffered through the press scrums and talks, and especially through King's presence. While he was cordial, and relations had improved between the two men since King's trip to Britain, Churchill's private doctor, Lord Moran, revealed the stark difference in the two leaders: "'The great thing in politics,' said our host later, 'is to avoid mistakes.' I could almost see the P.M. [Churchill] sniffing as Mackenzie King, looking at us through his pince-nez, which were tethered to a button-hole by a long black ribbon, made this pronouncement. King had never been a man to take risks, and this prudent outlook no doubt accounts for some lack of fervour on the P.M.'s part. The two men are, of course, quite friendly, but the P.M. is not really interested in Mackenzie King. He takes him for granted."[13] Churchill tolerated King—although at times he was said to have referred to him as that "little son of a bitch"—but he did not go out of his way to cultivate a close relationship, as he did with Roosevelt, whom he liked despite mistrusting him, and whom he needed to keep arming and supporting Britain.[14]

Perhaps the most lasting legacy of the trip was a photograph. Churchill was garrulous and bad tempered after a long day. Canadian photographer Yousuf Karsh had little time to capture his image. He snapped Churchill and King together, but had only a few more minutes to frame Churchill alone, who was already scowling and looking forward to a much-needed scotch. Karsh was unhappy with the first image. As Churchill continued to glower in his suit and waistcoat, the mischievous Karsh reached over and snatched the cigar from Churchill's jaws. The old man, startled, clamped down his teeth, and gave a sour, determined glare. Churchill's set mouth revealed a grim tenacity and the photograph became one of the iconic images of the Second World War.

The other photographs taken that day never resonated in the same way, although a series of portraits of King and Churchill together captured a certain magic. Both wartime leaders had a hardened look. An innocent observer looking at them might imagine, for a moment, that King and Churchill were cut from the same cloth. In some ways they were, as they grappled with their unified, yet at the same time unique, war efforts.

WHITE CANADIANS HAD A LONG HISTORY of nativism and racism against Asians. Head taxes, riots, and ill will had plagued relations with Chinese and Japanese immigrants, who often were singled out as different, unwanted, and undesired. The war against Japan triggered a new round of persecution against Japanese Canadians in particular, nearly 23,000 of whom lived on the west coast.

King was no friend to Japanese Canadians, even though he had had greater involvement with the "Oriental question" than any politician of his time.[15] In 1907, he had been a commissioner appointed to examine the aftermath of race riots in Vancouver, and he had participated in several commissions that investigated Asian immigration and the opium trade. Although he was not a racist, he was surrounded by several in cabinet, including his friend Ian Mackenzie, who often whispered poisonous words and, at one point, publicly gloated that "there would not be a single Japanese left in British Columbia once the war with Japan ended."[16] While Mackenzie may have influenced the prime minister, more damning to Japanese Canadians was that King had time and time again traded on expediency rather than doing the right thing.

King was, quite simply, willing to sacrifice Japanese Canadians if it meant avoiding conflict with the British Columbia wing of his party. While few MPs stood up in the House of Commons to defend Japanese Canadians against the monstrous slander that was directed against them, King's willingness to let bad things happen to the innocent appears inconsistent with his stated belief in helping the common man, as professed in his 1918 book, *Industry and Humanity*. But more important was the book's message that, wherever possible, strife, disharmony, and discord were to be avoided, and peace was to be sought at almost any price.[17]

In 1942, King offered a few platitudes in his speeches about the need to be aware that naturalized Japanese Canadians had rights, but his sympathy did not lie with the victims.[18] On February 20, the U.S. government announced that Japanese Americans were to be moved inland so that they could not aid a Japanese invasion force. With this example before them, and in the context of the calamitous announcement that the British fortress of Singapore had fallen, Canada followed suit four days later, with an order-in-council requiring all persons of Japanese ancestry living in British Columbia to be moved to isolated towns in the interior.[19] Men, women, and children were rounded up like prisoners, herded into trucks, and driven away. Although a small minority of Japanese Canadians sympathized with Japan—one RCMP report suspected a mere 30 out of 20,000—the vast majority were innocent Canadians. Those few who tried to fight back were put in internment camps.[20]

King also denied entry into the country to Jews who were fleeing persecution in Germany. Canada had a long-standing anti-Semitic immigration policy, and it was not uncommon to hear Jews described as parasites, schemers, subversives, and the dregs from other nations. In the late 1930s, the King administration, urged on by racist public servants and the influential Quebec Catholic Church, refused admittance to desperate Jews fleeing Hitler's repressive regime. Canada had no refugee policy, and consequently no administrative method for identifying those in desperate need.[21] This led to heinous events such as the turning back of the ship M.S. *St. Louis,* which was carrying 937 Jews seeking safety in May 1939. Again, King was not overtly racist, and certainly less bigoted than most white Canadians of his age, but he refused to do anything for these defenceless asylum-seekers, and doing nothing meant consigning 254 of them, including children, to their deaths.[22] For King, it was always easier to do nothing, to sacrifice a minority to satisfy the demands of the majority (except in the case of Quebec), and to avoid conflict by doing the wrong thing.

The relocation of Japanese Canadians remains a stain on Canada's history. In the aftermath of the move, the government sold off Japanese Canadians' property, boats, and household possessions at low prices, an action that was nothing short of criminal.[23] While King could always justify his actions, claiming either to be following the will of the majority or political expediency, it is evident that his ill-treatment of these Canadians caused him little worry.

IN 1942, THE CANADIAN NAVY and its British counterpart were fighting a relentless battle in the Atlantic against the ferocious and skilled U-boats that were sending merchant ships to the bottom at a shocking rate. In the air, Canadians had gone from defending Britain to pressing the offensive against Germany. The bombing campaign was initially ineffective, with air crews rarely hitting specific military targets and suffering extremely high casualty rates; gradually, however, larger bombers, carrying heavier payloads, would deliver greater destruction. Only the army seemed to be without purpose, with some critics sneering that the Canadians in England were a force in waiting, better suited to fighting in bars than in battle. The pressure on King and the cabinet to get the army into action was cranked up as American forces were slated to fight in North Africa at the end of the year.

At home, the factories were producing astonishing quantities of war supplies, and the farms were feeding the Allied armies. In January 1942, King's cabinet agreed to what would be called the "billion-dollar gift," an enormous injection of funds into Britain to help it purchase Canadian-made war materiel. This colossal gift, measured on a per capita basis, exceeded American support provided through Lend-Lease, and lesser though significant Canadian aid was sent to Australia, China, and Russia, the last receiving more than $320 million in goods and war materiel.[24] Tens of millions more dollars were lent over the coming years. King believed that this incredible generosity, on top of Canada's assumption of the financial burden for the overseas RCAF squadrons and its swallowing of most of Britain's cost in the British Commonwealth Air Training Program, was enough to satisfy Canadians of his government's commitment to the war and to reduce the need for an overseas land force. It wasn't. A glum prime minister found that his colleagues, especially Ralston and Macdonald, did not believe that the $1-billion giveaway lessened Canada's moral duty to contribute fighting forces to the Allied war effort.[25] Regardless of the financial contribution, the question of support, as in the Great War, came down to men on the ground.

Much of English Canada was demanding a total war effort, which was usually interpreted as the implementation of conscription, while some French papers, like the influential *Le Devoir*, were at the other end of the spectrum, arguing that the war was imperialistic in nature and that Canada had no place fighting for or against either side.[26] King tried to check such ill-informed sentiments in Quebec, and he found the English-Canadian demand for conscription equally hard to justify, if only because Canada had already shifted to a nearly unlimited war effort, with its contributions significant on all fronts and with no seeming shortage of reinforcements. While King believed that conscription was a fairer way to distribute manpower across military and civilian sectors, he would not go so far as to send men overseas against their will.[27] But feeling the enormous pressure from English Canada and from within his own cabinet, he wondered if he might shift the burden of that decision to Canadians.

When King spoke on the first day of the new session of the Parliament, on January 22, 1942, he committed himself to action. Japan's entry into the war had changed everything. The rumour that Arthur Meighen was considering a return to politics, which terrified King, was another factor that forced him to be aggressive. The governor general, through the government's Speech from the Throne, told Canadians that the Mobilization Act needed to be amended to allow the government to conscript forces for overseas services, should circumstances arise. What those circumstances might entail, he did not make public, but the change to the act was a bold move, and King sought to protect himself from criticism by holding a national plebiscite.

In proposing a plebiscite—a national referendum to release the government from its previous pledge of no conscription—King took the Conservatives' best weapon away from them. However, the price he paid was in splitting his own cabinet, with Ralston and Macdonald on one side, Cardin on the other, and the other ministers divided between them. For King, release from his previous pledge did not necessarily mean that conscription would be immediately invoked. Ralston thought otherwise, believing that a vote in the affirmative freed the government from any manpower constraints, and could be acted on promptly. Here was the heart of the problem. Conscription was a last resort for King, only to be embraced if the Allies were in danger of losing the war; for Ralston, conscription was necessary if the armed forces were in desperate need of reinforcements.[28] King and Ralston were entrenched in positions on opposite sides of an ideological No Man's Land.

As the mechanics for implementing the plebiscite were being prepared, King continued to agonize over his nemesis. Meighen had made up his mind and was running in a by-election in a Conservative safe seat, York South, in Toronto. King hated Meighen, who had repeatedly embarrassed him over the years, often reducing him to sanctimonious gibberish in defence of his party or ideals. In his diary, King used apocalyptic language to describe Meighen's return, which, as he saw it, was "something that was truly vile and bad."[29]

The Liberals decided not to run a candidate against Meighen because that allowed them to avoid splitting the vote with the CCF candidate, Joseph Noseworthy, a high-school teacher. King resigned himself to new scars, taking little solace in reports that Noseworthy was connecting with working-class Torontonians and might stage a spectacular underdog win. On February 9, the unthinkable happened. Meighen was defeated by a wide margin.

It was a shocking reversal, and King was all the more thrilled because Louis St. Laurent was elected in a separate by-election, winning the seat held for decades by Laurier and then Lapointe. In King's mind, St. Laurent was associated in victory with the defeat of his greatest enemy, although God, too, according to King, had played a hand in sparing Canada division and strife under the cancerous thing that was Meighen.

Throughout March and April, the plebiscite remained a hot topic in Canada. While the Liberals tracked the positive commentary in English Canada, the question of releasing the government from its obligation was, not surprisingly, unpopular in Quebec. French-Canadian Liberal MPs treated the subject like a plague, while provincial newspaper editors connected the deaths of Lapointe and Senator Raoul Dandurand (in March 1942) with King's about-face on the conscription issue. "The time was coming when Canadians would realize that they no longer understood one another, that they despised and hated each other, that they forced two nations," remarked one critic of the government's policy.[30] Even with St. Laurent's arrival, the Liberal Party was too quickly burying its French-Canadian leaders.

The plebiscite gave Canadians a stark choice. Most interpreted a "yes" as support for overseas conscription, while "no" meant the government should stick to its promise. In the fiercely contested war of words leading up to the vote, Quebec was singled out in many English newspapers as a province full of slackers. The nation's decision was revealed on April 27. It was, of course, fractured. An overwhelming 64 percent of Canadians were in favour of releasing the government from its promise so that it could prosecute the war more fully, although there were large pockets of resistance, especially in the prairies. But the main dissenting minority was in Quebec, where 71 percent of the total population were against any change in policy, and some 85 percent of French Canadians.[31] A disappointed King, who somehow hoped that French Canada might be convinced of the government's desperate need for manoeuvring room on the question of manpower, shrank from the thought of isolating Quebec. While he had a mandate that freed him to act, King believed that to invoke conscription for overseas service simply because the majority had voted for it would, in Lord Durham's famous phrase, reduce English and French to "two nations warring in the bosom of a single state."[32] King delayed his decision, but much of English Canada, soon confused and then angry, lambasted him over his calculated inaction.

The plebiscite led to Bill 80, which would codify the changes to the Mobilization Act. It also set the warring factions against each other in the cabinet. Cardin and the Quebec wing wanted nothing do with Bill 80, which had been introduced to the House on May 11, while Ralston and his supporters, who included much of the influential Ontario wing, demanded the immediate introduction of overseas conscription, now that they had the legal and moral authority to move forward. Why waste time with a bill that released the government from the terms of a previous bill, Ralston argued, when a majority of Canadians had just voted in favour of this release? During these acrimonious debates, long-time critic of conscription T.A. Crerar, a minister in Borden's Unionist government and former leader of the Progressives, abandoned his anti-conscription stance, believing that all available men would be needed to win the war, and backed Ralston and Macdonald.

In early May, Cardin, already sick, claimed that the tension was too much for him to bear. The plebiscite had whittled away his influence in Quebec. He would not join the ranks of French-Canadian pariahs from Borden's previous government, men who could not walk down the streets of their hometown without fearing bodily harm. He resigned on May 9, despite King's pleading. Cardin played the good soldier for a while, but later attacked King and the party during the next round of the conscription crisis.

During the rancorous discussion, debates, and posturing over Bill 80, few MPs avoided the chance to leave their opinion on record. A great deal of passion and fury was expended by both sides. King's own contribution on June 10 was safe and unemotional. But he agonized over the reaction to it by the opposition and by members of his own party, especially Ralston, who, King felt, was preparing a broadside against him. In the course of his speech, King let drop the most famous political statement in Canadian history, "Not necessarily conscription, but conscription if necessary," which epitomized his habitual caution, obliqueness, and lack of commitment.[33] It was a perfectly Kingian statement, but it also reflected accurately his feeling on the complex subject. While others had the luxury of preening and staking out their territory, King was constrained by his own nature and by the desire to avoid upsetting any of the competing groups in his party, or society at large. His goal, as one contemporary observed, was to "hold off the evil day as long as possible."[34]

The Liberals survived the debates and Bill 80 passed on July 7, but they had paid for it with blood. Quebec felt betrayed, and forty-five French-speaking Liberal MPs voted against the bill. English Canada was braying for action. Cardin was gone, and Ralston, in demanding that conscription be brought in immediately, twice offered his resignation, the second time leaving his letter with King. The obstinate defence minister relented in response to King's pleading, but he would not let the matter of conscription drop, and his relationship with the prime minister was poisoned. King had survived another near fatal blow, guided by his patience and by political skills that allowed him to find the narrow common ground, even if occupying it had left him open to attack from opposition and friends and made him appear waffling and indecisive. The passing of Bill 80 freed King's hands for future action, but invoking conscription, in his mind, would still bring on "civil war."[35] King hunkered down and prepared for future battles over manpower. Few would call him a warlord, but Canada was very different from Germany or Britain, and it needed a different type of war leader, one who could manage the domestic pressure of an increasingly disunited nation.

KING AND CANADA WERE THROWN into a new crisis in August 1942, when elements of the 2nd Canadian Division launched a major amphibious assault on the French coastal town of Dieppe. The Americans had been pressing the British to mount a cross-channel invasion: they were anxious to start fighting the Germans in strength in order to draw pressure off the Russian forces that were struggling against most of the German armies. Churchill and his senior staff regarded the idea as bad and mad, all their military appreciations suggesting that a lack of aircraft, firepower, landing craft, and a host of other deficiencies, from force structure to training, would leave any assault in bloody tatters on the French shore. The British argued for a continuation of the fighting in North Africa and of the strategic bombing campaign to wear down civilian morale, slow arms production, and force the Germans to draw back military resources from the Eastern Front to defend their cities.

King had few qualms about taking the battle to the German heartland, though from the start of the war he had believed that Canada's enemy was Hitler, not the German people. They were "slaves" to a militaristic government.[36] But he also knew that the hard hand of war had to be levelled against the German population before their war machine, run by millions of civilians and slave workers, could be broken. As the waves of bombers pounding the enemy cities reached a crescendo, King wrote: "... a concentrated bombing of Germany from the air by a tremendous force will probably be more effective in the end than any invasion of Europe ... Their people can be reduced to a state of terror through superior air forces."[37] While King fretted over the deaths of civilians, he would rather see Germans killed than Canadians. In this, he was surely siding with the vast majority—perhaps all but the most pacifist—of Canadians.

Canadian forces had been in England for almost three years, and the Canadian public, as well as many soldiers, were anxious to join the fighting. When Lieutenant-General Harry Crerar, then in temporary command of the Canadian Corps in England, caught wind that the British were planning an amphibious operation, he told them the Canadians sought some role in the raid.[38] Attack formations of the 2nd Division were trained vigorously over the summer months to prepare them for a water-borne assault. The operation, code-named Rutter, was scrubbed in early July because of poor weather and because German air attacks on the raid's ships had compromised the mission's secrecy.

But within a few weeks, Lord Louis Mountbatten, commander of the Combined Operations Headquarters, which had organized the raids, reinstated the operation, now known as Jubilee. On August 19, 1942, close to 5,000 Canadians frontally assaulted the heavily defended port of Dieppe and contiguous beaches with the intention of surprising the enemy, causing havoc, and then retreating before the Germans counterpunched. There were problems from the start. The RAF refused to send heavy bombers to pound Dieppe for fear that the airmen would suffer high casualties from the ground defences, and because of inter-service rivalries. The Royal Navy, too, was worried about losing its prize battleships, and therefore held most of them back. When the infantry touched down on the beaches, they ran into concentrated fire, often from enemy strongpoints situated on the high cliffs overlooking the open ground. As the Germans built up a hurricane of small arms, artillery, and mortar fire, the Canadians were slaughtered in the kill zone. Only 2,200 Canadians returned to England: 907 had been killed, 586 wounded, and 1,946 were taken prisoner.

King and his closest advisors knew nothing of the raid in advance: they were advised of the operation after the Canadians were committed to battle, and then received only a cautious message to the effect that the casualties had been heavy. A worried King noted in his diary: "one felt inclined to question the wisdom of the raid."[39] Two days later, on the 21st, as the media did its best to put a positive spin on the disaster, King noted grimly that the terrible loss of life "makes me sad at heart."[40] King believed that the debacle was another sign that the Canadian army should be kept from combat until the decisive moment. Ralston and the generals had been pressing for a more active role, but King continued to believe that the wiser course was to stay far from battle. A few months later, in December 1942, Ralston despaired:

"If the war ended now we would have to hang our heads in shame."[41] King did not see it this way. With the enormous exertions at home and with the navy and air force actively engaged in operations, King was not looking for another battle. He knew, even as he desired to put the brake on more reckless operations, that the army, navy, and air force would have much hard fighting and sustain cruel casualties before Germany was defeated.

CHAPTER 16

MAN WITH A MISSION, 1943–1944

While the country was still licking its collective wounds from Dieppe and fearing for the nearly 2,000 soldiers imprisoned in Nazi Germany, Canadians continued to do their part for the war effort. Canadian industry under Howe's direction was producing mountains of guns, ships, planes, and all manner of war supplies, and with compulsory military training, Canada was on a firm war footing. Limited liability was a distant memory. King, however, worried that the nation's resources were stretched too thin, with much of its army and air force, and most of its modern destroyers, overseas or committed to fierce battles.

The Dominion's vulnerability was revealed when U-boats penetrated the St. Lawrence River in early May 1942, sinking ships in the very heart of the country. Britain was desperate for even more of Canada's warships to protect American and British soldiers being ferried across the oceans to invade North Africa, and the RCN was further weakened when it agreed to send seventeen badly needed corvettes to support the operation. As U-boats continued to sink ships in Canadian waters throughout the summer, rumours abounded in Quebec that Ottawa had deliberately left the St. Lawrence vulnerable to punish French Canada.[1] Reeling from the losses, and lacking war vessels to hunt the U-boats, the government closed the St. Lawrence to ocean shipping on September 9, 1942, constricting trade significantly. While this appeared to be a stunning defeat for the navy, more sophisticated anti-submarine tactics and the increased deployment of bomber patrols gradually drove the U-boats from Canadian to American coastal waters where the pickings were easier.[2]

A few months later, in December, the RCN was pulled from North Atlantic convoy duty to rest the battered crews, re-equip the ships with modern sonar, and provide time for much-needed training. These actions were critical to relieving the overtaxed RCN, but there was no denying that, under the Canadian watch, more merchant ships had been lost in 1942 than when the better-equipped British or American navies escorted them across the Atlantic. The numbers were damning: by late 1942, 35 percent of the Allied escorts involved in the North Atlantic were Canadian, and the convoys they escorted suffered some 80 percent of Allied shipping losses in the last six months of that year.[3] The closing of the St. Lawrence, and to a lesser extent the temporary removal of the RCN escorts from convoy duty, along with the low number of RCN-attributed U-boat kills, meant that King could not rely on the navy, as he had hoped, to produce large-scale public relations victories. The navy's failure added moral fervour to the public's demand that the Dominion's other forces take the fight to the enemy.

Meanwhile, Ilsley struggled constantly to find ways to pay for the war. He was not helped by King, whose dislike of his tenacious minister hampered cooperation. King's attitude sprang partly from the debilitating insecurity that led him to mistrust competitors, and partly from a self-serving conviction that his colleagues suffered from deep inadequacies of character or performance. Despite King's hostility, Ilsley laboured day and night to find new ways to keep almost a million men and women in uniform; hundreds of warships, fighter planes, and bombers in action; and five overseas divisions of infantry and armour in play. Canada's incredibly generous $1-billion gift to the United Kingdom was followed by a mutual aid program that saw the transfer of another $2 billion in munitions and food, an act that put even greater pressure on the Canadian economy. Corporate taxes jumped from 18 to 40 percent in 1943, with excessive profits taxed almost at 100 percent.[4] That same year, Ilsley's March 2 budget raised personal taxes to their highest level, with upper-middle-class Canadians paying up to 47.6 percent of their incomes to Ottawa.[5] Ilsley squeezed more blood from stone, raising $12.5 billion by selling War Loans and Victory Bonds, most of which were held by Canadians. The defence ministers and Howe were generally not interested in financial problems, focusing instead on their own expanding fiefdoms. Ilsley was on his own, although he succeeded beyond all expectations and the Dominion remained on solid financial footing.

If finance was an ongoing challenge, manpower problems seemed insurmountable. In mid April, Ralston and Howe were again battling in the war committee over the allocation of the dwindling number of men for the army or industry. This was a struggle that would continue intermittently for the next two years. With most men and women working in various sectors across the economy, there were fewer Canadians available to go into the forces. A frustrated Howe raged that there was already a shortage of essential workers in the mining and forestry sectors, and that coal and steel production were in critical danger of not meeting their quota, all of which would curtail the output of Canadian war materiel.[6] Though King's preference was to side with Howe, he felt constrained in doing so openly because of his respect for Ralston, but also because any reduction of the army would be viewed by his enemies as evidence that he was "soft" on the war.[7] The dispute raged on for several weeks, with King mediating and delaying, ensuring that the bad will never erupted into internecine warfare, although it took its toll. Around this time, journalist Grant Dexter described the cabinet as "burnt out men."[8]

With his own cabinet disintegrating under the pressure, King refused to heed the calls by the newspapers or the opposition to bring Tories or CCFers into the government. King was a conciliator, but he was also deeply partisan. Like his grandfather, who fought against the Tories of his day, he hated Conservatives with a deeply ingrained passion. His outlook can be traced to his university education and the belief in liberal values and ideals that he acquired during his studies. Over the years, his commitment to liberalism had become almost evangelical: he was convinced that the Liberal Party had a historic mission to harmonize society, and that the other political entities were divisive in nature, outlook, and policy.[9] He kept the opposition parties out of his government, even though he was often condemned for putting petty politics before full commitment to winning the war. His self-belief allowed him to withstand it all. "I have defeated all their machinations," he gloated in the summer of 1943.[10]

IN MARCH 1943, King and the war cabinet were informed by Lieutenant-General Kenneth Stuart, chief of the general staff, that the invasion of Europe had been put off a year. The British had convinced the Americans to wait until sufficient resources and firepower could reduce the enemy's strongpoints in order to avoid the likelihood of another slaughter of Dieppe proportions. Instead, the Allies, having driven the German forces out of North Africa, would pursue a new front in the Mediterranean. With General McNaughton having famously remarked in October 1941 that the Canadian army was the "dagger pointed at the heart of Berlin," many believed that now was the time to use the blade.[11] Ralston, of course, wanted the army to participate in the new campaign, especially as the late-arriving Yanks had successfully fought in North-Western Africa as part of Operation Torch while the Canadians had continued to stew in England. King offered a withering assessment: "all our generals were concerned about was to be in at the kill," and he wanted Ralston to push back against the senior army command.[12] Ralston would not, and continued to press the prime minister for Canadian involvement.

King fretted over Ralston's and Stuart's drive for Canadian inclusion in a new theatre of war, but he positively recoiled at Ralston's suggestion that he raise the matter with Churchill. Here King was at his worst, refusing to intervene with the British to put Canadians in the campaign, because such action, in his words, "goes the whole length of placing me in the position, as head of the Canadian Government, of settling the strategy so far as Canadian troops are concerned."[13] This, surely, was one of King's stranger wartime statements, but he continued to cringe at the idea of having any involvement in setting the Allied strategy. In fact, King kept his military advisors at arm's length throughout much of the war. Unlike Churchill, who relied heavily on his chief of the imperial general staff, Sir Alan Brooke, King had avoided the military brass, as he always believed that any advice was part of an unspoken policy to garner glory for Canada but leave the nation exposed to conscription. His habit of backing away from any strategic involvement was unheroic to say the least and he refused to act in a way that allowed others to pin a single strategic decision on him. However, with regard to the army being committed to a new theatre of war, he sent out signals indicating that he would not be opposed to contributing a Canadian division to the forthcoming operation.[14]

Now that Canadians were irrevocably committed to fighting, there was no way to avoid loss of life. A chiefs-of-staff briefing to the war committee on June 18, 1943, predicted 115,000 Canadian casualties over the next sixteen months, the majority to be suffered by the army. "No word I have thus far heard," wrote King, "caused me a greater pain in my heart than the thought all of this implied in the lives of the men serving in the Army, and to our young country."[15] The distressing briefing was a firm indication to King that Canada would not get out of the war without heavy losses; equally troubling, such predictions of casualties might also negate the promises of the military men that the government would not have to turn to conscription.[16]

The Allies landed in southern Sicily almost unopposed on July 10, 1943. Fierce fighting developed over the next six weeks, however, as British, American, and Canadian forces marched north through the dust and heat, engaging German forces—and accepting the surrender of Italians—among the poverty-stricken Sicilians. Lack of water made life in the field miserable, while malaria laid low thousands. The Canadians were bloodied in battles at Valguarnera, Leonforte, and Agira, although they fought well in a harsh environment against a skilled enemy. But for King, what apparently mattered most was not that the Canadians had proven their mettle or that they had suffered 2,310 casualties, of whom 562 were killed in action; his chief concern was more about the credit given to Canada at the start of the operation.

For some time, King had been angered by Churchill's habit of speaking almost solely about British forces, and either ignoring the contributions of the dominions or to simply subsume them within the Empire's war effort. While King continued to see Churchill as "the one man who had saved the British Empire," and understood Churchill's need to counterbalance the American war machine by showing the Empire as a unified force, he agonized over his counterpart's reluctance to share information with the dominions and his rare acknowledgment of Canadian accomplishments.[17] This high-handedness enraged King, but he never pressed Churchill to change, his inclination being to sniff a little and to assume that his quiet sighs would be picked up by the British warlord. Often they were not, or they were ignored. King interpreted this obstinacy as the long-standing superciliousness adopted by the British with respect to their supposed inferiors. In 1943, he focused considerable attention on the perceived affronts, which left his government more vulnerable to the slightly rejuvenated opposition.

The ugly issue of recognition had revealed itself most forcefully at the time of the invasion of Sicily. A few days before the landing, the Canadians saw an advance copy of the official announcement and were shocked that it mentioned only that the United States and United Kingdom were committing troops to battle. King and Ralston complained that there was no reference to Canada, but the cagey British, claiming the need for secrecy, refused to commit to an amendment. Behind the scenes, the Canadian high commissioner to London, Vincent Massey, worked his connections and they were sympathetic.[18] But Massey's intervention was either not communicated to King or Ralston, or was lost in a flurry of telegrams, and the two Canadian war leaders remained indignant. Canada was pushing itself to the extreme, sending men, materiel, and billions in cash to Britain, but was getting little recognition in return. Minor insults over the Sicily landing became the focus of pent-up rage.

The cabinet ordered special delegates to Washington to impress upon the Americans the need for inclusion in the announcement, and while King waited he fumed to his diary about the difference between the British and Americans: "Was it any wonder that our people ... were antagonized at the English, and were beginning to be more and more friendly with the Americans?"[19] Roosevelt, however, was less helpful than King had hoped: he informed the Dominion representatives that he could not mention the Canadians, if the British, or the commander in the field, General Dwight Eisenhower, cited security reasons. Ralston urged King to press Churchill, but a placid, even compliant King, seemingly satisfied at having made his point, left his outrage on record and did not press matters further. He should have. As Lester Pearson was to sneer privately, King's meekness was akin to "the strong glove over the velvet hand."[20]

Throughout the day of the July 10 invasion, news flashes from Britain and the United States were picked up by Canadian newsrooms, which called on King for a comment. The British had, in fact, announced Canadian participation, but somehow this had not been communicated to King, who was still labouring under the assumption that he could not talk to the press about the Canadian part in the invasion. So when the inquiries came in, the humiliated King was forced to scurry for cover and pretend to be out of reach of his secretaries. Later in the day, after being informed that Roosevelt had highlighted Canadian involvement, a relieved King offered a public speech. King had been right to demand that Canada receive recognition, and he smouldered in the incident's aftermath, brooding over having to beg for scraps from the foot of the masters' table. None of this boded well for Canada's role in the North Atlantic Triangle, as mediator between Britain and the United States.

THE CONFUSION OVER THE ANNOUNCEMENT of the Sicily invasion had resulted in a significant strain in the relationship between Canada and Britain, but there was an opportunity to ease tension a few weeks later when Churchill and Roosevelt descended for a second time on Quebec in August 1943. Where once Canada and King had played a role in bringing together the great powers, now the discussion between the United States and Britain was closed to outside parties. King accepted the exclusion, and he well knew that Canada could not expect (and indeed he did not want) any influence over the Allies' grand strategy. Nonetheless, the Canadian prime minister would prosper politically from hosting the event and from being seen with his famous friends, who generally went out of their way to ensure that he was photographed with them. Still, he wailed privately about the unfortunate tendency of many Canadians to call Churchill and Roosevelt "our leaders."[21]

While King and his military staff were only on the periphery of these important meetings, even being on the fringe meant that secrets were heard and high-level discussions revealed. Churchill had convinced the Americans to move the fighting front from liberated Sicily to the Italian mainland, a theatre of battle he termed the "soft underbelly of Europe." Most of the Canadian generals expected King to avoid another commitment, but he was now a convert to the Mediterranean campaign, especially as casualties had been fairly low in Sicily. His personal justification for supporting the continuing campaign, however, revealed his poor understanding of the Allied high command's strategy. He wrote on October 21, for instance, that he thought it a good idea for the Canadians to fight in Italy to get some experience, but also so that when the "main assault comes" on Europe, "instead of our men bearing the brunt of the assault it will be divided between British, Americans, and ourselves."[22] At no time would anyone in Allied planning have thought to send only the Canadians in to reclaim Europe. Perhaps King, who recoiled at even knowing what his army was doing let alone asking for influence over it, was conflating the memory of Dieppe with the prospect of other dreaded amphibious landings. Whatever the case, over the coming months, an armoured division and corps headquarters would be added to form a Canadian Corps in Italy.[23] But this splitting of the Canadian army led to friction with the army commander, General A.G.L. McNaughton, who wanted to ensure a unified fighting force for the eventual invasion of Europe and worried about an increase in casualties if his army fought in two theatres of war.

There had been significant hostility between McNaughton and Ralston in the previous months. McNaughton bristled at Ralston's micromanagement of the army, remarking intemperately that he "had to get permission to blow [his] nose from Ralston," and, later, when intemperance became insubordination, he told journalists that the minister was unfit to oversee the army, because he lost sight of the big picture by meddling in the army's operations.[24] There were other problems. McNaughton was a popular leader, but the British felt that he had never mastered command of a corps, let alone an army. Moreover, his fierce defence of Canadian national interests, especially his insistence that the army fight together, infuriated the British. From early 1943, and especially after McNaughton's perceived failure in Spartan—a large training exercise in which the Canadians showed significant problems in staff work and logistical planning—the British chief of the imperial general staff, General Sir Alan Brooke, actively undermined McNaughton with the Canadian government.[25] Ralston saw no reason to support the Dominion's troublesome and beleaguered general overseas.

By December 1943, the overmatched McNaughton resigned and was eventually replaced by General Harry Crerar. The King government knew Crerar intimately, although he had been severely criticized when he was chief of the general staff for advocating that Canadian forces garrison the Hong Kong colony and subsequently for agreeing to Canadian involvement in the Dieppe operation. He was also a little too brazen in seeking McNaughton's job, his naked ambition separated only a hairsbreadth from disloyalty. Crerar would prove a competent army commander, although more of a manager than a warrior. His command style ensured that he was overshadowed by the monstrous egos of other Allied senior commanders, such as the British field marshal, Bernard Montgomery, or the American general, George Patton, just as King was diminished in comparison to Churchill and Roosevelt. Crerar's methodical if unglamorous ways should have made him a natural ally of King, but the prime minister viewed him with suspicion because Crerar was the architect of the "big army" concept and so, by implication, a potential proponent of conscription. He would be watched.

AS THE WAR DRAGGED INTO its fourth year, general anxiety among Canadians deepened. Luxury goods disappeared from the stores. A thriving black market made meat, liquor, and other commodities available, but only to those who could afford them.[26] There was a housing shortage in most major urban centres as rural Canadians moved there for jobs, with the lack of building materials and workers keeping new housing starts to a minimum.[27] The scarcity of housing became so critical that the King government had to intervene, but the issue was never satisfactorily resolved, and many Canadians were crowded into small and overpriced dwellings.

Labour disputes were increasingly bitter. King found himself pitted against his powerful ministers, especially the no-nonsense Howe, who ran industry hard with his "dollar-a-year men." In early January 1943, King felt "left alone" in cabinet "to debate the side of the workers," and worried that the coarsening effects of the war were hardening the party and dragging it towards the ideological camp of the hated Tories.[28] There were several strikes throughout this period that Howe wanted to break by using either police or legislation, but King sought to temper his minister's desire to smash rather than work with labour. The workers' unrest that peaked in 1943 was eased when the King government set up a new labour relations board and, in February 1944, passed an order-in-council that recognized the rights of workers to organize and engage in collective bargaining in federally regulated industries.[29] This was a monumental achievement in labour relations and would be the legislative foundation for much of organized labour's resurgence in the twentieth century.

King made advances for workers, but he was increasingly frustrated by the party's gradual repudiation of his core values. With the Liberals as the nation's war party, the CCF was pushing its way from the far left closer to the centre, and opinion polls in the summer of 1943 revealed them to be passing the Liberals in popularity.[30] A Gallup poll of the same year found that a surprising 71 percent of Canadians responded that they wanted to "see great reforms in this country after the war," while another reported that Canadians faced the uncertain postwar future with a "feeling akin to dread."[31] King saw the signs and acted aggressively.

King urged the war cabinet to instigate a series of social policies to aid the most needy across the nation. Most of his ministers, seeing these measures as a way to keep the CCF down and the Tories out, and to reward Canadians at the same time, were open to King's policy shift, although almost all were too busy guiding their massive departments to devote much energy to the seemingly distant future. It was King, with his eyes on the next election, who refused to let his plans for a social security network languish.

The fighting, of course, was far from being over, and countless families were grieving. King felt this pain, too, for in September 1943, his brother Max's son, Surgeon Lieutenant William Lyon Mackenzie King II, was killed while serving on the destroyer HMCS *St. Croix*. King was shocked by the loss of his nephew, whose death epitomized for him the waste of youth in war. After absorbing the terrible news on September 27, King gave an emotional speech to his colleagues, imploring them "to keep uppermost in their minds ... the men who were giving their lives at sea, on land and in the air and the homes and families from which they came."[32]

While King was rarely viewed as a friend to the Canadian combatants overseas, he believed a debt was owed to those who risked their lives for their country. He was also aware of their collective voting clout in a postwar Canada. Was he a political opportunist or simply a leader who believed that the veterans should be rewarded? Probably he was both, but in his public addresses and private reflections, he genuinely desired to support veterans. At a Liberal caucus meeting before his nephew's death, he had spoken forcefully about the need "of giving first place in everything to the man who was offering his life voluntarily for the service of his country," and throughout the summer and fall he fretted over what could be done for overseas service personnel and their families.[33]

While there had been a committee on reconstruction since March 1941, King believed that a new department was required to ensure the smooth transition from war to peace, and to guide the airmen, sailors, soldiers, and other personnel back into the civilian working ranks. Early in the new year, on January 11, 1944, the cabinet agreed to set up three new departments: reconstruction, veterans affairs, and national health and welfare. The indomitable Howe would manage reconstruction, while the cheerful scallywag Ian Mackenzie took veterans affairs, and the up-and-comer Brooke Claxton—a Great War veteran and forward-thinking MP from Montreal—received national health and welfare. King sought to avoid the chaos of 1919 and the failure of the Borden government to properly reward veterans.

King wasn't waiting until after the war to prepare Canada for the peace. "Men who have fought in this war, and others who have borne its privations and sufferings, will never be satisfied with a return to the conditions which prevailed before 1939," he told an audience at midpoint in the war.[34] The next year, in March 1943, he was encouraged and inspired by the Marsh Report, known officially as "The Report on Social Security for Canada," by the committee on reconstruction. Dr. L.C. Marsh, a director of social policy research at McGill University, echoed similar studies in the United Kingdom and the United States when he advocated for a compassionate government to care for all members of society, arguing for security against sickness, old age, unemployment, and a child allowance for families. Many of these progressive ideas reflected notions described in *Industry and Humanity*, at least in King's mind, and he saw in them an opportunity to fulfill his life's work. While it took time for King to warm to the idea—he told a close aide at one point that family allowances would be a greater threat to national unity than any other measure he could think of except conscription—he eventually pushed hard for the program that created a minimum monthly payout to Canadian families of $5 to $8 per child, depending on age.[35] Ralston, Macdonald, and Ilsley were uninterested in the social program, while Crerar and Howe were dead set against what became known as the "baby bonus," but most of the cabinet was supportive. In addition to its political utility in stealing thunder from the left, they understood that the program offered some relief from the wage ceiling, and would serve as a monthly reminder that it was a Liberal government that was issuing the cheques to keep Canada prosperous. As J.W. Pickersgill told one reporter, "We are going to the left and with a vengeance."[36] The program came with the enormous price tag of $200 million and posed a major organizational challenge in setting up a national registry for 3.5 million children.[37] This would have been an insurmountable challenge before the war, but with the expanded federal bureaucracy, and the country at full employment, it was now possible. As King told the House of Commons a few months later, "The new order is not going to have things done as charity. What is to be done will be done as a matter of right."[38]

When King faced opposition to his proposed policy in the cabinet, he did not seek unanimity as he did on almost all other matters. In promoting his social agenda, he saw himself "as a man with a mission" and bullied and blasted his way forward.[39] With his experience, skill, and passion, he imposed his will on the many powerful ministers who were lined up against the legislation.[40] In the end, as King suspected, the opposing ministers did not feel strongly enough to resign over the family allowance legislation. On January 27, 1944, King unveiled his new social policy. It was good for Canadians and would inject money into the postwar economy at the grassroots, and it put those funds in the hands of mothers, to whom the cheques were sent (except in Quebec, where they went to husbands).[41] This was another coup for King and the Liberals. From mid-1943, King's wartime strategy was a postwar strategy, one through which he sought to fulfill his "life work."[42] He would win the war and then he would win the peace.

KING HAD REMARKABLE STAMINA for a man of his age, but he was always very cautious about overextending himself. He took naps every day and slept regularly in his single bed, rarely having an interrupted night. Although he had given up alcohol for the duration of the war (and backslid only a few times), he ate heavily—some said like a glutton—and was then forced to exercise out of guilt. Usually the exercise took the form of calisthenics undertaken in the morning or at night and involved stretching and light exertion. He continued to read voraciously in his book-lined study, with its dark wood and bearskin rug, where he was always overseen by the illuminated portrait of his mother. King was a bibliophile, and even during the war he tracked down rare books or wrote to authors for signed copies of their work. He had read or thumbed through most of the 2,500 books in his collection. History, politics, literature, and poetry excited his imagination, as well as official government publications and self-help books, although not novels.[43] A careful and thoughtful reader, King was often moved by relevant or poignant passages, to which he drew attention with pencilled vertical lines along the margins. While he read his Bible every day, there is little evidence that he ever picked up a military history or work on strategy during the course of the war.

His diary remained his private duty. He dictated entries to his loyal secretary, J. Edouard Handy, at the close of every day. The multi-page entries must have taken the good part of an hour, and perhaps longer, but it was his ritual. And he had his other yearnings. Anxious and overworked, King continued to seek spiritual and supernatural assistance, hungering for meaning in everyday occurrences. His diary is filled with portents and symbols. He constantly saw significance in the way clock-face hands lined up or the pattern formed by tea leaves in a cup. In these signs, he drew reassurance from beyond this world, encouraging him to go forward despite the crushing and difficult questions he faced daily.[44] In just one of many examples, John Diefenbaker was with a group of concerned Conservatives who went to King's office in June 1940 when they heard that Paris had fallen to the Germans. They found King in his office—he had slept there overnight. When they questioned him about the rumours, the pyjama-clad prime minister read the dispatches and confirmed their fears. But, as Diefenbaker described, King calmly "stepped towards the fire-place on the east wall of the office, his eyes fixed on the mantel clock. There was silence. I was standing beside him. He turned to me, 'Diefenbaker, we can't lose. We shall win the war.' It was twenty after ten."[45] King had seen something in the clock face. Diefenbaker, in turn, found something equally deep, although far more disturbing, in King's moony face.

Clocks, tea leaves, and visions offered comfort, but so too did his dog, Pat. Even after the canine passed away, King believed that its spirit watched over him. While allowances can be made for King and his need for spiritual support, his heartfelt conviction that the spirits were looking out for him and that he was being guided by unseen forces reveal a neurotic and lonely man. King met with fewer mediums, clairvoyants, palm readers, and fortune tellers during the war years, due to his heavy workload, but he could not deny himself completely, and these sessions helped to soothe him. At the same time, he knew there was danger in consulting mediums. He was under more scrutiny from the press now, and he had more enemies too. If his spiritual search had ever been revealed to the public, he would have suffered devastating criticism.

King continued to spend time at Kingsmere. He had first visited the property, which was about 12 kilometres as the crow flies from Parliament Hill, in 1900 and he had bought it shortly thereafter. He added to the estate over time, and soon formed

A determined and resolute Sir Robert Borden, who has emerged as Canada's warlord.

LIBRARY AND ARCHIVES CANADA, PA-117660

A young William Lyon Mackenzie King stands by his venerable and venerated leader, Sir Wilfrid Laurier. King's support of Laurier during the 1917 election laid the foundation for his own control of the party over the coming decades.

LIBRARY AND ARCHIVES CANADA, C018586[1]

William Lyon Mackenzie King sitting for a formal portrait after capturing the leadership of the Liberal Party in 1919.

LIBRARY AND ARCHIVES CANADA, A028137[1]

LIBRARY AND ARCHIVES CANADA, PA119007

An uncomfortable-looking W.L.M. King standing by Nazi officials at an event in Berlin. In June 1937, King visited the Nazi dictator, Adolf Hitler, to persuade him to abandon his aggression towards his neighbours. Hitler received King politely, but utterly ignored his suggestion of taking the path to peace.

King stands with his friend and long-time Quebec lieutenant, Ernest Lapointe, at a celebration of the twentieth anniversary of his leadership of the Liberal Party in 1939.

LIBRARY AND ARCHIVES CANADA, C-024720

This 1939 cartoon conveys the pathetic state of the Canadian military through a hockey analogy. Canada found itself at war, but grossly unprepared for the "big game."

AUTHOR'S COLLECTION

This poster captures the sentiment of most Canadians in 1939: "It's our war." While many Canadians were still deeply linked to Britain, Canada would fight as an ally, not a colony.

AUTHOR'S COLLECTION

King in his book-lined study staring reverentially at a portrait of his mother. King believed that she watched over him from the spirit world.

LIBRARY AND ARCHIVES CANADA, C-075053

LIBRARY AND ARCHIVES CANADA, A152440

WHERE'S JOE? M965.199.4567 © McCORD MUSEUM

TOP: The prime minister was uncomfortable with carrying out inspections like these and with giving speeches to military personnel.
ABOVE: This cartoon captures King as an insignificant little boy trying to break into the grown-up conversation of cigarette-smoking American president Franklin D. Roosevelt and cigar-chomping British prime minister Winston Churchill. The cartoon reflected the harsh reality that Canada was pushed out of most discussions between the Americans and the British following the United States' entry into the war as an ally in December 1941.

LIBRARY AND ARCHIVES CANADA, C014171

LIBRARY AND ARCHIVES CANADA, C031186

TOP: Canadian soldiers are marched into captivity after the disastrous Dieppe raid of August 19, 1942. King and his cabinet had exercised no control over the raid and the prime minister believed it revealed the army high command's recklessness.
ABOVE: Roosevelt, King, and Churchill at the Citadel in Quebec City during the August 1943 Quadrant Conference. Although the Canadians hosted the event, they were excluded from the high-level strategic talks. But King showed political wisdom in being photographed with the recognizable Western wartime leaders.

LIBRARY AND ARCHIVES CANADA, PA-132649

AUTHOR'S COLLECTION

TOP: Minister of National Defence J.L. Ralston greeting a Canadian soldier in England. King and Ralston became fierce opponents during the war, as Ralston supported the need for a large army and conscription.
ABOVE: American-published *True Comics* featured W.L.M. King in this May 1942 issue. "King of Canada" was the most famous Canadian of his day and rightly noted as a good friend to the United States.

This 2004 Aislin drawing of W.L.M. King portrays a strong figure and reveals a nuanced appreciation of Canada's longest-serving prime minister. King may have been a scallywag, but, as the glint in his eye reveals, he was also much more.

an obsession with stone ruins, which he gathered, in pieces or whole, from rundown estates across Ottawa and the Dominion. He placed stone gnomes, donkeys, and rabbits along the treeline or had them poking out among the crumbling stone monuments that dotted the landscape. "The Temple" and the "Abbey Ruin" were two of his favourite ruins, and he continually acquired more over time, using his influence to gather and collect all manner of oddities. He even harassed the very able and busy Lester Pearson, while he was first secretary in the Canadian High Commission in London, sending him secret telegrams that revealed after decoding that he wanted relics from the wreck of Westminster Hall after it had been bombed. Pearson was forced to use his connections, no doubt sighing deeply, to acquire the broken stone for his prime minister.[46]

"In his personal relations with people," wrote T.A. Crerar, "Mr. King could be affable and agreeable, but there was always a barrier across which no one was invited. And so in the sanctum of his heart he was a lonely man."[47] King lamented his isolation from friends and family, and had increasingly become "conscious of the loneliness which years can bring."[48] While he enjoyed being on his own during the few breaks from his busy duties, it is more than a little sad to think of William Lyon Mackenzie King alone in Laurier House, where neighbours reported hearing him singing hymns at night, his warbling voice reverberating throughout the empty halls.

ONE OF KING'S MOST PRESSING CONCERNS was the close integration of American and Canadian military forces on Dominion soil. The Permanent Joint Board on Defence had been tasked with organizing a plan to meet the chaotic situation should Britain be overrun in an amphibious assault, which would have seen strategic control of Canadian forces pass to the Americans. But after Britain's survival in late 1940, a second plan, labelled ABC-22, witnessed the Americans pressing for strategic control of Canadian forces on both coasts. Much to his credit, and in an effort that no doubt required him to screw up his courage to the sticking point, King refused Roosevelt and the American brass the right to command Canadian military forces in the defence of North America.

This the Americans accepted with ill grace. However, to placate the United States in its desire to secure the west coast against Japanese invasions, and to support isolated Alaska, Ottawa agreed to the construction of a new road to link the most northern state to those south of the forty-ninth parallel. The Americans promised to take care of everything. The project cost close to $150 million and brought a welcome injection of capital and infrastructure, but it also caused concern as thousands of friendly invaders poured across the border. The Americans went too far when their soldiers answered the phones with the cheeky greeting, "army of occupation."[49] After Malcolm MacDonald prodded King to be a little more wary of the American presence on Canadian soil, the prime minister insisted that Canada pay the lion's share of costs and reclaim control over its sovereign territory.[50] King spoke forcefully in late 1942 of ensuring that the United States did not drag Canada into its orbit: "I want to see Canada continue to develop as a nation to be, in time, as our country certainly will, the greatest of nations of the British Commonwealth."[51] He continued to be worried about this to the end of the war and beyond. Canada was growing up quickly, and it had to take responsibility for its own borders and how it would manoeuvre within the alliance against Hitler.

King's defence of Canadian sovereignty showed leadership, but he continued to reveal his reluctance to be involved in the strategic direction of the war. He had dodged this responsibility before the Americans entered the conflict, when Ottawa had much more influence with London; now, with Britain the junior partner to the United States, Canada had little hope of being heard. However, while Canada would never be a military superpower, it was a food power, and it had punched far above its weight in supplying the Allies with wartime materiel. Shouldn't Canada have greater influence in these fields? Was it to be a simple hewer of wood and carrier of water? From 1942 onwards, key members of the Department of External Affairs stiffened the prime minister's resolve as he pushed for inclusion in the Anglo-American combined boards that coordinated much of the Allied war effort. After much stonewalling, Canada finally received a position on the Combined Production and Resources Board and Combined Food Board, in late 1942 and early 1943. This may have been, according to one historian, a "rather empty honour," as they were the least influential of the boards, but even these small victories were a significant step forward for the Dominion, and no other middle power was recognized in the same way.[52] Canada's new voice was justified under the "functional principle," a concept that the nation carried into the postwar era. In promoting this principle, Canada acknowledged that it did not rank in military prowess with the great powers, but that it demanded an influence in fields where its contribution was significant.

AFTER SEVERAL YEARS OF THE Russians holding out against the Nazi war machine, and then finally turning the tide, with the Battle of the Atlantic nearly won and bombers pounding German cities, the Allies finally launched the invasion of Europe on D-Day, June 6, 1944. Canadians were in the vanguard of battle as one of the five Allied divisions to storm the beaches. Despite the significant Canadian contribution, the D-Day landings revealed again, as if it were necessary, that Canada was not an equal partner in the war. King had been awakened a little after dawn on that fateful day and told, much to his surprise, that Canadian forces had been committed to the invasion of Europe.[53] For King to be completely unaware of the operation's timing is shocking, to say the least. Never was there a greater sign that his administration was completely out of touch with the Allied direction of the war.

The truth is that King had avoided assuming a role in the military decision making in the mistaken belief that responsibility came with chains.[54] But the prime minister was already chained to the war, and by refusing to press for some influence in the realm of grand strategy, he missed the opportunity for Ottawa to have some authority over the Allied war effort, and even how Canada's airmen, sailors, and soldiers would be committed to battle. Pearson observed of King that he accepted the dictates from London "with a mild complaint or none at all."[55] Let it be said that no one would have handed King the reins of strategic control—which were firmly in American and British hands, with the Soviets fighting their own war on the Eastern Front—but Canada had earned a right to be consulted and to be a part of the discussion. King abdicated without a fight.

Canadian forces were fully engaged in the Normandy invasion. RCN destroyers and minesweepers supported the landings, and

RCAF bombers and fighters targeted strongpoints or swept the coast, while land forces fought their way deep into the German positions on the first day of battle. Over the coming seven weeks, Allied forces drove the Nazi forces back, but always with heavy casualties. By August 21, 1944, the Allies had closed the bag on much of the German army, killing or capturing 300,000 men, and destroying some 2,000 tanks, light vehicles, and artillery pieces. Some 18,444 Canadians had been killed or wounded in the fighting, but their sacrifice seemed to portend the end of the war.[56]

In September, Churchill and Roosevelt met again at Quebec. Their discussions were intended to decide the strategy for the Pacific campaign, the shape of a postwar world, and the role of a defeated Germany in Europe. King was excluded from the strategic talks, but again he benefitted from peripheral discussions. He was candid enough in his diary to observe that "the close relationship of Churchill, the President and myself cannot fail to be of help to me politically."[57] King noted gleefully that after five years of war, "Canada has emerged in every sense of the word into a world power."[58] It was too grandiose a statement, but Canada was an important second-tier power in the Allied structure. It had achieved this status through service and sacrifice, and through King's skill in handling the war effort on the home front.

CHAPTER 17

THE CRISIS, 1944

King spent much of the summer of 1944 looking towards a future election. He had turned his sights on political victory now that the Germans were on the verge of military defeat. King and his cabinet based their assessment on an August 3 briefing by Chief of the General Staff Lieutenant-General Kenneth Stuart, who had returned from an overseas trip and reported that the war might be over sooner than expected.[1] The Canadian casualties had been heavy, but according to army reports, they were manageable and within the accepted limits.

The war in the Pacific was far from over, but Canadians had little interest in the fight against Japan.[2] Britain's concern was more complicated and it hoped to offer limited support, so that, in Churchill's mind, it could reclaim lost colonies and possessions when it was over. The Americans, however, were content to win that war on their own and, indeed, bluntly said as much to the Canadians.[3] But King's defence ministers, echoing their service chiefs, demanded to be involved, partly to be in at the kill, and partly to stand by the country's allies, but mainly as justification for maintaining a large postwar fighting force. The question of whether or not to commit forces to the Pacific led to several stormy meetings in September 1944, with King set against his defence ministers—at one point railing that he "would not allow waste of a single life for the sake of appearance" and that the government's "duty was to save lives."[4] King did not win the argument, although he reduced the force. In the end, it was decided that a compromise infantry division of volunteers would be sent to the Pacific after the war in Europe was won, as well as RCAF squadrons and warships.[5]

Even if Canada would not commit a large force to the Pacific, it was fighting in multiple theatres. The RCN continued to escort convoys across the Atlantic and in the dreaded Murmansk run to supply Russia, as well as to hunt German U-boats and surface raiders in the English Channel and along the French coast. The army remained split, with one corps fighting in Italy and the other, as part of the First Canadian Army, battling through Normandy and then pushing north to clear essential German-held ports along the French coast. And the bombers continued to rain hell down on the increasingly pulverized German cities. Thousands of additional troops were in England in administrative or logistical roles. The size and cost of Canada's military preoccupied King. He and Howe talked at length about how to repurpose the roughly 70,000 NRMA conscript home-defence soldiers in Canada by quickly demobilizing them and getting them into industry, which was beginning in some sectors to transition from manufacturing war supplies to domestic items. Though Howe and King were shifting their focus to postwar prosperity, Ralston thought it premature to demobilize any troops, especially the NRMA soldiers, partially because they would take the best jobs before the fighting men returned home. This would only lead to anger and unrest. King empathized with his argument, but had to balance the two arms of the war effort: overseas services and home-front production. There was never an easy solution, especially with Ralston obstinately pressing his case. While Howe was no wallflower, King characterized his battles with Ralston as a "test of endurance."[6] Ralston, in turn, was supremely frustrated in his dealings with the prime minister, telling Grant Dexter that he hated King's "guts more than ever."[7]

In mid September, word circulated through returned veterans, back channels, and then newspaper accounts that the Canadian army's fighting formations in Italy and France were dangerously depleted of front-line troops. Too many battalions in the line had taken significant losses in combat and the army was plagued by a shortage of trained replacements. The effect of this at the sharp end was disastrous. Under-strength regiments that went into battle had fewer men to cover ground, lay down fire, and defend against counterattacks. According to rumours, the heavy casualties were forcing authorities to send poorly trained Canadian infantrymen to France in order to bring the shattered regiments up to strength, and men were losing their lives because they were inadequately trained. The cabinet murmured in disbelief. How could the army be out of men, if tens of thousands were in uniform in England and uncommitted to battle, and the RCAF had already begun to demobilize unneeded flyers? However, the stories of neglect and shortages prompted the conscientious Ralston to go overseas for a three-week tour, first to Italy and then to France.

On October 13, Ralston sent a telegram to King from England, warning the prime minister that they had to meet upon his return to Canada. King blanched. This could only mean that the situation was desperate and that his minister would argue for conscription. King nearly wept at the madness of having to fight another conscription battle with the war all but won. "It would be a criminal thing," he lamented in his diary, "and would destroy the entire War Record."[8]

Ralston and King met in the prime minister's parliamentary office at 5 P.M. on October 18, almost as soon as the defence minister's plane touched down. Ralston was reluctant to broach the difficult subject, and admitted a few days earlier to a friend that he was "despondent and lonely" and had lost his "good humour," but he was compelled to raise the issue. He told King that the fighting in Italy and France had been more costly than anticipated and that Field Marshal Bernard Montgomery, the British army group commander, now believed that the Germans, obstinate, experienced, and fanatical in the defence of occupied Western Europe, would hold out until the spring of 1945.[9] After taking a moment to regroup, Ralston launched into the heart of the matter. He had met wounded soldiers in hospitals, and he had been shaken by those who spoke of their units being down more than 50 percent in strength, with the survivors fighting for their lives.[10] Canadians were dying unnecessarily because of a lack of reinforcements. Ralston told King that it was finally necessary to invoke conscription. Even though he was expecting the news, the prime minister was shocked and retreated behind his multiple layers of defence, noting that the cabinet would need to discuss the traumatic effects of such an action. And so began two weeks of infighting between King and Ralston, in a divisive campaign that nearly destroyed the prime minister and the Liberal Party.

OVER THE COMING DAYS, King railed at the position in which he found himself. At every turn over the last five years he had questioned the high command and his ministers over whether the addition of another division or brigade, or the establishment of more squadrons or warships, would put a strain on voluntary enlistment. At each meeting, the prime minister reminded Ralston, the military advisors had guaranteed that his government would not have to force young men to serve against their will.[11] Now, the promises were revealed to be lies at worst or major errors at best. King quickly saw this in conspiratorial terms, as he often did when he was under stress. The military, having deceived him, was now forcing the government towards a decision that would destroy the country's fragile unity and doom his political career. With the "ring being drawn steadily tighter around Germany," King lamented, "the people of Canada would hardly understand why we should resort to conscription."[12] He would lose Quebec to Duplessis, he would lose the West to the CCF, and the Liberals would be shattered for the second time in as many generations over the same agonizing issue.

Ralston understood this. He did not want to knife his own party. He could only respond that the military assessments had been wrong, or had changed with the circumstances of the battlefield, and that the fighting had taken more lives than expected. Whatever the case, Canadian soldiers were dying because of a lack of trained reinforcements. King had no response to that, although he believed in his heart that conscription would lead to civil war. What was he to do: abandon the soldiers or risk the unity of the country?

Battle lines were drawn. Ralston, Macdonald, and Ilsley, with the powerful Howe and T.A. Crerar, were set against the rest of the cabinet. Although they were outnumbered, the pro-conscriptionists were the most influential ministers with the greatest wartime responsibilities; if they resigned, the party would collapse. King also promised to resign over the issue, however, which would inevitably lead to a coalition government. Macdonald and the others actively sought a compromise, with little success. Ralston would not back down. In his mind, the lives of Canadian soldiers were at stake. Frustration mounted and most of the ministers carried resignation letters. King tried every trick he had learned during his decades of political experience, but in the end he could only delay: he pushed decisions into the next day's meeting, and then to the one afterwards, but all the while the party was reeling towards ruin.

Throughout this agonizing period, Power led several ministers in consultation with Department of Defence officials to find, either in Canada or abroad, the necessary men to serve in the infantry battalions through voluntary means. Tens of thousands were identified in England, but they were not trained to be infantryman, and to send them to the front was a sure death sentence. It was later revealed that the Canadian army's fighting arms made up only 34.2 percent of the force, while the "headquarters and overhead" elements constituted 28.3 percent, compared to 11.6 percent in the U.S. army.[13] There were simply far too many Canadian administrative soldiers, resulting in an army with too much tail and not enough teeth. The disproportion was partly the legitimate result of Canada's insistence on sustaining a small, separate army in the field, but such details were lost on King, who seethed at the incompetence. If the army had enough men, but had failed to allocate them properly, why did the Canadian people have to suffer the consequences? Lieutenant-General

Kenneth Stuart was hauled before the cabinet and forced to admit that he had erred in assessing the number of reinforcements required to keep fighting units up to strength in Normandy, and that his earlier reports had misled the cabinet, including a critical one of August 3, which guaranteed that reinforcement personnel were available for three months at "the intensive battle casualty rate."[14] A smug King was triumphant in having absolved himself from blame, but it changed nothing. The situation was desperate.

Ralston urged the cabinet to pass an order-in-council reassigning the trained NRMA soldiers from home defence to overseas service. King refused. That was conscription, even if it was limited. Yes, replied Ralston, and the nation had freed the government's hand to do exactly this in the 1942 plebiscite. King laid out his case to the cabinet: he would not argue in favour of conscription, because it was not necessary to win the war.[15] In this regard, he was right: the Allies did not need the Canadians in order to win the war. But as the prime minister raged that conscription was betraying a trust to all Canadians—by which, as always, he meant French Canada—he had almost nothing to say about the Canadians fighting in Northwest Europe, especially the costly Scheldt campaign that saw the death and maiming of hundreds of Canadians each day throughout October, a situation made all the worse because units were under strength. Conscription was not needed to win the war, but it was needed to save the lives of Canadian soldiers at the front.

In a search for compromise, King—supported by his military advisor since August 1944, Lieutenant-General Maurice Pope—suggested reducing the overseas army that was being mauled in battle. Why not pull a division from the line, disband it, and use the men as reinforcements? Or, why not reduce the number of rifle companies in a battalion from four to three?[16] Ralston and senior military staff believed these manoeuvres would be devastating to the fighting spirit of the troops—as it had been when such reorganizations were carried out in British divisions during the Great War—and that the reduction in strength would have an impact on Supreme Allied Commander Dwight Eisenhower's ability to prosecute the war.[17] That argument must have sounded weak to King's ears, especially as the Americans were fielding dozens of combat divisions. A few days later, King floated a timid message to Churchill, asking about his plans for the disposition of the Canadian army, hoping perhaps that Churchill would tell him not to worry, that the Canadians would be put into a safe corner. Churchill did no such thing. He said bluntly that the Canadians would be in heavy fighting, as were all the Allied forces. King realized that he would have no support from the British in finding a solution to the conscription crisis.[18] For one of the first times, King felt disadvantaged by his lack of influence over the strategic direction of the war. During the cabinet discussions on October 19, for instance, King complained that with Canadians in battle, his government was "entitled to know what was involved in the [Allied] strategy" for taking the battle to Germany.[19] No minister had the courage to remind King that he had never wanted any influence and that now it was too late.

King was convinced that Ralston was to blame for the reinforcement crisis because he let his generals run him.[20] King reminded the cabinet that it had been Ralston who had split the army, sending half of it to Italy, where it was engaged in fierce battles that ran up casualties. General A.G.L. McNaughton had warned against fighting in two theatres and had been overruled and sent home. Perhaps the general had more political sense than his minister? The prime minister continued to think highly of McNaughton and had been considering him as a candidate to be the first Canadian-born governor general. King was motivated in this action by his desire to defang him politically, because Liberal sources had told him the Tories were wooing McNaughton to lead a coalition government. Now King wondered if the popular general might replace Ralston as minister of national defence.

After a week of high stress, Chubby Power remarked that King at times was exhausted and "not reasoning very well." The ministers who opposed him on conscription—Ralston, Macdonald, Ilsley, Crerar, and Howe—were also the ministers who had never embraced King's social legislation. In the heat of the sustained battle, King now drew a connection between the issues, reinforcing in his mind the idea that they were plotting against him.[21] The Great War again offered warnings, and King harkened back to his hero Laurier in his time of crisis, when "his supposedly strongest colleagues left him, one by one, and joined their political enemies and became a party of conscription."[22] Even as he talked half-heartedly of resigning, King was determined to stand his ground against the "conscriptionists," which is how he now described them, in order to "fight for the peoples' rights in this country."[23] King could never acknowledge, even to himself, the legitimacy of the opposing view, that the conscriptionists were fighting for the soldiers' rights—and lives—overseas.

On October 31, King met with McNaughton. The general was anxious to serve. He continued to carry a grudge against Ralston and Stuart for his professional demise as army commander and he was now pleased to repay the favour. Although he was not privy to relevant reports or recent intelligence, the general assured King that if he was minister he would find a way to convince the NRMA men to enlist. Almost incomprehensibly, he also blamed the high numbers of Canadian casualties on a shortage of guns and shells, making it appear to the unmilitary King that it had again been incompetence that put him, as war leader, in this precarious situation. McNaughton was wrong, but he was very good at soothing the anxious prime minister.[24] King had found his replacement for Ralston. He left McNaughton after swearing him to secrecy and telling him that he would call on him soon.

The appalling situation came to a head on November 1. King informed the governor general and his key confidant St. Laurent that he would have to remove Ralston, whom he had described a few days earlier as "inhumanly determined to get his own way."[25] The prime minister then lined up his supporters in cabinet, calling them on the phone and asking them to follow his lead in the meeting later in the day. At the cabinet meeting, a tired Ralston reiterated the issues, but his voice quivered and he seemed beaten.[26] King raised all the same objections. He was hoping that Ralston would offer his resignation, as he had in the past, which King would then accept. Ralston did not; indeed, he was more conciliatory and open to solutions than he had seemed to be before. King sweated and looked for an opening as the meeting dragged on for hours. No such opportune moment occurred, but he struck anyway, telling the cabinet the issue had to come to a conclusion that night. With tension rising in the room, King told the now silent ministers that Ralston had told them repeatedly that the NRMA men would not enlist without conscription, but King believed McNaughton could rally them to volunteer. A white-knuckled King referred back to Ralston's 1942 resignation letter, which he had kept, and said that the deed was done. He would now accept Ralston's letter. "A chill of frozen silence" filled the room, wrote one observer.[27] With great dignity, Ralston rose, shook hands with several of his friends, and then with King, and left the cabinet forever.

After throwing Ralston on his sword, King pleaded with the other ministers—especially Macdonald, Ilsley, and Howe—to stand by the government. Macdonald wavered but did not go. He remarked later that as he watched King politically execute his friend he had felt like punching the prime minister in the face, but he believed that McNaughton ought to have a chance to raise the recruits that were needed.[28] At the same time, King had seized the initiative, moving so rapidly that these powerful and angry men had been stopped in their tracks.[29] King's firing of Ralston was one of the most dangerous political gambles of his long career, but, as always, he had prepared the path, sized up his opponents, and acted boldly when he had to. "It was a scene I shall never forget, nor will those who were present," wrote King to his diary.[30] That was a classic King understatement. One of the shocked ministers sitting at the table later described King's expulsion of Ralston as "the most cold-blooded thing I have ever seen."[31]

IT WAS A BRUTAL AFFAIR, but it was the right decision. Ralston's obstinacy had split the cabinet. He had been unable to control the manpower situation within the army and he fought openly against the government's conscription policy. He had his reasons, all honourable and justifiable in his mind, but in the end either he or King had to go. The perennial survivor King knew how that would end. However, while Ralston was gone, he was not dead. Out of cabinet, he could attack the government, rally MPs to his cause, and continue to fight for conscription. The key to diluting

Ralston's impact, thought King, was getting McNaughton to enlist the necessary 16,000 Zombies (as the NRMA soldiers were known widely and unaffectionately because they had no "soul" or "heart") for overseas service as quickly as possible.[32]

The cabinet meeting on November 2 was a tense affair. Journalists were already hunting for the story of what had occurred the previous day. King might have been confronted by mass resignations, but McNaughton's commanding presence saved him. The new minister of national defence made a good impression on the cabinet. He was fresh, spoke with authority, and offered a way forward. The burned-out ministers, King recounted, were relieved. King and McNaughton were nearly inseparable over the next couple of days, while they tried to get a handle on the reinforcement issue. McNaughton also took the time to even an old score, quickly dispatching Kenneth Stuart.[33]

Throughout the crisis, from late October through the first two weeks of November, King's diary conspicuously lacks any observation related to the fighting overseas. Yet in Italy, and especially in the Scheldt campaign, Canadian ground troops were involved in vicious battles, resulting in thousands of casualties.[34] Given the detail and complexity of King's diary, it is fair to say that not only were the soldiers not on his mind but he completely ignored them.

After only a few days, pressure began to build again in support of conscription. Newspapers brayed at the government's failure to resolve the crisis. The Legion accused the Liberals of causing unnecessary deaths overseas. Some English Canadians muttered darkly that Quebec controlled the fate of the nation.[35]

Ralston issued his first statement about his firing on November 12. While it was not an outright attack on the government, he noted that he had been asked to resign because his solution to cabinet in resolving the reinforcement crisis was ignored. He also corrected a statement made by King in the House of Commons on November 8, in which the prime minister had predicted that there would be a shortage of reinforcements in the months to come. Ralston said that was untrue, that the shortage was being felt now, and that only by sending trained men to Europe could the crisis be resolved in time.[36] King was worried about Ralston's statement and its effect on the public, and went so far as to lie to himself in his diary, writing that Ralston had maligned him by suggesting that King "had asked him to resign."[37] This was one of many strange instances in which King invented a story to ease his own troubled conscience. He waited for further political fallout, thinking that he might yet receive Macdonald's resignation and then become the focus of a two-pronged public attack by his former ministers. It did not happen, although the naval minister placed before King a letter that demanded some action be taken on the reinforcement issue. The pressure continued to mount.

McNaughton struggled with his task. The Zombies were not enlisting for overseas service, and his passionate pleas only left him the butt of mean-spirited attacks. Ontario's new Conservative premier, George Drew, wrote nastily to McNaughton, "Your latest move destroys the last vestiges of respect I had for you ... Now I would not insult a yellow dog by calling you one."[38] Between November 14 and 19, McNaughton was informed by several of his senior district commanders that it would be impossible to raise the necessary 16,000 reinforcements through voluntary means. He put on a brave face to the media, suggesting optimistically that the voluntary principle was still viable. In a clear sign of their desperation, several outraged generals wrote to headquarters to protest that McNaughton had misrepresented their views. There was, they repeated, no chance of getting the NRMA soldiers to volunteer.

King sought an escape route, even as public opinion polls showed that 57 percent of Canadians favoured conscription.[39] He could not break his promise to the nation's citizens, and neither would he hand over the reins of government to the Conservatives, but the pressure from his ministers and the newspapers was relentless. On the 19th, for instance, Macdonald harangued King for procrastinating and Ilsley accused him of "gambling with human lives."[40] King limped out of the cabinet meeting, never feeling so alone.

A MONTH OF MOUNTING ANXIETY came to a head on November 22, when McNaughton phoned King to say that voluntary recruitment had failed. This defeat was a blow to McNaughton, who felt he had let down the cabinet as well as the prime minister, but King kept searching for a compromise. At a Liberal caucus meeting that day, King gave a fighting speech that went on for half an hour, and convinced the MPs that he would never surrender to the conscriptionists. There were many cheers, but Ralston and dozens of others looked on with silent disdain. King felt their stares. When he finished defending his principles and those of the Liberal Party, the venerable T.A. Crerar rose slowly to speak, and in the process caught Ralston's eye. King noticed the unspoken message and interpreted it as the start of some sort of conspiratorial action. Something snapped in the prime minister. King leapt to his feet, waved his arms, and mumbled that the caucus meeting was over. It was a startling exit. Even as the prime minister fled the room, Chubby Power wrote that "everyone was under the impression that King would remain firm in his attitude not to send the Zombies overseas."[41] But something in Crerar's manner had shaken King to the core, and he must have believed that the minister was about to submit the first in a chain of resignations.[42] In the period between the caucus and a cabinet meeting scheduled for later that evening, Parliament met and King received permission to bring McNaughton before the House to explain the recruitment situation. He gave no sign of bending.

But at the cabinet meeting that night, King shocked his colleagues. After repeating McNaughton's admission of failure, King now said passionately that "conscription was necessary." The reason for the flip-flop, said King, was a generals' revolt that threatened the very fabric of the nation. The country would be lost to a military coup if he did not relent, although King's flimsy evidence was only the actions of a few disgruntled generals who had gone to the press to express their outrage over the government's failure to bring in conscription. St. Laurent described to a journalist how a wild-eyed King had talked to him before the cabinet meeting, ranting about the military uprising, trying to persuade him of its severity. "I had to pretend I believed him. I even had to pretend that I believed that he himself believed what he was saying."[43] A sympathetic St. Laurent supported his chief, even though he did not believe a word of the military conspiracy.[44]

Like King's belief that conscription would unleash civil war—of which there is not a single credible bit of evidence beyond hyperbolic Quebec nationaliste speeches—the prime minister, in a bid to justify his about-face and save himself, invented the threat of a military revolution. In his mind, he was compelled to introduce limited conscription to avoid this inevitability, and even worse disasters. His statement to the cabinet late on November 22 moved from the self-serving to the ludicrous. At one point he pleaded, "I did not intend to have on my conscience the thought that I had not done everything possible to ensure the lives of the men overseas."[45] King had convinced himself that he was the champion of the fighting man at the front.

King met the Liberal caucus on the 23rd and revealed his reversal. Most of the MPs were gobsmacked into silence, and his secret was kept until later in the day when he announced in the House that an order-in-council would send 16,000 NRMA conscripts overseas. King noted that several dozen of his Quebec MPs sat with anguished expressions on their faces. The Conservatives, too, refused to cheer, although they were bewildered by the announcement, which broke their most powerful weapon against the Liberals. The Conservative leader, R.B. Hanson, shouted out "surrender" to King, but many Conservatives must have been murmuring about their own defeat.

THE CONSERVATIVES HAD BEEN OUTMANOEUVRED again and were in a foul mood. McNaughton, who only weeks before had been courted to possibly lead the party, came into the House that same day to explain the failure in recruiting. He was attacked relentlessly by the opposition parties, especially the Tories, who heaped "derision, scorn and fury" on the man who many of them believed had saved the King government.[46] McNaughton stood bravely in the face of these taunts and challenges, in a session that lasted throughout the afternoon and late into the night; it was an agonizing day for the minister, who had to defend his previous on-record support of volunteerism and then back the case for conscription. "King sat by coolly and watched McNaughton being ripped to shreds in the House defending a military policy of which he was not the author, his glory hanging in rags and tatters," recounted one dismayed journalist.[47] The Tories' venting of their frustration on McNaughton deflected much of the criticism from King, who left the House feeling better than he had in a month. William Lyon Mackenzie King had lived to fight another day.

On November 23, there was a mutiny by a small group of French and English NRMA soldiers at Terrace, British Columbia, who refused to follow orders and seized weapons to defend themselves. The Liberal cabinet was shocked, much as the Borden government had been dismayed by the 1918 Easter Riots in Quebec City; the incident at Terrace reinforced King's fear of a military revolution.[48] Although the riots were quelled after a few days, with no bloodshed, a shaken King again confirmed in his own mind the necessity of limited conscription, as opposed to the Tory demand for a general call-up of all available men. He had embraced the lesser evil and, as in 1935 election, he believed the choice was between "King or chaos."

Ironically, the Canadian land formations in Northwest Europe, having lost thousands of men in the fighting at the Scheldt, had been pulled out of the line to rest over the winter. The reinforcements were still needed to bring units up to strength, but the urgency was no longer there. In the end, of the roughly 13,000 NRMA soldiers who were sent overseas, only 2,463 were integrated into the fighting units.[49] While many received a rough initial reception, by most accounts they fought well. The movement of I Canadian Corps from the Italian front in February 1945 to join the First Canadian Army under General Harry Crerar gave the Canadians extra punch, with II Canadian Corps fighting into Germany in the final months of the war while I Corps liberated the Netherlands.

The conscription crisis came to an end in the first week in December, when the government survived a vote of confidence in the House. King lost one of his best ministers, Chubby Power, who refused to accept conscription and resigned after King's announcement to caucus, and McNaughton had been badly mauled during the ordeal. The Quebec wing of the party felt betrayed, but those MPs also knew they had few other options but to stick with King. Nonetheless, King knew he was lucky to escape with his political skin. He concluded piously in his diary that "some day the world will know some of the things that I have prevented."[50] In King's mind, he had averted civil war and a military coup, convinced Quebec to accept the inevitable, kept the Liberal Party united, and supported Canadian service personnel overseas. In reality, civil war and a military coup were never a possibility; moreover, few soldiers believed that they had been backed by the government, and certainly not in a timely fashion. King had, however, fought to support Quebec in his long, public, but ultimately unsuccessful rearguard action against conscription, and he had kept the Liberal Party from disintegrating during the crisis. One can only conclude that King's concern for Quebec and its support for the Liberal Party was far more important to him than any anxiety over the overseas soldiers and unnecessary combat deaths.

CHAPTER 18

KING AND COUNTRY, 1945–1950

William Lyon Mackenzie King went into 1945 aware that the war was coming to an end and that it was an election year. He had seen the country through calamitous times, and despite having been boxed into a corner and forced to bring in limited conscription, the aftermath of the crisis was less poisonous than the grim years following the Great War. This man of peace, who had been thrust into war, would return to his proper sphere, where he could, in his own words, promote "human welfare and social reform."[1]

King set about creating the winning conditions for his party. He was adamant about not having an election during the war. He felt it would detract from supporting the service personnel overseas, and he was wily enough to know that an election that came on the heels of victory over the Nazis would likely bring some rewards from the electorate. But he needed help. He had relied heavily on Minister of National Defence A.G.L. McNaughton over the last tumultuous months. An early 1945 opinion poll revealed that McNaughton was King's second most recognized minister, only slightly less well known than Ilsley and far more than Howe and Macdonald.[2] McNaughton's charisma, intellect, and experience had allowed Ralston's commanding presence to be overshadowed. It was important to get the former general elected.

A seat was found for McNaughton, but the Tories and CCF decided to run candidates against him in a February 5, 1945, by-election. King was horrified by this instance of partisan malice, pleading with the leaders to put aside their differences and allow McNaughton to be elected for the good of the country. The opposition parties were having none of that: they sensed disarray in the Liberal cabinet and they were going for the jugular. After a fierce and brutal campaign, in which McNaughton was denigrated relentlessly, he lost the election by a significant margin.[3] King reeled personally at McNaughton's defeat, which was interpreted widely as a snub against him, but pulled himself together, as he always did, and soldiered on.

King's cabinet was in shambles. McNaughton had been defeated but still served as minister of national defence until he lost again in the next election. Ralston had been fired, Power had resigned, Ilsley was ill and disillusioned, and Macdonald was set to exit the cabinet in April 1945, anxious to flee the loathsome presence of King and reassume as provincial leader in Halifax. The core of the cabinet was disintegrating. But the end was near overseas, too. In early May, the war crashed to a halt in Europe. Italy had been crushed two years earlier and now the German air force and navy had been shattered, its armies beaten decisively, and its cities reduced to smouldering ruins. Only Japan held on, although it had no hope in its lopsided battle with the United States.

BY WAR'S END, a full 10 percent of the Canadian population had served in uniform, and millions more supported the war from the home front. The Royal Canadian Navy had joined the Royal Navy in taking on the unglamorous if critical role of safeguarding the North American logistical lifeline to Britain, and was also fighting in many other theatres. A quarter of Bomber Command aircrews were composed of Canadians. The army had fought in Sicily, Italy, Northwest Europe, and Germany, and had liberated the Netherlands. While any price had to be paid for victory, the final tally revealed that the war had cost Canada $18 billion, with almost one-fifth of that amount going to Britain in the form of financial aid.[4] Canada's support of Britain, calculated on a per capita basis, was five times greater than the funds and supplies transferred from the United States to Britain under Lend-Lease.[5] During the course of the war, Canada produced $9 billion worth of war materiel, or almost 8 percent of the British Commonwealth's total supplies from all sources, making it the fourth largest producer among the Allies.[6] Canada had entered the conflict anxious to limit its liability in terms of expending blood and treasure; it ended the war having served in multiple theatres of battle, committed billions of dollars of munitions and supplies to Allied nations, and made a name for itself in what became an unlimited war effort. Canada was truly an arsenal of democracy.

In the aftermath of war, Canadians surveyed the ashes of Germany, the humiliation of France, the destitution of Britain, and realized that they had largely escaped the hard hand of war. The worldwide death toll was still being compiled, but eventually it would rise to some 50 million, including the horrors of the Holocaust that saw the Nazis systematically murder six million

Jews and others they found undesirable, forever darkening world history. Canada's 45,000 dead and 55,000 wounded paled in comparison to the totals suffered by other belligerents. Yet each son and daughter lost, every uncle, father, and neighbour who lay buried overseas left a gaping hole in families, communities, and the nation.

Canada had gone into the war nearly bankrupt, financially and perhaps morally, after the brutal Depression years. The country was broken. Throughout the 1930s, Canadians had done their best to avoid the wars of Europe, but in the end, they had rallied to protect Britain. But this was also Canada's war. Canadians had entered it united and exited it bruised and battered, but with an earned confidence. Rich in natural resources, influential because of its relationships with Britain and the United States, and equipped with armed forces that, at least for a few months after war's end, were ranked amongst the most hard-hitting in the world, Canada seemed destined to make a difference.

This Canadian desire to wield its new influence would be tested in San Francisco, when King led a delegation to the founding conference of the United Nations (UN), which was held from April 25 to June 26, 1945. The United Nations was to replace the failed League of Nations, an international body to promote dialogue and diplomacy, international law, and security. For King, this was an opportunity to represent Canada at a critical time in history and, like Borden, to push for a stronger leadership role in the international sphere. But King was not Borden. At San Francisco, Canada's was a muted voice: the country had middle-power status but was unsure how to exert it. King's fretfulness over international commitments and his tentative wartime leadership made him easy to ignore in its aftermath. The Ottawa delegation was more anxious to please than to rock the boat, and the Australians took the lead in demanding more influence. King's address at the plenary session consisted of his regular, moralizing bunk, and had little impact. Predictably, King scurried away from the conference to fight the June election, feeling he had done well for the world. He had the audacity to write later, albeit privately, that much of the foundation and most of the guiding principles for the United Nations could be found in his book *Industry and Humanity*.[7]

THE ELECTION WOULD BE A TRIAL for the prime minister and the Liberal Party. King was old, and it showed. Polls seemed to suggest that Canadians wanted a change. Yet while many professed to dislike King, he was trusted and safe. Uninspiring, yes, but Canadians knew who they were getting. This might not have been enough to tip the balance with the electorate, but King was aided again by the Conservatives, who hoisted themselves with their own petard by campaigning on conscription for the Pacific campaign that was expected to drag on bloodily for another eighteen months. The Conservative Party leaders seemed to have suffered a collective lobotomy, and their platform revealed an utterly bizarre misreading of the war-weary public mood. The CCF, too, had slipped from their high popularity in 1943, as King had spiked their guns with his skilful adoption of social programs. Canadians were worried about the future and wanted to be cared for; the Liberal campaign slogans of "Build a New Social Order" and "Liberal Policies Create Jobs" resonated with them.[8]

The June 1945 election was King's last. Although the King government had already prepared key legislation to ease the transition of service personnel back to civvy street, the prime minister remained mistrusted by the overseas forces. Those serving overseas understood that King had sacrificed them for the sake of unity, or, as was more commonly sneered, for Quebec. A poem written by a soldier summed up the feelings of many of his comrades:

> Mackenzie King is my shepherd,
> I am in want,
> He maketh me abide by his fallacies,
> He leadeth me into troubled waters,
> He polluteth my soul,
> He leadeth the country into destruction
> For his Party's sake
> For he is with me.
> His diplomacy and policies they frighten me,
> He prepareth a reduction in production
> In the presence of mine enemies.
> He anointeth my salary with taxes.
> My expenses runneth over,
> Surely a willy-nilly complex shall follow me
> All the days of my life,
> And I shall live in the shadow of Quebec Forever.[9]

The men who had served overseas may have ridiculed the prime minister, but Canadians sided with the Liberals, again, and more military personnel voted Liberal than for any other party. Was it a case of party first and leader second? A lack of suitable choices? Perhaps an off-the-cuff slogan coined by Chubby Power was closer to the mark: "Not necessarily Mackenzie King, but

Mackenzie King if necessary."[10] The Conservatives made gains in Ontario, but not enough in the West, and Quebec remained a wasteland, with the party polling only 8.4 percent of the popular vote.[11] The Liberals won 125 of the 245 Commons seats; the Conservatives took 67; the CCF, 28; Social Credit, 13; and independents, a dozen.

Two of King's Conservative enemies had lamented their defeat in the 1940 election to "the fat little jelly fish out at Kingsmere," wondering how "he seems to come out on top."[12] The bewildered sentiment would have been shared by Meighen and all the other former comers who had been left in their political graves. And now, against the odds, King had survived to fight another day. While the Liberal victory was meagre, it was nonetheless a win. In Britain, meanwhile, Winston Churchill, the epitome of grit, determination, and triumph, was swept out of power in July 1945. King was the only Allied wartime leader to last throughout the Second World War, aside from Stalin, who had the political advantage of murdering any opponent who sought to stand against him.

As the combatants were transitioning back to civilian life, the war in the Pacific also was coming to an end. King had tried to avoid sending a military force to that theatre of war, but he had eventually compromised with his ministers, and an infantry division, along with several warships and RCAF squadrons, was being prepared to move and fight as the Allies closed the ring around the already shattered Japanese empire. However, King hoped that the war would be ended before Canadians were committed to battle, by the Americans' dropping of their atomic bombs. King had been briefed about these weapons and shuddered at their destructive power: "I feel that we are approaching a moment of terror to mankind," which could result in the "destruction of civilization."[13] The deployment of the bombs in August 1945 forced the Japanese surrender in the face of atomic Armageddon, and saved Canadian forces from being fully committed to the campaign. The Second World War was over.

AFTER THE GREAT WAR, veterans had felt cheated of recognition, rights, and recompense; the King government was well aware of the danger of bringing home another disillusioned generation of civilian-warriors. To compensate and reward those who had served their country, King's government rolled out the Veterans Charter, a compendium of legislation and programs for veterans that included job training, preferential hiring for government positions, grants to start businesses or buy homes, paid access to education, land grants, and hospital care and rehabilitation. Some 650,000 veterans entered the job market in the first year after the end of the war, and this successful transition from war to peace led to a baby boom (encouraged by King's family allowance grants, which were first distributed in mid-1945). These developments combined to usher in a period of economic growth and social stability.[14] By February 1947, an astonishing 33,800 veterans were enrolled in universities. In comparison, a total of only 35,164 students filled the ranks of all Canadian universities at the start of the war.[15] An affluent Canada, whose gross domestic product rose from $5.6 billion in 1939 to $11.8 billion in 1945, allowed the King government to ensure that the nation received what a future generation would call a peace dividend. The Veterans Charter, and all that it represented, was one of King's greatest legacies.[16]

As the world buried its dead, it was unthinkable that the years of hardship and bloodshed might be followed by more conflict, but the Soviet Empire, led by the West's wartime ally, Joseph Stalin, was aggressively consolidating its gains in Eastern Europe. What would befall shattered Europe? Canada was largely immune to the communist threat, or so King and most Canadians believed. But the defection of a low-level cipher clerk from the Soviet embassy in Ottawa in early September 1945 set off an international incident, and reminded Canadians again that they no longer lived in a "fire-proof house." Igor Gouzenko fled with pilfered documents that revealed the existence of Moscow-controlled spies in Canada, the United States, and Britain. While Soviet agents scoured Ottawa to silence him, he convinced the RCMP to take him into protective custody. King was shocked by Gouzenko's revelations, as almost everyone else was, but then, predictably, he did not want to do anything. He panicked at the thought that this incriminating evidence would pit the Soviet Union against the Western Allies, with Canada as a prime target. Perhaps Gouzenko might be persuaded to commit suicide? Yet, despite King's trepidation, the Canadians passed information to the British and Americans over the next five months and then a sting operation was mounted, leading to the arrest of Soviet moles in multiple countries.[17]

The discovery of a worldwide enemy spy ring was a key incident in the early days of the Cold War, and although King had wobbled at the start, he eventually rose to the occasion. In King's mind, the new threat posed by the Soviets meant that the West needed to unite in matters of defence. In a new take on the North Atlantic Triangle, King believed Canada to be "the link that would keep the other two great powers united."[18] This was an ambitious and unlikely outcome, but reflected the thinking of the influential mandarins at the Department of External Affairs, who believed that Canada had emerged as a middle power whose voice and actions would be heard and felt outside of the nation's borders. Neutrality was not an option, and Canada was soon drawn into North American and European defence arrangements.

BY 1946, A CLOSE ADVISOR noted that King's "energies were diminishing," but judging from the seventy-two-year-old's diary, he still kept a heavy work schedule.[19] While always anxious to assist the British and Americans, and conscious of the need to be united against the Soviet threat, King was gravitating back towards his guarded internationalism. Despite having been accused all of his life of turning too freely towards the Americans, King remained wary of them, especially now that Britain's near economic helplessness left Canada so much more exposed in North America. J.W. Pickersgill remembered his surprise when a conspiratorial King whispered after the war that "the secret aim of every American leader, including Franklin Roosevelt, [was] to dominate Canada and ultimately to possess the country."[20] While King remained suspicious of British imperialists, he would not turn his back on the British people, and he sought to support the country's battered economy through robust postwar trade, which would also create a market for Canadian goods.[21] Cranky and cautious, King was nonetheless instrumental in ensuring that the cabinet provided a March 1946 reconstruction loan to Britain, which, at $1.25 billion, amounted to an astonishing 10 percent of Canada's gross national product. King wanted to prop up Britain, but he was less generous than during the war, demanding a low interest rate this time, largely because Whitehall continued to act as a great power and not the debtor nation that it had become. King had not abandoned Britain, though its financial crisis forced him to embrace North American trade markets.[22]

In January 1947, while speaking in Toronto, Louis St. Laurent, the new secretary of state for external affairs and heir apparent to King, declared Canada's willingness to assert its new status and influence, and to turn its back on its parochial, irresponsible, and isolationist past. In what became known as the Gray Lecture, St. Laurent made clear that, while concern over national unity would still guide the government, the Liberals had staked out an internationalist policy. Historians have credited St. Laurent's undersecretary, Lester Pearson, with driving the process, but it also had the support of the prime minister. King saw potential threats in every shadow, in the form of imperial wars or military commitments, but he ultimately stood behind the cabinet and, especially, St. Laurent.[23]

Journalist Bruce Hutchison, who generally respected King, spoke for many when he wrote that by 1947 the old man "had ceased to be prime minister" in everything but title.[24] But King continued to have some bite left in him, as seen, for example, in his scuttling of a 1948 trade deal with the United States that he believed was dangerous because it would bind Canada too closely to its neighbour. It was a belief he came to naturally, based on his past history, and perhaps supernaturally, through a secret visit to a medium in London who channelled the spirit of Roosevelt. The president, who had died in the last months of the war, apparently now warned King against unnamed but nefarious American agents who sought to exert control over Canada through economic penetration. It was advice that King accepted, even though Roosevelt's spirit called King "Mac," which he had never done throughout his life.[25] King pondered the warning, and perhaps the need for safety in alliances, and so he allowed Canadian delegates to engage in the "ABC" talks involving the United States, Britain, and Canada, which laid the foundation for the North Atlantic Treaty.

While King was often prodded in these final years, he did not abdicate the throne. He used inertia to his advantage, as he had done through most of his political life. He was not easily cornered. While he allowed St. Laurent and others to guide him, with varying degrees of force, towards decisions, sometimes he pushed back. In 1947, he lost the battle to withhold Canadian observers, who were to monitor elections in Korea and report on the growing tension between the recently divided communist north and capitalist south, but he refused to be drawn into the 1948 Berlin Airlift, an American-led mission that dropped food and supplies behind the Soviet-erected barrier around much of Berlin. King saw both of these events as perilously similar to the 1922 Chanak Crisis, albeit involving different empires and different enemies.[26] In spite of King's age, growing fragility, and slow disengagement, Cabinet Secretary Arnold Heeney wrote in his memoirs, "Mackenzie King's dominance of his cabinet persisted well into 1948."[27]

KING STAYED TOO LONG. Even though he was tired of holding political office, he was scared to let go. He no longer knew how to be anything but a politician. In his final years, he dithered, and occasionally anguished, over making decisions, and was an eternal nitpicker and fault-finder when reading documents or letters prepared for him by his staff. He fretted over his finances. Although King had received gifts and money from the party faithful throughout his life, he almost never carried cash and rarely paid for anything. He cried poverty to friends and associates, and perhaps had convinced himself that he lived in the margins, having sacrificed prosperity for the nation.[28] He made a convincing story of it, and more than a few were surprised when the miser died with an estate valued at over $700,000. As one close observer noted of the grasping, annoying old man who had grown more priggish and hard to please at the end of his life, King "does not grow in stature in one's eyes."[29]

King retired in November 1948, handing over control to Louis St. Laurent, his chosen successor. Unlike many of his predecessors—and Borden would be included here—he bequeathed a party that was rejuvenated, scandal-free, and on a solid footing to enjoy another decade of rule before it imploded. This was just one of King's legacies, but perhaps his most important is that he left a far stronger Canada than the one he had inherited. Canada had grown into an influential and wealthy nation under the leadership of William Lyon Mackenzie King.

KING'S POLITICAL REIGN had lasted an astonishing 7,829 days, longer than any other leader in the Commonwealth's long history. Yet in retirement he was lost. He had cultivated few friends, and most colleagues remained in the hectic life of politics, enjoying the success that King had forged for the party. After a short rest, King planned to occupy his time by composing his memoirs. Macdonald and Laurier had left their legacy to other writers, albeit sympathetic ones, while Borden had taken matters into his own hands.

Now, King's version of the past, more than anything, would be his final political engagement. He would settle old scores, justify his actions, and leave his mark on history. However, although assistants corralled records and notes, King found himself too weary to go through more than a few at a sitting. He was even beyond the point of reading his diary and converting it into a publishable manuscript, although, as he told one professional acquaintance, if his memoirs were never published he would not be forgotten to history, for "the whole story of my life is in the diaries."[30] For a time, he focused on the letters and correspondence that he wished to burn, but the pack-rat King merely marked them, unable to actually destroy the material, and he never made much headway in the work.[31] A $100,000 grant from the Rockefeller Foundation in June 1949, in support of a series of biographies or memoirs on the public and private life of King, allowed for the hiring of additional researchers and official historians, but King was unable to direct the work as he had once hoped.

His government had brought in the Canadian Citizenship Act—which conferred Canadian citizenship as a status separate from British subjecthood—in 1946 and it came into force the next year, with King receiving the first certificate in January. Canada's first citizen died on July 22, 1950, at age seventy-five. His death provoked only muted public mourning.[32] Somewhat strangely for one who had lived in Ottawa for half a century, he was buried in Toronto, with his family, although this perhaps reflects again the long reach of his grandfather and parents. Arnold Heeney remarked on King's death, "I certainly felt respect and gratitude, but I doubted that many felt affection for that great but strange man."[33]

DESPITE HIS MORE THAN twenty-two years in power, the king of contradictions was easy to dislike, and easier to dismiss. He was never an inspirational figure, and he did not push others to be better. He simply gave them the tools and stood back. He had neither the flash and charisma of Macdonald and Laurier, nor the senatorial gravitas of Borden. When King was gone and his political skills buried with him, it was hard to find anyone who spoke kindly of the inscrutable and unloved leader. One journalist noted that many of King's closest political colleagues remembered him with "bitter animosity."[34] The long-time Liberal Kirk Cameron wrote meanly of King: "He was a political, mental, and maybe a physical Hermaphrodite ... He never conceived anything. He never created anything. Almost without exception his political wins were fortuitous or vicarious."[35] It was a viciously wrong-headed comment, but others felt the same way.

Almost immediately after King's death, the respected *Maclean's* journalist Blair Fraser shocked the nation by publishing a 1951 exposé. "The Secret Life of Mackenzie King, Spiritualist" revealed King's passion for communicating with the dead by table-rapping, his use of mediums, and all manner of other personal oddities that had remained hidden throughout his life.[36] The piece set tongues a-wagging. How had his strange obsessions been hidden from the Canadian public? Had King been a gullible and neurotic old man, or worse, a lonely, raving lunatic, who had allowed quacks to guide the Dominion's interests? The spiritual revelations provoked much snickering commentary, and almost no one stood up to defend the man who was now condemned as a sad, slightly comical figure.

King was also damned as a sellout. During the war, a desperate Canada had been driven into the arms of the Americans due to Britain's near financial collapse and its ongoing security issues. The Ogdensburg Agreement and Hyde Park Declaration provided increased security and financial stability to Canada during the early part of the war so that it could continue to support Britain. King had been responsible for this, and these deals were among his most important contributions to the war effort. While he had been almost universally lauded for his actions by contemporaries who understood how he had eased several threats against the nation, after his death King was increasingly condemned by a generation of historians and commentators who argued that he had recklessly transformed the nation into a satellite of the United States. It is hard to imagine how any other Canadian leader, in those desperate circumstances, could have acted differently.

With his plodding personality, mincing manner, and unprepossessing drabness, King brought out the worst in his critics. His reputation was buried under a growing avalanche of eviscerating words and conjured images of the weirdo who had done nothing while in power except dull Canada's best desires and hold back the country's potential. But what potential had that been, especially in a financially ruined, Depression-wracked nation? Would Canada have embraced greatness more quickly by sending young men to their deaths on battlegrounds from North Africa to New Guinea? King had led the nation and kept it from disintegrating during the war, but his tactics had been unheroic, unheralded, and, for the most part, unappreciated. Yet perhaps the most damaging blow to his reputation came from King's own hand. The assiduousness of his commitment to his diary, kept up year after year, revealed its importance as a record of events, but also as a cathartic tool. The final irony of this multi-volume "secret" document is that King's life was revealed like that of no other figure in Canadian history. And because there is that sustained insight into the man, his odd preoccupations have been ridiculed, his foibles derided, his private eccentricities exposed.

Perhaps it would have been better—or fairer—if the diaries had not survived his death. They almost did not. King saved almost everything that came across his desk—from menus to dental X-rays to his dogs' licenses—and his personal archives, when finally reconstituted from numerous buildings, attics, basements, and houses, consisted of over two million pages of correspondence and documents. But it was the diaries that mattered most. King had told close friends as the end neared that he wanted them destroyed except for the parts that he had flagged. But he never had time to mark the 30,000 pages. So his literary executors were left in the terrible position of either fulfilling his wishes by burning one of the most important historical records in the nation's history, or leaving them intact in violation of King's expressed wishes. After several years of discussion, the executors—all close acquaintances and men with an appreciation of King's place in history—eventually decided to save the diaries, although a few of the very personal records related to King's spiritual encounters were destroyed. A number of official histories were commissioned, and the diaries were published in an abridged form—the four-volume *Mackenzie King Record*—and, now that they have been digitized by the Library and Archives of Canada, they remain available for all. However, historian J.L. Granatstein was correct to observe in 1969 that "Mackenzie King is unquestionably our most maligned prime minister."[37]

Five years later, an academic symposium was held to mark King's one-hundredth birthday. One of the underlying themes of the conference was a lament that Canadians had all but forgotten King.[38] "Who loved King? Practically nobody," wrote Great War veteran and historian Arthur Lower. "Who else could have got us through the storm? Nobody."[39] The storm's fury had elapsed by the early 1970s, and so too had the memory of King's adept handling of the country as it was lashed during the war. King had been reduced to a caricature.

In 1976, one of Canada's most respected historians, Colonel C.P. Stacey, further damaged King's reputation. Stacey served as army official historian for years and had written dependable, even majestic, books on the Second World War and almost every other topic in Canadian military history. A careful historian in research and judgment, Stacey was astonished to stumble upon King's hidden life in the diaries. In Stacey's hands, this leader of tedium and boredom, of compromise and calculated confusion, became angst-ridden over prostitutes, hysterical about his personal misfortunes, and bizarrely involved in the occult. In the bestseller *A Very Double Life*, Stacey's dislike of King was palpable, and he portrayed Canada's longest-serving prime minister as a pathetic figure.

Historians such as J.L. Granatstein, Blair Neatby, and Norman Hillmer have toiled to resuscitate King's legacy since the 1960s, reminding their readers to look beyond the sometimes repellent personality of the man and to highlight the skills of a master political tactician who did more than any other individual to shape twentieth-century Canada. Yet their scholarship has been overwhelmed by a steady stream of books, novels, and documentaries that have continued to focus on the tormented man rather than the triumphant politician. King's reputation remains that of the oddball who talked to his dead dog and mum, who built strange ruins, who sought guidance in clock faces, and who chose to scurry for political cover rather than lead the nation. "Weird Willie" is firmly embedded in public memory.

CONCLUSION

A few weeks after Borden's retirement, one Calgary journalist wrote, "Sir Robert Borden may have been an outstanding figure in Canadian public life, being even a leader in Imperial councils during the war, but he seems to have lacked the arts which most appeal to the popular imagination. For example, one never hears and never will hear a personal anecdote about Borden. His biography, when written, will be dull. It will ... bore the people to death."[1] Boring Canadians to their graves? The judgment is more than a little harsh, and through Borden's private diary, his correspondence, and the observations of others, the complexity of the war leader is revealed. It is fair to say, however, that Borden has never received the recognition he deserved for guiding the country through the most traumatic and challenging event up to that point in Canada's history.

When Borden is depicted in our history books or remembered at all, it is as an indecisive, unemotional man, floundering and flailing from one bad decision to another on the uncontrollable tide of war. For decades after the war, Liberal Party supporters, some contemporary commentators, and French-Canadian nationalistes portrayed Borden's decision to introduce conscription as merely an opportunistic ploy to win the election.[2] Robert Borden and Arthur Meighen were subjected to monstrous accusations, including, in Quebec, the suggestion that the Conservative leaders were engaging in a genocidal battle to annihilate the French race.[3] The conscription wound never healed; it was methodically reopened in elections over the next three decades and, periodically, ever since.

Borden may have left a poisoned chalice for his successors, and perhaps the nation, but his goal had always been wartime victory. Could there be any other way when a nation was fighting for its very survival, as he and a majority of Canadians believed? Could Canada be only partially committed to a war in which tens of thousands of Canadians had already been killed, and more wounded in body and mind? Could Borden and the government implore young men to enlist and then abandon them to their fate in undermanned formations at the front when others did not join them in service to King and country? Borden did not initially or automatically come to the conclusion that the goal of victory had to subsume all other decisions made by him or his, but the cumulative effects of the war drove him to that position. In the Great War for Civilization, as many contemporaries called it—revealing the near-apocalyptic terms in which it was viewed—Borden would agonize over but not shrink from interning a few thousand enemy aliens, disregarding the demands of French Canada, or forcing young Canadians to fight overseas against their will.

Borden, unlike King, has been portrayed as coming down on the wrong side of history in pressing for conscription. Yet Canada had never faced as grim a year as 1917, when its own total of men killed in action surpassed 30,000 and the Allies faltered on all fronts, and when there was a very real likelihood that the war could be lost. There were other options besides conscription, such as reducing Canada's land army commitment or simply pulling back from the firing line, but such actions, Borden believed, would leave a stain on the nation's character and would amount to a betrayal of both the country's allies and its fallen dead. Canada had built its reputation during the war through success and sacrifice. Borden was not about to endanger that legacy, with greater political autonomy within the British Empire as its potential reward. Borden and his ministers could have recognized earlier, perhaps, that a different type of manpower allocation system was necessary—one that was more efficient and that acknowledged not only that the Canadian total war effort required soldiers overseas but also that it needed men and women in factories, in fields, and in homes taking care of families. How best to balance these different demands was never fully determined in the total equation of war. But then again, the exact same challenge emerged during the Second World War, when human resource shortages were just as calamitous, and when the government possessed a far more efficient and sizeable bureaucracy, as well as the Great War's lessons upon which to build.[4] Organizing a controlled economy during the Great War was beyond the state's capacity. In the end, Borden saw conscription as a way of sharing the burden of the war more evenly among Canadians, mobilizing the full resources of the nation effectively, and supporting the troops overseas no matter the cost. Borden made his choice, and it was the right one.

One of the fundamental questions raised in assessing Borden's wartime leadership pertains to how far democratic nations are willing to go in the pursuit of victory. The Borden government censored the press, muted free speech, and disenfranchised tens of thousands of Canadians. Habeas corpus was suspended, and control over the collective body of male citizenry was the ultimate intrusion (by forcing men into the army and potentially into harm's way). At what point, it is worth asking, does patriotic rhetoric become cover and justification for excessive intervention and force by the state against its citizens? Borden wrote in his diary during the bitter 1917 election campaign that he placed "winning of the war above every other consideration."[5] So did many Canadians, but at what cost to the social fabric? There was no easy answer, but some contemporaries, and later generations of commentators, believed that Borden had sacrificed too much. They may have been right, but Borden was leading a majority of Canadians in what he and they believed was a fight for survival, and in supporting the British Empire, which was, for English Canada, deeply entwined with its sense of self, place, and identity. Canada and the Empire were not separate entities at that time, and to argue that one could be severed from the other—politically or emotionally—is to misconstrue a very complex relationship.

Looking back on the war, Sir Robert wrote in 1933 that Canada entered "the portal of full nationhood ... due to the valour, the endurance and the achievement of the Canadian Army in France and Belgium which inspired our people with an impelling sense of nationhood never before experienced."[6] Frank Underhill, war veteran, historian, and certainly no conservative or Conservative sympathizer, noted that the Canadian Corps "was the greatest national achievement of the Canadian people since the Dominion came into being; and its story is to be cherished not only as the proof of Canadian military capacity but as the noblest example yet given of the ability of Canadians to ...

accomplish great ends ... The four years' career of her fighting troops in France forms the real testimony to Canada's entrance into nationhood, the visible demonstration that there has grown upon her soil a people not English nor Scottish nor American but Canadian."[7] Another veteran, Arthur Lower, wrote that, while the war had taken a terrible toll on the nation, "In the trenches of France and Flanders, the spirit of Canadian nationalism was born. It was carried back to Canada in the knapsacks of Canadian troops and there taking firm hold, hastened the slow process by which a community comes to self-consciousness."[8] The war had pressed Canadians to take important steps forward, but it was a long path from colony to nation, and it would take longer still to change the mindset of the country's people, politicians, and governments. For some, the nation changed too much; for others, not enough. Either way, Canada had moved significantly towards autonomy and a firmer sense of what it meant to be Canadian. And it had been led there by Sir Robert Borden.

But what had been sacrificed in the drive for victory? Had Canada won the war only to lose the peace? The creation and success of the Canadian Expeditionary Force, which allowed Canada to flex its muscles and achieve new confidence within the Empire-wide war effort, led to an emerging sense of nationalism, but this accomplishment must be balanced against the darker legacy of the war's aftermath, when the nation was impoverished and divided, grief-stricken, and battle-haunted. No one was certain about what had been lost in the fight to the finish, but one thing became clear: Canada would in future be a far harder country to govern, to lead, and to hold together.

WILLIAM LYON MACKENZIE KING was an uninspiring leader, much like Borden in the first half of the war, but unlike Borden, he did not go through a significant transformation. Perhaps King knew, more than Borden, who he was from the very start. He believed from a young age until his death that he was a man of destiny, one who would lead the Liberal Party and navigate the nation through trials, dissent, and grief without splitting the country. Unlike the international statesman Borden was to become, King was content to rule Canada, and almost everything he did during his career was designed to deny his political opponents power so they did not destroy all that he had created. Much of his partisan thinking had emerged from or been confirmed by watching Borden and Meighen take the country apart in the search for victory in the Great War.

Yet King was not simply reactive. Nor did he achieve six electoral victories over three decades by chance. Mediocrities do not win multiple majorities, and the magnitude of King's success requires some analysis. At the most basic level, King owned the political centre. Part of his genius was in declawing his enemies by incorporating their ideas into his party's program. Ilsley's budget of August 1942 raised taxes significantly for Canadians, and in the process came close to adopting the CCF battle cry of "conscription of wealth." King's expansion of the army, his visits to the United Kingdom, and his toughness on dissidents were all attempts during the war to reduce the effectiveness and influence of the Conservatives, who had used these issues to hammer the government. King's great talent, believed Jack Pickersgill, "was not in originating new policies, but in adapting the ideas of others at the moment when the public would accept them as solutions of political problems."[9] But his political canniness could extend to ruthlessness. "He rarely hesitated to sacrifice liberal principles, turn the sharpest of corners, and discard loyal colleagues and old friends," wrote one contemporary critic.[10] His blind eye to the suffering of Jews and Japanese Canadians was in keeping with his lifelong aim of avoiding conflict. King lost no sleep over such decisions.

The extent of King's political survival was astonishing. Yet while prime ministers are to be judged in many ways, one measure of their success must be the quality of their opponents. Borden had Laurier, and both were regarded as titans. King faced strong opponents in Meighen and Bennett, but during the war years the Conservatives could put up only a succession of less formidable men who could be counted on to support the wrong policy and to allow the foxy King to wedge them into peripheral political spaces. Yet even good leaders have been done in by their own unruly party, wayward ministers, global economic downturns, and the effects of war. King led from the rear, but he had a razor-sharp instinct for knowing when to go from the back to the front of the line, and how to champion the ideas and policies that mattered to him.

With his power base in Quebec, it is ironic that King barely spoke French and had little affinity for that unique province.[11] And so he always sought a Quebec lieutenant, in whom he invested authority and influence. But he was not controlled by Lapointe or, later, St. Laurent. A lieutenant was essential, but they were not generals. And the percentage of the Liberal caucus made up of Quebec MPs dropped over time, from a high of 76 percent in 1917 to 47 percent in 1926 to 34 percent in 1940.[12] Quebec had a strong voice in the Liberal cabinet, but King had the final say, though he had that rare gift of controlling his own instincts for the sake of party unity. Yet King had no unbreakable rules, as evidenced by his flip-flop in the 1944 conscription crisis, a point at which he sacrificed the NRMA soldiers and angered Quebec when he deemed it necessary to stave off national defeat.

King used the talents of his colleagues freely. He relied heavily on his cabinet ministers and senior bureaucrats, of which he had some of the very best in Canadian history. His advisors and secretarial staff were worked mercilessly, and when they protested or sought relief, he could be vain and vindictive. He was even harder on his close acquaintances, seemingly riding Skelton and Lapointe to their deaths. The collapse of others around him, especially the bull-like Ralston and Ilsley, reminded him of the need to conserve his own strength. He did, but at the expense of others' strength. In the aftermath of Skelton's funeral in January 1941, he wrote, "I am positive I would have been in my grave before this," if not for having delegated responsibility to the dead man and "avoided trying to gain too much in the way of power for myself."[13] There was a fine line between delegation and exploitation; King frequently crossed it.

But with regard to gathering power, King was the centre of the government and responsible for allowing or quashing most decisions made during the course of the war. Nonetheless, his influence remains obscured in popular memory by his turn towards the supernatural and spiritual. Why did King so readily participate in seances, consult mediums, and obsess about symbols and numbers? His proclivity to seek guidance from the spirits left him open to ridicule in death, even though there is little evidence that the messages from beyond had an impact on his policy decisions other than confirming what he had already decided. While twenty-first-century Canadians are likely more accepting of

King's eccentricities, narcissism, and spiritual beliefs than those of seventy years ago, it is still peculiar fare. No other Canadian of his stature and influence has ever had such proclivities, as far as we know. King did not live a double life, as some have suggested: his spiritualism underpinned his political values. However, his sense of mission, rather than his chats with the departed, was the driving force in his life. Some historians have gone to great pains to explain away the significance of King's seeking of supernatural guidance, while others have used his searches as nails with which to crucify him. Despite his political acumen and steadfast vision, King was plagued by self-doubt and strange urges. He was an odd fellow. But that is different from being a loony, lonely caricature, as he has often been portrayed.

King's opportunism has left generations wondering if he was more interested in political survival than in leading the nation. For King, however, the two goals went hand in hand: effectively prosecuting the war was always intertwined with political survival, since he believed fervently that only he and the Liberals could lead and keep the nation unified. King's obfuscation in matters of defence and diplomacy often led to a blurring of messages or to baffling statements, for which he was roundly condemned at the time and has been ever since, but his vision was remarkably consistent. Before the war, he refused to be drawn into colonial or imperial wars, but would defend Britain if it was truly threatened; throughout the conflict, he sought to do anything in his power to support Britain, but would not endanger his nation's unity. And despite the dodging and weaving, equivocating and vacillating, he fulfilled that mission.

Notwithstanding his vision, King was hamstrung by caution. His philosophy might have been "Not necessarily action, but action when necessary." This lack of assertiveness was profoundly disappointing for many Canadians, who ached for a rousing wartime leader. His trusted advisor, Norman Robertson, who had evidently worked too closely with the prime minister, was said to have "despised" King and remarked that "I never saw a touch of greatness in him."[14] Many others did, not least in his political longevity, and there were some like Lester Pearson, who noted that he did not recognize King's strengths until later in life, when he, as a prime minister, faced similar pressures. Pearson commented that King was "aware that his posture was often neither heroic nor dramatic. Nailing your colours to both sides of a fence seldom is; but it may be better than nailing your colours to one side if in so doing, you bring down the fence."[15] That said, no one mistook King for Churchill, exhorting all to fight on the beaches, fight in the streets, and never surrender. But King led a country that was not on the firing lines. Canadians would never have to die on their own beaches while repelling an invasion or battle furiously night after night against continual bombardment of their homeland cities from the air. And although some Canadians may have been disenchanted with King, his failure to move them emotionally with stirring rhetoric did not appear to detract from their commitment to the war effort. Canadians must have taken solace in King's other leadership qualities: political experience, fiscal conservatism, consensus building, and the ability to lead a strong cabinet. In September 1939, he was thrust into the role of war leader, for which he was neither trained nor ready; his watchfulness allowed him to seek a cautious path forward, and usually it was the right one.

When King was forced to leave the comfortable ground of limited liability, he did so tentatively, but always with the idea of standing by Britain. And soon, under his leadership, Canada's wartime exertions were awe-inspiring. The sending of 1.1 million citizens to war put an enormous strain on the nation, yet still Canadians produced an avalanche of war materiel and food. The fighting forces overseas punched far above their weight. The Dominion of Canada contributed as much as it did because of a motivated citizenry, a stable government, strong ministers, a cemented relationship with the United States, and King's steadiness at the helm of state.

J.W. Dafoe thought little of King in the 1920s. But by the midpoint of the war, he wrote, "My relations with King have never got to the point of warm friendship, but they have been close enough to give me an impression, which grows with every contact, that there is more to this man than I have thought."[16] Indeed, there was. Luck, chance, and timing are all important in politics; but good politicians such as King make their own luck out of the welter of decisions and factors that can derail policy, platform, or party. As one studies King and his actions, it is clear that there was more to the man, not the least of which is how he skilfully carried his nation through the trials of war.

"THE HISTORIAN WILL NOT DO JUSTICE to history and to Sir Robert Borden if he fails to appraise Sir Robert as Canada's greatest Prime Minister," wrote one journalist in 1920. "Lacking the magnetism and picturesqueness of Sir John Macdonald and Sir Wilfrid Laurier, he probably would not have been so successful had he been Prime Minister in their day. In the piping times of peace Canada demanded magnetism and picturesqueness in her leaders."[17] But could Macdonald or Laurier have filled the bill in

Sir Robert's time? We will never know the answer to that probing question, but neither Macdonald nor Laurier had his mettle tested in a world war, while King and Borden faced unique challenges in the history of their country.

By whatever criteria we assess Borden and King, we must gauge them within the context of their time. The two leaders faced unique situations, were supported by different bureaucracies and ministers, and had dissimilar relations with the Americans, the British, and their own people. Some have called the world wars one long war that spanned 1914 to 1945. There is some merit in that concept, as there is much continuity between the wars, but too many historical square pegs must be rammed into circular holes to make the construct work. Nonetheless, in their respective wars, the prime ministers faced similar challenges. Both had to raise armed forces from a civilian base. Both had to deal with the grief of a suffering nation whose young were being cut down on foreign fields. Both confronted the complexities of financing war, the challenges of dealing with allies, the management of internal dissent, and the agonizing appraisal of how far the nation could be pushed in the pursuit of victory.

King and Borden offer us different visions of how our leaders respond to crises. Both men were restrained, patient, and generally conciliatory. Yet time and again they beat the long odds, whistling past the political graves of opponents who had underestimated their endurance, skill, and ruthlessness. King saw himself as a rebel, but for almost all of his long political career he was more of a moderate when it came to finance, social policy, and government intervention.[18] Borden, conversely, saw himself as a reformer before the war, but that changed during the conflict, when he was transformed into a hard-bitten warlord. King was a shameless idealist who always turned to pragmatism when confronted with political realities; Borden was a no-nonsense pragmatist who succumbed in the end to idealism by gambling the nation's fate when striving for the rewards of greater influence and independence. Borden grew into the role of statesman, even as he shed his responsibility as a consensus-shaping politician—a transformation demonstrated most clearly by his willingness to sacrifice his party's future prosperity to ensure that the soldiers overseas were supported. King could never do that to the Liberal Party. Not only was he deeply partisan, but he truly believed that the Liberals were a force for good and harmony. To hand over influence to the Conservatives was to embrace that which was most repugnant to him. The dark danger of Conservatism was a hyperbolic narrative that King had constructed for himself, and others, over a lifetime, and that he never abandoned.

Borden had no precedent to follow during the Great War: he was forced to confront one challenge after another, and none so monumental as the manpower question that led to conscription and then to national disunity. King's primary motivation was to avoid what Borden had done, and almost every decision he made was an attempt to keep from alienating Quebec through another crisis over army recruits. Yet the world wars left no easy choices and, as they dragged on and the fighting forces suffered heavy casualties, the majority of Canadians on the home front demanded that the full resources of the nation be thrown into winning the war, no matter the cost. So, in spite of King's long struggle, he was forced in the end to walk down Borden's path to conscription. That is not to say that the two leaders viewed conscription similarly. They didn't. In broad strokes, it can be said that Borden sided with the soldiers at the cost of jeopardizing unity at home, while King did the opposite, choosing unity over the lives of the soldiers overseas.

The captions on the official portraits of Borden and King hanging outside the House of Commons are right to focus on their wartime leadership. Both of these prime ministers heaved against the maelstrom, occasionally stumbling, but almost always finding traction in an ever-shifting world of domestic politics and external war. One can scarcely imagine two more different leaders. In trying to sum up King's impact on Canada, one prominent historian described him as the "leader who divided us least."[19] Faint praise, but praise nonetheless given the difficulty of governing a country like Canada. No one would employ such a phrase to describe Borden. He perhaps *divided* us most in his quest for victory. With regard to questions of foreign policy and the Dominion's commitment to victory during the Great War, Borden believed the crisis required that domestic policies be subsumed to the international war. For King, it was always the domestic that trumped the international, regardless of the pressure or strain on the Allied war effort. Borden was most proud of what he accomplished, primarily the guiding of Canada onto the world stage, while King saw his legacy in what he prevented, particularly the avoidance of irreparable damage to national unity.

Warlords are typically portrayed as militaristic, aggressive, and ruthlessly backed by military power, with violence and destruction used to achieve their goals. During the world wars, Canada required a different type of civilian leader. The Dominion was never on the front lines of battle, except when faced with the real but relatively minor threat to shipping posed by U-boats in Canadian waters during the Second World War, but a majority of citizens demanded a nearly unlimited war effort in support of

Britain and its allies. Forced to learn their jobs during times of intense crisis, Borden and King more often than not found the right delicate balance between financing the war, ensuring home front production, raising armed forces, and gradually ramping up the nation towards a total war effort. At the outset of the two wars, no one could have predicted the enormous exertions that would be required of Canadians in the years that immediately followed, but the final contributions were staggering. Borden and King had almost no role to play in personally directing their fighting forces or in setting military strategy, but almost all of the critical logistical, financial, and manpower issues fell under their control. So, too, did almost everything else in the militarized nation. As Canada's war leaders, Borden and King were adept at wielding power. They were thus very much warlords, albeit in a Canadian way, and though their leadership approaches differed significantly in both style and substance, they guided their country to victory in the two most traumatic events in Canadian history. Like the fierce determination glowing from their eyes, even as old men, in their official portraits, Borden and King both, in unique ways that reflected their different personalities, saw what had to be done, and then did it. They were forever changed by the world wars and so was their country.

BIBLIOGRAPHY

PRIMARY SOURCES, UNPUBLISHED

Library and Archives Canada, Ottawa, Government Records

RG 2, Records of the Privy Council Office
RG 9, Records of the Department of Militia and Defence
RG 24, Records of the Department of National Defence

Library and Archives Canada, Ottawa, Private Records

C.C. Ballantyne papers, MG 27 II-D-1
Lord Beaverbrook papers, MG 27 II-G-1
Sir Robert Borden papers, MG 26 H
Loring Christie papers, MG 30 E44
Harry Crerar papers, MG 30 E157
Sir George Foster papers, MG 27 II-D-7
C.D. Howe papers, MG 27 III-B-20
A.E. Kemp papers, MG 27 II-D-9
William Lyon Mackenzie King papers, MG 26 J
Sir Sam Hughes papers, MG 27 II-D-23
Sir Wilfrid Laurier papers, MG 26 G
Ian Mackenzie papers, MG 27 III-B-5
Sir George Perley papers, MG 27 II-D-12

J.L. Ralston papers, MG 27 III-B-11
Newton Rowell papers, MG 27 II-D-3
Louis St. Laurent papers, MG 26 L
Sir Thomas White papers, MG 27 II-D-18
Sir John Willison papers, MG 30 D29

Canadian War Museum, Ottawa
Sir Richard Turner collection, 19710147-001

Queen's University Archives, Kingston
T.A. Crerar papers
Norman Rogers papers
C.G. Power papers
Grant Dexter papers

MONOGRAPHS AND BOOKS

Abella, Irving and Harold Troper. *None Is Too Many: Canada and the Jews of Europe, 1933–1948*. Toronto: Lester & Orpen Dennys, 1982.

Adachi, Ken. *The Enemy that Never Was: A History of the Japanese Canadians*, 2nd ed. Toronto: McClelland & Stewart, 1991.

Argyle, Ray. *Turning Points: The Campaigns that Changed Canada*. Toronto: White Knight, 2004.

Armstrong, Elizabeth. *The Crisis of Quebec, 1914–18*. New York: Columbia University Press, 1937.

Armstrong, John. *The Halifax Explosion and the Royal Canadian Navy: Inquiry and Intrigue*. Vancouver: University of British Columbia Press, 2002.

Aster, Sidney (ed.). *The Second World War as a National Experience*. Ottawa: The Canadian Committee for the History of the Second World War, 1981.

Avery, Donald. *Dangerous Foreigners: European Immigrant Workers and Labour Radicalism in Canada, 1896–1932*. Toronto: McClelland & Stewart, 1979.

Bangarth, Stephanie. *Voices Raised in Protest: Defending North American Citizens of Japanese Ancestry, 1942–49*. Vancouver: University of British Columbia Press, 2008.

Beck, J. Murray. *Pendulum of Power: Canada's Federal Elections*. Scarborough: Prentice-Hall of Canada, 1968.

Becker, John Harold. *Silhouettes of the Great War: The Memoirs of John Harold Becker*. Ottawa: CEF Books, 2001.

Bellamy, Matthew. *Profiting the Crown: Canada's Polymer Corporation, 1942–1990*. Montreal: McGill-Queen's University Press, 2005.

Bennett, Captain S.G. *The 4th Canadian Mounted Rifles, 1914–1919*. Toronto: Murray Printing Company, 1926.

Bercuson, David J. *True Patriot: The Life of Brooke Claxton, 1898–1960*. Toronto: University of Toronto Press, 1993.

Berger, Carl. *The Sense of Power: Studies in the Ideas of Canadian Imperialism, 1867–1914*. Toronto: University of Toronto Press, 1971.

Berger, Carl. *The Writing of Canadian History: Aspects of English-Canadian Historical Writing, 1900–1970*. Toronto: Oxford University Press, 1976.

Berger, Carl (ed.). *Conscription 1917*. Toronto: University of Toronto Press, 1969.

Betcherman, Lita-Rose. *Ernest Lapointe: Mackenzie King's Great Quebec Lieutenant*. Toronto: University of Toronto Press, 2002.

Betcherman, Lita-Rose. *The Swastika and the Maple Leaf: Fascist Movements in Canada in the Thirties*. Toronto: Fitzhenry & Whiteside, 1975.

Bliss, Michael. *A Canadian Millionaire: The Life and Business Times of Sir Joseph Flavelle, Bart., 1858–1939*. Toronto: Macmillan of Canada, 1978.

Bliss, Michael. *Right Honourable Men: The Descent of Canadian Politics from Macdonald to Mulroney*. Toronto: HarperCollins, 1994.

Borden, Sir Robert. *Canada and the Commonwealth*. Oxford: Clarendon Press, 1929.

Borden, Sir Robert. *Canadian Constitutional Studies*. Toronto: University of Toronto Press, 1922.

Borden, Sir Robert Laird. *Robert Laird Borden: His Memoirs*, 2 volumes. Toronto: Macmillan Co. of Canada, 1938.

Borden, Sir Robert Laird. *Robert Laird Borden: His Memoirs*, volume I. Introduction by Heath Macquarrie. Toronto: McClelland & Stewart, 1969.

Borden, Henry (ed.). *Letters to Limbo*. Toronto: University of Toronto Press, 1971.

Bothwell, Robert. *Alliance and Illusion: Canada and the World, 1945–1984*. Vancouver: University of British Columbia Press, 2007.

Bothwell, Robert. *Eldorado: Canada's National Uranium Company*. Toronto: University of Toronto Press, 1984.

Bothwell, Robert. *Loring Christie: The Failure of Bureaucratic Imperialism*. New York: Garland Publishing, 1988.

Bothwell, Robert. *The Penguin History of Canada*. Toronto: Penguin Canada, 2006.

Bothwell, Robert, Ian Drummond, and John English. *Canada, 1900–1945*. Toronto: University of Toronto Press, 1987.

Bothwell, Robert and William Kilbourn. *C.D. Howe: A Biography*. Toronto: McClelland & Stewart, 1979.

Bourassa, Henri. *The Duty of Canada at the Present Hour*. Montreal, 1915.

Bourrie, Mark. *The Fog of War: Censorship of Canada's Media in World War Two*. Vancouver: Douglas & McIntyre, 2011.

Bouvier, Patrick. *Déserteurs et insoumis: les Canadiens français et la justice militaire, 1914–1918*. Outremont: Athéna, 2003.

Boyko, John. *Bennett: The Rebel Who Challenged and Changed a Nation*. Toronto: Key Porter, 2010.

Brennan, Patrick H. *Reporting the Nation's Business: Press-Government Relations during the Liberal Years, 1935–1957*. Toronto: University of Toronto Press, 1994.

Bridle, Augustus. *The Masques of Ottawa*. Toronto: Macmillan Co. of Canada, 1921.

Bridle, Augustus. *Sons of Canada: Short Studies of Characteristic Canadians*. Toronto: Macmillan Co. of Canada, 1916.

Brown, Robert Craig. *Robert Laird Borden: A Biography. Volume I: 1854–1914*. Toronto: Macmillan of Canada, 1975.

Brown, Robert Craig. *Robert Laird Borden: A Biography. Volume II: 1914–1937*. Toronto: Macmillan of Canada, 1980.

Brown, Robert Craig and Ramsay Cook, *Canada 1896–1921: A Nation Transformed*. Toronto: McClelland & Stewart, 1974.

Bryce, Robert. *Canada and the Cost of World War II: The International Operations of Canada's Department of Finance, 1939–1947*. Montreal: McGill-Queen's University Press, 2005.

Buchan, John. *Memory Hold-the-Door*. London: Hodder & Stoughton, 1945.

Burns, E.L.M. *Manpower in the Canadian Army, 1939–1945*. Toronto: Irving and Company Limited, 1956.

Busby, Brian (ed.). *Great Canadian Speeches: Words that Shaped a Nation*. London: Arcturus Publishing, 2008.

Caccia, Ivana. *Managing the Canadian Mosaic in Wartime: Shaping Citizenship Policy, 1939–1945*. Montreal: McGill-Queen's University Press, 2010.

Canada, Government of. *Canada's War Effort, 1914–1918*. Ottawa: Director of Public Information, 1918.

Carnegie, David. *History of Munitions Supply in Canada 1914–1918*. Toronto: Longmans, 1925.

Chapnick, Adam. *The Middle Power Project: Canada and the Founding of the United Nations*. Vancouver: University of British Columbia Press, 2005.

Cook, Tim. *At the Sharp End: Canadians Fighting the Great War. Volume I: 1914–1916*. Toronto: Viking, 2007.

Cook, Tim. *The Madman and the Butcher: The Sensational Wars of Sam Hughes and General Arthur Currie*. Toronto: Allen Lane, 2010.

Cook, Tim. *Shock Troops: Canadians Fighting the Great War. Volume II: 1917–1918*. Toronto: Viking, 2008.

Copp, Terry. *Cinderella Army: The Canadians in Northwest Europe, 1944–1945*. Toronto: University of Toronto Press, 2006.

Creighton, Donald. *Canada's First Century, 1867–1967*. Toronto: Macmillan of Canada, 1970.

Creighton, Donald. *The Forked Road: Canada 1939–1957*. Toronto: McClelland & Stewart, 1976.

Crowley, Terry. *Marriage of Minds: Isabel and Oscar Skelton Reinventing Canada*. Toronto: University of Toronto Press, 2003.

Cuff, Robert and J.L. Granatstein. *Canadian-American Relations in Wartime: From the Great War to the Cold War*. Toronto: Hakkert, 1975.

Dafoe, J.W. *Clifford Sifton in Relation to His Times*. Toronto: The Macmillan Company of Canada, 1931.

Dafoe, J.W. *Laurier: A Study in Canadian Politics*. Toronto: McClelland & Stewart, 1963 [original in 1922].

Dancocks, Daniel. *The D-Day Dodgers: The Canadians in Italy, 1943–1945*. Toronto: McClelland & Stewart, 1991.

Dawson, R. MacGregor. *The Conscription Crisis of 1944*. Toronto: University of Toronto Press, 1961.

Dawson, R. MacGregor. *William Lyon Mackenzie King: A Political Biography, Volume I: 1874–1923*. Toronto: University of Toronto Press, 1958.

Dickson, Paul. *A Thoroughly Canadian General: A Biography of General H.D.G. Crerar*. Toronto: University of Toronto Press, 2007.

Diefenbaker, John G. *One Canada: The Crusading Years, 1895–1956*. Toronto: MacMillan of Canada, 1975.

Dilks, David. *The Great Dominion: Winston Churchill in Canada, 1900–1954*. Toronto: Thomas Allen, 2005.

Donaldson, Gordon. *Eighteen Men: The Prime Ministers of Canada*. Toronto: Doubleday, 1985.

Drummond, Ian M. and Norman Hillmer. *Negotiating Freer Trade: The United Kingdom, the United States, Canada, and the Trade Agreements of 1938*. Waterloo: Wilfrid Laurier University Press, 1989.

Durflinger, Serge Marc. *Fighting from Home: The Second World War in Verdun, Quebec*. Vancouver: University of British Columbia Press, 2006.

Dutil, Patrice and David MacKenzie. *Canada 1911: The Decisive Election that Shaped the Country*. Toronto: Dundurn, 2011.

Dziuban, S.W. *The Military Relations between the United States and Canada, 1939–1945*. Washington: United States Army in World War II, Special Studies, 1959.

Eayrs, James. *In Defence of Canada. Volume II: Appeasement and Re-Armament*. Toronto: University of Toronto Press, 1965.

Eggleston, Wilfrid. *While I Still Remember*. Toronto: Ryerson Press, 1968.

Ellis, Charles Howard. *The Origin, Structure & Working of the League of Nations*. Boston: Houghton Mifflin Company, 1929.

English, John. *Borden: His Life and World*. Toronto: McGraw-Hill Ryerson, 1977.

English, John. *The Decline of Politics: The Conservatives and the Party System, 1901–20*. Toronto: University of Toronto Press, 1977.

English, John, Kenneth McLaughlin, and P. Whitney Lackenbauer (eds.). *Mackenzie King: Citizenship and Community*. Toronto: Robin Brass Studio, 2002.

English, John and J.O. Stubbs (eds.). *Mackenzie King: Widening the Debate*. Toronto: Macmillan of Canada, 1977.

Esberey, Joy E. *Knight of the Holy Spirit: A Study of William Lyon Mackenzie King*. Toronto: University of Toronto Press, 1980.

External Affairs, Department of. *Documents on Canadian External Relations*, volume 1. Ottawa: Information Canada, 1968.

External Affairs, Department of. *Documents on Canadian External Relations*, volume 8. Ottawa: Information Canada, 1976.

Ferns, Henry and Bernard Ostry. *The Age of Mackenzie King: The Rise of the Leader*. London: William Heinemann, 1955.

Fisher, Susan. *Boys and Girls in No Man's Land: English-Canadian Children and the First World War*. Toronto: University of Toronto Press, 2011.

Francis, Daniel. *Canada's Red Scare*. Vancouver: Arsenal Pulp Press, 2010.

Fullerton, Douglas. *Graham Towers and His Times*. Toronto: McClelland & Stewart, 1986.

Gibson, Frederick W. and Barbara Robertson (eds.). *Ottawa at War: The Grant Dexter Memoranda, 1939–1945*. Winnipeg: Manitoba Record Society, 1994.

Glazebrook, George. *Canadian External Relations*. Toronto: Oxford University Press, 1950.

Graham, Roger. *Arthur Meighen, A Biography: The Door of Opportunity*, volume 1. Toronto: Clarke, Irwin & Company, 1960.

Graham, Roger. *Arthur Meighen, A Biography: And Fortune Fled*, volume 2. Toronto: Clarke, Irwin & Company, 1963.

Granatstein, J.L. *Canada's War: The Politics of the Mackenzie King Government, 1939–1945*, 2nd ed. Toronto: University of Toronto Press, 1990.

Granatstein, J.L. *The Generals: The Canadian Army's Senior Commanders in the Second World War*. Toronto: Stoddart Publishing Co., 1993.

Granatstein, J.L. *How Britain's Weakness Forced Canada into the Arms of the United States*. Toronto: University of Toronto Press, 1989.

Granatstein, J.L. *The Last Good War: An Illustrated History of Canada in the Second World War, 1939–1945*. Vancouver: Douglas & McIntyre, 2005.

Granatstein, J.L. *Mackenzie King: His Life and World*. Toronto: McGraw-Hill Ryerson, 1977.

Granatstein, J.L. *A Man of Influence: Norman A. Robertson and Canadian Statecraft, 1929–1968*. Ottawa: Denau, 1981.

Granatstein, J.L. *The Ottawa Men: The Civil Service Mandarins, 1935–1957*. Toronto: Oxford University Press, 1982.

Granatstein, J.L. *Yankee Go Home? Canadians and Anti-Americanism*. Toronto: HarperCollins, 1996.

Granatstein, J.L. and Norman Hillmer. *For Better or For Worse: Canada and the United States to the 1990s*. Toronto: Copp Clark Pitman, 1991.

Granatstein, J.L. and Norman Hillmer. *Prime Ministers: Ranking Canada's Leaders*. Toronto: HarperCollins, 1999.

Granatstein, J.L. and J.M. Hitsman. *Broken Promises: A History of Conscription in Canada*. Toronto: Oxford University Press, 1977.

Granatstein, J.L. and Desmond Morton, *Canada and the Two World Wars*. Toronto: Key Porter Books, 2003.

Granatstein, J.L. and Dean F. Oliver, *The Oxford Companion to Canadian Military History*. Toronto: Oxford University Press Canada, 2011.

Gray, Charlotte. *Mrs. King: The Life and Times of Isabel Mackenzie King*. Toronto: Viking, 1997.

Greenfield, Nathan. *The Damned: The Canadians at the Battle of Hong Kong and the POW Experience, 1941–45*. Toronto: HarperCollins, 2010.

Greenhous, Brereton et al. *The Crucible of War 1939–1945: The Official History of the Royal Canadian Air Force*, Volume 3. Toronto: University of Toronto Press, 1994.

Gregory, Adrian. *The Last Great War: British Society and the First World War.* Cambridge: Cambridge University Press, 2008.

Hadley, Michael. *U-boats against Canada*: *German Submarines in Canadian Waters*. Montreal: McGill-Queen's University Press, 1985.

Hadley, Michael and Roger Sarty. *Tin-pots and Pirate Ships: Canadian Naval Forces and German Sea Raiders, 1880–1918*. Montreal: McGill-Queen's University Press, 1991.

Hall, H. Duncan and C.C. Wrigley. *Studies of Overseas Supply.* London: H.M. Stationery Office, 1956.

Hamelin, Marcel (ed.). *The Political Ideas of the Prime Ministers of Canada*. Ottawa: The Vanier Lectures, 1969.

Hardy, Reginald. *Mackenzie King of Canada*: *A Biography*. Toronto: Oxford University Press, 1949.

Harris, Stephen J. *Canadian Brass: The Making of a Professional Army, 1860–1939*. Toronto: University of Toronto Press, 1988.

Hatch, F.J. *Aerodrome of Democracy: Canada and the British Commonwealth Air Training Plan, 1939–1945*. Ottawa: Directorate of History, Monograph Series 1, 1983.

Haycock, R.G. *Sam Hughes: The Public Career of a Controversial Canadian, 1885–1916*. Ottawa: Canadian War Museum, 1986.

Heeney, Arnold. *The Things that Are Caesar's: Memoir of a Canadian Public Servant*. Toronto: University of Toronto Press, 1972.

Henderson, George F. *W.L. Mackenzie King: A Bibliography and Research Guide*. Toronto: University of Toronto Press, 1998.

Henderson, T. Stephen. *Angus L. Macdonald: A Provincial Leader*. Toronto: University of Toronto Press, 2007.

Hilliker, J.F. *Documents on Canadian External Relations,* volume 10. Ottawa: Information Services, 1980.

Hillmer, Norman and J.L. Granatstein. *From Empire to Umpire: Canada and the World to the 1990s*. Toronto: Copp Clark Longman, 1994.

Hopkins, J. Castell. *The Book of the Union Government*. Toronto: Annual Review of Publishing, 1918.

Hopkins, J. Castell. *Canadian Annual Review, 1914*. Toronto: Annual Review of Publishing, 1915.

Hutchison, Bruce. *The Far Side of the Street*. Toronto: Macmillan of Canada, 1976.

Hutchison, Bruce. *The Incredible Canadian: A Candid Portrait of Mackenzie King*. Toronto: Longmans Canada, 1970 [original, 1952].

Hutchison, Bruce. *Mr. Prime Minister, 1867–1964*. Toronto: Longmans Canada Limited, 1964.

Iarocci, Andrew. *Shoestring Soldiers: The 1st Canadian Division at War, 1914–1915*. Toronto: University of Toronto Press, 2008.

Johnston, Charles. *E.C. Drury: Agrarian Idealist*. Toronto: University of Toronto Press, 1986.

Keshen, Jeff. *Saints, Soldiers and Sinners: Canada's Second World War.* Vancouver: University of British Columbia Press, 2004.

Keshen. Jeffrey A. *Propaganda and Censorship during Canada's Great War.* Edmonton: University of Alberta Press, 1996.

Kilbourn, William. *A Guide to the Peaceable Kingdom*. Toronto: Macmillan of Canada, 1970.

King, William Lyon Mackenzie. *Industry and Humanity: A Study in the Principles Underlying Industrial Reconstruction*. Toronto: Thomas Allen, 1918.

King, William Lyon Mackenzie. *Industry and Humanity: A Study in the Principles Underlying Industrial Reconstruction*. With an introduction by David Jay Bercuson. Toronto: University of Toronto Press, 1973.

King, William Lyon Mackenzie. *The Secret of Heroism: A Memoir of Henry Albert Harper*. New York: Fleming H. Revell, 1906.

Knight, Amy. *How the Cold War Began: The Gouzenko Affair and the Hunt for Soviet Spies*. Toronto: McClelland & Stewart, 2005.

Kordan, Bohdan S. *Enemy Aliens, Prisoners of War: Internment in Canada during the Great War*. Montreal: McGill-Queen's University Press, 2002.

Laurendeau, Andre. *Witness for Quebec*. Toronto: Macmillan of Canada, 1973.

Lay, Rear-Admiral H. Nelson. *Memoirs of a Mariner*. Stittsville: Canada's Wings, 1982.

Lefevbre, Florent. *The French-Canadian Press and the War*. Toronto: Ryerson Press, 1942.

Levine, Allan. *King: William Lyon Mackenzie King: A Life Guided by the Hand of Destiny*. Vancouver: Douglas & McIntyre, 2011.

Levitt, Joseph. *Henri Bourassa on Imperialism and Bi-culturalism, 1900–1918*. Toronto: Copp Clark, 1970.

Lloyd George, David. *The Truth about the Peace Treaties,* volume I. London: Victor Gollancz, 1938.

Lloyd George, David. *War Memoirs of David Lloyd George*, volume IV. London: I. Nicholson and Watson, 1936.

Lower, Arthur. *My First Seventy-Five Years*. Toronto: The Macmillan Co. of Canada, 1967.

Ludwig, Emil. *Mackenzie King: A Portrait Sketch*. Toronto: Macmillan Co. of Canada, 1944.

Lyddon, Colonel W.G. *British War Missions to the United States, 1917–1918*. Oxford University Press, 1938.

Malone, Richard S. *A Portrait of War, 1939–1943*. Toronto: Collins, 1983.

Malone, Richard S. *A World in Flames, 1944–1945*. Toronto: Collins, 1984.

Macfarlane, John. *Ernest Lapointe, Mackenzie King and Quebec's Voice in Canadian Foreign Policy*. Toronto: University of Toronto Press, 1999.

Mackenzie, David (ed.). *Canada and the First World War: Essays in Honour of Robert Craig Brown*. Toronto: University of Toronto Press, 2005.

Macmillan, Margaret. *Paris 1919*. New York: Random House, 2001.

Macphail, Andrew. *The Medical Services: Official History of the Canadian Forces in the Great War 1914–19*. Ottawa: F.A. Acland, 1925.

Mansergh, Nicholas. *Survey of British Commonwealth Affairs: Problems of External Policy, 1931–1939*. London: Oxford University Press, 1952.

Martin, A.W. and Patsy Hardy (eds.). *Dark and Hurrying Days: Menzies' 1941 Diary*. Canberra: National Library of Australia, 1993.

Martin, Lawrence. *The Presidents and the Prime Ministers. Washington and Ottawa Face to Face: The Myth of Bilateral Bliss, 1867–1982*. Toronto: Doubleday, 1982.

Martin, Paul. *A Very Public Life: Far from Home*. Ottawa: Deneau, 1983.

Massey, Vincent. *What's Past Is Prologue: The Memoirs of the Right Honourable Vincent Massey*. Toronto: Macmillan Co. of Canada, 1963.

McCormack, A. Ross. *Reformers, Rebels and Revolutionaries: The Western Canadian Radical Movement, 1899–1919*. Toronto: University of Toronto Press, 1977.

McGregor, Fred A. *The Fall and Rise of Mackenzie King, 1911–1919*. Toronto: Macmillan Co. of Canada, 1962.

McKercher, B.J.C. and Lawrence Aronsen (eds.). *The North Atlantic Triangle in a Changing World*. Toronto: University of Toronto Press, 1996.

McLaughlin, K.M. *The Germans in Canada*. Ottawa: Canadian Historical Association, 1985.

McMullin, Stan. *Anatomy of a Séance: A History of Spirit Communication in Central Canada*. Montreal: McGill-Queen's University Press, 2004.

Meighen, Arthur. *Unrevised and Unrepented*. Toronto: Clarke, Irwin & Company, 1949.

Miller, Carman. *A Knight in Politics: A Biography of Sir Frederick Borden*. Montreal: McGill-Queen's University Press, 2010.

Miller, J.O. (ed.). *The New Era in Canada: Essays Dealing with the Upbuilding of the Canadian Commonwealth*. Toronto: J.M. Dent, 1917.

Milner, Marc. *Canada's Navy: The First Century*. Toronto: University of Toronto Press, 1999.

Morton, Desmond. *Fight or Pay: Soldiers' Families in the Great War*. Vancouver: University of British Columbia Press, 2004.

Morton, Desmond. *A Peculiar Kind of Politics: Canada's Overseas Ministry in the First World War*. Toronto: University of Toronto Press, 1982.

Morton, Desmond and J.L. Granatstein. *Marching to Armageddon: Canadians and the Great War, 1914–1919*. Toronto: Lester & Orpen Dennys Limited, 1989.

Morton, Desmond and Glenn Wright. *Winning the Second Battle: Canadian Veterans and the Return to Civilian Life, 1915–1930*. Toronto: University of Toronto Press, 1987.

Moss, Mark. *Manliness and Militarism: Educating Young Boys in Ontario for War*. New York: Oxford University Press, 2001.

Mount, Graeme S. *Canada's Enemies: Spies and Spying in the Peaceable Kingdom*. Toronto: Dundurn Press, 1993.

Neary, Peter. *On to Civvy Street: Canada's Rehabilitation Program for Veterans of the Second World War*. Montreal: McGill-Queen's University Press, 2011.

Neatby, Blair. *William Lyon Mackenzie King: The Lonely Heights, Volume II: 1924–1932*. Toronto: University of Toronto Press, 1970.

Neatby, Blair. *William Lyon Mackenzie King: The Prism of Unity, Volume III: 1933–1939*. Toronto: University of Toronto Press, 1975.

Neatby, H. Blair. *The Politics of Chaos: Canada in the Thirties*. Toronto: Macmillan of Canada, 1972.

Neiberg, Michael. *Fighting the Great War: A Global History*. Cambridge: Harvard University Press, 2005.

Nicholson, G.W.L. *Canadian Expeditionary Force: The Official History of the Canadian Army in the First World War*. Ottawa: Queen's Printer, 1964.

Nolan, Brian. *King's War: Mackenzie King and the Politics of War, 1939–1945*. Toronto: Random House, 1988.

O'Leary, Grattan. *Recollections of People, Press, and Politics*. Toronto: MacMillan of Canada, 1977.

Owram, Doug. *The Government Generation: Canadian Intellectuals and the State, 1900–1945*. Toronto: University of Toronto Press, 1986.

Pearson, Lester B. *Mike: The Memoirs of the Right Honourable Lester B. Pearson, Volume I, 1897–1948*. Toronto: University of Toronto Press, 1972.

Perras, Galen. *Franklin Roosevelt and the Origins of the Canadian–American Security Alliance, 1933–1945*. Westport: Greenwood Press, 1998.

Petrou, Michael. *Renegades: Canadians in the Spanish Civil War*. Vancouver: University of British Columbia Press, 2008.

Pickersgill, J.W. *The Mackenzie King Record*, 4 volumes. Toronto: University of Toronto Press, 1960–1970.

Pickersgill, J.W. *Seeing Canada Whole: A Memoir*. Toronto: Fitzhenry & Whiteside, 1994.

Pope, Maurice (ed.). *Public Servant: The Memoirs of Sir Joseph Pope.* Toronto: Oxford University Press, 1960.

Pope, Maurice. *Soldiers and Politicians: The Memoirs of Lt.-Gen. Maurice A. Pope.* Toronto: University of Toronto Press, 1962.

Prang, Margaret. *N.W. Rowell: Ontario Nationalist.* Toronto: University of Toronto Press, 1975.

Pratte, André. *Wilfrid Laurier.* Toronto: Penguin Canada, 2011.

Preston, R.A. *Canada and "Imperial Defence": A Study in the Origins of the British Commonwealth's Defence Organization, 1867–1919.* Durham: Durham University Press, 1967.

Rea, J.E. *T.A. Crerar: A Political Life.* Montreal: McGill-Queen's University Press, 1997.

Read, Daphne (ed.). *The Great War and Canadian Society: An Oral History.* Toronto: New Hogtown Press, 1978.

Reynolds, David. *The Creation of the Anglo-American Alliance, 1937–1941.* Chapel Hill: University of North Carolina Press, 1982.

Reynolds, Louise. *Mackenzie King: Friends & Lovers.* Victoria: Trafford, 2005.

Rickard, John Nelson. *The Politics of Command: Lieutenant-General A.G.L. McNaughton and the Canadian Army, 1939–1943.* Toronto: University of Toronto Press, 2010.

Riddell, Walter (ed.). *Documents on Canadian Foreign Policy, 1917–1939.* Toronto: Oxford University Press, 1962.

Ritchie, Charles. *Diplomatic Passport: More Undiplomatic Diaries, 1946–1962.* Toronto: Macmillan of Canada, 1981.

Roazen, Paul. *Canada's King: An Essay in Political Psychology.* Oakville: Mosaic Press, 1998.

Roberts, Barbara. *Why Do Women Do Nothing to End the War? Canadian Feminist-Pacifists and the Great War.* Ottawa: Canadian Research Institute for the Advancement of Women, 1985.

Robertson, Gordon. *Memoirs of a Very Civil Servant: Mackenzie King to Pierre Trudeau.* Toronto: University of Toronto Press, 2000.

Roskill, Stephen. *Hankey, Man of Secrets I, 1877–1918.* London: Collins, 1970.

Sarty, Roger. *The Maritime Defence of Canada*. Toronto: The Canadian Institute of Strategic Studies, 1996.

Saywell, John T. *Just Call Me Mitch: The Life of Mitchell F. Hepburn*. Toronto: University of Toronto Press, 1991.

Schull, Joseph. *Laurier: The First Canadian*. Toronto: Macmillan Co. of Canada, 1965.

Skelton, Oscar Douglas. *Life and Letters of Sir Wilfrid Laurier*. Toronto: Oxford University Press, 1921.

Stacey, C.P. *Arms, Men and Governments: The War Policies of Canada, 1939–1945*. Ottawa: Queen's Printer, 1970.

Stacey, C.P. *Canada and the Age of Conflict: A History of Canadian External Policies. Volume I: 1867–1921*. Toronto: Macmillan of Canada, 1977.

Stacey, C.P. *Canada and the Age of Conflict: A History of Canadian External Relations. Volume II: 1921–1948, The Mackenzie King Era*. Toronto: University of Toronto Press, 1981.

Stacey, C.P. *Historical Documents of Canada. Volume V: The Arts of War and Peace, 1914–1945*. Toronto: Macmillan of Canada, 1972.

Stacey, C.P. *Mackenzie King and the Atlantic Triangle*. Toronto: Macmillan of Canada, 1977.

Stacey, C.P. *Six Years of War: The Canadian Army in Canada, Britain and the Pacific; The Official History of the Canadian Army in the Second World War*, volume 1. Ottawa: The Queen's Printer, 1955.

Stacey, C.P. *A Very Double Life: The Private World of Mackenzie King*. Toronto: Macmillan of Canada, 1976.

Stanley, George. *Canada's Soldiers, 1604–1954: The Military History of an Unmilitary People*. Toronto: Macmillan of Canada, 1954.

Stevenson, Michael D. *Canada's Greatest Wartime Muddle: National Selective Service and the Mobilization of Human Resources during World War II*. Montreal: McGill-Queen's University Press, 2001.

Stursberg, Peter. *The Sound of War: Memoirs of a CBC Correspondent*. Toronto: University of Toronto Press, 1993.

Swettenham, John. *McNaughton, Volume II, 1939–1943*. Toronto: Ryerson Press, 1969.

Swettenham, John. *McNaughton, Volume III, 1944–1966*. Toronto: Ryerson Press, 1969.

Theobald, Andrew. *The Bitter Harvest of War: New Brunswick and the Conscription Crisis of 1917*. New Brunswick: Goose Lane, 2008.

Thompson, Dale C. *Louis St. Laurent: Canadian*. New York: St. Martin's Press, 1968.

Thompson, John Herd. *The Harvests of War: The Prairie West, 1914–1918*. Toronto: McClelland & Stewart, 1978.

Thornton, Martin. *Sir Robert Borden*. London: Haus, 2010.

Tucker, G.N. *Naval Service of Canada: Official History, Volume 1*. Ottawa: King's Printer, 1952.

Underhill, F.H. *In Search of Canadian Liberalism*. Toronto: Macmillan Co. of Canada, 1961.

Urquhart, M.C. and K.A.H. Buckley. *Historical Statistics of Canada*. Toronto: Macmillan Co. of Canada, 1965.

Vance, Jonathan. *Maple Leaf Empire: Canada, Britain, and Two World Wars*. Toronto: Oxford University Press, 2011.

Wade, Mason. *The French-Canadians*, volume II. Toronto: Macmillan Co. of Canada, 1968.

Waiser, Bill. *Saskatchewan: A New History*. Calgary: Fifth House Ltd, 2005.

Wallace, W. Stewart. *The Memoirs of the Rt. Hon. Sir George Foster*. Toronto: Macmillan Co. of Canada, 1933.

Ward, Norman (ed.). *A Party Politician: The Memoirs of Chubby Power*. Toronto: Macmillan Co. of Canada, 1966.

Wardhaugh, Robert A. *Behind the Scenes: The Life and Work of William Clifford Clark*. Toronto: University of Toronto Press, 2010.

Wardhaugh, Robert A. *Mackenzie King and the Prairie West*. Toronto: University of Toronto Press, 2000.

White, Sir Thomas. *The Story of Canada's War Finance*. Montreal: The Canadian Bank of Commerce, 1921.

Wilmott, H.P. *Empires in the Balance: Japanese and Allied Pacific Strategies to April 1942*. Maryland: Naval Institute Press, 1982.

Wilson, Barbara. *Ontario and the First World War, 1914–1918*. Toronto: University of Toronto Press, 1977.

Young, Scott and Astrid Young. *Silent Frank Cochrane: The North's First Great Politician*. Toronto: Macmillan of Canada, 1973.

ARTICLES

Auger, Martin. "On the Brink of Civil War: The Canadian Government and the Suppression of the 1918 Quebec Easter Riots." *The Canadian Historical Review* 89.4 (2008) 503–40.

Auger, Martin F. "'A Tempest in a Teapot': Canadian Military Planning and the St. Pierre and Miquelon Affair, 1940–1942." *Acadiensis* 13.1 (2003) 47–72.

Baker, W.M. "A Case Study of Anti-Americanism in English-Speaking Canada: The Election Campaign of 1911." *The Canadian Historical Review* 51.4 (1970) 426–49.

Balzer, Timothy. "'In Case the Raid is Unsuccessful ...': Selling Dieppe to Canadians." *The Canadian Historical Review* 87.3 (2006) 409–30.

Barton, Brandey. "Public Opinion and National Prestige: The Politics of Canadian Army Participation in the Invasion of Sicily, 1942–1943." *Canadian Military History* 15.2 (2006) 23–34.

Beatty, David. "The 'Canadian Corollary' to the Monroe Doctrine and the Ogdensburg Agreement of 1940." *The Northern Mariner* 1 (1994) 3–22.

Béland, François. "Frederick Debartzch Monk." *Dictionary of Canadian Biography Online*.

Blake, Raymond. "Mackenzie King and the Genesis of Family Allowances in Canada, 1939–1944," in Raymond Blake and Jeff Keshen (eds.) *Social Welfare Policy in Canada*. Mississauga: Copp Clark Ltd., 1995, 244–54.

Bliss, Michael. "War Business as Usual: Canadian Munitions Production 1914–1918," in N.F. Dreisziger (ed.) *Mobilization for Total War:*

The Canadian, American and British Experience, 1914–1918, 1939–1945. Waterloo: Wilfred Laurier University Press, 1981, 45–55.

Bothwell, Robert. "The Canadian Isolationist Tradition." *International Journal* 54.1 (1998) 76–87.

Bothwell, Robert. "'Who's Paying for Anything these Days?' War Production in Canada, 1939–1945," in N.F. Dreisziger (ed.) *Mobilization for Total War*. Waterloo: Wilfrid Laurier University Press, 1981, 57–69.

Bothwell, Robert and John English. "Canadian Trade Policy in the Age of American Dominance and British Doctrine, 1943–1947." *The Canadian Review of American Studies* 8.1 (1977) 52–65.

Bothwell, Robert and John English. "'Dirty Work at the Crossroads': New Perspectives on the Riddell Incident." *Historical Papers* 7.1 (1972) 263–85.

Bourrie, Mark. "The Myth of the 'Gagged Clam': William Lyon Mackenzie King's Press Relations." *Global Media Journal—Canadian Edition* 3.2 (2010) 13–30.

Bray, R. Matthew. "A Conflict of Nationalisms: The Win the War and National Unity Convention, 1917." *Journal of Canadian Studies* 15.4 (1980–1981) 18–30.

Bray, R. Matthew. "Fighting as an Ally: The English-Canadian Patriotic Response to the Great War." *The Canadian Historical Review* 61.2 (1980) 141–68.

Brookfield, Tarah. "Divided by the Ballot Box: The Montreal Council of Women and the 1917 Election." *The Canadian Historical Review* 89.4 (2008) 473–501.

Brown, E.K. "Mackenzie King of Canada." *Harper's Magazine* (January 1943) 192–200.

Brown, Robert Craig. "Frank Broadstreet Carvell." *Dictionary of Canadian Biography Online*.

Brown, Robert Craig. "Sir Robert Borden." *Dictionary of Canadian Biography Online*.

Brown, Robert Craig. "Sir Robert Borden, the Great War, and Anglo Canadian Relations," in J.L. Granatstein (ed.) *Towards a New World: Readings in the History of Canadian Foreign Policy*. Toronto: Copp Clark, 1992, 28–46.

Brown, Robert Craig. "Sir Robert Borden, the Great War and Anglo-Canadian Relations," in John S. Moir (ed.) *Character and Circumstance*. Toronto: Macmillan of Canada, 1970, 201–24.

Brown, Robert Craig. "'Whither Are We Being Shoved?' Political Leadership in Canada during World War I," in J.L. Granatstein and R.D. Cuff (eds.) *War and Society in North America*. Toronto: Thomas Nelson and Sons, 1971, 104–19.

Brown, Robert Craig and Robert Bothwell. "The Canadian Resolution," in Michael Cross and Robert Bothwell (eds.) *Policy by Other Means: Essays in Honour of C.P. Stacey*. Toronto: Clarke and Irwin, 1972, 163–77.

Brown, R.C. and D. Loveridge, "Unrequited Faith: Recruiting the CEF 1914–1918." *Revue Internationale d'Historie Militaire* 51 (1982) 53–79.

Byers, Daniel. "The Conscription Election of 1917 and its Aftermath in Orillia, Ontario." *Ontario History* 83 (1991) 275–96.

Byers, Daniel. "Mobilising Canada: The National Resources Mobilization Act, the Department of National Defence, and Compulsory Military Service in Canada, 1940–1945." *Journal of the Canadian Historical Association* 7.1 (1996) 175–203.

Case, Captain Gordon C. "The Lessons of Munich: Mackenzie King's Campaign to Prepare Canada for War." *Canadian Military Journal* 5.4 (2004–2005) 73–82.

Clarke, Nic. "'You Will Not Be Going To This War': The Rejected Volunteers of the First Contingent of the Canadian Expeditionary Force." *First World War Studies* 1.2 (2010) 161–84.

Comeau, Robert. "L'opposition à la conscription au Québec," in Roch Legault and Jean Lamarre (eds.) *La Première Guerre mondiale et le Canada*. Montréal: Méridien, 1999, 91–109.

Cook, George L., "Sir Robert Borden, Lloyd George and British Military Policy, 1917–1918." *The Historical Journal* 14 (1971) 371–95.

Cook, Ramsay. "Dafoe, Laurier, and the Formation of the Union Government." *The Canadian Historical Review* 42.3 (1961) 185–208.

Cook, Ramsay. "J.W. Dafoe at the Imperial Conference, 1923." *The Canadian Historical Review* 51.1 (1960) 19–40.

Copp, Terry. "The Decision to Reinforce Hong Kong: September 1941." *Canadian Military History* 20.2 (2011) 3–13.

Copp, Terry. "Ontario 1939: The Decision for War," in Norman Hillmer et al. (eds.) *A Country of Limitations: Canada and the World in 1939*. Ottawa: Canadian Committee for the History of the Second World War, 1996, 109–19.

Corry, J.A. "The Growth of Government Activities in Canada, 1914–1921." *Canadian Historical Association Annual Report* (1940) 63–73.

Courtney, John C. "Prime Ministerial Character: An Examination of Mackenzie King's Political Leadership." *Canadian Journal of Political Science* 9.1 (1976) 77–100.

Couture, Paul M. "The Vichy-Free French Propaganda War in Quebec, 1940 to 1942." *CHA Historical Papers* (1978) 200–16.

Crerar, Thomas A. "The Incredible Canadian: An Evaluation." *International Journal* 8.3 (1953) 151–6.

Crowley, Terry. "The Thin Raiment of the North Atlantic Triangle: Canada and the Decision for War, 1938–1939." *London Journal of Canadian Studies* 20 (2004–2005) 27–44.

Cuff, Robert D. "The Toronto Eighteen and the Election of 1911." *Ontario History* 42 (December 1965) 169–80.

Dennis, Patrick. "A Canadian Conscript Goes to War—August 1918." *Canadian Military History* 18.1 (2009) 21–36.

Dickson, Paul. "Harry Crerar and an Army for Strategic Effect." *Canadian Military History* 17.1 (2008) 37–48.

Dickson, Paul. "The Politics of Army Expansion." *Journal of Military History* 60.2 (1996) 271–98.

Dryden, Jean E. "The Mackenzie King Papers: An Archival Odyssey." *Archivaria* 6 (1978) 40–69.

Duffy, Dennis. "Love among the Ruins: The King of Kingsmere." *American Review of Canadian Studies* 37.3 (2007) 355–70.

Egerton, George. "The Lloyd George War Memoirs: A Study in the Politics of Memory." *Journal of Modern History* 60.1 (1988) 55–94.

English, J.A. "Not an Equilateral Triangle: Canada's Strategic Relationship with the United States and Britain, 1939–1945," in B.J.C. McKercher and L. Aronsen (eds.) *The North Atlantic Triangle in a Changing World: Anglo-American-Canadian Relations, 1902–1956*. Toronto: University of Toronto Press, 1996, 147–83.

Esberey, Joy E. "Personality and Politics: A New Look at the King–Byng Dispute." *Canadian Journal of Political Science* 6.1 (1973) 37–55.

Esberey, Joy E. "Prime Ministerial Character: An Alternative View." *Canadian Journal of Political Science* 9.1 (1976) 101–6.

Fedorowich, Kent. "'Cocked Hats and Swords and Small, Little Garrisons': Britain, Canada and the Fall of Hong Kong, 1941." *Modern Asian Studies* 37.1 (2003) 111–57.

Fedorowich, Kent. "Sir Gerald Campbell and the British High Commission in Wartime Ottawa, 1938–1940." *War in History* 18.3 (2011), 357–85.

Fitzhardinge, L.F. "Hughes, Borden, and Dominion Representation at the Paris Peace Conference." *The Canadian Historical Review* 49.2 (1968) 160–9.

Fraser, Blair. "The Secret Life of Mackenzie King, Spiritualist." *Maclean's* (15 December 1951), 7–9, 60–1.

Gibson, James A. "Mr. Mackenzie King and Canadian Autonomy, 1921–1946." *Report of the Annual Meeting of the Canadian Historical Association* 30.1 (1951), 12–21.

Granatstein, J.L. "Conscription in the Great War," in David MacKenzie (ed.) *Canada and the First World War: Essays in Honour of Robert Craig Brown*. Toronto: University of Toronto Press, 2005, 62–75.

Granatstein, J.L. "Financing the Liberal Party, 1935–1945," in Michael Cross and Robert Bothwell (eds.) *Policy by Other Means*. Toronto: Clarke and Irwin, 1972, 179–200.

Granatstein, J.L. "Happily in the Margins: Mackenzie King and Canada at the Quebec Conference," in David Woolner (ed.) *The Second Quebec Conference Revisited, Waging War, Formulating Peace: Canada, Great Britain and the United States in 1944–1945*. New York: St. Martin's Press, 1998, 49–63.

Granatstein, J.L. "King and Country." *International Journal* 24.2 (1969).

Granatstein, J.L. "Settling the Accounts. Anglo-Canadian War Finance, 1943–1945." *Queen's Quarterly* 83 (1976) 234–49.

Granatstein, J.L. and Robert Bothwell, "'A Self-Evident National Duty': Canadian Foreign Policy, 1935–1939." *Journal of Imperial and Commonwealth History* 3.2 (1975) 212–33.

Hallahan, Kirk. "W.L. Mackenzie King: Rockefeller's 'Other' Public Relations Counsellor in Colorado." *Public Relations Review*, 29.4 (2003) 401–14.

Harris, Stephen. "From Subordinate to Ally: The Canadian Corps and National Autonomy, 1914–1918." *Revue Internationale d'Historie Militaire* 51 (1982) 109–30.

Haycock, Ronald. "'Done in our Own Country': The Politics of Canadian Munitioning," in B.D. Hunt and R.G. Haycock (eds.) *Canada's Defence: Perspectives on Policy in the Twentieth Century.* Toronto: Copp Clark Pitman, 1993, 44–68.

Henderson, T. Stephen. "Angus L. Macdonald and the Conscription Crisis of 1944." *Acadiensis* 27.1 (1997) 85–104.

Hennessy, Michael A. "The Industrial Front: The Scale and Scope of Canadian Industrial Mobilization during the Second World War," in Bernd Horn (ed.) *Forging a Nation: Perspectives on the Canadian Military Experience.* St. Catharines: Vanwell, 2002, 135–54.

Hillmer, Norman. "The Anglo-Canadian Neurosis: The Case of O.D. Skelton," in Peter Lyon (ed.) *Britain and Canada: Survey of a Changing Relationship*. London: Frank Cass, 1976, 61–84.

Hillmer, Norman. "The Cunning of Restraint: General J.H. MacBrien and the Problems of Peacetime Soldiering." *Canadian Defence Quarterly* 8.4 (1979) 40–7.

Hillmer, Norman, "Defence and Ideology: The Anglo-Canadian Military 'Alliance' in the 1930's." *International Journal* 23 (1978) 588–612.

Hillmer, Norman. "O.D. Skelton and the North American Mind." *International Journal* 60.1 (2004) 93–110.

Hillmer, Norman. *"The Outstanding Imperialist": Mackenzie King and the British*. London: Canadian House Lecture Series, Number 4.

Holland, Robert. "The British Empire and the Great War, 1914–1918," in Judith Brown and William Louis (eds.) *The Oxford History of the British Empire. Volume 4: The Twentieth Century*. Oxford: Oxford University Press, 1999.

Hoogenraad, Maureen. "Mackenzie King in Berlin." *The Archivist* 20.3 (1994) 19–21.

Hooker, M.A. "Serving Two Masters: Ian Mackenzie and Civil-Military Relations in Canada, 1935–1939." *Journal of Canadian Studies* 21 (1986).

Hughes, Sam H.S. "Sir Sam Hughes and the Problem of Imperialism." *Report of Annual Meeting of the Canadian Historical Association* 29.1 (1950) 30–41.

Hyatt, A.J.M. "Sir Arthur Currie and Conscription: A Soldier's View." *The Canadian Historical Review* 50.3 (1969) 286–96.

Isitt, Benjamin. "Mutiny From Victoria to Vladivostok, December 1918." *The Canadian Historical Review* 87.2 (2006) 223–64.

Kaprielian-Churchill, Isabel. "Armenian Refugees and their Entry into Canada, 1919–1930." *The Canadian Historical Review* 71.1 (1990) 80–108.

Kealey, Gregory. "State Repression of Labour and the Left in Canada, 1914–20: The Impact of the First World War." *The Canadian Historical Review* 73.3 (1992) 281–314.

Keshen, Jeffrey. "Getting it Right the Second Time Around," in Peter Neary and J.L. Granatstein (eds.), *The Veterans Charter and Post-*

World War II Canada. Montreal: McGill-Queen's University Press, 1998, 62–9.

Keyserlingk, Robert H. "Mackenzie King's Spiritualism and His View of Hitler in 1939." *Journal of Canadian Studies* 20.4 (1985–1986) 26–44.

Kitchen, Martin. "The German Invasion of Canada in the First World War." *The International History Review* 7.2 (1985) 245–60.

Lewis, John. "Canada at War," in *Canada in the Great World War*, volume II. Toronto: United Publishers of Canada, 1921, 20–48.

MacFarlane, John. "Double Vision: Ernest Lapointe, Mackenzie King and the Quebec Voice in Canadian Foreign Policy, 1935–1939." *Journal of Canadian Studies* 34.1 (1999) 93–111.

MacFarlane, John. "Mr. Lapointe, Mr. King, Quebec and Conscription." *Beaver* 75.2 (1995) 26–31.

Mackenzie, Hector. "'Arsenal of the British Empire'? British Orders for Munitions Production in Canada, 1936–39." *Journal of Imperial and Commonwealth History* 31 (2003) 46–73.

Mackenzie, Hector. "King's Exit: The Prime Minister and Canada's International Relations, 1945–1948." *London Journal of Canadian Studies* 24 (2008–2009) 105–30.

Mackenzie, Hector. "The Path to Temptation: The Negotiation of Canada's Reconstruction Loan to Britain in 1946." *Canadian Historical Association Papers* (1982) 196–220.

Mackenzie, Hector. "Shades of Gray? The Foundations of Canadian Policy in World Affairs." *The American Review of Canadian Studies* 37.4 (2007) 459–73.

Macmillan, Margaret. "Canada and the Peace Settlements," in David Mackenzie (ed.) *Canada and the First World War*. Toronto: University of Toronto Press, 2005, 379–408.

Macquarrie, Heath N. "The Formation of Borden's First Cabinet." *The Canadian Journal of Economics and Political Sciences* 23.1 (1957) 90–104.

Marsden, Paul. "The Costs of No Commitments: Canadian Economic Planning for War," in Norman Hillmer et al. (eds.) *A Country of*

Limitations: Canada and the World in 1939. Ottawa: Canadian Committee for the History of the Second World War, 1996, 199–216.

Martin, Ged. "Mackenzie King, the Medium and the Messages." *British Journal of Canadian Studies* 4.1 (1989) 109–35.

Massie, Justin. "North Atlantic Quadrangle: Mackenzie King's Lasting Imprint on Canada's International Security Policy." *London Journal of Canadian Studies* 24 (2008–2009) 85–105.

McCulloch, Tony. "The North Atlantic Triangle: A Canadian Myth?" *International Journal* 66.1 (2010–2011) 197–207.

McDowall, Duncan. "Spinning the Past: Prime Ministerial Memoirs." *Queen's Quarterly* 115.1 (2008) 117–32.

Miller, Ian. "Toronto's Response to the Outbreak of War, 1939." *Canadian Military History* 11.1 (2002) 5–23.

Millman, Brock. "Canada, Sanctions and the Abyssinian Crisis of 1935." *The Historical Journal* 40.1 (1997) 143–68.

Millman, Brock. "A Counsel of Despair: British Strategy and War Aims, 1917–18." *Journal of Contemporary History* 36.2 (2001) 241–70.

Milner, Marc. "The Royal Canadian Navy and 1943: A Year Best Forgotten?," in Paul Dickson (ed.) *1943: The Beginning of the End*. Waterloo: Wilfrid Laurier University Press, 1995, 123–36.

Morton, Desmond. "The Cadet Movement in the Moment of Canadian Militarism, 1909–1914." *Journal of Canadian Studies* 13.2 (1978) 56–68.

Morton, Desmond. "The Canadian Veterans' Heritage from the Great War," in Peter Neary and J.L. Granatstein (eds.) *The Veterans Charter and Post-World War II Canada*. Montreal: McGill-Queen's University Press, 1998, 15–31.

Morton, Desmond. "French Canada and the Canadian Militia, 1868–1914." *Social History/histoire sociale* 3 (April 1969) 32–50.

Morton, Desmond. "French Canada and War, 1868–1917: The Military Background to the Conscription Crisis of 1917," in J.L. Granatstein and R.D. Cuff (eds.) *War and Society in North America*. Toronto: Thomas Nelson and Sons Canada Limited, 1971, 84–103.

Morton, Desmond. "Polling the Soldier Vote: The Overseas Campaign in the Canadian General Election of 1917." *Journal of Canadian Studies* 10.4 (1975) 39–58.

Munro, Ross. "Conscription in Canada," in *Canada in the Great World War,* volume II. Toronto: United Publishers of Canada, 1921, 87–105.

Naylor, R.T. "The Canadian State, the Accumulation of Capital, and the Great War." *Journal of Canadian Studies* 16 (1981) 26–55.

Neatby, H. Blair. "Mackenzie King and French Canada." *Journal of Canadian Studies* 11.1 (1976) 3–13.

Neilson, Keith. "Canada and British War Finance, 1914–1917," in Bernd Horn (ed.) *Forging a Nation: Perspectives on the Canadian Military Experience*. St. Catharines: Vanwell, 2002, 109–22.

Niergarth, Kirk. "'This Continent Must Belong to the White Races': William Lyon Mackenzie King, Canadian Diplomacy and Immigration Law, 1908." *International History Review* 32.4 (2010) 599–617.

Offer, Avner. "The Working Classes, British Naval Plans and the Coming of the Great War." *Past and Present* 107 (1985) 204–26.

Pearson, Lester B. "Reflections on Inter-War Canadian Foreign Policy." *Journal of Canadian Studies* 7.2 (1972) 36–42.

Pollock, Fred. "Roosevelt, the Ogdensburg Agreement, and the British Fleet: All Done with Mirrors." *Diplomatic History* 5 (1981) 203–19.

Prang, Margaret. "Clerics, Politicians and the Bilingual Schools Issue in Ontario, 1910–1917." *The Canadian Historical Review* 41 (1960) 281–307.

Preston, Adrian W. "Canada and the Higher Direction of the Second World War, 1939–1945," in B.D. Hunt and R.G. Haycock (eds.) *Canada's Defence: Perspectives on Policy in the Twentieth Century*. Toronto: Copp Clark, 1993, 98–102.

Quiney, Linda. "Bravely and Loyally They Answered the Call: St. John Ambulance, the Red Cross, and the Patriot Service of Canadian Women during the Great War." *History of Intellectual Culture* 5.1 (2005) 1–19.

Ramkhalawansingh, Ceta. "Women during the Great War," in Janice Acton et al.(eds.). *Women and Work: Ontario, 1850–1930.* Toronto: Canadian Women's Educational Press, 1974, 261–303.

Rea, J.E. "'Clay from Feet to Forehead': The Mackenzie King Controversy." *Beaver* 73.2 (1993) 27–34.

Rea, J.E. "The Conscription Crisis: What Really Happened?" *Beaver* 74.2 (1994) 10–19.

Reid, Escott. "Mr. Mackenzie King's Foreign Policy, 1935–1936." *The Canadian Journal of Economics and Political Science* 3.1 (1937) 86–97.

Rickard, John Nelson. "The Test of Command: McNaughton and Exercise 'Spartan,' 4–12 March 1943." *Canadian Military History* 8.3 (1999) 22–38.

Robin, Martin. "Registration, Conscription, and Independent Labour Politics, 1916–1917," in Carl Berger (ed.) *Conscription 1917.* Toronto: University of Toronto Press, 1969.

Roy, Reginald H. "From the Darker Side of Canadian Military History: Mutiny in the Mountains—The Terrace Incident." *Canadian Defence Quarterly* 6.2 (1976) 42–55.

Sangster, Joan. "Mobilizing Canadian Women for War," in David Mackenzie (ed.) *Canada and the First World War.* Toronto: University of Toronto Press, 2005, 157–94.

Sarty, Leigh. "The Limits of Internationalism: Canada and the Soviet Blockade of Berlin, 1948–1949," in J.L. Black and Norman Hillmer (eds.) *Nearly Neighbours, Canada and the Soviet Union: From Cold War to Détente and Beyond.* Kingston: Ronald P. Frye & Company, 1989, 56–74.

Sarty, Roger. "The 'Battle We Lost at Home' Revisited: Official Military Histories and the Battle of the St. Lawrence." *Canadian Military History* 12. 1 & 2 (2003) 41–50.

Sarty, Roger. "Mr. King and the Armed Forces," in Norman Hillmer et al. (eds.) *A Country of Limitations: Canada and the World in 1939.* Ottawa: Committee for the Study of the Second World War, 1996, 217–46.

Siemiatycki, Myer. "Munitions and Labour Militancy: The 1916 Hamilton Machinists' Strike." *Labour/Le Travailleur* 3 (1978) 131–51.

Sloane, Neville. "Chamberlain, Appeasement and the Role of the British Dominions." *London Journal of Canadian Studies* 23 (2007–2008) 67–80.

Smith, David Edward. "Emergency Government in Canada." *The Canadian Historical Review* 50.4 (1969) 429–48.

Soward, F.H. "Sir Robert Borden and Canada's External Policy, 1911–1920." *Canadian Historical Association, Annual Report* (1941) 65–82.

Stacey, C.P. "The Canadian–American Permanent Joint Board on Defence, 1940–1945." *International Journal* 9.2 (1954) 107–24.

Stacey, C.P. "The Divine Mission: Mackenzie King and Hitler." *The Canadian Historical Review* 61.4 (1980) 502–12.

Stacey, C.P. "Laurier, King, and External Affairs," in John Moir (ed.) *Character and Circumstance: Essays in Honour of Donald Grant Creighton*. Toronto: Macmillan Co. of Canada, 1970, 85–98.

Stevenson, John A. "The Career of Mackenzie King." *The Political Quarterly* 21.4 (1950) 395–410.

Stewart, Andrew. "The 1939 British and Canadian 'Empire Air Training Scheme' Negotiations." *Round Table* 93 (2004) 739–54.

Theobald, Andrew. "Divided Once More: Social Memory and the Canadian Conscription Crisis of the First World War." *Past Imperfect* 12 (2006) 1–19.

Turley-Ewart, John A. and Robert Craig Brown, "Sir Edward Albert Kemp." *Dictionary of Canadian Biography Online*.

Vince, M.A.R. "Development in the Legal Status of the Canadian Military Forces, 1914–1919, as Related to Dominion Status." *The Canadian Journal of Economics and Political Science* 20.3 (1954) 357–70.

Waite, P. B. "Mr. King and Lady Byng," *Beaver* 77.2 (1997) 24–30.

Walker, Richard. "The Revolt of the Canadian Generals, 1944: The Case for the Prosecution," in Howard G. Coombs (ed.) *The Insubordinate and the Noncompliant: Case Studies of Canadian Mutiny and Disobedience, 1920 to the Present*. Toronto: The Dundurn Group, 2007, 55–100.

Walker, James W. St.G. "Race and Recruitment in World War I: Enlistment of Visible Minorities in the Canadian Expeditionary Force." *The Canadian Historical Review* 70.1 (1989) 1–26.

Whitaker, Reginald. "The Liberal Corporatist Ideas of Mackenzie King." *Labour/Le Travail* 2 (1977) 137–69.

Whitaker, Reginald. "Official Repression of Communism during World War II." *Labour/Le Travail* 17 (1986) 135–68.

Whitaker, Reginald. "Political Thought and Political Action in Mackenzie King." *Journal of Canadian Studies* 13.4 (1978–1979) 40–60.

Wigley, Philip and Norman Hillmer. "Defining the First British Commonwealth: The Hankey Memoranda and the 1926 Imperial Conference." *Journal of Imperial and Commonwealth History* 8.1 (1979) 105–16.

Willms, A.M., "Conscription 1917: A Brief for the Defence." *The Canadian Historical Review* 37.4 (1956) 338–51.

Woolner, David B. "Mackenzie King and the St. Pierre and Miquelon Crisis of 1941." *London Journal of Canadian Studies* 24 (2008–2009) 42–84.

Young, W.R. "Conscription, Rural Depopulation, and the Farmers of Ontario, 1917–19." *The Canadian Historical Review*, 53.3 (1972) 289–320.

Young, William R. "Academics and Social Scientists versus the Press: The Politics of the Bureau of Public Information and the Wartime Information Board, 1939–1945." *Historical Papers* (1978) 217–40.

Young, William R. "Building Citizenship: English Canada and Propaganda during the Second World War." *Journal of Canadian Studies* 16.3 & 4 (1981) 121–32.

THESES AND DISSERTATIONS

Alain, Robert. "Sir Thomas White and Canada's Participation in the Great War." MA thesis: Queen's University, 1975.

Barker, Stacey Joanne. "'Save Today What Our Allies Need Tomorrow': Food Regulation in Canada during the First World War." MA thesis: Carleton University, 2003.

Bedore, Margaret Elizabeth. "The Infamous Charts of Mackenzie King from *Industry and Humanity*." MA thesis: Queen's University, 2003.

Bedore, Margaret Elizabeth. "The Reading of Mackenzie King." PhD thesis: Queen's University, 2008.

Campbell, J.R. "James Layton Ralston and Manpower for the Canadian Army." MA thesis: Wilfrid Laurier University, 1986.

Ferraro, Patrick. "English Canada and the Election of 1917." MA thesis: McGill University, 1971.

Holt, Richard. "Filling the Ranks: Recruiting, Training and Reinforcements in the Canadian Expeditionary Force 1914–1918." PhD thesis: Western University, 2011.

Johnston, Iain Edward. "Anglo-Canadian Relations within the Context of Imperial Defence, 1935–1940." MA thesis: Cambridge University, 2010.

LeBlanc, Bernard Charles. "A Reluctant Recruit: Angus L. Macdonald and Conscription, 1940–1945." MA thesis: Queen's University, 1987.

Maker, John. "A Home Away from Home: Citizenship and National Identity in the Canadian Army Overseas, 1939–1945." PhD thesis: University of Ottawa, 2010.

McSheffrey, Marion. "The Khaki Election: A New Perspective, The Ottawa Valley in 1917." MA thesis: University of Calgary, 2005.

Sauntry, Victor. "Canadian Newspapers and the Paris Peace Conference, 1919." MA thesis: University of Waterloo, 2008.

Sloane, W.N. "The Paradox of Unity: Winston Churchill, Mackenzie King and Anglo-Canadian Relations, 1940–45." PhD thesis: University of East Anglia, 2007.

Slobodin, Thomas Brent. "A Tangled Web: The Relationship between Mackenzie King's Foreign Policy and National Unity." PhD thesis: Queen's University, 1986.

Street, Kori. "Bankers and Bomb Makers: Gender Ideology and Women's Paid Work in Banking and Munitions during the First World War in Canada." PhD thesis: University of Victoria, 2000.

Trowbridge, Robert. "War-Time Rural Discontent and the Rise of the United Farmers of Ontario 1914–1919." MA thesis: University of Waterloo, 1964.

Waddell, Christopher Robb. "The Wartime Prices and Trade Board: Price Control in Canada in World War II." PhD thesis: York University, 1981.

Waugh, Alyse. "'Once a Soldier: Always a Man': The Military Hospitals Commission and Society, 1915–1928." MA thesis: Carleton University, 2011.

Wood, James A. "The Sense of Duty: Canadian Ideas of the Citizen Soldier, 1896–1917." PhD thesis: Wilfrid Laurier University, 2006.

ENDNOTES

PROLOGUE

1 The original King diaries are at the Library and Archives Canada (LAC). They have been digitized and are available online as part of the LAC's online resources; they will be cited in this book as King diary, 17 May 1945.
2 LAC, Sir Robert Borden papers, MG 26 H, R6113-46-1-E, personal diary [hereafter Borden diary], 16 May 1915.
3 Sir John A. Macdonald was minister of militia and defence in Canada East and West before Confederation.
4 The phrases come from George Stanley, *Canada's Soldiers, 1604–1954: The Military History of an Unmilitary People* (Toronto: Macmillan, 1954) and William Kilbourn, *A Guide to the Peaceable Kingdom* (Toronto: Macmillan Co. of Canada, 1970).

CHAPTER 1

1 Sir Robert Borden, *Robert Laird Borden: His Memoirs,* volume I [hereafter *Memoirs*] (Toronto: Macmillan Co. of Canada, 1938) 3.
2 Dictionary of Canadian Biography Online [hereafter DCB online], Robert Craig Brown, "Sir Robert Borden."
3 Borden, *Memoirs*, I/11–12.

4 Gordon Donaldson, *Eighteen Men: The Prime Ministers of Canada* (Toronto: Doubleday, 1985) 80.
5 Robert Craig Brown, "The Political Ideas of Robert Borden," in Marcel Hamelin (ed.), *The Political Ideas of the Prime Ministers of Canada* (Ottawa: The Vanier Lectures, 1969) 88.
6 LAC, Sir Robert Borden papers [hereafter Borden papers], MG 26 H, microfilm reel C-4432, Borden to Thompson, 13 October 1933, 152735.
7 Borden, *Memoirs*, I/19.
8 DCB online, "Sir Robert Borden."
9 John English, *Borden: His Life and World* (Toronto: McGraw-Hill Ryerson, 1977) 50.
10 Augustus Bridle, *The Masques of Ottawa* (Toronto: Macmillan Co. of Canada, 1921) 28.
11 John English, *The Decline of Politics: The Conservatives and the Party System, 1901–1920* (Toronto: University of Toronto Press, 1977) 34.
12 Borden, *Memoirs*, I/42.
13 Borden, *Memoirs*, I/43.
14 Borden, *Memoirs*, I/47.
15 J.M. Beck, *Pendulum of Power: Canada's Federal Elections* (Toronto: Prentice-Hall of Canada, 1968) 96.
16 DCB online, "Sir Robert Borden."
17 Borden, *Memoirs*, I/74.
18 Michael Bliss, *Right Honourable Men: The Descent of Canadian Politics from Macdonald to Mulroney* (Toronto: HarperCollins, 1994) 47.
19 J.W. Dafoe, *Clifford Sifton in Relation to His Times* (Toronto: Macmillan Co. of Canada, 1931) 271.
20 DCB online, "Sir Robert Borden."
21 Beck, *Pendulum of Power*, 107.
22 Borden, *Memoirs*, I/229.

23 Desmond Morton and J.L. Granatstein, *Marching to Armageddon* (Toronto: Lester & Orpen Dennys, 1989) 8; Borden papers, reel C-4209, Hughes to MacArthur, 23 March 1911, 7829.
24 Borden, *Memoirs,* I/230.

CHAPTER 2

1 See Carman Miller, *A Knight in Politics: A Biography of Sir Frederick Borden* (Montreal: McGill-Queen's University Press, 2010).
2 Arthur Lower, *From Colony to Nation* (Toronto: Longmans, Green & Company, 1946) 451.
3 Michael Hadley and Roger Sarty, *Tin-pots and Pirate Ships: Canadian Naval Forces and German Sea Raiders, 1880–1918* (Montreal: McGill-Queen's University Press, 1991) 57.
4 André Pratte, *Wilfrid Laurier* (Toronto: Penguin Canada, 2011) 183–4.
5 Cited in Beck, *Pendulum of Power*, 122.
6 Borden, *Memoirs*, I/287.
7 Scott Young and Astrid Young, *Silent Frank Cochrane: The North's First Great Politician* (Toronto: Macmillan of Canada, 1973) 120.
8 J.L. Granatstein, *Yankee Go Home? Canadians and Anti-Americanism* (Toronto: HarperCollins, 1996) 61.
9 W.M. Baker, "A Case Study of Anti-Americanism in English-Speaking Canada: The Election Campaign of 1911," *The Canadian Historical Review* 51.4 (1970) 426–49.
10 English, *Borden: His Life and World*, 67.
11 Ross Munro, "Conscription in Canada," in *Canada in the Great World War,* volume II (Toronto: United Publishers of Canada, 1921) 87.
12 Patrice Dutil and David MacKenzie, *Canada 1911: The Decisive Election that Shaped the Country* (Toronto: Dundurn, 2011) 214.
13 Heath Macquarrie introduction to Sir Robert Borden, *Robert Laird Borden: His Memoirs,* volume I (Toronto: McClelland & Stewart, 1969) xii.
14 Bliss, *Right Honourable Men*, 54.

15 J.W. Dafoe, *Laurier: A Study in Canadian Politics* (Toronto: McClelland & Stewart, Carleton Library, 1963 [original in 1922]) 44.

16 M.C. Urquhart and K.A.H. Buckley, *Historical Statistics of Canada* (Toronto: Macmillan Co. of Canada, 1965) 27.

17 See Carl Berger's *The Sense of Power: Studies in the Ideas of Canadian Imperialism, 1867–1914* (Toronto: University of Toronto Press, 1971) and R.A. Preston, *Canada and "Imperial Defence": A Study in the Origins of the British Commonwealth's Defence Organization, 1867–1919* (Durham, N.C.: Durham University Press, 1967).

18 W. Stewart Wallace, *The Memoirs of the Rt. Hon. Sir George Foster* (Toronto: Macmillan Co. of Canada, 1933) 155–6.

19 Borden papers, C-4364, Borden to Drummond, 14 October 1911, 82033.

20 Borden diary, 26 February 1916.

21 Borden, *Memoirs*, I/231.

22 DCB online, François Béland, "Frederick Debartzch Monk."

23 Heath N. Macquarrie, "The Formation of Borden's First Cabinet," *The Canadian Journal of Economics and Political Sciences* 23.1 (February 1957) 99.

24 Dutil and MacKenzie, *Canada 1911*, 214.

25 English, *The Decline of Politics*, 78–9; Borden papers, reel C-4212, Chase-Casgrain to Borden, 17 September 1913, 11084.

26 DCB online, "Sir Robert Borden."

27 Borden, *Memoirs*, I/430.

28 Bridle, *The Masques of Ottawa*, 30.

29 Sam H.S. Hughes, "Sir Sam Hughes and the Problem of Imperialism," *Report of Annual Meeting of the Canadian Historical Association* 29.1 (1950) 37.

30 On Hughes, see R.G. Haycock, *Sam Hughes: The Public Career of a Controversial Canadian, 1885–1916* (Ottawa: Canadian War Museum, 1986); on the militia, see James A. Wood, "The Sense

of Duty: Canadian Ideas of the Citizen Soldier, 1896–1917" (PhD thesis: Wilfrid Laurier University, 2006).

CHAPTER 3

1 C.P. Stacey, *Canada and the Age of Conflict: A History of Canadian External Policies, Volume 1: 1867–1921* (Toronto: Macmillan of Canada, 1977) 172.
2 Borden, *Memoirs*, I/456.
3 Borden, *Memoirs*, I/278.
4 John Herd Thompson, *The Harvests of War: The Prairie West, 1914–1918* (Toronto: McClelland & Stewart, 1978) 28.
5 Order-in-council, 4 August 1914; Thomas White, *The Story of Canada's War Finances* (Montreal: The Canadian Bank of Commerce, 1921) 5–8.
6 Maurice Pope (ed.), *Public Servant: The Memoirs of Sir Joseph Pope* (Toronto: Oxford University Press, 1960) 246–7.
7 Borden diary, 4 August 1914.
8 J. Castell Hopkins, *Canadian Annual Review, 1914* [hereafter *CAR 1914*] (Toronto: The Annual Review of Publishing, 1915) 142.
9 *CAR 1914*, 138.
10 Order-in-council 1914, 4 August 1914.
11 G.N. Tucker, *Naval Service of Canada: Official History*, volume I (Ottawa: King's Printer, 1952) 290.
12 Order-in-council 2067, 6 August 1914.
13 House of Commons debates [hereafter Hansard], 18 August 1914, 10.
14 Robert Craig Brown and Ramsay Cook, *Canada 1896–1921: A Nation Transformed* (Toronto: McClelland & Stewart, 1974) 213; Brown, "The Political Ideas of Robert Borden," 94.
15 Hansard, 19 August 1914, 22.
16 War Measures Act, Statutes of Canada, 1914, c.2; Borden, *Memoirs*, I/458.
17 *CAR 1914*, 154.

18 See David Edward Smith, "Emergency Government in Canada," *The Canadian Historical Review* 50.4 (December 1969) 429–48; Lower, *Colony to Nation*, 473.
19 Borden, *Memoirs*, I/461.
20 *CAR 1914,* 158.
21 Margaret Prang, *N.W. Rowell: Ontario Nationalist* (Toronto: University of Toronto Press, 1975)160.
22 Andrew Macphail, *The Medical Services: Official History of the Canadian Forces in the Great War 1914–19* (Ottawa: F.A. Acland, 1925) 190.
23 Borden papers, C-4232, speech, 18 December 1914, 17702.
24 Borden papers, C-4238, Memorandum of points in General Alderson's letter, 4 December 1914, 22857.
25 *CAR 1914,* 152.
26 Borden diary, 28 January 1916.
27 Department of External Affairs, *Documents on Canadian External Relations* [hereafter *DCER*], volume I (Ottawa: Information Canada, 1968) 59.
28 See Tim Cook, *The Madman and the Butcher: The Sensational Wars of Sam Hughes and General Arthur Currie* (Toronto: Allen Lane, 2010) 103–8; also see, David Carnegie, *History of Munitions Supply in Canada 1914–1918* (Toronto: Longmans, 1925).
29 Borden, *Memoirs*, I/462.
30 *CAR 1914*, 276.
31 J.L. Granatstein and Desmond Morton, *Canada and the Two World Wars* (Toronto: Key Porter Books, 2003) 17.
32 *Toronto Globe*, 7 August 1914.
33 Martin Kitchen, "The German Invasion of Canada in the First World War," *The International History Review*, 7(2) (May 1985) 245–6; Borden papers, C-4388, Nixon to Hazen [August 1914] 105969–70.
34 Borden papers, C-4202, Borden to White, 22 October 1914, 2472.
35 *Ottawa Citizen*, 23 November 1914.
36 *CAR 1914*, 189.

37 Pope (ed.) *Public Servant*, 257–8.

38 Smith, "Emergency Government in Canada," 436; Borden papers, C-4432, Memorandum for his Excellency [by Borden, no date, c. 1915] 152496.

39 Bohdan S. Kordan, *Enemy Aliens, Prisoners of War: Internment in Canada during the Great War* (Montreal: McGill-Queen's University Press, 2002).

40 Robert Bothwell, *Loring Christie: The Failure of Bureaucratic Imperialism* (New York: Garland Publishing, 1988) 84; Robert Craig Brown, "Sir Robert Borden, the Great War and Anglo-Canadian Relations," in John S. Moir (ed.), *Character and Circumstance* (Toronto: Macmillan of Canada, 1970) 204–5.

41 Sir Robert L. Borden, "Speech to the Winnipeg Canadian Club December 29th 1914," in Brian Busby (ed.) *Great Canadian Speeches: Words that Shaped a Nation* (London: Arcturus Publishing, 2008) 59.

42 Borden, *Memoirs*, I/viii.

CHAPTER 4

1 On Second Ypres, see Andrew Iarocci, *Shoestring Soldiers: The 1st Canadian Division at War, 1914–1915* (Toronto: University of Toronto Press, 2008).

2 Borden diary, 25 and 27 April 1915.

3 J.A. Corry, "The Growth of Government Activities in Canada, 1914–1921," *Canadian Historical Association Annual Report* (1940), 63–4.

4 Daphne Read (ed.), *The Great War and Canadian Society: An Oral History* (Toronto: New Hogtown Press, 1978) 185.

5 See Desmond Morton, *Fight or Pay: Soldiers' Families in the Great War* (Vancouver: University of British Columbia Press, 2004).

6 *CAR 1915*, 337.

7 English, *The Decline of Politics*, 68–9.

8 Sir Thomas White, "Before the Toronto Bankers' Education Association, on Wednesday, January 25th, 1922," *Journal of the*

Canadian Bankers Association, 29 (1922) 360; Hansard, 20 August 1914, 25.

9 LAC, Thomas White papers, MG 27 II-D-18, White to Williams-Taylor, 24 August 1916, 2087.

10 *CAR 1914*, 246 and *CAR 1916*, 354.

11 LAC, Sir George Foster papers, MG 27 II-D-7, diary [hereafter Foster diary], 15 February 1916.

12 Bridle, *The Masques of Ottawa*, 110.

13 White, *The Story of Canada's War Finance*, 58; Robert Alain, "Sir Thomas White and Canada's Participation in the Great War" (MA thesis: Queen's University, 1975) 86–97.

14 Keith Neilson, "Canada and British War Finance, 1914–1917," in Bernd Horn (ed.), *Forging a Nation: Perspectives on the Canadian Military Experience* (St. Catharines: Vanwell, 2002) 111.

15 *CAR 1917*, 294.

16 LAC, A.E. Kemp papers [hereafter Kemp papers], MG 27 II-D-9, v. 39, file 9, clippings, *Telegram*, 26 November 1914.

17 Borden diary, 7 March 1916.

18 Borden, *Memoirs*, I/480–1; DCB online, John A. Turley-Ewart and Robert Craig Brown, "Sir Edward Albert Kemp."

19 Hansard, 15 April 1915, 2613–17.

20 For some of the challenges of the committee, and its internal workings, see LAC, Sam Hughes papers [hereafter Hughes papers], MG 27 II-D-23, v. 3, file 6, Minutes of the Shell Committee; Michael Bliss, "War Business as Usual: Canadian Munitions Production 1914–1918," in N.F. Dreisziger (ed.), *Mobilization for Total War: The Canadian, American and British Experience, 1914–1918, 1939–1945* (Waterloo: Wilfred Laurier Press, 1981) 47.

21 DCB online, Robert Craig Brown, "Frank Broadstreet Carvell"; Young and Young, *Silent Frank Cochrane*, 139.

22 On Hughes, see Borden diary, 17 April 1915; on Flavelle, see LAC, Sir John Willison papers, MG 30 D29, Flavelle to Willison, 31 July 1918.

23 Ronald Haycock, "'Done in our Own Country': The Politics of Canadian Munitioning," in B.D. Hunt and R.G. Haycock (eds.), *Canada's Defence: Perspectives on Policy in the Twentieth Century* (Toronto: Copp Clark Pitman, 1993) 62–3.

24 Borden diary, 22 January 1916 and 2 February 1916.

25 Foster diary, 8 October 1915.

26 Michael Bliss, *A Canadian Millionaire: The Life and Business Times of Sir Joseph Flavelle, Bart., 1858–1939* (Toronto: Macmillan of Canada, 1978) 274; Robert Craig Brown, "'Whither Are We Being Shoved?' Political Leadership in Canada during World War I," in J.L. Granatstein and R.D. Cuff (eds.), *War and Society in North America* (Toronto: Thomas Nelson and Sons, 1971) 105; Foster diary, 7–8 October 1915; Borden diary, 26 February 1916.

27 *CAR 1915*, 175.

28 Borden papers, C-4214, G.H. Bradbury to Borden, 24 October 1916.

29 Andrew Theobald, *The Bitter Harvest of War: New Brunswick and the Conscription Crisis, 1917* (New Brunswick: Goose Lane, 2008) 47.

30 See Desmond Morton, "French Canada and the Canadian Militia, 1868–1914," *Social History-histoire sociale* (April 1969) 32–50.

31 Elizabeth Armstrong, *The Crisis of Quebec, 1914–18* (New York: Columbia University Press, 1937) 72.

32 For the question of language and schools, see Margaret Prang, "Clerics, Politicians and the Bilingual Schools Issue in Ontario, 1910–1917," *The Canadian Historical Review* XLI (December 1960) 281–307.

33 *CAR 1915*, 298.

34 Joseph Levitt, *Henri Bourassa on Imperialism and Bi-culturalism, 1900–1918* (Toronto: Copp Clark, 1970) 162; CAR *1914*, 515.

35 Henri Bourassa, *The Duty of Canada at the Present Hour* (Montreal, 1915) n.p.

36 Henri Bourassa, *The Duty of Canada at the Present Hour* (Montreal, 1915) n.p; Joseph Schull, *Laurier: The First Canadian* (Toronto: Macmillan Co. of Canada, 1965) 560.
37 Borden diary, 9 May 1915.
38 Donald Avery, *Dangerous Foreigners: European Immigrant Workers and Labour Radicalism in Canada, 1896–1932* (Toronto: McClelland & Stewart, 1979) 163, note 21.
39 Granatstein and Morton, *Canada and the Two World Wars*, 8–19; Barbara Wilson, *Ontario and the First World War, 1914–1918* (University of Toronto Press, 1977) lxx–lxxxiv; K.M. McLaughlin, *The Germans in Canada* (Ottawa: Canadian Historical Association, 1985) 12–13.
40 Bliss, *Right Honourable Men*, 80.
41 Bruce Hutchison, *Mr. Prime Minister, 1867–1964* (Toronto: Longmans Canada Limited, 1964) 149.
42 Borden, *Memoirs*, I/viii.
43 *Montreal Star*, 8 December 1914.
44 Borden diary, 1 July 1915.
45 Sir Robert Borden, *Letters to Limbo* (Toronto: University of Toronto Press, 1971) 78–9.
46 See Brown, "Sir Robert Borden, the Great War and Anglo-Canadian Relations," 207–8, 210; *DCER*, volume I, 104.
47 Borden diary, no date, [June 1915].
48 C.P. Stacey, *Canada and the Age of Conflict: A History of Canadian External Policies*, volume I (Toronto: Macmillan of Canada, 1977) 188.
49 CWM, Sir Richard Turner collection, 19710147-001, diary, 27 July 1915.
50 *CAR 1915*, 181.
51 Borden, *Memoirs*, I/508–9.
52 Col. J.G. Adami, *The War Story of the C.A.M.C., 1914–15* (Toronto: The Musson Book Company, 1918) introduction [by Sir Robert Borden].
53 *CAR 1915*, 182.

CHAPTER 5

1 Dafoe, *Laurier*, 93.
2 For women in the workforce, see Kori Street, "Bankers and Bomb Makers: Gender Ideology and Women's Paid Work in Banking and Munitions during the First World War in Canada" (PhD thesis: University of Victoria, 2000).
3 R.C. Brown and D. Loveridge, "Unrequited Faith: Recruiting the CEF 1914–1918," *Revue Internationale d'Historie Militaire* 51 (1982) 53–79.
4 Brown, *Borden*, II/27.
5 Borden diary, 8 June 1916.
6 Borden papers, speech, 22 December 1915, 175538.
7 Borden diary, 24 December 1915.
8 Urquhart and Buckley, *Historical Statistics of Canada*, 14.
9 R.T. Naylor, "The Canadian State, the Accumulation of Capital, and the Great War," *Journal of Canadian Studies* 16 (Fall–Winter, 1981) 39–40.
10 Borden, *Memoirs*, I/528. For the half-million recruitment figure, order-in-council, 12 January 1916.
11 White, *The Story of Canada's War Finances*, 31.
12 *CAR 1915*, 227.
13 *CAR 1915*, 219.
14 *DCER*, volume I, 104; Stacey, *Canada in the Age of Conflict*, 191–2.
15 J.L. Granatstein and J.M. Hitsman, *Broken Promises: A History of Conscription in Canada* (Toronto: Oxford University Press, 1977) 35; John Lewis, "Canada at War," in *Canada in the Great World War*, volume II (Toronto: United Publishers of Canada, 1921) 41.
16 Richard Holt, "Filling the Ranks: Recruiting, Training and Reinforcements in the Canadian Expeditionary Force 1914–1918" (PhD thesis: Western University, 2011) 66–8.
17 R. Matthew Bray, "A Conflict of Nationalisms: The Win the War and National Unity Convention, 1917," *Journal of Canadian Studies* 15.4 (1980–1981, Winter) 19.

18 A.M. Willms, "Conscription 1917: A Brief for the Defence," *The Canadian Historical Review* 37.4 (1956) 343.
19 Borden papers, C-4390, Borden to Hughes, 31 January 1916, 108855.
20 For the failures in attempting to organize a system, see Holt, "Filling the Ranks," chapter 2.
21 Robert Trowbridge, "War-Time Rural Discontent and the Rise of the United Farmers of Ontario 1914–1919" (MA thesis: University of Waterloo, 1964) 44.
22 Avner Offer, "The Working Classes, British Naval Plans and the Coming of the Great War," *Past and Present* 107 (1985) 204.
23 See W.R. Young, "Conscription, Rural Depopulation, and the Farmers of Ontario, 1917–19," *The Canadian Historical Review*, LIII.3 (September 1972) 289–320.
24 *Saturday Night*, 8 August 1914.
25 Hansard, 11 February 1915, 86; *CAR 1917*, 296–7; Borden diary, 12 February 1916; Bliss, *A Canadian Millionaire*, 272.
26 See the debates and discussions for White and others in Hansard, 25 July 1917.
27 For the tax levels, see Urquhart and Buckley, *Historical Statistics of Canada*, 99. Also see *Canada's War Effort, 1914–1918* (Ottawa: Director of Public Information, 1918) 11.
28 Brown and Cook, *A Nation Transformed*, 233.
29 Avery, *Dangerous Foreigners*, 70.
30 Alain, "Sir Thomas White," 19–20.
31 Granatstein and Morton, *Canada and the Two World Wars*, 56.
32 See Morton, *Fight or Pay*.
33 Borden, *Memoirs*, I/524; Borden diary, 26 November 1915.
34 Borden papers, C-4310, "The Truth about Two Railways," (pub. no. 28).
35 Donald Creighton, *Canada's First Century, 1867–1967* (Toronto: Macmillan of Canada, 1970) 130.
36 Borden diary, 6 April 1916.

37 Borden diary, 9 May 1916.
38 Borden, *Memoirs*, II/566.
39 Bliss, *A Canadian Millionaire*, 273.
40 See, for example, Canadian War Museum Military History Research Centre [hereafter MHRC], *Shell and Fuse Scandals: A Million Dollar Rake-off*, pub. no. 49 (Ottawa: Central Liberal Information Office, n.d. [1916]); MHRC, *War Contract Scandals*, pub. no. 44 (Ottawa: Central Liberal Information Office, n.d. [1915]).
41 Hughes papers, v. 1, file 8, Hughes to Borden, 24 July 1916.
42 Stephen J. Harris, *Canadian Brass: The Making of a Professional Army, 1860-1939* (Toronto: University of Toronto Press, 1988) 107–10.
43 Borden papers, Borden to Perley, 14 March 1916, 4302–3.
44 Borden diary, 3 April 1916.
45 Foster diary, 29 August 1916.
46 Borden diary, 1 June 1916.
47 For the overseas administrative mess, see Desmond Morton, *A Peculiar Kind of Politics: Canada's Overseas Ministry in the First World War* (Toronto: University of Toronto Press, 1982).
48 LAC, Lord Beaverbrook papers, MG 27 II G 1, Series E, reel A-1765, Sims to Aitken, 8 June 1916.
49 See Donald M.A.R. Vince, "Development in the Legal Status of the Canadian Military Forces, 1914–1919, As Related to Dominion Status," *The Canadian Journal of Economics and Political Science* 20.3 (August 1954) 357–70.
50 LAC, Lord Beaverbrook papers, MG 27 II G 1, Series E, reel A-1764, Hughes to Aitken, 26 October 1916; Hughes papers, v. 1, file 9, Borden to Hughes, 9 November 1916; Borden, *Memoirs*, II/568.
51 Macquarrie, "The Formation of Borden's First Cabinet," 96, note 17.
52 Borden diary, 29 February 1916 and 20 January 1916.

CHAPTER 6

1 MHRC, *Correspondence of General Sir Sam Hughes, Ex-minister of Militia and the Right Hon. Sir Robert Borden at the Time Sir Sam Resigned* (Ottawa: Government publication, 1916).
2 Foster diary, 6–7 July 1917.
3 LAC, Sir George Perley papers, MG 27 II-D-12, v. 8–12, Borden to Perley, 13 June 1917.
4 George L. Cook, "Sir Robert Borden, Lloyd George and British Military Policy, 1917–1918," *The Historical Journal* 14.2 (June 1971) 373.
5 Stephen Roskill, *Hankey, Man of Secrets I, 1877–1918* (London: Collins, 1970) 348.
6 Norman Hillmer and J.L. Granatstein, *From Empire to Umpire: Canada and the World to the 1990s* (Toronto: Copp Clark Longman, 1994), 59.
7 Bothwell, *Loring Christie*, 113.
8 Brown, *Borden*, II/77.
9 Borden, *Memoirs*, II/666.
10 See Brock Millman, "A Counsel of Despair: British Strategy and War Aims, 1917–18," *Journal of Contemporary History* 36.2 (April 2001) 247–8.
11 Sir James Edmonds, *Military Operations France and Belgium, 1917*, volume II (Imperial War Museum, n.d.) viii.
12 Borden papers, C-4314, Borden to Blount, 20 April 1917, 35374.
13 *CAR 1917*, 286.
14 Borden, *Memoirs*, II/678.
15 David Lloyd George, *War Memoirs of David Lloyd George*, volume IV (London: I. Nicholson and Watson, 1933–36) 1760–3.
16 Robert Borden, "The Imperial Conference," *Journal of the Royal Institute of International Affairs* 6.4 (July 1927) 200.
17 *CAR 1917*, 289.
18 R. Craig Brown and Robert Bothwell, "The Canadian Resolution," in Michael Cross and Robert Bothwell (eds.), *Policy by Other*

Means: Essays in Honour of C.P. Stacey (Toronto: Clarke and Irwin, 1972) 163–77.

19 Stephen Harris, "From Subordinate to Ally: The Canadian Corps and National Autonomy, 1914–1918," *Revue Internationale d'Historie Militaire* 51 (1982) 116.

20 Kemp papers, v. 120, file 26 (a), Memo, Department of Militia and Defence, 7 July 1917.

21 LAC, RG 24, v. 1843, GAQ 10-47c, "Memorandum Relating to the Military Situation in Canada on the 1st of May 1917."

22 For the unfit soldiers, see Nic Clarke, "'You Will Not Be Going To This War': The Rejected Volunteers of the First Contingent of the Canadian Expeditionary Force," *First World War Studies* 1.2 (2010) 161–84.

23 Borden papers, C-4322, Borden to Kemp, 22 March 1917, 43479.

24 Borden papers, Speech to the Canadian Club of Ottawa, 16 September 1915, 175510.

25 Borden diary, 16 May 1915.

26 Kemp papers, v. 53, file 8, Kemp to Borden, 10 April 1917.

27 The Military Service Council, *For the Defence of Canada* (October 1917) 25.

28 Roger Graham, *Arthur Meighen, A Biography: The Door of Opportunity,* volume 1 (Toronto: Clarke, Irwin & Company, 1960) 117.

29 Borden diary, 17 May 1917.

30 Bridle, *The Masques of Ottawa*, 28.

31 Foster diary, 27 July 1917. Also see, Brown, "The Political Ideas of Robert Borden," 101–2; English, *The Decline of Politics*, 36.

32 See Hansard, 18 May 1917; also see R.C. Brown and D. Loveridge, "Unrequited Faith: Recruiting the CEF 1914–1918," *Revue Internationale d'Historie Militaire* 51 (1982) 63.

33 Toronto *Globe*, 19 May 1917

34 *CAR 1917*, 493.

35 Borden diary, 25 May 1917.

36 Prang, *N.W. Rowell*, 189.

37 LAC, Sir Wilfrid Laurier papers [hereafter Laurier papers], MG 26 G, Calder to Laurier, 29 January 1917, 194676.
38 H.S. Ferns and B. Ostry, *The Age of Mackenzie King: The Rise of the Leader* (London: William Heinemann, 1955) 227.
39 Oscar Douglas Skelton, *Life and Letters of Sir Wilfrid Laurier*, volume II (Toronto, 1921) 183.
40 For Meighen's speech, although slightly abbreviated, see Arthur Meighen, *Unrevised and Unrepented* (Toronto: Clarke, Irwin & Company, 1949) 71–86.
41 Brown and Loveridge, "Unrequited Faith: Recruiting the CEF 1914–1918," 53–79.
42 *CAR 1917*, 328–9.
43 Borden papers, C-4319, Reid to Borden, 9 June 1917, 40497.
44 Borden papers, C-4319, Laurier to Borden, 6 June 1917, 40047A; Prang, *N.W. Rowell*, 190.
45 Laurier papers, Laurier to Sir John Gibson, 1 January 1917, 194349.

CHAPTER 7

1 Hansard, 11 June 1917, 2195.
2 Borden papers, C-4323, Patenaude to Borden, 8 June 1917, 43947.
3 Borden papers, C-4323, Borden to Patenaude, 13 June 1917, 43960.
4 Schull, *Laurier*, 567.
5 Skelton, *Life and Letters of Sir Wilfrid Laurier*, volume II, 169.
6 Margaret Macmillan, "Canada and the Peace Settlements," in David Mackenzie (ed.), *Canada and the First World War* (Toronto: University of Toronto Press, 2005) 383.
7 R. MacGregor Dawson, *William Lyon Mackenzie King: A Political Biography, 1874–1923* (Toronto: University of Toronto Press, 1958) 260; Ferns and Ostry, *The Age of Mackenzie King*, 235–6.
8 Borden papers, C-4319, Borden to Rogers, 17 August 1917, 40890–4; and Ibid., Rogers to Borden, 18 August 1917, 40896–7; English, *The Decline of Politics*, 147–50.
9 Hansard, 27 June 1917, 2709–15.
10 Halifax *Herald*, 20 November 1917.

11 Dafoe, *Laurier*, xviii. The *Manitoba Free Press* changed its name in 1931 to the *Winnipeg Free Press*.

12 Robert Holland, "The British Empire and the Great War, 1914–1918," in Judith Brown and William Louis (eds.), *The Oxford History of the British Empire. Volume 4: The Twentieth Century* (Oxford: Oxford University Press, 1999) 117–18.

13 Kemp papers, v. 193, file Borden Correspondence, Borden to Kemp, 20 November 1925.

14 Borden papers, C-4314, Premier's Message to the People, 29 June 1917, 35332.

15 See Desmond Morton, "Polling the Soldiers' Vote: The Overseas Campaign in the Canadian General Election of 1917," *Journal of Canadian Studies* 10.4 (November 1975) 39–58.

16 See Ceta Ramkhalawansingh, "Women during the Great War," in Janice Acton et al., *Women and Work: Ontario, 1850–1930* (Toronto: Canadian Women's Educational Press, 1974) 261–303; and Joan Sangster, "Mobilizing Canadian Women for War," in David Mackenzie (ed.), *Canada and the First World War* (Toronto: University of Toronto Press, 2005) 157–94.

17 See Barbara Roberts, *Why Do Women Do Nothing to End the War? Canadian Feminist-Pacifists and the Great War* (Ottawa: Canadian Research Institute for the Advancement of Women, 1985).

18 Tarah Brookfield, "Divided by the Ballot Box: The Montreal Council of Women and the 1917 Election," *The Canadian Historical Review* 89.4 (December 2008) 475.

19 *CAR 1917*, 332.

20 Patrick Ferraro, "English Canada and the Election of 1917" (MA thesis: McGill University, 1971) 58; Schull, *Laurier*, 589; English, *The Decline of Politics*, 153–4.

21 Brookfield, "Divided by the Ballot Box," 488; also see Hansard, 10 September 1917, 5583.

22 *St. John Daily Telegram and Sun*, 7 September 1917.

23 Hansard, 10 September 1917, 5584–5.

24 Borden papers, C-4403, Harvey to Borden, 18 August 1917, 123235–7.

25 Foster diary, 8 October 1917.

26 *London Free Press*, 30 November 1917.

27 *Calgary Daily Herald*, 15 December 1917.

28 Robert Bothwell, Ian Drummond, and John English, *Canada, 1900–1945* (Toronto: University of Toronto Press, 1987) 131.

29 Ramsay Cook, "Dafoe, Laurier, and the Formation of the Union Government," *The Canadian Historical Review* XLII.3 (September 1961) 197.

30 Norman Ward (ed.), *A Party Politician: The Memoirs of Chubby Power* (Toronto: Macmillan Co. of Canada, 1966) 61–2.

31 Augustus Bridle, *Sons of Canada*: *Short Studies of Characteristic Canadians* (Toronto: Macmillan Co. of Canada, 1916) 12.

32 Stephen Leacock, "Our National Organization for the War," in J.O. Miller (ed.), *The New Era in Canada: Essays Dealing with the Upbuilding of the Canadian Commonwealth* (Toronto: J.M. Dent, 1917) 413.

33 Charles Johnston, *E.C. Drury: Agrarian Idealist* (Toronto: University of Toronto Press, 1986) 52.

34 Bill Waiser, *Saskatchewan: A New History* (Calgary: Fifth House Ltd, 2005) 219–20.

35 *CAR 1917*, 625.

36 Kemp papers, v. 70, file 18: United Farmers of Ontario to Kemp, 22 March 1917; J. Castel Hopkins, *The Book of the Union Government* (Toronto: The Canadian Annual Review Limited, 1918) 77.

37 *CAR 1917*, 347.

38 Kealey, "State Repression of Labour," 281–314.

39 Myer Siemiatycki, "Munitions and Labour Militancy: The 1916 Hamilton Machinists' Strike," *Labour/Le Travailleur* 3 (1978) 131–51.

40 A. Ross McCormack, *Reformers, Rebels and Revolutionaries: The Western Canadian Radical Movement, 1899–1919* (Toronto: University of Toronto Press, 1977) 128.
41 Thompson, *Harvests of War*, 117.
42 Captain S.G. Bennett, *The 4th Canadian Mounted Rifles, 1914–1919* (Toronto: Murray Printing Company, 1926) 94.
43 John Harold Becker, *Silhouettes of the Great War: The Memoirs of John Harold Becker* (Ottawa: CEF Books, 2001) 134.
44 See Morton, "Polling the Soldiers Vote."
45 Borden diary, 25 September 1917.
46 McSheffrey, "The Khaki Election," 57; Ray Argyle, *Turning Points: The Campaigns that Changed Canada* (Toronto: White Knight, 2004) 177; Brookfield, "Divided by the Ballot Box," 494.
47 See the results in Patrick Ferraro, "English Canada and the Election of 1917" (MA thesis: McGill University, 1971); Beck, *Pendulum of Power*, 148; Granatstein and Hitsman, *Broken Promises*, 81.
48 *Ottawa Journal*, 18 December 1917.
49 *London Free Press*, 18 December 1917.
50 Hansard, 18 May 1917, 1541.

CHAPTER 8

1 *CAR 1917*, 361.
2 For food rationing, see Stacey Joanne Baker, "Save Today What Our Allies Need Tomorrow: Food Regulation in Canada during the First World War" (MA thesis: Carleton University, 2003).
3 Foster diary, 2 February 1918.
4 For the Halifax disaster, see John Armstrong, *The Halifax Explosion and the Royal Canadian Navy: Inquiry and Intrigue* (Vancouver: University of British Columbia Press, 2002).
5 Kemp papers, v. 129, file B-3, Borden to Kemp, 14 March 1918.
6 Robert Cuff and J.L. Granatstein, *Canadian–American Relations in Wartime: From the Great War to the Cold War* (Toronto: Hakkert, 1975) 70–1.
7 Borden diary, 5 February 1916.

8 Borden diary, 18 October 1914.

9 Kemp papers, v. 129, file B-3, Borden to Kemp, 14 March 1918.

10 Schull, *Laurier*, 588.

11 "Local Tribunals Are Tightening Up on Exemptions," Toronto *News*, 10 November 1917.

12 Granatstein and Hitsman, *Broken Promises*, 83–5. The British faced their own challenges in adjudicating the tribunals; see Adrian Gregory, *The Last Great War: British Society and the First World War* (Cambridge: Cambridge University Press, 2008) 103–8.

13 *CAR 1917*, 341

14 Gordon Donaldson, *Eighteen Men: The Prime Ministers of Canada* (Toronto: Doubleday Canada, 1985) 92.

15 Patrick Bouvier, *Déserteurs et insoumis: les Canadiens français et la justice militaire, 1914–1918* (Outremont: Athéna, 2003).

16 See Martin Auger, "On the Brink of Civil War: The Canadian Government and the Suppression of the 1918 Quebec Easter Riots," *The Canadian Historical Review* 89.4 (2008) 503–40.

17 Brown and Cook, *Canada, 1896–1921: A Nation Transformed*, 306.

18 Borden, *Memoirs*, II/786–92.

19 Hansard, 2 April 1918, 237–8; Hansard, 5 April 1918, 401; order-in-council, PC 834, 4 April 1918.

20 Order-in-council, PC 1241, 22 May 1918; also see Jeffrey Keshen, *Propaganda and Censorship during Canada's Great War* (Edmonton: The University of Alberta Press, 1996) 65–126.

21 Kemp papers, v. 129, file B-3, Borden to Kemp, 24 April 1918; Ibid., Borden to Kemp, 3 May 1918; Armstrong, *The Crisis of Quebec,* 243.

22 For government restraint, see Smith, "Emergency Government in Canada," 447–8.

23 Foster diary, 28 May 1918.

24 *The Industrial Banner*, 30 November 1917.

25 English, *The Decline of Politics*, 183.

26 George L. Cook, "Sir Robert Borden, Lloyd George and British Military Policy, 1917–1918," *The Historical Journal* 14.2 (June 1971) 381.
27 Borden, *Memoirs*, II/786–92; Borden papers, C-4333, Borden to Kemp, 11 April 1918, 56085.
28 Johnston, *E.C. Drury*, 51.
29 Keshen, *Propaganda and Censorship*, 52.
30 Borden diary, 3–4 May 1918.
31 Tim Cook, *Shock Troops: Canadians Fighting the Great War, Volume II: 1917–1918* (Toronto: Viking, 2008) 400.
32 On the MSA numbers, see G.W.L. Nicholson, *Canadian Expeditionary Force: The Official History of the Canadian Army in the First World War* (Ottawa: Queen's Printer, 1964) 551; also see Patrick Dennis, "A Canadian Conscript Goes to War—August 1918," *Canadian Military History* 18.1 (Winter 2009) 21–36; Colonel W.G. Lyddon, *British War Missions to the United States, 1917–1918* (Oxford University Press, 1938) 203.
33 Kemp papers, v. 129, file B-3, Borden to Kemp, 3 May 1918.
34 See A.J.M. Hyatt, "Sir Arthur Currie and Conscription: A Soldier's View," *The Canadian Historical Review* 50.3 (1969) 286–96.
35 Borden diary, 12 June 1918; *DCER*, volume I, 201–3.
36 See F.H. Soward, "Sir Robert Borden and Canada's External Policy, 1911–1920," *Canadian Historical Association, Annual Report* (1941) 73–5; Borden diary, 12 June 1918.
37 Brown, "'Whither Are We Being Shoved?,'" 104.
38 Brown, *Borden*, II/139; also see *DCER*, volume I, 331.

CHAPTER 9

1 Borden diary, 11 November 1918.
2 LAC, C.C. Ballantyne papers, MG 27 II D 1, volume 1, Borden to Ballantyne, 3 December 1918.
3 Brown, *Borden*, II/135; memo in LAC, Loring Christie papers, MG 30 E44, v. 2, 'Memorandum,' n.d., nos. 1419–22. Also, see Bothwell, *Loring Christie*, 218–9.

4 *DCER*, volume I, 218, Borden to Lloyd George, 29 October 1918.

5 See L.F. Fitzhardinge, "Hughes, Borden, and Dominion Representation at the Paris Peace Conference," *The Canadian Historical Review* 49.2 (June 1968) 160–9.

6 Brown, *Borden*, II/151.

7 On English Canadian newspapers, see Victor Sauntry, "Canadian Newspapers and the Paris Peace Conference of 1919: A Study of English-Language Media Opinion" (MA thesis: Waterloo University, 2008).

8 David Lloyd George, *The Truth about the Peace Treaties,* volume I (London: Victor Gollancz, 1938) 207.

9 Borden diary, 1 December 1918.

10 Stephen Harris, "From Subordinate to Ally: The Canadian Corps and National Autonomy, 1914–1918," *Revue Internationale d'Historie Militaire* 51 (1982) 110.

11 Lawrence Martin, *The Presidents and the Prime Ministers, Washington and Ottawa Face to Face: The Myth of Bilateral Bliss, 1867–1982* (Toronto: Doubleday, 1982) 83.

12 DCB online, "Sir Robert Borden."

13 Macmillan, "Canada and the Peace Settlements," 381.

14 See L.F. Fitzhardinge, "Hughes, Borden, and Dominion Representation at the Paris Peace Conference," *The Canadian Historical Review* 49.2 (June 1968) 160–9.

15 Martin Thornton, *Sir Robert Borden* (London: Haus, 2010) 6.

16 Charles Howard Ellis, *The Origin, Structure & Working of the League of Nations* (Boston: Houghton Mifflin Company, 1929) 489.

17 On Article X, see Department of External Affairs, *Documents on Canadian External Relations, The Paris Peace Conference of 1919*, volume II (Ottawa, 1967) 58; Borden papers, C-4449, series of memorandum, 173241–57.

18 Michael Neiberg, *Fighting the Great War: A Global History* (Cambridge: Harvard University Press, 2005) 225. Also, see

Margaret Macmillan, *Paris 1919* (New York: Random House, 2001).

19 Charles J. Doherty and Arthur L. Sifton signed on behalf of Canada.

20 Theobald, *The Bitter Harvest of War*, 95.

21 See Daniel Francis, *Seeing Reds: The Red Scare of 1918–1919, Canada's First War on Terror* (Vancouver: Arsenal Pulp Press, 2010).

22 See Order-in-council; also see Borden papers, reel C-4334, Cahan to Borden, 14 September 1918, 56668.

23 Borden papers, C-4402, Speech of the Hon. Arthur Meighen.... [1920], 2878.

24 Brown, *Borden*, II/166–7.

25 Janice P. Dickin McGinnis, "The Impact of Epidemic Influenza: Canada, 1918–1919," *Historical Papers* 12.1 (1977) 128.

26 Desmond Morton, "The Canadian Veterans' Heritage from the Great War," in Peter Neary and J.L. Granatstein (eds.), *The Veterans Charter and Post-World War II Canada* (Montreal: McGill-Queen's University Press, 1998) 24.

27 *The Veteran* 1.1 (December 1917) 8.

28 See Desmond Morton and Glenn Wright, *Winning the Second Battle: Canadian Veterans and the Return to Civilian Life, 1915–1930* (Toronto: University of Toronto Press, 1987); Borden papers, C-4240, MHC to Borden, 27 March 1915; and Alyse Waugh, "'Once a Soldier: Always a Man': The Military Hospitals Commission and Society, 1915–1928" (MA thesis: Carleton University, 2011).

29 Morton, "The Canadian Veterans' Heritage from the Great War," 26–7.

30 LAC, Newton Rowell papers, MG 27 II-D13, v. 5, Rowell to Borden, 28 October 1918.

31 Robert Bothwell, *The Penguin History of Canada* (Toronto: Penguin Canada, 2006) 313.

32 Bothwell, Drummond, and English, *Canada, 1900–1945*, 179.

33 Hansard, 2 September 1919, 13–25.

34 Brown, *Borden*, II/179.

35 See Brown, *Borden*, II/179–83; also Borden diary, 20 June to 7 July, 1919.
36 "Who Is the Greatest Living Canadian?" *Maclean's*, 15 May 1927.
37 Borden papers, reel C-4432, Gray to Borden, 4 September 1934, 152608.
38 Borden papers, reel C-4434, Borden to Lloyd George, 9 May 1932, 155067.
39 Borden papers, reel C-4434, Borden to Lord Grey, 24 July 1931, 152636.
40 Borden, *Letters from Limbo*, vi.
41 Heath Macquarrie introduction to Sir Robert Borden, *Robert Laird Borden: His Memoirs*, volume I (Toronto: McClelland & Stewart, 1969) xvi.
42 Duncan McDowall, "Spinning the Past: Prime Ministerial Memoirs," *Queen's Quarterly* 115.1 (2008) 117–32.
43 On Lloyd George's memoirs, George Egerton, "The Lloyd George War Memoirs: A Study in the Politics of Memory," *Journal of Modern History* 60.1 (March 1988) 55–94; Borden papers, Borden to Connaught, 9 July 1930, 152340.
44 Borden papers, C-4430, Borden to Bovey, 23 August 1934, 150501.
45 Borden, *Letters from Limbo*, vi.

CHAPTER 10

1 See, for example, John C. Courtney, "An Examination of Mackenzie King's Political Leadership," *Canadian Journal of Political Science* 9.1 (March 1976) 80.
2 For King's intellectual underpinnings, see Reginald Whitaker, "The Liberal Corporatist Ideas of Mackenzie King," *Labour/Le Travail* 2 (1977) 137–69.
3 King diary, 19 November 1896 and 6 December 1896.
4 For two opposing views on King's sexuality, see C.P. Stacey, *A Very Double Life: The Private World of Mackenzie King* (Toronto: Macmillan, 1976) 41–3; and Bliss, *Right Honourable Men*, 123–9.

5 See Charlotte Gray, *Mrs. King: The Life and Times of Isabel Mackenzie King* (Toronto: Penguin Canada, 1997) for an evocative retelling of King's early years.
6 William Lyon Mackenzie King, *The Secret of Heroism: A Memoir of Henry Albert Harper* (New York: Fleming H. Revell, 1906) 65–8.
7 See the painful speech to the House, Hansard, 20 April 1920.
8 Kirk Hallahan, "W.L. Mackenzie King: Rockefeller's "Other" Public Relations Counsellor in Colorado," *Public Relations Review* 29.4 (2003) 401–14. For a negative portrayal of King, see H.S. Ferns and Bernard Ostry, *The Age of Mackenzie King: The Rise of the Leader* (London: William Heinemann, 1955).
9 Paul Roazen, *Canada's King: An Essay in Political Psychology* (Oakville: Mosaic Press, 1998) 77.
10 Roazen, *Canada's King*, 81.
11 King diary, 21 September 1931.
12 William Lyon Mackenzie King, *Industry and Humanity: A Study in the Principles Underlying Industrial Reconstruction* (Toronto: Thomas Allen, 1918).
13 See Margaret Bedore, "The Infamous Charts of Mackenzie King from *Industry and Humanity*" (MA thesis: Queen's University, 2003).
14 For King's publications, see the excellent bibliography, George F. Henderson, *W.L. Mackenzie King: A Bibliography and Research Guide* (Toronto: University of Toronto Press, 1998).
15 H. Blair Neatby, "Mackenzie King and French Canada," *Journal of Canadian Studies* 11.1 (February 1976) 3–13.
16 Bruce Hutchison, *The Far Side of the Street* (Toronto: Macmillan of Canada, 1976) 72.
17 Bliss, *Right Honourable Men*, 135–6.
18 Vincent Massey, *What's Past Is Prologue: The Memoirs of the Right Honourable Vincent Massey* (Toronto: Macmillan Co. of Canada, 1963) 80.
19 J.L. Granatstein, *Mackenzie King: His Life and World* (Toronto: McGraw-Hill Ryerson, 1977) 39.

20 King diary, 24 October 1938.
21 Skelton, *Life and Letters of Sir Wilfrid Laurier*, volume II, 293.
22 Dawson, *William Lyon Mackenzie King,* 409.
23 For King's worry about imperial fervour in Canada, see King diary, 17–19 September 1922.
24 King diary, 19 October 1922.
25 Gregory A. Johnson and David A. Lenarcic, "The Decade of Transition: The North Atlantic Triangle during the 1920s," in B.J.C. McKercher and Lawrence Aronsen (eds.), *The North Atlantic Triangle in a Changing World* (Toronto: University of Toronto Press, 1996) 95.
26 C.P. Stacey, "Laurier, King, and External Affairs," in John Moir (ed.), *Character and Circumstance: Essays in Honour of Donald Grant Creighton* (Toronto: Macmillan Co. of Canada, 1970) 91–2; Dafoe, *Laurier*, 46–7.
27 Thomas Brent Slobodin, "A Tangled Web: The Relationship between Mackenzie King's Foreign Policy and National Unity" (PhD thesis: Queen's University, 1986) 86–7.
28 C.P. Stacey, *Historical Documents of Canada, Volume V: The Arts of War and Peace, 1914–1945* (Toronto: Macmillan, 1972) 437.
29 Granatstein, *Mackenzie King: His Life and World*, 113.
30 Ramsay Cook, "J.W. Dafoe at the Imperial Conference, 1923," *The Canadian Historical Review* 51.1 (March 1960) 20–1.
31 Hutchison, *The Far Side of the Street*, 68.
32 Robert A. Wardhaugh, *Mackenzie King and the Prairie West* (Toronto: University of Toronto Press, 2000) 110.
33 See J.B. Esberey, "Personality and Politics: A New Look at the King-Byng Dispute," *Canadian Journal of Political Science* 6.1 (March 1973) 37–55.
34 Allan Levine, *King: William Lyon Mackenzie King, A Life Guided by the Hand of Destiny* (Vancouver: Douglas & McIntyre, 2011) 159.
35 King diary, 14 September 1926.

36 See the excellent online exhibition, *A Real Companion and Friend: The Diary of William Lyon Mackenzie King* at the Library and Archives of Canada website.

37 Stacey, *A Very Double Life*, photo caption, no. 16.

38 See, for example, Janet Oppenheim, *The Other World: Spiritualism and Psychical Research in England, 1850–1914* (Cambridge: Cambridge University Press, 1985); Stan McMullin, *Anatomy of a Séance: A History of Spirit Communication in Central Canada* (Montreal: McGill-Queen's University Press, 2004).

39 F.A. McGregor, *The Fall and Rise of Mackenzie King, 1911–1919* (Toronto: Macmillan Co. of Canada, 1962) 331.

40 Louise Reynolds, *Mackenzie King: Friends & Lovers* (Victoria: Trafford, 2005) 184.

41 King diary, 17 August 1939 and 16 August 1940; Blair Neatby, *William Lyon Mackenzie King: The Prism of Unity, Volume III: 1932–1939* (Toronto: University of Toronto Press, 1976) 407–8.

42 King diary, 16 June 1931.

43 Sir Robert Borden, *Canada and the Commonwealth* (Oxford: Clarendon Press, 1929) 128.

44 Robert Bothwell, "The Canadian Isolationist Tradition," *International Journal* 54.1 (Winter 1998–1999) 76.

45 Massey, *What's Past Is Prologue*, 112. Also see, James A. Gibson, "Mr. Mackenzie King and Canadian Autonomy, 1921–1946," *Report of the Annual Meeting of the Canadian Historical Association* 30.1 (1951) 14.

46 Norman Hillmer, *'The Outstanding Imperialist': Mackenzie King and the British* (London: Canadian House Lecture Series, Number 4) 6–7.

47 Philip Wigley and Norman Hillmer, "Defining the First British Commonwealth: The Hankey Memoranda and the 1926 Imperial Conference," *Journal of Imperial and Commonwealth History* 8.1 (October 1979) 105–16.

48 Granatstein, *Mackenzie King: His Life and World*, 113.

49 Blair Neatby, *William Lyon Mackenzie King: The Lonely Heights*, Volume II (Toronto: University of Toronto Press, 1963) 321.
50 For Bennett, see John Boyko, *Bennett: The Rebel Who Challenged and Changed a Nation* (Toronto: Key Porter, 2010).
51 J.M.S. Careless, *Canada: A Story of Challenge* (Toronto: Macmillan Co. of Canada, 1963) 367.
52 King diary, 23 May 1933 and 3 December 1933.

CHAPTER 11

1 Robert Bothwell and John English, "'Dirty Work at the Crossroads': New Perspectives on the Riddell Incident," *Historical Papers* 7.1 (1972) 263.
2 Lester B. Pearson, *Mike: The Memoirs of the Right Honourable Lester B. Pearson, Volume I, 1897–1948* (Toronto: University of Toronto Press, 1972) 71.
3 Norman Hillmer, "The Anglo-Canadian Neurosis: The Case of O.D. Skelton," in Peter Lyon (ed.), *Britain and Canada: Survey of a Changing Relationship* (London: Frank Cass, 1976) 65.
4 King diary, 11 September 1929 and 13 November 1938; C.P. Stacey, *Mackenzie King and the Atlantic Triangle* (Toronto: Macmillan of Canada, 1977) 27
5 King diary, 22 August 1935.
6 Brock Millman, "Canada, Sanctions and the Abyssinian Crisis of 1935," *The Historical Journal* 40.1 (March 1997) 149; John A. Munro, "Loring Christie and Canadian external relations, 1935–1939," *Journal of Canadian Studies* 7.2 (1972) 30.
7 W. Riddell (ed.), *Documents on Canadian Foreign Policy, 1917–1939* (Toronto: Oxford University Press, 1962) 554–5; Hansard, 11 February 1936.
8 King diary, 26 August 1936.
9 Granatstein, *Mackenzie King: His Life and World*, 124.
10 Escott Reid, "Mr. Mackenzie King's Foreign Policy, 1935–1936," *The Canadian Journal of Economics and Political Science* 3.1 (February 1937) 90.

11 See Michael Petrou, *Renegades: Canadians in the Spanish Civil War* (Vancouver: University of British Columbia Press, 2008).
12 Stacey, *Mackenzie King and the Atlantic Triangle*, 49.
13 Norman Hillmer, "O.D. Skelton and the North American Mind," *International Journal* (Winter 2004–2005) 93.
14 Ian M. Drummond and Norman Hillmer, *Negotiating Freer Trade: The United Kingdom, the United States, Canada, and the Trade Agreements of 1938* (Waterloo: Wilfrid Laurier University Press 1989).
15 David Beatty, "The 'Canadian Corollary' to the Monroe Doctrine and the Ogdensburg Agreement of 1940," *The Northern Mariner* 1 (1994) 9.
16 S.W. Dziuban, *The Military Relations between the United States and Canada, 1939–1945* (Washington: United States Army in the World War II, Special Studies, 1959) 4.
17 For multiple warnings by senior military officials about the need to protect Canadian sovereignty or hand over autonomy to the Americans, see Galen Perras, *Franklin Roosevelt and the Origins of the Canadian-American Security Alliance, 1933–1945* (Westport: Greenwood Press, 1998) 1–23.
18 King diary, 17 and 20 June 1895.
19 Hillmer, "The Anglo-Canadian Neurosis: The Case of O.D. Skelton," 63.
20 Nicholas Mansergh, *Survey of British Commonwealth Affairs: Problems of External Policy, 1931–1939* (London: Oxford University Press, 1952) 83.
21 King diary, 7 June 1937.
22 Maureen Hoogenraad, "Mackenzie King in Berlin," *The Archivist* 20.3 (1994) 20; and C.P Stacey, "The Divine Mission: Mackenzie King and Hitler," *The Canadian Historical Review* 61.4 (1980) 502–12.
23 King diary, 29 June 1937.
24 B.J.C. McKercher, "World Power and Isolationism: The North Atlantic Triangle and the Crises of the 1930s," in B.J.C. McKercher

and Lawrence Aronsen (eds.), *The North Atlantic Triangle in a Changing World* (Toronto: University of Toronto Press, 1996) 134.

25 Keith Feiling, *The Life of Neville Chamberlain* (London: Macmillan Co. of Canada, 1946) 381.

26 Neville Sloane, "Chamberlain, Appeasement and the Role of the British Dominions," *London Journal of Canadian Studies* 23 (2007–2008) 74–5.

27 On fence-sitting, see Kent Fedorowich, "Sir Gerald Campbell and the British High Commission in Wartime Ottawa, 1938–1940," *War in History* 18.3 (2011) 359; James Eayrs, *In Defence of Canada, Volume II: Appeasement and Re-Armament* (Toronto: University of Toronto Press, 1965) 65.

28 King diary, 13 September 1938.

29 J.L. Granatstein and Robert Bothwell, "A Self-Evident National Duty: Canadian Foreign Policy, 1935–1939," *Journal of Imperial and Commonwealth History* 3.2 (1975) 221; also see Terry Crowley, "The Thin Raiment of the North Atlantic Triangle: Canada and the Decision for War, 1938–1939," *London Journal of Canadian Studies* 20 (2004–2005) 27–44.

30 King diary, 27 and 28 September 1938.

31 LAC, Ian Mackenzie papers, MG 27 III-B-5, v. 29, file x-4, Memorandum on the Defence of Canada, 7 January 1938.

32 M.A. Hooker, "Serving Two Masters: Ian Mackenzie and Civil-Military Relations in Canada, 1935–1939," *Journal of Canadian Studies* 21 (1986) 44–6.

33 Iain Edward Johnston, "Anglo-Canadian Relations within the Context of Imperial Defence, 1935–1940," (MA thesis: Cambridge University, 2010) 66.

34 Roger Sarty, *The Maritime Defence of Canada* (Toronto: The Canadian Institute of Strategic Studies, 1996) 112.

35 J.L. Granatstein, *The Last Good War: An Illustrated History of Canada in the Second World War, 1939–1945* (Vancouver: Douglas & McIntyre, 2005) 6; King diary, 14 November 1938.

36 Norman Hillmer, "Defence and Ideology: The Anglo-Canadian Military 'Alliance' in the 1930s," in B.D. Hunt and R. G. Haycock (eds.), *Canada's Defence: Perspectives on Policy in the Twentieth Century* (Toronto: Copp Clark Pitman, 1993) 92–3.

37 Queen's Archives, T.A. Crerar papers, box 119, file 9, King to Crerar, 12 September 1938; King diary, 31 August 1938.

38 Malcolm J. MacDonald, "King: The View from London," in John English and J.O. Stubbs (eds.), *Mackenzie King: Widening the Debate* (Toronto: MacMillan of Canada, 1977) 45.

39 Norman Hillmer, "The Pursuit of Peace: Mackenzie King and the 1937 Imperial Conference," in John English and J.O. Stubbs (eds.), *Mackenzie King: Widening the Debate* (Toronto: MacMillan of Canada, 1977) 158.

40 Neatby, *William Lyon Mackenzie King*, volume III, 297.

41 Captain Gordon C. Case, "The Lessons of Munich: Mackenzie King's Campaign to Prepare Canada for War," *Canadian Military Journal* (Winter 2004–2005) 79–80.

42 Hansard, 20 March 1939, 2943.

43 Hansard, 30 March 1939.

44 King diary, 27 September 1938 and 19 January 1939.

CHAPTER 12

1 C.P. Stacey, *Arms, Men and Governments: The War Policies of Canada, 1939–1945* (Ottawa: Queen's Printer, 1970) 2.

2 King diary, 1 September 1939.

3 Wilfrid Eggleston, *While I Still Remember* (Toronto: Ryerson Press, 1968) 253–4; King diary, 1 September 1939.

4 Patrick Brennan, *Reporting the Nation's Business: Press-Government Relations during the Liberal years, 1935–1957* (Toronto: University of Toronto Press, 1994) 29.

5 King diary, 1 September 1939.

6 King diary, 1 September 1939.

7 Robert H. Keyserlingk, "Mackenzie King's Spiritualism and His View of Hitler," *Journal of Canadian Studies* 20.4 (1985–1986) 35–7.

8 Stacey, *A Very Double Life*, 190–1.

9 Maurice Pope, *Soldiers and Politicians: The Memoirs of Lt.-Gen. Maurice A. Pope* (Toronto: University of Toronto Press, 1962) 138.

10 Lita-Rose Betcherman, *Ernest Lapointe: Mackenzie King's Great Quebec Lieutenant* (Toronto: University of Toronto Press, 2002) 276–7.

11 Ian Miller, "Toronto's Response to the Outbreak of War, 1939," *Canadian Military History* 11.1 (Winter 2002) 6–7.

12 King diary, 7 September 1939.

13 Betcherman, *Ernest Lapointe*, 280–1.

14 Hansard, 8 September 1939; King diary, 9 September 1939.

15 King diary, 24 November 1939; Ward (ed.), *A Party Politician*, 351.

16 Lita-Rose Betcherman, *The Swastika and the Maple Leaf: Fascist Movements in Canada in the Thirties* (Toronto: Fitzhenry & Whiteside, 1975); Reg Whitaker, "Official Repression of Communism during World War II," *Labour/Le Travail* 17 (1986) 135–68.

17 King diary, 5 September 1939; Frederick W. Gibson and Barbara Robertson (eds.), *Ottawa at War: The Grant Dexter Memoranda, 1939–1945* (Winnipeg: Manitoba Record Society, 1994) 9.

18 King diary, 5 September 1939.

19 Perras, *Franklin Roosevelt and the Origins of the Canadian Security Alliance*, 55.

20 E.K. Brown, "Mackenzie King of Canada," *Harper's Magazine* 186 (January 1943) 196.

21 Gibson and Robertson (eds.), *Ottawa at War*, 39.

22 King diary, 13 September 1939.

23 J.W. Pickersgill, *Seeing Canada Whole: A Memoir* (Toronto: Fitzhenry & Whiteside, 1994) 164.

24 J.A. English, "Not an Equilateral Triangle: Canada's Strategic Relationship with the United States and Britain, 1939–1945," in

B.J.C. McKercher and L. Aronsen (eds.), *The North Atlantic Triangle in a Changing World: Anglo-American-Canadian Relations, 1902–1956* (Toronto: University of Toronto Press, 1996) 160.

25 Reginald Hardy, *Mackenzie King of Canada: A Biography* (Toronto: Oxford University Press, 1949) 315.

26 Arnold Heeney, *The Things that Are Caesar's: Memoir of a Canadian Public Servant* (Toronto: University of Toronto Press, 1972) 76.

27 Paul Martin, "King: The View from the Backbench," in John English and J.O. Stubbs (eds.), *Mackenzie King: Widening the Debate* (Toronto: MacMillan of Canada, 1977) 38–9.

28 King diary, 19 September 1939.

29 J.L. Granatstein, *Ottawa Men: The Civil Service Mandarins, 1935–1957* (Toronto: Oxford University Press, 1982); Doug Owram, *The Government Generation: Canadian Intellectuals and the State, 1900–1945* (Toronto: Univeristy of Toronto Press, 1986).

30 Bliss, *Right Honourable Men*, 139.

31 J.L. Granatstein, *How Britain's Weakness Forced Canada into the Arms of the United States* (Toronto: University of Toronto Press, 1989) 25; also see, Thomas A. Crerar, "The Incredible Canadian: An Evaluation," *International Journal* 8.3 (Summer 1953) 155.

32 Heeney, *The Things that Are Caesar's*, 48.

33 Pickersgill, *Seeing Canada Whole*, 289.

34 King diary, 22 February 1940.

35 William Lyon Mackenzie King papers, MG 26 J [hereafter King papers], memorandum, "Canadian War Policy," [authored by O.D. Skelton], 24 August 1939, 1550073.

36 English, "Not an Equilateral Triangle," 147–83; John Maker, "A Home Away from Home: Citizenship and National Identity in the Canadian Army Overseas, 1939–1945," (PhD thesis: University of Ottawa, 2010) 36–43.

37 LAC, Harry Crerar papers, MG 30 E157, v. 23, "Chiefs of Staff Committee Memorandum—Canada's National Effort (Armed Forces) in the Early Stages of a Major War," 29 August 1939; King diary, 1, 2, and 5 September 1939.

38 Robert Bryce, *Canada and the Cost of World War II: The International Operations of Canada's Department of Finance, 1939–1947* (Montreal: McGill-Queen's University Press, 2005) 22–3; King diary, 18 September 1939.

39 Queen's Archives, Norman Rogers papers, box 8, Record of Visit to the UK, 18 April to 9 May 1940, 19 April 1940, 5–6; 24 April, 36–37; Hector Mackenzie, "'Arsenal of the British Empire'? British Orders for Munitions Production in Canada, 1936–39," *Journal of Imperial and Commonwealth History* 31 (2003) 46–73.

40 J.W. Pickersgill, *The Mackenzie King Record,* volume I (Toronto: University of Toronto Press, 1960) 30; King diary, 17 September 1939.

41 King diary, 1 September 1939.

42 For Roosevelt administration's actions and relationship towards the British, see David Reynolds, *The Creation of the Anglo-American Alliance, 1937–1941* (Chapel Hill: University of North Carolina Press, 1982).

43 J.R. Campbell, "James Layton Ralston and Manpower for the Canadian Army," (MA thesis: Wilfrid Laurier University, 1986) 24–5; Granatstein, *The Generals*, 61–2; King diary, 28 August 1941.

44 Roger Sarty, "Mr. King and the Armed Forces," Norman Hillmer et al. (eds.), *A Country of Limitations: Canada and the World in 1939* (Ottawa: Committee for the Study of the Second World War, 1996) 239–40.

45 A.W. Martin and Patsy Hardy (eds.), *Dark and Hurrying Days: Menzies' 1941 Diary* (Canberra: National Library of Australia, 1993) 124–5.

46 Richard S. Malone, *A Portrait of War, 1939–1943* (Toronto: Collins Publishers, 1983) 74.

47 King diary, 25 September 1939.

48 Bruce Hutchison, *The Incredible Canadian: A Candid Portrait of Mackenzie King* (Toronto: Longmans Canada, 1970 [original, 1952]) 262.

49 King diary, 25 and 28 September 1939.

50 J.L. Granatstein, "Financing the Liberal Party, 1935–1945," in Michael Cross and Robert Bothwell (eds.), *Policy by Other Means* (Toronto: Clarke and Irwin, 1972) 188–9.
51 Betcherman, *Ernest Lapointe*, 288–9.
52 MacFarlane, *Ernest Lapointe*, 156.
53 Queen's Archives, C.G. Power papers, box 86, file 2, F.W. Gibson interview with Power, [formation of 1935 cabinet], 17 January 1961, transcripts, 30–1.
54 Paul Martin, *A Very Public Life: Far from Home* (Ottawa: Deneau, 1983) 237.
55 King diary, 17 October 1939.
56 Gibson and Robertson (eds.), *Ottawa at War*, 19.
57 See F.J. Hatch, *Aerodrome of Democracy: Canada and the British Commonwealth Air Training Plan, 1939–1945* (Ottawa: Directorate of History, Monograph Series 1, 1983) 17.
58 Pickersgill, *The Mackenzie King Record,* volume I, 43.
59 Gibson and Robertson (eds.), *Ottawa at War*, 3. For other challenges, see Andrew Stewart, "The 1939 British and Canadian 'Empire Air Training Scheme' Negotiations," *Round Table* 93 (2004) 739–54.
60 Pearson, *Mike, Volume I*, 152.
61 Pickersgill, *The Mackenzie King Record,* volume I, 51–2.
62 Brereton Greenhous et al., *The Crucible of War 1939–1945: The Official History of the Royal Canadian Air Force*, volume III (Toronto: University of Toronto Press, 1994) 16–43.
63 Kent Fedorowich, "Sir Gerald Campbell and the British High Commission in Wartime Ottawa, 1938–1940," *War in History* 18(3) 378; also see Heeney, *The Things that Are Caesar's*, 62, and Terry Crowley, *Marriage of Minds: Isobel and Oscar Skelton Reinventing Canada* (Toronto: University of Toronto Press, 2003), 247.
64 J.L. Granatstein and Dean F. Oliver, *The Oxford Companion to Canadian Military History* (Toronto: Oxford University Press, 2011) 64.
65 John T. Saywell, *Just Call Me Mitch: The Life of Mitchell F. Hepburn* (Toronto: University of Toronto Press, 1991) 437.

66 Pickersgill, *Seeing Canada Whole*, 182–3; King diary, 18 January 1940.
67 King diary, 23 January 1940.
68 King diary, 27 January 1940.
69 J.L. Granatstein, *Canada's War: The Politics of the Mackenzie King Government, 1939–1945*, 2nd ed. (Toronto: University of Toronto Press, 1990) 73.
70 Gibson and Robertson (eds.), *Ottawa at War*, 42.

CHAPTER 13

1 King diary, 10 June 1939.
2 King diary, 10 May 1940.
3 Fedorowich, "Sir Gerald Campbell," 378.
4 John Buchan, *Memory Hold-the-Door* (London: Hodder and Stoughton, 1945) 289.
5 For the challenges of early economic planning, see Paul Marsden, "The Costs of No Commitments: Canadian Economic Planning for War," in Norman Hillmer et al. (eds.), *A Country of Limitations: Canada and the World in 1939* (Ottawa: Canadian Committee for the History of the Second World War, 1996) 199–216.
6 Hansard, 14 June 1940.
7 J.L. Granatstein, "Arming the Nation: Canada's Industrial War Effort, 1939–1945," (Ottawa: paper prepared for the Canadian Council of Chief Executives, 2005) 7.
8 Robert Bothwell, "'Who's Paying for Anything These Days?' War Production in Canada, 1939–1945," in N.F. Dreisziger (ed.), *Mobilization for Total War* (Waterloo: Wilfrid Laurier University Press, 1981) 62.
9 Robert Bothwell, *Eldorado*: *Canada's National Uranium Company* (Toronto: University of Toronto Press, 1984); Matthew Bellamy, *Profiting The Crown*: *Canada's Polymer Corporation, 1942–1990* (Montreal: McGill-Queen's University Press, 2005).
10 Granatstein, *Mackenzie King: His Life and World*, 149.
11 Ward (ed.), *A Party Politician*, 122–3.

12 King diary, 10 June 1940.

13 T. Stephen Henderson, "Angus L. Macdonald and the Conscription Crisis of 1944," *Acadiensis* 27.1 (Autumn 1997) 86.

14 Bryce, *Canada and the Cost of World War II*, 4–5.

15 Robert A. Wardaugh, *Behind the Scenes: The Life and Work of William Clifford Clark* (Toronto: University of Toronto Press, 2010) 144 and 179.

16 Granatstein, *Canada's War*, 106.

17 King diary, 11 July 1940.

18 Ivana Caccia, *Managing the Canadian Mosaic in Wartime: Shaping Citizenship Policy, 1939–1945* (Montreal: McGill-Queen's University Press, 2010) 29.

19 For Houde's speech, see Hansard, 3 August 1940, 2402.

20 Mark Bourrie, *Fog of War: Censorship of Canada's Media in World War Two* (Vancouver: Douglas & McIntyre, 2011) 120–2; Pickersgill, *Seeing Canada Whole*, 198.

21 King diary, 10 September 1939

22 King diary, 29 May 1940; Campbell, "James Layton Ralston," 51–3; Pickersgill, *The Mackenzie King Record,* volume I, 76.

23 King diary, 24 May 1940.

24 King papers, H-1558, "Discussion of Possible Eventualities," 29 May 1940, C281914–19; King diary, 26 May 1940.

25 The term came from historian John B. Brebner, *North Atlantic Triangle: The Interplay of Canada, the United States and Great Britain* (New York: Columbia University Press, 1945); also see, Tony McCulloch, "The North Atlantic Triangle: A Canadian Myth?" *International Journal* LXVI.1 (Winter 2010–11) 197–207.

26 King diary, 26 May 1940.

27 King diary, 30 May 1940.

28 J.L. Granatstein and Norman Hillmer, *For Better or For Worse: Canada and the United States to the 1990s* (Toronto: Copp Clark Pitman, 1991) 137; *DCER*, volume VIII, 85–6.

29 King diary, 16 June 1940.

30 King diary, 6 June 1940.

31 King diary, 17 August 1940.
32 Colonel C.P. Stacey, "The Canadian–American Permanent Joint Board on Defence, 1940–1945," *International Journal* 9.2 (Spring 1954) 107–24; the war committee adopted the Ogdensburg Agreement on 20 August 1940.
33 Fred Pollock, "Roosevelt, the Ogdensburg Agreement, and the British Fleet: All Done with Mirrors," *Diplomatic History* 5 (1981) 203–19.
34 King diary, 22 August 1940.
35 King diary, 11 December 1941.
36 Stacey, *Arms, Men and Governments*, 48.
37 Queen's Archives, Grant Dexter papers, box 19, folder 177, "Explanation on the History and Function of the Army Council."
38 King diary, 4 December 1940.
39 King diary, 6 December 1940.
40 King diary, 14 January 1941.
41 Granatstein, *Canada's War*, 173–4; King diary, 22 October 1940.
42 King diary, 6 January 1941; Hutchison, *The Incredible Canadian*, 289.
43 Wardaugh, *Behind the Scenes*, 200–5.
44 King papers, W.C. Clark to King, 9 April 1941, C288013–33.
45 King diary, 17 April 1941.
46 See the argument in Granatstein, *How Britain's Weakness Forced Canada*.
47 Pickersgill, *The Mackenzie King Record*, volume I, 200.
48 Douglas Fullerton, *Graham Towers and His Times* (Toronto: McClelland & Stewart, 1986) 143.

CHAPTER 14

1 Serge Marc Durflinger, *Fighting from Home: The Second World War in Verdun, Quebec* (Vancouver: University of British Columbia Press, 2006) 181.

2 J.D. Ketchum and J.S.A. Bois, "Morale in Canada," in Goodwin Watson (ed.), *Civilian Morale* (New York: Houghton Mifflin, 1942) 253.
3 Peter Stursberg, *The Sound of War: Memoirs of a CBC Correspondent* (Toronto: University of Toronto Press, 1993) 81.
4 Ward (ed.), *A Party Politician*, 188–9.
5 Mac Johnston, *Corvettes Canada: Convoy Veterans of WWII Tell their True Stories* (Toronto: McGraw-Hill Ryerson, 1994) 2.
6 King diary, 10 June 1941; T. Stephen Henderson, *Angus L. Macdonald: A Provincial Leader* (Toronto: University of Toronto Press, 2007) 102–3.
7 See Mark Bourrie, "The Myth of the 'Gagged Clam': William Lyon Mackenzie King's Press Relations," *Global Media Journal—Canadian Edition* 3.2 (2010) 13–30.
8 Bourrie, *The Fog of War*, 38.
9 King diary, 30 April 1940.
10 MacDonald, "King: The View from London," 47.
11 Gibson and Robertson (eds.), *Ottawa at War*, 193.
12 King diary, 6 August 1941.
13 King diary, 12 August 1941; also see Douglas Brinkley and David R. Facey-Crowther (eds.), *The Atlantic Charter* (New York: St. Martin's Press, 1994).
14 Rear-Admiral H. Nelson Lay, *Memoirs of a Mariner* (Stittsville: Canada's Wings, 1982) 144; King diary, 19 August 1941.
15 King diary, 24 August 1941.
16 King diary, 28 August 1941.
17 Canadian Military Headquarters Report No. 44, Visits of Rt. Hon. W.L. Mackenzie King to Canadian Troops in England, 2–4 [available online at the Directorate of History and Heritage]; King diary, 23 August 1941.
18 King diary, 23 August 1941.
19 King diary, 26 August 1941.
20 King diary, 26 August 1941.
21 King diary, 26 August 1941.

22 King diary, 10 October 1941.
23 J.W. Pickersgill, "Mackenzie King's Political Attitudes and Political Policies: A Personal Impression," in John English and J.O. Stubbs (eds.), *Mackenzie King: Widening the Debate* (Toronto: MacMillan of Canada, 1977) 16.
24 Granatstein, *Mackenzie King: His Life and World*, 152; William R. Young, "Mobilizing English Canada for War: The Bureau of Public Information, the Wartime Information Board and the View of the Nation during the Second World War," in Sidney Aster (ed.), *The Second World War as a National Experience* (Ottawa: The Canadian Committee for the History of the Second World War, 1981) 202–3.
25 For the program, see Christopher Robb Waddell, "The Wartime Prices and Trade Board: Price Control in Canada in World War II," (PhD thesis: York University, 1981).
26 Paul Dickson, "Harry Crerar and an Army for Strategic Effect," *Canadian Military History* 17.1 (Winter 2008) 42.
27 *Public Opinion Quarterly* 6 (Spring 1942) 158.
28 MacFarlane, *Ernest Lapointe*, 12.
29 King diary, 14 November 1941.
30 King diary, 6 November 1941.
31 Henderson, *Angus L. Macdonald*, 104–5.
32 MacDonald, "King: The View from London," 52.
33 King diary, 7 December 1941.
34 Kent Fedorowich, "'Cocked Hats and Swords and Small, Little Garrisons': Britain, Canada and the Fall of Hong Kong, 1941," *Modern Asian Studies* 37.1 (February 2003) 111–57; quote from Terry Copp, "The Decision to Reinforce Hong Kong: September 1941," *Canadian Military History* 20.2 (Spring 2011) 11.
35 For a description of the battle, see Nathan Greenfield, *The Damned: The Canadians at the Battle of Hong Kong and the POW Experience, 1941–45* (Toronto: HarperCollins, 2010).
36 King diary, 21 January 1942.

CHAPTER 15

1 H.P. Wilmott, *Empires in the Balance: Japanese and Allied Pacific Strategies to April 1942* (Maryland: Naval Institute Press, 1982) 333.
2 For the view of Mackenzie's constituents, see LAC, Ian Mackenzie papers, MG 27, III–B-5, v. 24, file 67-25, pt. 1 to pt. 4.
3 RG 2, 7C, v. 6, Cabinet War Committee Minutes, 2 December 1941.
4 King diary, 2 December 1941.
5 Pearson, *Mike, Volume I*, 153.
6 King papers, "Personal View with Respect to 1941–42 Proposed Programme of the Army," 3 December 1941, 244478; J.L. Granatstein, *The Generals: The Canadian Army's Senior Commanders in the Second World War* (Toronto: Stoddart Publishing. Co., 1993) 223–4; J.E. Rea, *T.A. Crerar: A Political Life* (Montreal: McGill-Queen's University Press, 1997) 208–10.
7 On the strength, see C.P. Stacey, *Six Years of War: The Canadian Army in Canada, Britain and the Pacific; The Official History of the Canadian Army in the Second World War*, volume 1 (Ottawa: The Queen's Printer, 1955) 19, 522–3. On the formation of the Canadian army, see Paul Dickson, "The Politics of Army Expansion: General H.D.G. Crerar and the Creation of First Canadian Army, 1940–41," *The Journal of Military History* 60 (April 1996) 271–98.
8 King diary, 25 December 1941.
9 For the controversy, see David B. Woolner, "Mackenzie King and the St. Pierre and Miquelon Crisis of 1941," *London Journal of Canadian Studies* 24 (2008–2009) 42–84; and Martin F. Auger, "'A Tempest in a Teapot': Canadian Military Planning and the St. Pierre and Miquelon Affair, 1940–1942," *Acadiensis* 33.1 (Fall 2003) 68–70.
10 Paul M. Couture, "The Vichy–Free French Propaganda War in Quebec, 1940 to 1942," *Historical Papers* (1978) 200–16; Justin Massie, "North Atlantic Quadrangle: Mackenzie King's Lasting Imprint on Canada's International Security Policy," *London Journal of Canadian Studies* 24 (2008–2009) 97–8.

11 Pickersgill, *The Mackenzie King Record,* volume I, 409.
12 John G. Diefenbaker, *One Canada: The Crusading Years, 1895–1956* (Toronto: MacMillan of Canada, 1975) 202.
13 David Dilks, *The Great Dominion: Winston Churchill in Canada, 1900–1954* (Toronto: Thomas Allen, 2005) 216.
14 Granatstein, *Canada's War*, 119.
15 Stephanie Bangarth, "Mackenzie King and Japanese Canadians," in John English et al. (eds.), *Mackenzie King: Citizenship and Community* (Toronto: Robin Brass, 2002) 100; and Stephanie Bangarth, *Voices Raised in Protest: Defending North American Citizens of Japanese Ancestry, 1942–49* (Vancouver: University of British Columbia Press, 2008).
16 Pickersgill, *Seeing Canada Whole*, 263.
17 Whitaker, "The Liberal Corporatist Ideas of Mackenzie King," 151; see the introduction by David Jay Bercuson in William Lyon Mackenzie King's *Industry and Humanity* (Toronto: University of Toronto Press, 1973) xxii; Esberey, *Knight of the Holy Cross*, 198.
18 King diary, 19 February 1942.
19 Order-in-council 1486, 24 February 1942.
20 Pope, *Soldiers and Politicians*, 177.
21 On refugee policy, see Isabel Kaprielian-Churchill, "Armenian Refugees and their Entry into Canada, 1919–1930," *The Canadian Historical Review* 71.1 (Spring 1990) 80–108.
22 Irving Abella and Harold Troper, *None Is Too Many: Canada and the Jews of Europe, 1933–1948* (Toronto: Lester & Orpen Dennys, 1982); Richard Foot, "Canada's Shame Memorialized," *The Ottawa Citizen*, 20 January 2011.
23 See Ken Adachi, *The Enemy that Never Was: A History of the Japanese Canadians*, 2nd ed. (Toronto: McClelland & Stewart, 1991).
24 Bryce, *Canada and the Cost of World War II*, 156–7; Granatstein, *Canada's War*, 312–14.
25 King diary, 2 January 1942.

26 Florent Lefevbre, *The French-Canadian Press and the War* (Toronto: Ryerson Press, 1942) 23–30.
27 Pickersgill, "Mackenzie King's Political Attitudes," 18.
28 King diary, 31 January 1942; LAC, J.L. Ralston papers, MG 27 III-B-11, v. 54, file Plebiscite, 1942, "Conversation Ralston and I had with P.M., Saturday, January 31 [1942]."
29 King diary, 9 February 1942.
30 Andre Laurendeau, *Witness for Quebec* (Toronto: Macmillan of Canada, 1973) 52.
31 See Granatstein and Hitsman, *Broken Promises*, 163–71.
32 King diary, 27 April 1942.
33 Hansard, 10 June 1942, 3236.
34 Hardy, *Mackenzie King of Canada*, 202.
35 King diary, 11 May 1942.
36 Pickersgill, *The Mackenzie King Record*, volume I, 17.
37 King diary, 7 September 1942.
38 For Crerar and Dieppe, see Paul Dickson, *A Thoroughly Canadian General: A Biography of General H.D.G. Crerar* (Toronto: University of Toronto Press, 2007).
39 King diary, 19 August 1942.
40 King diary, 21 August 1942. Also see Timothy Balzer, "'In Case the Raid is Unsuccessful ...': Selling Dieppe to Canadians," *The Canadian Historical Review* 87.3 (2006) 409–30.
41 Marc Milner, "The Royal Canadian Navy and 1943: A Year Best Forgotten?," in Paul Dickson (ed.), *1943: The Beginning of the End* (Waterloo: Wilfrid Laurier University Press, 1995) 126.

CHAPTER 16

1 Michael Hadley, *U-boats against Canada*: *German Submarines in Canadian Waters* (Montreal: McGill-Queen's University Press, 1985) 103.
2 Roger Sarty, "The 'Battle We Lost at Home' Revisited: Official Military Histories and the Battle of the St. Lawrence," *Canadian Military History* 12.1 & 2 (Winter/Spring 2003) 41–50.

3 Marc Milner, *Canada's Navy: The First Century* (Toronto: University of Toronto Press, 1999) 109–12.

4 J.L. Granatstein, "Settling the Accounts: Anglo-Canadian War Finance, 1943–1945," *Queen's Quarterly* 83 (Summer 1976) 246; Granatstein and Oliver, *The Oxford Companion to Canadian Military History*, 454.

5 Wardaugh, *Behind the Scenes*, 248.

6 King diary, 14–16 April 1943; Robert Bothwell and William Kilbourn, *C.D. Howe: A Biography* (Toronto: McClelland & Stewart, 1979) 167.

7 Granatstein and Hitsman, *Broken Promises*, 195.

8 David J. Bercuson, *True Patriot: The Life of Brooke Claxton, 1898–1960* (Toronto: University of Toronto Press, 1993) 120.

9 Reginald Whitaker, "Political Thought and Political Action in Mackenzie King," *Journal of Canadian Studies* 13.4 (Winter 1978–1979) 47; Esberey, *Knight of the Holy Cross*, 144–5.

10 King diary, 25 June 1943.

11 John Swettenham, *McNaughton, Volume II,* 1939–1943 (Toronto: Ryerson Press, 1969) 185.

12 Queen's Archives, Grant Dexter papers, box 3, folder 21 (c), memorandum [conversation with W.L.M. King], 28 February 1942.

13 King diary, 15 March 1943.

14 King diary, 11 March 1943 and 15 March 1943.

15 King diary, 18 June 1943.

16 For a repetition of this message to the caucus, see King diary, 25 September 1943.

17 See W. Neville Sloane, "The Paradox of Unity: Winston Churchill, Mackenzie King and Anglo-Canadian Relations, 1940–1945" (PhD thesis: University of East Anglia, 2007) 3, 12, 76; King diary, 11 August 1943.

18 Brandey Barton, "Public Opinion and National Prestige: The Politics of Canadian Army Participation in the Invasion of Sicily, 1942–1943," *Canadian Military History* 15.2 (Spring 2006) 29.

19 King diary, 8 July 1943.

20 J.L. Granatstein, "Happily on the Margins: Mackenzie King and Canada at the Quebec Conferences," in David B. Woolner (ed.), *The Second Quebec Conference Revisited: Waging War, Formulating Peace: Canada, Great Britain, and the United States in 1944–1945* (New York: St. Martin's Press, 1998) 54.
21 Stacey, "Mackenzie King and the Atlantic Triangle," 54.
22 King diary, 21 October 1943.
23 On the Italian campaign, see Daniel Dancocks, *The D-Day Dodgers: The Canadians in Italy, 1943–1945* (Toronto: McClelland & Stewart, 1991).
24 John Rickard, *The Politics of Command: Lieutenant-General A.G.L. McNaughton and the Canadian Army, 1939–1943* (Toronto: University of Toronto Press, 2010) 47; Gibson and Robertson (eds.), *Ottawa at War*, 284.
25 John Nelson Rickard, "The Test of Command: McNaughton and Exercise 'Spartan,' 4–12 March 1943," *Canadian Military History* 8.3 (Summer 1999) 22–38.
26 Jeff Keshen, *Saints, Soldiers and Sinners: Canada's Second World War* (Vancouver: University of British Columbia Press, 2004).
27 John Bacher, *Keeping to the Marketplace: The Evolution of Canadian Housing Policy* (Montreal: McGill Queen's University Press, 1993) 120–2.
28 King diary, 14 January 1943.
29 Order-in-council, 1003, 17 February 1944.
30 Granatstein, *Mackenzie King: His Life and Times*, 173.
31 Blair Fraser, "Political Ferment in Canada," *Foreign Affairs* 23.1 (October 1944) 79; John English, "Politics and the War: Aspects of the Canadian National Experience," in Sidney Aster (ed.), *The Second World War as a National Experience* (Ottawa: The Canadian Committee for the History of the Second World War, 1981) 55–6.
32 King diary, 27 September 1943.
33 King diary, 9 June 1943.

34 LAC, Ian Mackenzie papers, MG 27 III–B-5, v. 41, file G-25-15, "The Rt. Hon. W.L. Mackenzie King, Address to the American Federation of Labor, 9 October 1942."

35 Pickersgill, *Seeing Canada Whole*, 233; also see King diary, 1 October 1943.

36 Gibson and Robertson (eds.), *Ottawa at War*, 441–2.

37 David J. Bercuson, *True Patriot: The Life of Brooke Claxton, 1898–1960* (Toronto: University of Toronto Press, 1993) 132–3.

38 Hansard, 17 July 1944, 5335.

39 King diary, 15 July 1944.

40 J.L. Granatstein, "King and his Cabinet: the War Years," John English and J.O. Stubbs (eds.), *Mackenzie King: Widening the Debate* (Toronto: MacMillan of Canada, 1977) 184–5.

41 See James Struthers, "Family Allowances, Old Age Security, and the Construction of Entitlement in the Canadian Welfare State, 1943–1951," in Peter Neary and J.L. Granatstein (eds.), *The Veterans Charter and Post-World War II Canada* (Montreal: McGill-Queen's University Press, 1998) 179–204. Also see Raymond Blake, "Mackenzie King and the Genesis of Family Allowances in Canada, 1939–1944," in Raymond Blake and Jeff Keshen (eds.), *Social Welfare Policy in Canada* (Mississauga: Copp Clark Ltd., 1995) 244–54.

42 King diary, 6 June 1943.

43 Margaret Elizabeth Bedore, "The Reading of Mackenzie King," (PhD thesis: Queen's University, 2008) 12.

44 Dawson, *William Lyon Mackenzie King*, 252–3.

45 John G. Diefenbaker, *One Canada: The Crusading Years, 1895–1956* (Toronto: MacMillan of Canada, 1975) 199.

46 On Kingsmere, see Dennis Duffy, "Love among the Ruins: The King of Kingsmere," *American Review of Canadian Studies* 37.3 (2007) 355–70; Pearson, *Mike, Volume I*, 187–8.

47 Thomas A. Crerar, "The Incredible Canadian: An Evaluation," *International Journal* 8.3 (Summer 1953) 155.

48 King diary, 23 October 1943.

49 King diary, 29 March 1943.

50 Curtis Nordman, "The Army of Occupation: Malcolm MacDonald and the U.S. Military Involvement in the Canadian Northwest," in Kenneth Coates (ed.), *The Alaska Highway: Papers of the 40th Anniversary Symposium* (Vancouver: University of British Columbia Press, 1985) 92.

51 King diary, 30 December 1942; Granatstein and Bothwell, "A Self-Evident National Duty," 224–5.

52 Stacey, *Arms, Men and Governments*, 332. Also see J.L. Granatstein, "Hume Wrong's Road to the Functional Principle," in Keith Neilson and Roy A. Prete (eds.), *Coalition Warfare: An Uneasy Accord* (Waterloo: Wilfrid Laurier University Press, 1983).

53 King diary, 6 June 1944.

54 For a fierce condemnation of King, see Adrian W. Preston, "Canada and the Higher Direction of the Second World War," in B.D. Hunt and R.G. Haycock (eds.), *Canada's Defence* (Toronto: Copp Clark Pitman, 1993) 98–118.

55 Pearson, *Mike, Volume I*, 215.

56 Terry Copp, *Cinderella Army: The Canadians in Northwest Europe, 1944–1945* (Toronto: University of Toronto Press, 2006) 5.

57 King diary, 12 August 1944.

58 King diary, 10 September 1944.

CHAPTER 17

1 King diary, 3 August 1944.

2 King diary, 31 August 1944.

3 Stacey, *Arms, Men and Governments*, 56–7.

4 King diary, 20 September 1944; J.F. Hilliker (ed.), *DCER*, volume 10 (Ottawa: Information Services, 1980) 465; Henderson, *Angus L. Macdonald*, 128–9.

5 For King's push back against the navy, see Roger Sarty, "The Ghosts of Fisher and Jellicoe: The Royal Canadian Navy and The Quebec Conferences," in David B. Woolner (ed.), *The Second Quebec Conference Revisited: Waging War, Formulating Peace: Canada,*

Great Britain, and the United States in 1944–1945 (New York: St. Martin's Press, 1998) 160–3.

6 King diary, 22 September 1944.

7 Granatstein, "King and his Cabinet," 188.

8 King diary, 13 October 1944.

9 Richard S. Malone, *A World in Flames, 1944–1945* (Toronto: Collins, 1984) 145–6.

10 See Hansard, 29 November 1944, for a later account of his perception during the October crisis.

11 See, for example, King's papers, "Personal View with Respect to 1942–1943 Proposed Programme of the Army," 3 December 1941, 244478; and King diary, 18 October 1944.

12 King diary, 18 October 1944.

13 E.L.M. Burns, *Manpower in the Canadian Army, 1939–1945* (Toronto: Irving and Company Limited, 1956) 18.

14 King diary, 19 October 1944; Cabinet War Committee Minutes, 3 August 1944.

15 King diary, 20 October 1944.

16 Pope, *Soldiers and Politicians*, 248–51.

17 Henderson, "Angus L. Macdonald and the Conscription Crisis of 1944," 90–1.

18 Dilks, *The Great Dominion*, 358; J.W. Pickersgill, *The Mackenzie King Record,* volume II (Toronto: University of Toronto Press, 1968) 167.

19 King diary, 19 October 1944.

20 King diary, 26 October 1944; Pickersgill, *The Mackenzie King Record,* volume II, 151.

21 King diary, 27 October 1944; Dale C. Thompson, *Louis St. Laurent: Canadian* (New York: St. Martin's Press, 1968) 144–5.

22 King diary, 30 October 1944.

23 King diary, 30 October 1944.

24 See meetings in King diary, 31 October 1944 and 1 November 1944.

25 King diary, 26 October 1944.

26 Henderson, "Angus L. Macdonald and the Conscription Crisis of 1944," 93.
27 Heeney, *The Things that Are Caesar's*, 70.
28 Gibson and Robertson (eds.), *Ottawa at War*, 489; and Bernard Charles LeBlanc, *A Reluctant Recruit: Angus L. Macdonald and Conscription, 1940–1945* (MA thesis: Queen's University, 1987) 77–8.
29 R. MacGregor Dawson, *The Conscription Crisis of 1944* (Toronto: University of Toronto Press, 1961) 51.
30 King diary, 1 November 1944.
31 Granatstein, *Mackenzie King: His Life and World*, 164.
32 Daniel Byers, "Mobilising Canada: The National Resources Mobilization Act, the Department of National Defence, and Compulsory Military Service in Canada, 1940–1945," *Journal of the Canadian Historical Association* 7.1 (1996) 175–203.
33 Stacey, *Arms, Men, and Governments*, 437–8.
34 LAC, J.L. Ralston papers, MG 27 III-B-11, v. 86, file Conscription, Stuart-Murchie reports, "'C.G.S.' Reinforcement Situation, 2 August 1944."
35 Mason Wade, *The French-Canadians,* volume II (Toronto: Macmillan, 1968) 1042–3.
36 LAC, J.L. Ralston papers, MG 27 III-B-11, v. 86, file Resignation, November 1944, [Ralston's speech], 12 November 1944.
37 King diary, 12 November 1944.
38 Granatstein, *The Generals*, 81.
39 Granatstein and Hitsman, *Broken Promises*, 222–3.
40 King diary, 19 November 1944.
41 Queen's Archives, C.G. Power papers, box 12, file 2, Notes on Discussion on the Conscription Crisis, 22 November 1944.
42 Rea, *T.A. Crerar*, 228–9.
43 Grattan O'Leary, *Recollections of People, Press, and Politics* (Toronto: MacMillan of Canada, 1977) 91.
44 See Richard Walker, "The Revolt of the Canadian Generals, 1944: The Case for the Prosecution," in Howard G. Coombs (ed.), *The*

Insubordinate and the Noncompliant: Case Studies of Canadian Mutiny and Disobedience, 1920 to the Present (Toronto: The Dundurn Group, 2007) 55–100.

45 King diary, 22 November 1944.

46 John Swettenham, *McNaughton, Volume III, 1944–1966* (Toronto: Ryerson Press, 1969) 63.

47 O'Leary, *Recollections of People, Press, and Politics*, 90.

48 Reginald H. Roy, "From the Darker Side of Canadian Military History: Mutiny in the Mountains—The Terrace Incident," *Canadian Defence Quarterly* 6.2 (Autumn 1976) 42–55.

49 Stacey, *Arms, Men and Governments*, 481–2.

50 King diary, 8 December 1944.

CHAPTER 18

1 Granatstein, *Mackenzie King: His Life and Times*, 182.

2 *Public Opinion Quarterly* (1945) 88.

3 Diefenbaker, *One Canada*, 217.

4 Granatstein, *How Britain's Weakness Forced Canada...*, 39.

5 Michael A. Hennessy, "The Industrial Front: The Scale and Scope of Canadian Industrial Mobilization During the Second World War," in Bernd Horn (ed.), *Forging a Nation: Perspectives on the Canadian Military Experience* (St. Catharines: Vanwell, 2002) 140.

6 H. Duncan Hall and C.C. Wrigley, *Studies of Overseas Supply* (London: H.M. Stationery Office, 1956) 46.

7 Adam Chapnick, *The Middle Power Project: Canada and the Founding of the United Nations* (Vancouver: University of British Columbia Press, 2005) 126–31, 140.

8 Bercuson, *True Patriot*, 135.

9 Canadian Letters and Images Project, Maurice Melville Maloney papers, unnamed poem.

10 Pickersgill, *Seeing Canada Whole*, 267.

11 Beck, *Pendulum of Power*, 253.

12 Brian Nolan, *King's War: Mackenzie King and the Politics of War, 1939–1945* (Toronto: Random House, 1988) 45.

13 King diary, 12 April 1944, 24 February 1945, and 27 July 1945.

14 Jeffrey Keshen, "Getting it Right the Second Time Around," in Peter Neary and J.L. Granatstein (eds.), *The Veterans Charter and Post-World War II Canada* (Montreal: McGill-Queen's University Press, 1998) 72.

15 Peter Neary, "Canadian Universities and Canadian veterans of World War II," in Peter Neary and J.L. Granatstein (eds.), *The Veterans Charter and Post-World War II Canada* (Montreal: McGill-Queen's University Press, 1998) 120–2.

16 See Peter Neary, *On to Civvy Street: Canada's Rehabilitation Program for Veterans of the Second World War* (Montreal: McGill-Queen's University Press, 2011).

17 See Amy Knight, *How the Cold War Began: The Gouzenko Affair and the Hunt for Soviet Spies* (Toronto: McClelland & Stewart, 2005).

18 King diary, 9 July 1946.

19 Gordon Robertson, *Memoirs of a Very Civil Servant: Mackenzie King to Pierre Trudeau* (Toronto: University of Toronto Press, 2000) 62.

20 Pickersgill, "Mackenzie King's Political Attitudes," 18.

21 King diary, 18 February 1946; and Robert Bothwell and John English, "Canadian Trade Policy in the Age of American Dominance and British Doctrine, 1943–1947," *The Canadian Review of American Studies* 8.1 (Spring 1977) 61.

22 See Hector Mackenzie, "The Path to Temptation: The Negotiation of Canada's Reconstruction Loan to Britain in 1946," *Canadian Historical Association Papers* (1982) 196–220; Hector Mackenzie, "King's Exit: the Prime Minister and Canada's International Relations, 1945–1948," *London Journal of Canadian Studies* 24 (2008–2009) 118.

23 See Hector Mackenzie, "Shades of Gray? The Foundations of Canadian Policy in World Affairs," *The American Review of Canadian Studies* 37.4 (2007) 459–73.

24 Hutchison, *The Incredible Canadian*, 425.

25 Ged Martin, "Mackenzie King, the Medium and the Messages," *British Journal of Canadian Studies* 4.1 (1989) 118–9.

26 See Robert Bothwell, *Alliance and Illusion: Canada and the World, 1945–1984* (Vancouver: University of British Columbia Press, 2007) 73–89; Leigh Sarty, "The Limits of Internationalism: Canada and the Soviet Blockade of Berlin, 1948–1949," in J.L. Black and Norman Hillmer (eds.), *Nearly Neighbours, Canada and the Soviet Union: from Cold War to Détente and Beyond* (Kingston: Ronald P. Frye & Company, 1989) 56–74.

27 Heeney, *The Things that Are Caesar's*, 93.

28 Joy E. Esberey, *Knight of the Holy Spirit: A Study of William Lyon Mackenzie King* (Toronto: University of Toronto Press, 1983) 219–220.

29 Charles Ritchie, *Diplomatic Passport: More Undiplomatic Diaries, 1946–1962* (Toronto: Macmillan of Canada, 1981) 11.

30 McGregor, *The Fall and Rise of Mackenzie King, 1911–1919*, 15.

31 Jean Dryden, "The Mackenzie King Papers: An Archival Odyssey," *Archivaria* 6 (Summer 1978) 51.

32 J.L. Granatstein and Norman Hillmer, *Prime Ministers: Ranking Canada's Leaders* (Toronto: HarperCollins, 1999) 100.

33 Heeney, *The Things that Are Caesar's*, 94–5.

34 Hutchison, *Mr. Prime Minister*, 202.

35 J.E. Rea, "'Clay from Feet to Forehead': The Mackenzie King Controversy," *The Beaver* (April–May 1993) 30.

36 Blair Fraser, "The Secret Life of Mackenzie King, Spiritualist," *Maclean's* (15 December 1951) 7–9, 60–1.

37 J.L. Granatstein, "King and Country," *International Journal* 24.2 (Spring 1969) 374.

38 H. Blair Neatby, "Mackenzie King and the Historians," in John English and J.O. Stubbs (eds.) *Mackenzie King: Widening the Debate* (Toronto: MacMillan of Canada, 1977) 1.

39 Arthur R.M. Lower, *My First Seventy-Five Years* (Toronto: The Macmillan Co. of Canada, 1967) 274.

CONCLUSION

1 Brown, "'Whither Are We Being Shoved?,'" 106.
2 See Carl Berger, "Introduction," *Conscription 1917* (Canadian Historical Readings, No. 8) viii; Willms, "Conscription 1917," 338–9.
3 Graham, *Arthur Meighen*, volume 1, 128.
4 See Michael D. Stevenson, *Canada's Greatest Wartime Muddle: National Selective Service and the Mobilization of Human Resources during World War II* (Montreal: McGill-Queen's University Press, 2001).
5 Borden diary, 29 September 1917.
6 Borden, *Letters to Limbo*, 6.
7 Carl Berger, *The Writing of Canadian History: Aspects of English-Canadian Historical Writing, 1900–1970* (Toronto: Oxford University Press, 1976) 58–9.
8 Lower, *From Colony to Nation*, 457–9.
9 Pickersgill, "Mackenzie King's Political Attitudes," 29.
10 John A. Stevenson, "The Career of Mackenzie King," *The Political Quarterly* 21.4 (October 1950) 396.
11 King diary, 15 July 1943.
12 MacFarlane, *Ernest Lapointe*, 125–6.
13 King diary, 28 January 1941.
14 J.L. Granatstein, *A Man of Influence: Norman A. Robertson and Canadian Statecraft, 1929–1968* (Ottawa: Deaneau, 1981) 202.
15 Lester B. Pearson, "Relations on Inter-War Canadian Foreign Policy," *Journal of Canadian Studies* 7.2 (1972) 39.
16 Wardhaugh, *Mackenzie King and the Prairie West*, 230.
17 Kemp papers, v. 129, file B-3, *New York Sun*, 6 January 1920, "Borden Held as Greatest Canadian Prime Minister."
18 Gibson, "Mr. Mackenzie King and Canadian Autonomy, 1921–1946," 20.
19 F.H. Underhill, *In Search of Canadian Liberalism* (Toronto: Macmillan Co. of Canada, 1961) 127.

ACKNOWLEDGMENTS

It is a pleasure to work as a historian at the Canadian War Museum and to confront daily the happy challenges of presenting the nation's complex past. One could not hope for better colleagues, and I have benefited from their rich and varied knowledge. While this book was written on my own time, I am grateful for the ongoing support of senior management at the Canadian War Museum, especially Dr. Dean Oliver, James Whitham, and Mark O'Neill.

Jonathan Webb's edits made this a far better book, and I enjoyed our tussling over the text, removing the extraneous, and clarifying the confusing. I have had the pleasure of working with Tara Tovell on *Warlords* and my last three books, and her skill at line and copy editing has saved me from numerous errors, while always helping to sharpen the story. At Penguin Canada, I have been lucky to work with Diane Turbide, who has a strong vision for presenting literary non-fiction and encouraging the writing of Canadian history. I'd also like to thank my friend and agent, Rick

Broadhead, who puts his considerable expertise and energy into working on my behalf.

Professor Terry Copp, Dr. Roger Sarty, and Michael Bechthold at the Laurier Centre for Military Strategic and Disarmament Studies shared a number of photographs. I am especially grateful to Dr. Kathryn Rose, the Laurier Centre's former archivist and now a librarian at Memorial University, who shared with me the transcripts to Sir Robert Borden's diary. Dr. Bill Waiser of the University of Saskatchewan provided some cartoons, and Dr. David Bercuson of the University of Calgary invited me to give the Ross Ellis Lecture in Military and Strategic Studies, which helped to crystallize some of my thoughts relating to Sir Robert Borden.

I was very lucky to be able to call upon historians to read and comment on the manuscript. These included some of the most senior scholars in the country, many of whom laid the foundation for studying Borden and King. Dr. John English, Dr. J.L. Granatstein, and Dr. Norman Hillmer read the manuscript and shared their deep knowledge of Canadian history. Dr. John MacFarlane offered insight into the relationship between Lapointe and King, as well as other useful commentary and queries. My friend Eric Brown also provided a thorough edit. This small community of scholars is indicative of the larger one that is generous with time and willing to share knowledge and give support. The errors that remain are mine alone.

My father, Dr. Terry Cook, offered detailed edits in style and content. He, more than anyone in my life, has taught me how to write. His ongoing support, with that of my mother, Dr. Sharon Cook, who juggles a busy professional life of being an educator, professor, historian, and expert babysitter, is very gratifying. My brother, Graham, who was wise enough to escape the clutches of history and become a successful lawyer, remains a source of inspiration.

During the final stages of this book, I was diagnosed with a serious illness. While this was a difficult time, I remain amazed by the outpouring of sympathy, friendship, and assistance given freely by friends, colleagues, and extended family. Our friends in the Manor Park community provided playdates for my girls and meals for us. Kind words and missives came in from across the country and around the world. The friends on my hockey team, The Red Army, always provided good cheer and bad chat in the dressing room, and I thank them for their generosity during my illness and, as ever, their backchecking and shot-blocking.

To Sarah, who offered unflagging support and love, along with our three daughters, Chloe, Emma, and Paige, I am eternally grateful. They allow me to stay in the writing trenches and emerge to smiles and hugs. They are worth the fight.

INDEX